Paved with Good Intentions

PAVED WITH GOOD INTENTIONS

The American Experience and Iran

BARRY RUBIN

New York • Oxford
OXFORD UNIVERSITY PRESS
1980

Copyright © 1980 by Oxford University Press, Inc.

Library of Congress Cataloging in Publication
Rubin, Barry M
Paved with good intentions.
Includes index.
1. United States—Foreign relations—Iran.
2. Iran—Foreign relations—United States. I. Title.
E183.8.T55R83   327.73055   80-16888
ISBN 0-19-502805-8

First printing September 1980
Second printing October 1980

Printed in the United States of America

To Kathy

Artificial sprites
As by the strength of their illusion
Shall draw him on to his confusion
He shall spurn fate, scorn death and bear:
His hopes 'bove wisdom, grace and fear:
And you all know security
Is mortal's chiefest enemy.
                "MacBeth"

Preface

Responding to a press-conference question in February, 1980 about the United States role in the 1953 return to power of the shah, President Carter replied that the events were not worth going into because they were "ancient history." Clearly this was a tactical response—there was no sense adding fuel to the fire while fifty-three Americans were still being held hostage. Yet there was no lack of interest within the American public in the angry charges coming daily out of Iran or in the debate within the United States between those who supported these allegations of American perfidy and those who did not.

On the contrary, there was a strong and widespread interest in calm evaluation and better understanding. But first the public wanted the facts. What exactly had the nation done to cause the current leaders of Iran to hold the United States in such utter contempt, to charge it with such rank imperialism, and to lay at the doorstep of the White House all the sins of its own former monarch?

The temptation to see the history of United States-Iranian relations as a story of heroes and villains, of a few missed op-

ix

portunities, of colorful incidents and obvious lessons should
be avoided. Before reading conclusions into this story, one
ought to examine all the evidence—what happened in Iran in
1978 is unintelligible to those who know nothing of what occurred in 1953. Similarly, it is just as impossible to evaluate
the events of 1953 without reference to the special relationship between the United States and Iran that had preceded
them.

A country's behavior, as the Iranian crisis so vividly demonstrates, is not merely a product of a rational pursuit of
objective national interests. Rather, it is the result of the interaction of the collective historical experience of the nation
with the individual life experiences of its citizens. The former
creates a nation's political course, the latter shapes its political consciousness. Whether or not the interaction contributes
to the effective fulfillment of a nation's objective interests is
an important question, though not always the controlling
question.

There is also a rather common occurrence in politics that
might be called the vector principle. A boat sets off for the
opposite shore of a river but because of various unconsidered
currents ends up several miles downstream. American
policies often seemed in theory, if not in execution, directed
toward reasonably obtainable, rational goals but failed
nonetheless because they did not take fully into account the
currents of Iranian and Middle East politics.

In part, United States error may be traced to the triumph of
a single-minded strategy over political realities. It involved
overdependence on seemingly changeless factors, unwarranted
reliance on the strength of the status quo, and an excessively
cynical view of considerations presented as moralistic. Certainly, some dictatorships prosper—not all decay—and some
are replaced by worse alternatives. Nevertheless, the competence and popularity of foreign governments with whom the
United States must deal are factors contributing to or threatening the realization of American foreign policy goals.

Blindless toward these realities was heightened by
bureaucratic factors within the United States government—the

discouragement of internal debate and honest reporting in the
Nixon-Ford administrations and the breakdown of coordination and discipline during the Carter years. These often-
neglected considerations played a central role in American
misperceptions.

Especially remarkable is the extent to which years of
American-Iranian relations were built on mutual ignorance
and misperceptions. American strategists saw Iran as a chess
piece on the international political game board: capable of
making potent military and diplomatic moves in support of
the grand strategy without reference to its own internal tensions. The shah's regime and its enemies shared many serious
errors about the nature of the United States and its foreign
policy. To them, Washington had either to be savior or satan.
The road to the hell of the hostage crisis was often paved for
the United States with good intentions, coupled with exceed-
ingly bad judgment.

How was the United States transformed in Iranian eyes from
their nation's savior, in the 1940s, to the world-devouring
satan of the Khomeinist era? An answer to this question, it
seems, will tell much about the triumphs and tragedies of
American foreign policy toward the Third World over the past
thirty-five years.

This book was generated by my research as a historian in
the evolution of Middle East politics and United States policy
on the one hand and from my work as a political analyst of
contemporary developments on the other.

In addition to the use of archival material—much of it only
recently declassified—and of other primary sources, I have interviewed well over one hundred people involved with this
story. These include past and present American officials from
the Defense Department, State Department, National Security
Council, the United States Embassy in Tehran, and the CIA, as
well as many Iranians, both those who served under the shah,
as soldiers or diplomats, and those now part of the new Islamic Iranian government. Since these were mostly off-the-
record talks, they cannot be footnoted.

Naturally, however, personal descriptions and interpretations of events were cited only with caution and with corroboration from other sources. I wish to thank all of those who gave generously of their time and candidly and courageously of their thoughts on this subject.

I especially want to thank Jay La Monica, Devon Gaffney, and Marc Goodman for their moral support and material assistance. Susan Meisel helped on research and Bonnie Koenig compiled the chronology. My editor, Susan Rabiner, also labored above and beyond the call of duty.

To avoid overwhelming the reader with footnotes, I have generally attributed only direct quotes. In most cases, the bibliography should serve as a guide for those wishing to do further study. Again, for clarity I have generally used the transliterations of Iranian names most commonly employed by the Western media.

Washington, D.C.   B.R.
July, 1980

Contents

Paved with Good Intentions

1
A Friendship Is Born

At the beginning of this century, few Persian officials had even heard of the United States. Until an American diplomat talked him out of his plan, one adventurous nineteenth-century shah planned to travel to the New World by an over-land route. On the other side, Americans knew as little of Per-sia. As late as 1943, General Patrick Hurley, President Roosevelt's envoy to the Middle East, kept confusing Iran with neighboring Iraq.

Despite increasing political, economic, and cultural interac-tion over more recent years, neither country bothered to learn a great deal about the other. One could not even assume that those in the highest reaches of government were well in-formed. In the crisis-ridden months during and after Iran's Is-lamic Revolution of 1978–79, the consequences of this mutual ignorance would be clearly apparent. The revolution's violent anger toward the United States can be made intelligible only through reference to a long history of previous relations little known to most Americans.

The first twentieth-century contacts between the two peo-ple were characterized by special bonds of concern.

American missionaries and diplomats who viewed Persia
firsthand in the early 1900s were saddened by what they saw.
Compromised from within by a greedy and oppressive ruling
clique and from without by the imperialistic behavior of Russia and Great Britain, the country seemed barely able to survive as an independent nation. To Persian intellectuals, who
were beginning to delve into Western political history and
thought, America's distance and disinterestedness were fascinating. This new force on the horizon, a rising international
power, might be useful as a lever against the massive weight
of Anglo-Russian domination. And possibly more important,
that peculiar American concept of a constitutionally restricted
government appealed to an intellectual class that no longer
trusted its rulers to serve the interests of the nation. Limiting
the power of the shah might end the humiliating situation in
which the people and resources of Persia were daily sold or
leased out to foreign interests by the ruling clique. Why
should not Persia take its rightful place in the glittering new
century of industrialization, science, national pride, and mo-
torcars? Both Americans and Persians came to believe that
indeed the United States—with its growing power and yet
with no national interest in Persia's resources—might come to
play some special, beneficial role in rescuing Persia from its
humiliating servitude and in restoring it to some semblance of
its past glory.

Persia had indeed fallen a long way. Twenty-five hundred
years earlier, the country had produced a great and innovative
civilization that dared to dream of conquering all the known
world. It had defeated the dreaded Assyrians, built an empire of unsurpassed splendor, and had come close to conquering Greece. The early shahs had truly been the time's "king of
kings." Only Alexander the Great had been able to overcome
them. Beginning in 334 B.C., in three titanic battles that constituted Persia's first defeat at Western hands, Alexander's
forces smashed Persian armies outnumbering his force by up
to five-to-one.

A half-millennium later, the Sasanids started Persia on another flourishing era that lasted from the third to the seventh
centuries A.D. This dynasty was destroyed by an invasion of

the Arabs, newly converted and united by Islam. Yet the Muslim triumph, which ended Persia's political independence, simultaneously transformed and broadened her cultural influence. As the Muslim religion came to change the Persian life, Persian language, arts, bureaucracy, and political methods came to dominate the Islamic Empire. The merger was as tight as that between dye and cloth. As an eleventh-century Persian poet wrote, "I draw glory from the best of forebears and religion from the best of Prophets. I based my pride on both sides, the majesty of the Persians and the religion of the Arabs." [1]

The complex relationship between Islam and Iranian nationalism was partially resolved in the sixteenth century when the Safavid dynasty brought to power a particularly Iranian interpretation of Islam in the tradition of its Shi'a branch. Religion and politics had always been tightly blended in Persian life—the pre-Islamic kings with Zoroastrianism, the Abbasid caliphs with Islam, and the Safavids with Shi'a Islam. Within this context, however, the monarch usually tried to subordinate the clerical hierarchy. Often he succeeded, but the penalty for any too-outspoken deviation from Islamic principles might be religious revolt.

In pragmatic political terms it was far more important that a Persian ruler be properly pious than that he be democratic or even nationalistic. The Western view of consensual governance had evolved through a long history of conflict, first between nobles and kings, and then between middle and ruling classes and had no counterpart in Middle East societies. In Persia certainly, the principle of autocracy was never so challenged. Further, the competing claims of secular nationalism and religious authority, a dichotomous tension that had been resolved in the West through the Reformation and by a series of victories by secular forces over those of the Vatican, were never settled in Iran. These two fundamental differences, therefore, between Western and Iranian-Islamic perceptions of governance lie at the center of many misunderstandings regarding the shah's fall and the nature of the revolution that displaced him.

Two particularly important concepts in this regard—the

right to revolt against unjust rulers and the existence of organized religious power centers outside state authority—were more strongly developed in Shi'a Islam than they were in the majoritarian Sunni sect. Shi'ism was at the same time more mystical and more devoted to charismatic leadership. Persian Shi'ism had a definite hierarchy of religious authorities that stood apart from the governmental chain of command.

This politically freestanding hierarchy made it possible for religious leaders, known as mullahs, to lead a revolution, while Shi'a doctrine provided a defensible rationale for opposition to the shah. As early as the 680s A.D., Shi'a mullahs were fomenting revolutions to build a new order of social justice. They justified their uprisings by the sayings of the Prophet Muhammad: "At the end of time there will be tyrannical amirs, vicious viziers, treacherous judges, and lying jurists. Whoever lives to that time should not serve them, not as inspector, nor as collector, nor as treasurer, nor as policeman."[2]

Shi'a leaders, like Muhammad's grandson Zayd ibn Ali, summoned their followers, "to wage Holy War against oppressors and defend those who have been abased, to give pay to those who are deprived of it, and to share the booty equally among those who are entitled to it, to make good the wrongs done by the oppressors," and to aid the legitimate representatives of Islam against usurpers.[3]

Within this tradition, Iranian religious leaders were free to attack the shah's government and policies on the grounds that they were unjust and contrary to Islam. Tens of millions of Iranians, particularly those living in the rural villages and even the many peasants who had recently migrated to the cities, accepted these clerical proclamations as guides to proper behavior toward their king.

Iranian history also demonstrates a striking contrast between the fragility of dynasties and the remarkable durability of the nation. Time after time, revolts or invasions threw down mighty kings while the country's Persian core retained its distinctiveness and sense of identity. Doubtless this history owed much to Persia's climate and terrain. Bounded by mountains and deserts, the Persian homeland was often isolated on the great central plateau. Located on the crossroads of trade routes, Persia was often temptingly easy to conquer, but it was much harder to change or to rule.

Most of Iran's land has been unfit for agriculture, hospitable solely to pastoral nomadic tribes loyal to their own chiefs and hostile to a distant central government that represented only unpopular taxation and military conscription. Great regional cities strove for autonomy, while non-Persian peoples who lived on the periphery—Arabs in the southwest, Turks and Kurds in the northwest, and Baluchs in the southeast—had little affection for or allegiance to any Persian shah or nation.

The experience of centuries seemed to teach that rulers used an iron hand or they did not long remain in power. The alternative to strong central authority was chaos. Unfriendly foreign powers stalked the borders, seeking only an opportunity for conquest. Outlying provinces awaited only their opportunities to break away.

The decline of the Qajar dynasty in the nineteenth century coincided with the arrival of the Russians from the north and the British from the south. The former, expanding their great land empire, were continuing their historic march toward warm waters. The British sought to secure transport routes through the Persian Gulf and their imperial lifeline to India.

Both powers conspired, usually against each other, with tribes and factions of Persian politicians. Even without such interventions the shahs were becoming weaker, more corrupt, and more disliked by all classes of the population. With foreign involvement, Persia also became a battlefield for great-power rivalry and it was Russian and British machinations that were blamed for keeping the discredited Qajars on the throne.

Xenophobia—hatred and dislike of foreigners—was not new to Persia. Islam had given the Persians a sense of moral superiority over the infidels and Persian nationalism had provided them with a sense of cultural superiority over other Muslims. Yet if Iranian political culture often exaggerated the impact of hated foreign interference, it also often stressed the importance of being on the right side of some powerful foreign patron. If an outside power had such overwhelming control, Iranian politicians would do well to secure its backing. Thus, the early constitutionalists curried British support, the fortunes of the Tudeh (Communist) Party waxed and waned with the apparent power of the Soviet Union in the 1940s, and the United States itself became the object of the affections of a whole group of Iranian suitors.

The first Americans were too exotic for the political intriguers to worry about. American missionaries, who first arrived in 1829, worked only with the Christian minority communities, but they won widely held reputations for courage and humanitarianism. The schools and clinics they established helped open Iran to modern ideas. It was to protect these missionaries that the first United States diplomatic mission was established in 1883.

Beyond this minimal presence, the United States had no interest in further involvement. Given the proximity and intensity of British and Russian power, the wisest course seemed careful neutrality and consistent nonintervention. Iran however was not standing still. Modernization and constitutionalism appealed to some Persians; opposition to foreign encroachment and hatred of the oppressive shah motivated more. By 1906 the Qajar shah had been forced to promise constitutional government, an achievement hailed by American missionaries and diplomats.

Despite this promising start, the constitutionalist forces found that they could not depend upon British support. London had no incentive to back a major reform effort in Persia; its eyes were on wider geopolitical considerations. For almost a century, British and Russian interests had collided over a long belt of strategic territory stretching from the Ottoman Empire through Persia and Afghanistan and even into distant Tibet. This struggle, dubbed "the Great Game," involved the consolidation of Russia's ever-expanding southern borders against British attempts to provide security for their sea routes and their Indian Empire.

With Germany's rise as Britain's main rival in Europe, however, this periodic confrontation increasingly seemed like an unnecessarily distracting side issue. Thus, in 1907, Britain resolved its differences with Russia. Tibet was neutralized, Russia abandoned its interest in Afghanistan, and Persia was partitioned into three segments. Czarist Russia would exercise primary influence in the north; Britain staked out the south; and Tehran was designated a neutral zone.

This action demoralized the reformers and emboldened the shah, who had been egged on by the Russians. Indeed, St. Petersburg continued to support him in violation of their agreement, but London, motivated by wider considerations, was willing to look the other way. The shah's attempted counter-revolution led to a see-saw battle. The city of Tabriz, a hotbed of anti-shah activity, successfully revolted; between 1909 and 1912 the constitutionalists again briefly held power.

The official American role in these exciting events was quite limited, but the sympathy of individual Americans created goodwill among Persian democrats. This, in turn, provided a basis for Iranian hope of further American aid. Two quite different men symbolize this incipient hope: Howard C. Baskerville and W. Morgan Shuster.

Baskerville, a twenty-one-year-old Princeton graduate, was a teacher at the American mission school in Tabriz. Like many of his colleagues he sympathized with the constitutionalists. The local American consul, while sharing some of Baskerville's views, was duty bound to inform him that the United States must remain neutral in the ensuing civil war. He asked the outspoken young teacher to refrain from making any more public speeches. Baskerville was hardly in a position to offer the local forces real help against the surrounding pro-shah tribes, the consul added, since his entire military experience consisted of watching American troops drill years earlier.

But Baskerville persisted in attacking the shah. Ignoring pleas from the State Department and the Mission Board, he resigned his job in April, 1909. Now he threw himself into full-time support for the revolution. Enrolling his Iranian students as soldiers, Baskerville began to train constitutionalist militia units.

Less than two weeks later he was dead, shot down on the edge of the city while charging a royalist barricade, a victim of

his own tactical recklessness. Nevertheless, the American consul remarked, he had given his life in a good cause. Baskerville's funeral was turned into a nationalist demonstration,
with three thousand people attending in tribute. His life and
death, quickly forgotten in the United States, has often been
cited by followers of both the shah and the Ayatollah Khomeini as a fine example of United States-Iranian friendship.[4]

The temporary victory of the constitutionalists, sparked by
the Tabriz revolt, created its own monumental tasks in the
three years before the shah returned to full power. Administrative and financial institutions could barely keep Iran going;
foreign loans and technicians were badly needed. Where
could the constitutionalists turn? Toward the United States, of
course, and the new regime made contact with President William Howard Taft. Neither Britain nor Russia would object
since the only alternative seemed to be increased influence by
their German rivals. America would not pose any threat, London and St. Petersburg reasoned.

Taft, however, saw no reason for official American involvement. He would do no more than recommend W. Morgan
Shuster to be Iran's financial adviser. A handsome young
Washington lawyer, Shuster had held similar jobs for the
United States government in Cuba and in the Philippines before his return to private practice in 1908. Intrigued by this
new challenge, Shuster quickly signed a three-year contract,
chose four assistants, and boarded ship for Persia. He had no
idea of the steep odds facing him.

Shuster's mission was an exercise in frustration, since any
real reform of Persian finances would have threatened the
power and position of bureaucrats, reactionary politicians,
and landlords, to say nothing of the Russians and British. "I
thought I had been up against a few difficult circumstances in
my brief career before this," Shuster later wrote, "but everything in the past looks like child's play alongside the present
task."

As would Franklin Roosevelt much later, Shuster clung to
a strong faith that American honesty, persistence, and technology could help transform Iran into a modern democratic

nation. His efforts, however, were constantly blocked, not only by the foreign imperialist powers, but by the obstructionism of powerful antireform Persians as well.

He burned with righteous indignation against the shortsightedness of the old Persian elite and against the "uncivilized" behavior of the British and Russians, who were strangling Iran. His sympathies were with the constitutionalists and the Persian people who were "fighting for a chance to live and govern themselves instead of remaining the serfs of wholly heartless and corrupt rulers." [5]

After Shuster's first year in Iran the Russians forced his dismissal. Shortly afterward the shah succeeded in crushing the constitutional regime and disbanded the Majlis (parliament). Shuster's removal had been one step in the restoration of the shah's autocratic powers. Commented Stanislaw Poklevski-Koziell, the Russian minister in Tehran, "It was a monumental error to bring Americans to this country. I know them. I know for what they stand . . . and you can't make them 'fit' in this country." Americans, the British and Russians agreed, were simply too idealistic and unrealistic to deal with Iran. Their reformist meddling unbalanced the status quo. [6]

However, the upheavals that took place around the time of the First World War did far more to undermine the Iranian status quo than a hundred Shusters. Iran's declaration of neutrality was ignored by all belligerents and wartime strains further weakened the Qajar dynasty. The constitutionalists sided with the Germans to avenge themselves on the shah's supporters. Russian power in Iran melted away as that country underwent revolution and civil war. By 1918 British primacy seemed unchallengeable.

This influence was greatly reinforced by the introduction of a new factor that would forever change Persia's fate—oil. Ten years earlier, in 1908, a British petroleum company, frustrated after many dry wells, had ordered a stop to exploration, but the determined engineer in charge, convinced that a rich field would soon be found, stalled for time. Sure enough, at almost the last moment, the drillers hit a gusher.

First Lord of the Admiralty Winston Churchill quickly understood the discovery's potential importance. The British fleet, competing against the kaiser's navy, was converting from coal to oil as part of its modernization program. Persian oil filled a prime strategic need and consequently the British government bought a controlling interest in the company. The Persian government received a 16 percent share in exchange for the concession. Given this distribution of power, the corporation took the name Anglo-Iranian Oil Company (AIOC).

AIOC earned its profits by exploring, pumping, refining, transporting, and marketing Persian oil. In doing so it brought much revenue to the Tehran regime. Yet there was also ample basis for Persian resentment toward the AIOC, which provided far more in benefits to the British than to the Persians.

While the company paid no taxes or import duties to Iran, it paid Britain income tax, corporation tax, and import duties. The British Navy bought AIOC oil at a discount. There were no Persian directors to check the company accounts, a situation that led to constant Persian accusations that the books were juggled to minimize the Iranian share of the profits. Relatively few Persians were trained for skilled or managerial positions. AIOC became a state within the state, controlling Persia's main resource and intervening in Persian politics. It is not surprising that Persian antagonism toward AIOC eventually grew to explosive proportions.

To break the British monopoly over oil production, Iranian leaders approached Washington on several occasions. Since the United States had no incentive to challenge British primacy and since Iran was far too peripheral for America in those isolationist years between the wars, there was little interest in accepting such offers.

Indeed, when the Iranian government had appealed to President Woodrow Wilson for help in obtaining a seat at the 1919 Versailles peace conference, Wilson brought up the matter with his allies, and when the British strongly opposed any invitation for Iran, Wilson dropped the issue. Shortly thereafter, when London tried to impose an unequal treaty on Tehran the United States objected but took no serious action.

The general bent of American attitudes, however, did not go completely unnoticed by certain Persian politicians, two of whom would later play an important role in building relations between the two countries. Both Qavam es-Sultanah, the most skilful political organizer of his generation, and Hussein Ala, Persia's minister to Washington, saw the potential of an American card in their country's hand. Over the course of the next thirty years both sought to play such a card on a variety of occasions.

Their first attempt to bring American companies into Persia to compete with AIOC failed. Some of the more adventuresome independent companies were willing to talk to the Persians but none wanted to challenge the international oil cartel, in which AIOC was a key member. By the 1920s the major petroleum-producing corporations had already divided up the available world market and wanted to prevent any increased production. Trespassing on a British sphere of influence could bring retaliation from AIOC. Even though the Persian government appointed Schuster as its agent to search for alternative partners for producing oil no deal could be organized.

The Persians had more success with a new mission of American financial advisors, led by Arthur Millspaugh, which worked in Iran between 1922 and 1927. Millspaugh had taught economics at several universities before joining the United States government, where he rose to become economic advisor to the Department of State. Although he enjoyed some success in Iran, many of his experiences were as frustrating as those faced by Shuster some fifteen years earlier.

But there was one very significant difference. The year before Millspaugh's arrival the remnants of Qajar rule had been destroyed finally by a dashing Persian army officer, Reza Pahlevi. After putting down a Russian-sponsored Communist revolt in the north, Pahlevi marched into Tehran. He quickly outmaneuvered the civilian politicians who had supported him and overcame the few brave voices favoring a republic. The culmination of this process came on December 12, 1925, when he had himself elected as shah. From such modest beginnings came the last royal dynasty in Persia's twenty-five-hundred-year history.

In an ironic twist that would not fully reveal itself for another fifty years, Reza Shah, as he became known, had toyed with a renewal of the republic. Shi'a religious leaders refused to consider such an idea. The republican form of government, after all, was a Western innovation in conflict with centuries of Persian tradition. Considering the chaos and total governmental breakdown that characterized Persian life at the end of Qajar rule, many believed that only an autocrat could restore order. With Reza Shah's ascension to the throne his six-year-old son, piously named Muhammad, became crown prince.

The Pahlevis, father and son, were never wildly popular in Persia—or Iran, as Reza Shah renamed the country to symbolize his hopes of creating a new, forward-looking state. Of course, public popularity had never been a requirement for ruling Iran and few shahs ever possessed widespread popular support. Their ability to inspire fear and respect had always been far more relevant. Essentially, Reza Shah was a despotic modernizer. He followed an ancient injunction of Persian politics: ruthlessly centralize power.

Of course, there was more to be done if one wanted to create a developed state. Although Reza Shah admired Kemal Ataturk, the father of modern Turkey, he could never match that neighboring ruler's organizational or propaganda abilities. Ataturk also had far better material to work with than had Reza Shah, but he managed to build an alternate Turkish secular culture, to lay the foundations for Turkish industry, and to put together a well-rooted national political party. Ataturk was unquestionably an autocrat. Yet by structuring a secure base of support he built an edifice that endured.

Reza Shah, in contrast, treated the urban middle class, out of which should have come his managers and technocrats, as he treated the unruly tribes. Not surprisingly, his state factories malfunctioned. Ataturk broke the clergy's power, weakened Turkey's pan-Islamic loyalties, and substituted in their place a strong (though nonaggressive) nationalism. Reza Shah expounded no cohesive national ideology. It was no mere question of relative harshness. Many of Ataturk's early colleagues ended up in prison; the leaders of the Turkish Communist Party were set adrift in a leaky boat on the stormy Black Sea. But Ataturk also found a place for Turkish merchants and intellectuals. He developed a philosophy of Turkism, complete with a rewriting of the nation's history; founded a series of social and political clubs, which could be seen even in the tiniest village; and tirelessly worked to motivate the Turkish people. In short, he was a twentieth-century politician.

Reza Shah operated more like a traditional monarch. He would not delegate authority. The bureaucracy trembled before him since anyone might be whisked off to prison at any moment for failing to comply with the shah's dictates. He preferred prestigious construction projects to more necessary irrigation work. He feared rather than promoted any mobilization of the people. He took land from the Qajars and from his rivals only to turn it into his own estates. His son would be strongly influenced by this style of ruling, though he did try at times to turn it to more beneficent ends.

Reza Shah provoked the hatred of the landlords and clergy without gaining, in exchange, the support of any segment of Iranian society outside his own army. The corruption he inherited from the Qajar years continued and even became institutionalized. Progress toward modernization was spotty and isolated. As his reign wore on and as he became increasingly dependent on the military, it, in turn, regularly received up to 50 percent of government allocations to guarantee its continued loyalty.

Arthur Millspaugh's dislike for Reza Shah stemmed from their clashes over fiscal reform. The regressive tax system could not be made more equitable because it was expressly designed to benefit the wealthy landlords. Quite logically, then, as long as Reza Shah refused to implement changes in the tax system, it was impossible to raise any revenue except by levies on the poor. To the shah, Millspaugh was an arrogant and overbearing foreigner who was trying to tell him how to run his country. This friction was not dissimilar to that which would often enter into relations between Reza Shah's son and later American advisors.

The very real distance between the two cultures and the sensitivity displayed by each to affronts by the other was graphically illustrated by several minor incidents during the years before World War II. On July 18, 1924, Robert Imbrie, the United States vice-consul in Tehran and a zealous amateur photographer, went with an American friend to take some snapshots at one of Tehran's public water fountains. A religious gathering was in progress and some of the people present called out to him not to take any pictures. As Imbrie closed the camera to put it away the case clicked. The crowd, assuming he had taken another photograph, attacked him.

When the two Americans tried to escape in a passing carriage, the mob ran after it, shouting that the men had poisoned the well and that they had killed several people. They stopped the carriage and while several policemen and soldiers tried to help the Americans, others joined the mob. After being badly beaten, the two were finally able to make their way to the hospital.

Meanwhile, outside the hospital, a mullah further stirred the passions of a gathering crowd against the two foreigners. Led by a number of soldiers, they finally rushed into the building, overwhelmed the guard, and broke into the operating room. Finding Imbrie there under treatment by a Persian doctor, they tore up bricks from the room's floor and began to batter Imbrie. Before they ran away, the attackers had inflicted one hundred thirty-eight wounds on him. Imbrie died shortly thereafter.[7]

So intense was the emotional hysteria in Tehran that the government was able only with great difficulty to punish those responsible. Local opinion blamed the murder on foreign machinations. Since American oil company representatives had been holding talks with the Persian government, the popularly accepted version ran that the British had murdered Imbrie to protect their monopoly by frightening off the Americans.

The second incident showed some insensitivity on the other side of the relationship. Ghaffar Djalal, Iran's minister in Washington, was arrested for speeding through the small town of Elkton, Maryland in November, 1935. Iran protested this violation of Djalal's diplomatic immunity and the local police chief and constable were fired. But Reza Shah was enraged when Secretary of State Cordell Hull told Djalal that despite immunity diplomats should obey traffic laws. The incident was viewed as an assault on Iran's dignity.

Relations were far more seriously threatened by a series of stories in American newspapers, particularly in the Hearst press, claiming that Reza Shah had been as a youth a stable boy in the British legation. Reza Shah's enemies always were spreading the most fantastic stories about him—that he was a Christian, a Russian, or, most commonly, that he had been installed by the British. Distortions of this type, unfortunately, have not disappeared from Iranian politics, and this practice allows foreign media reports to have an effect on domestic politics well beyond what individual reporters might imagine.

In response to the stable-boy stories, Iran issued an official protest and threatened to break diplomatic links. State Department officials replied with explanations of the constitutional guarantees allowing the American press to print what it chose to print. It was further noted that in America depicting someone as a self-made man was hardly an insult.

This did not apply, however, to hereditary monarchs claiming two-thousand-year-old thrones. To have been called a former stable boy was insult enough but to have been called a British stable boy was in anglophobic Iran intolerable! Iran's foreign minister could only suggest that America might consider choosing between freedom of the press and the friendship of Reza Shah. As a result, from 1936 through 1938, United States-Iranian relations were at a standstill. The continued remoteness of the two countries from each other was amply demonstrated by the fact that this breakdown had little effect on either.

On the eve of World War II it was difficult to imagine that the relative isolation of America from Iran would ever change. They seemed as distant and as mutually exotic as might any two countries on the planet. But the war and its aftermath would change all that forever.

By the late 1930s, Reza Shah had become increasingly authoritarian and unpopular. The puppet Majlis followed his wishes, the press was as controlled as any despotic government could wish, and quick arrests prevented the formation of any opposition. Nazi Germany, well aware of Iran's hatred toward Britain and Russia, courted Reza Shah throughout the decade. They bestowed on the Persians the honor of Aryan status and expanded trade between the two nations; Berlin flooded the country with agents and propaganda. Bribes were spread thickly among politicians and journalists.

Once the war began, German forces initially achieved victory after victory in Europe and also threatened the strategic Middle East. Nazi forces invading the Soviet Union advanced hundreds of miles eastward. In 1940–41 Allied fortunes were at their lowest ebb. The anti-Axis cause required the survival of the Soviet Union; the Soviet Union's survival depended on supplies from the still-neutral but strongly anti-Nazi United States. The most convenient and secure supply route ran to Russia's back door—via Reza Shah's newly completed Trans-Iran Railroad.

To secure this prize, to protect the oil fields, and to keep the country out of pro-German hands, British and Soviet troops invaded Iran in August, 1941. Although some of his 125,000 troops fought bravely, the shah's pampered army quickly faded away. Once more Iran was being treated as an Anglo-Russian colony; once again foreigners would designate the country's leader. Reza Shah was packed off to exile on the uncomfortable east African island of Mauritius, never to return. Muhammad Reza Shah ascended the "Peacock Throne," to be Iran's sovereign for the next thirty-seven years. Many were happy to see Reza Shah go. The tribes and local gentry hoped again to escape the central government's hand; others had personal grudges. Yet this invasion and the subsequent occupation was a traumatic experience for Iran and for the young new shah. Perhaps, he must have thought many times, some foreign army might one day sweep across Iran's borders with equal ease to displace him.

Over the next four and a half years, the shah sat on the throne without much political power. British and Soviet soldiers and civilians virtually ran the country. Prices rose 450 percent and famine swept large parts of Iran. As in their old 1907 agreement, the Russians controlled the north while the British controlled the south. With good reason, Persians felt not like an ally but a conquered people.[8]

In the face of this frightening situation Iranian leaders turned to the United States for guarantees and assurances. Although Tehran could not convince Washington to try to end the occupation—Allied victory was America's top priority—Roosevelt did agree to seek an Anglo-Russian declaration that the takeover was temporary and that Iran would be returned to full independence as quickly as possible after the war.

While protesting their innocence of any imperialist intentions, both the USSR and Britain were reluctant to make such a pledge. As the United States continued to pressure them, the two finally signed a treaty with Iran in January, 1942. Article Five stated that Allied forces should be withdrawn from Iranian territory "not later than six months" after the war's end.[9] While Tehran welcomed this promise for the future, it continued to complain about Soviet and British behavior in the present.

The Soviets excluded all Iranian troops from the north, imported goods without paying duty, and bought up food for export. With southern Iran dependent on northern crops, this last action led to famine in some of the most densely populated areas of the country. More ominously, Moscow stimulated separatist propaganda among the Turkish-speaking people of Azerbaijan, Iran's northwest province, and among the Kurdish minority. Soviet Communist agitators belonging to related ethnic groups on the Russian side of the border were infiltrated into Iran. Leaders of the Iranian Communist Party (the Tudeh, literally, "Masses" Party) were released from Reza Shah's prisons and given Soviet subsidies and encouragement. Journalists and non-Tudeh Majlis members were bribed. The old Russian imperialism had returned in a new and even more terrifying form.[10]

Many Iranians saw the British as only marginally better. "The British are pillaging us," remarked Iran's foreign minister, although the English were, in fact, working hard to supply Iran with food. American diplomats and intelligence agents tended to sympathize with the Iranians and were, sometimes unfairly, quite critical of London's behavior. The Americans blamed the large, bloody bread riots of December, 1942 on British policy. Again and again, in Tehran and Washington, Iran's leaders and diplomats passed the message to their American counterparts: they liked neither the British nor the Russians, especially the latter, but they "fully trusted" the United States. Iran could be saved only by a strong United States commitment.[11]

Throughout 1942 and 1943, the Office of Strategic Services (OSS), predecessor to the CIA, found Iranians "unhappy and very restive," feeling they were being "ravaged" by Britain and the Soviet Union. United States Ambassador Louis Dreyfus thought the Iranian attitude toward Britain to be "short-sighted and unrealistic," but would not entirely blame them for "refusing to cooperate with a nation at whose hands they have suffered so much." The lesson in all this, he continued, was that "relations based on force and exploitation rather than on mutual help and good will do not pay dividends when the day of reckoning arrives." Fortunately, he concluded, American relations with Iran were of the latter variety. When some of Dreyfus's reports were accidentally given to the British Foreign Office, British diplomats were so angry that they successfully pressed for his removal.[12]

The American attitude at this time was perhaps best summarized by a January, 1943 report from John Jernegan, a State Department Middle East expert. "Although Russian policy had been fundamentally aggressive and British policy fundamentally defensive in character, the result in both cases has been interference with the internal affairs of Iran." This state of affairs "created an ingrained distrust of both powers in the Iranian people. . . ."[13]

Not surprisingly, the anger and distrust generated by Allied actions boosted the effectiveness of German propaganda. Berlin radio broadcasts were so successful that the British once pressured local police to remove all radios from public places.

When it was found that this made it impossible for Iranians to listen to British broadcasts as well the radios were returned; the Soviets solved the problem by jamming the Nazi transmissions.

Movie audiences in the poor sections of south Tehran sometimes cheered war newsreels in the wrong places and even applauded Hitler's appearance on the screen. American concern mounted. One could not possibly win the love of Iranians by starving them, the State Department cautioned London. As the tide of battle turned in the Allies' favor, however, conditions in the south gradually improved. Moreover, with the arrival of thousands of American servicemen in Iran as part of the new Persian Gulf Command, established in January, 1943 to facilitate supplies to the Soviet Union, the United States earned more of a say in relations with Iran.

This had little immediate effect on the overall political situation. By late 1943, the much-abused Iranian government was on the edge of a breakdown; Secretary of State Hull told the president that it "may dissolve into chaos at any moment."[14] For the first time the United States government began to think of developing a coherent Iran policy. Two things were needed: a United States strategy for defining Iran's place in a postwar world and a clearer guarantee for Iranian independence.

The first requirement was partly met through the work of the State Department and the White House between August, 1943 and August, 1944. Iran had been an Anglo-Russian battleground for more than a century and, according to this analysis, would be so again as soon as the military situation eased. The weakness of the Iranian government and the presence of British and Soviet forces made this outcome more likely. Unless this conflict was checked, it would destroy Iranian independence, an eventuality not only contrary to the Atlantic Charter but also disastrous to any "equitable and lasting" postwar settlement. The only way to avoid this danger, the State Department warned, would be to strengthen Iran so "she will be able to stand on her own feet" and hold firm against the two European powers. Only the United States could provide effective aid to Iran and protect it from its two unwelcome guests.[15]

Roosevelt was enthusiastic. He was, the president wrote Hull, "thrilled by the idea of using Iran as an example of what we could do by an unselfish American policy. We could not take on a more difficult nation than Iran. I should like, however, to have a try at it." Neither the United States nor any other country should acquire a zone of influence, Roosevelt wrote British Prime Minister Winston Churchill in February, 1944, but "it will take thirty or forty years to eliminate the graft and the feudal system. Until that time comes, Iran may be a headache to you, to Russia and to ourselves."[16]

"That Iran is dominated by a powerful and greedy minority," reported the State Department, "is an obviously true statement." American advisors would seek to "break this stranglehold of the entrenched classes and to ensure for the mass of the Iranians a fairer share in the proceeds of their labor." President Roosevelt agreed with this analysis. In Iran, he told an aide, "One percent of the population ruled—and they were all grafters—while the other ninety-nine percent lived under the worst form of feudalism." But, "if we can get the right kind of American experts who will remain loyal to their ideals I feel certain that our policy of aiding Iran will succeed."[17]

One such adviser was Millspaugh, who returned to Tehran in January, 1943 as director-general of finance. He remained in the country until the end of the war, along with seventy other Americans who worked in the ministries of Finance, Treasury, Food and Price Stabilization, the national bank, customs, and in the reorganization of the national police. Although they made some progress on modernizing Iran's political structures, Millspaugh had a number of clashes with the shah. Foreshadowing the future, one such conflict was over the size of the army that the country could afford. The shah wanted 108,000 men; Millspaugh suggested 30,000. After Millspaugh's departure, the shah had his own way.

In short, America's practical interests seemed to require a

strong and independent Iran, free from the internal weaknesses and the dissensions that breed foreign intervention. A
weak Iran, Hull and Roosevelt concluded, might provoke conflict between the USSR and Britain or an imperialist partition
by the two. It would be far better for Iran to become an example of Allied cooperation in the postwar period. Since the
United States was popular among Iranians and had few material interests of its own in that country, Washington policymakers believed America would be the best guarantor of
this balance and the best guardian of Iran's sovereignty.

This deepening commitment was implemented at the December, 1943 Tehran conference, where Roosevelt, Churchill,
and Soviet Premier Joseph Stalin met for one of their major
wartime discussions. Stalin had refused to go any farther from
Soviet territory than Iran's capital. By traveling through the
Soviet-occupied north of the country he virtually never left
lands ruled by him. Stalin was the event's *de facto* host. Although Roosevelt did meet with the shah, it was the monarch
who was kept waiting for the audience.

Despite these indignities, the Tehran Declaration, in which
the three Great Powers promised to preserve Iran's unity and
independence and to promote development there, was an important gain for the Iranians. In later years Iranian governments would often refer to that document as the basis for an
American obligation to protect their country and to furnish
large-scale aid. The vagueness of the declaration made this
more wishful thinking than legal logic. Nevertheless, the
United States now was openly bound to deeper involvement
in Iran and to help enforce a troop withdrawal at the war's
end.

General Patrick Hurley, Roosevelt's envoy to the Middle
East, was the accord's main architect. To Hurley, whose
hatred for the British was as intense as his dislike for the Communists, the project offered an opportunity to check the ambitions of both countries. As soon as the signatures of the three
national leaders were on the accord, Hurley ran up to Admiral
William Leahy, Roosevelt's military advisor, exclaiming,

"Bill, I did it!" He was as happy, wrote Leahy, as a small boy who had just landed a big fish in the mill pond.[18] The fish was even bigger than Leahy thought.

That Iran might become a tinderbox was demonstrated by the crisis of autumn 1944, a crisis that also contributed to rising American suspicions of Moscow's intentions. Attempting to strengthen American involvement as a counterweight to the occupying powers, the Tehran regime once again invited American oil companies to negotiate for possible concessions in the north. Reacting to this encroachment on their perceived sphere of influence, the Soviets sent a delegation of their own. Although this group tried to browbeat the Iranians into granting them northern oil rights, they seemed far more interested in using the opportunity to bring in large numbers of Soviet technicians and to establish a Soviet-controlled school system.

The Russian emissary told Prime Minister Muhammad Saed that Moscow had at first offered Finland easy peace terms but later, after that country resisted, it was forced to accept much less favorable arrangements. Iran, he warned, should not make a similar mistake. "It appears that a crucial point in Russian penetration is at hand," the Office of Strategic Services reported, "and it is quite well established that the Russians are going to follow through by whatever means are necessary." These included bribing public officials, forcing a change in the cabinet, propaganda campaigns, labor strikes, restricting food shipments from northern Iran, and creating disturbances calling for Red Army intervention. Each of these tactics were employed in the following months.[19]

The Iranians resisted. Few believed that the Soviets really were interested in working oil fields in the north—to this day no petroleum has been found there. Equally unpersuasive was the Russian argument that they were asking only for treatment equal to that afforded the British AIOC in the south. The solution to having one such privileged guest at the table was not to invite a second to hold economic, military, and political power in another key region.

Prime Minister Saed, a veteran at dealing with such foreign

pressures, came up with an ingenious response: he postponed all negotiations for oil concessions until after the war. Both the Americans and Soviets would have to wait. One of the main supporters of this position was a Majlis member named Muhammad Mossadegh, who sponsored this law in parliament and who would later lead the fight to remove the AIOC as well.

The Soviets blamed the United States for the Iranian move, but Washington had neither fomented nor encouraged it beforehand. United States oil companies, after all, were the main victims of this action. Washington did, however, after the fact, support Iran's right to have chosen its own course of action without fear of retaliation.

With the oil concession refused them, Moscow threw what can only be described as a temper tantrum, deploying a whole range of menacing gestures. All grain shipments from the north were halted. A regiment of armed Soviet troops drove through the streets of the capital. Soviet newspapers and radio broadcasts launched nonstop attacks against the Saed regime. Moscow's ambassador even walked out of the diplomatic box during a Soviet-Iran soccer match to avoid speaking to Saed.

Tudeh marches were held demanding the government's resignation. When Iranian soldiers tried to line the parade routes, truckloads of Soviet troops forcibly displaced them. It was a lesson that Iranians would not soon forget. Although Saed finally resigned, these incidents produced resentment rather than surrender.

Soviet behavior also influenced American policy. Moscow's actions in Iran, as well as in neighboring Turkey and in Eastern Europe, heightened United States suspicions toward Stalin's postwar intentions. More and more Washington officials began to echo the views of State Department Soviet specialist George Kennan. The USSR, Kennan cabled from Moscow, could only conceive of its neighbors as either vassals or enemies and "if they do not wish to be the one, must reconcile themselves to being the other." As the Soviets gained the upper hand in one country after another, Kennan asked, would they know where to stop?[20]

W. Averell Harriman, the United States ambassador to Moscow, gradually reached similar conclusions. In a dispatch of September, 1944, he wrote Hull:

> What frightens me . . . is that when a country begins to extend its influence by strong-arm methods beyond its borders under the guise of security it is difficult to see how a line can be drawn. If the policy is accepted that the Soviet Union has a right to penetrate her immediate neighbors for security, penetration of the next immediate neighbors becomes at a certain time equally logical. . . .[21]

Six days later, in a report to the State Department Policy Committee, Adolph Berle made a parallel analysis. The Soviet Union sought to extend its influence throughout much of the Middle East. As long as this was done through friendly agreement, the United States had no objections; "but the Soviet doctrine that the governments must be 'friendly' is still obscure," Berle continued:

> If it is meant that these governments must not engage in intrigue against the Soviet Union there could be no possible objection: if it is meant that, by subsidizing guerrilla or other movements, virtual puppet governments are to be established, a different situation would prevail.[22]

In summarizing the lessons of the Iran oil crisis, Harriman wrote in January, 1945 that Moscow's policy seemed to be one of using occupation troops, secret police, local Communist parties, labor unions, sympathetic leftist organizations, cultural societies, and economic pressure to establish regimes outwardly independent but in practice subservient to the Kremlin. The overriding consideration of Soviet foreign policy was a preoccupation with security. Yet, Harriman noted, "the Soviet conception of 'security' does not appear cognizant of the similar needs or rights of other countries and of Russia's obligation to accept the restraints as well as the benefits of an international security system."[23]

The question was not whether Stalin's policy was offensive or defensive, aggressive or fearful—it was all these things at the same time in practice. Nor was it seen as especially Marxist in motivation, for there was a strong element of continuity with traditional czarist attempts to control Iran.

Nevertheless, the United States was not prepared to allow a Soviet takeover of all or part of Iran, not only because of the immediate consequences of the conquest for Iran itself, but also because such a step might mark the first stage of a Soviet advance into the rest of the Middle East. Moscow's encouragement to the Tudeh and separatist movements, its banning of American and Iranian officials from the north, and its treatment of the Tehran government all seemed to point in this direction. This was also the interpretation made by Iran's leaders.

Month by month into 1945 the situation worsened. With Allied armies closing in on Berlin, the war was clearly coming to an end. Would the Tehran Declaration be implemented and the foreign troops removed? Moscow sidestepped United States attempts to learn its intentions. The shah was nervous. When the Germans surrendered the Soviets pointed out that the Japanese were still fighting. Finally, in August, 1945, the Japanese gave up. The crisis could no longer be postponed.

Stalin's answer came quickly. In August the anti-Iran campaign in the Soviet press opened up like an artillery barrage. The new theme was clear. Moscow was backing the establishment of a separate puppet state in the northern province of Azerbaijan. A similar effort was underway in Kurdistan as well, though there a genuine nationalist movement played some part. Reports began to arrive in Washington of a Soviet-organized wave of terror in the north.

When the Soviets decided to create an Azerbaijani republic in late 1945, the task was entrusted to a veteran Communist, Jaafar Pishevari, and two Soviet officials, Arkadi Arkadievich Krasnykh, the consul-general in Tabriz, and Mirza Ibragimov, deputy president of the Azerbaijani Soviet Socialist Republic Council of Ministers. Several hundred Turkish-speaking Soviet Communists, indistinguishable from their Iranian kin, were sent to reinforce the weak local Tudeh group. One of them, a member of the Soviet MVD secret police, headed the equivalent body in the puppet regime whose army, ironically, was equipped with American Lend-Lease materiel down to the cloth for their uniforms.

A few weeks later, an influential group of Kurdish tribal chiefs were brought to Baku for a meeting with Jaafar Baghirov, prime minister of the Azerbaijani Soviet Socialist Republic. Baghirov lectured them on their need for self-determination. "As long as the Soviet Union exists," he told them, "the Kurds will have their independence." He promised military equipment and training, a printing press, and financial support. The Kurdish delegation was quickly ushered back to the railroad station, but not before each had been presented with a heavily framed, full-color photograph of Stalin. While the Azerbaijanis were mere Soviet agents, the Kurds accepted Moscow's support with some cynicism. They had their own nationalist movement and alliance with the USSR was a matter of expediency rather than loyalty.

Moscow also maintained a large espionage network in Iran. Agents moved freely from one country to the other using Soviet "safe houses" located near strategic border crossings. The Soviet ambassador in Tehran financed the Tudeh through the operations of the Iran-Soviet bank. A whole string of transport, petroleum, and import-export groups, as well as a chain of Soviet-operated hospitals provided cover for propaganda and bribery programs. All of these assets, plus the presence of many Red Army units in the north, presented a clear and present danger to Iran's future.[24]

Was the Soviet aim merely to annex Azerbaijan or was this a first step toward conquest of the entire country? American diplomats were not sure, but either way they agreed that this move had to be stopped. Iran, which had earlier been seen as a test case for postwar Anglo-American-Soviet cooperation, had now become a decisive battleground in the emerging Cold War. United States-Iranian relations, which had been so tenuous only five years earlier, had now become the centerpiece of a global crisis.

2
A Country Is Saved
1945–50

Trapped between two great powers, Britain and the USSR, Iranian leaders, including the young new shah, looked to the United States as a "third force" that would help maintain their nation's independence. World War II, which had greatly upset the international balance of power, provided the United States with both the ability and the motive to play such a role. Yet the United States assumed the task only after years of requests by Iranians to do so, during which time American leaders became convinced of Soviet insincerity toward Iran's right to independence. Thus it was that Iran became the first battlefield of the Cold War.

President Roosevelt had hoped to make the country an example of Big Three cooperation. There the United States would show Britain and the USSR that each party acting only with due respect for the interests of the other two would be a preferable and realistic alternative to a renewed Great Power conflict. A balance of power would share out influence while preventing excessive infringements on Iranian sovereignty.

By the end of the war, as American policymakers gradually became convinced of Moscow's aggressive designs toward

Iran, this optimistic plan was abandoned. Instead, the United States had to ally itself with London and Tehran to force out Soviet occupation troops and to counter Russian attempts to carve up Iran. Thus, Iran became a testing ground for the containment policy and a key experience in persuading Americans of Soviet bad faith.

Yet Iran was not seen during those first few postwar years as a weapon against the Soviet Union. Rather it was thought of as a weak domino, a defensive position that might be held only with some difficulty. Consequently, while opposing Soviet bullying, occupation zones, or puppet enclaves, the State Department also offered the carrot of good Soviet-Iranian relations, provided Moscow accept Iran's independence. But before this arrangement could be established, Washington would have to clearly demonstrate, as it did in the crisis of 1946–47, that it was willing to go to the brink of war to safeguard Iran's sovereignty.

The first three months of 1946 saw a complex international crisis develop out of the failure of American attempts at the Yalta, Potsdam, and the December, 1945 Moscow conferences to resolve Big Power conflicts over Iran. The tripartite treaty of January, 1942 had long before pledged that all foreign troops would be withdrawn within six months of Allied victory, but the Soviet Union refused to confirm its intention to keep that promise. Japan's capitulation in August, 1945 set the six-month deadline for the end of February, 1946 at the latest. What would the Russians do?

United States Ambassador Wallace Murray reported a high level of tension in Iran. Moscow's short-run objective, he believed, was the creation of a "buffer zone" in northern Iran, but its long-range aim was direct access to the Persian Gulf. This involved the establishment in power of a puppet Tehran government "led by men under Soviet influence amenable to Russian demands and hostile to other foreign nations." Soviet propaganda seemed to further indicate that the Russians might be paving the way for a coup d'etat. Such a development, which would create a potential threat to United States oil holdings in Saudi Arabia, Bahrein, and Kuwait, could be stopped only by a strong United States stand.[1]

American Soviet experts, intelligence officers, and military leaders all agreed with this assessment. The Joint Chiefs of Staff saw Soviet policy as a continuation of czarist attempts since the fifteenth century "to dismember Iran." The Soviets, like the czars, sought control of raw materials and the principal routes connecting Europe and the Far East. Iran had never been a threat to Moscow; only Russian expansionism motivated their conflict.[2]

The United States press also began to adopt these new attitudes. Iran was extremely important, wrote the *Washington Post's* Barnet Nover in a New Year's Day column, because it "will throw light on Russian ambitions in the Middle East." Nover concluded:

> Should Russia retain her present foothold on Iran the presumption will be hard to avoid that she will sooner or later seek to go further. When it comes to carrying out a policy of strategic imperialism history proves abundantly that the appetite grows with the eating.[3]

Soviet behavior seemed to foretell the worst. While the last American troops left Iran on January 1, 1946, and Britain announced it would meet the March 1 deadline, Moscow refused to set a date for its withdrawal. Shortly thereafter, the Russians established a puppet Kurdish state alongside their Azerbaijan satellite. Kurdish leaders were invited to the USSR, and were ordered to set up their own regime under Soviet tutelage. Moscow's third step seemed even more threatening: Soviet propaganda indicated that this might be only the beginning. Radio Moscow proclaimed on January 18: "Is it only the Azerbaijanis who demand the same standards of living and reasonable political freedom as are enjoyed by all nations of Europe? No! The people of Gilan and Mazandiron as well as the vast masses in Tehran are voicing the same demands."[4]

The threat was unmistakable. Iran's future might lie along the road down which Romania and Bulgaria had been taken.

Qavam es-Sultanah, the wily politician who early on had conceived of Iran's American card, acted cautiously to avoid this fate. He talked to the Soviets about their demands for autonomy for Azerbaijan, a joint oil company, and the continued presence of Soviet troops in Iran, while simultaneously complaining to the United Nations Security Council about Moscow's behavior and seeking American support.

As reports mounted of continued Soviet troop buildups in Iran, American leaders became convinced of the need to back Iran's resistance. Secretary of State James Byrnes told a State Department meeting that the Russians were about to add military invasion to subversion. Byrnes concluded the meeting by pounding his fist into his other palm and remarking, "Now we'll give it to them with both barrels."[5]

These events coincided with the general intensification of international tension. Stalin's February 9 "election speech" stressed communism's incompatibility with capitalism and implied that future wars were inevitable. Two weeks later, Kennan finally won the State Department's attention with his famous cable predicting Soviet attempts to expand further. "Where individual governments stand in [the] path of Soviet purposes," he wrote, "pressure will be brought for their removal from office."[6]

Faced with Republican claims that President Truman's policy was one of appeasement, Byrnes replied with a strong speech of his own on February 28. The United States would not stand aside in the face of aggression, he warned. That same day he suggested the dispatch of an American naval task force to show the flag in the area. Prime Minister Winston Churchill, speaking in Fulton, Missouri with Truman's endorsement, described the descent of an "iron curtain" across Europe. The press also accepted this analysis. "Where does the search for security end and where does expansion begin?" asked The New York Times in reference to Soviet policy.[7]

On March 2 the Russians, seeming to retreat slightly, announced that they would withdraw a portion of their troops from Iran; the rest would remain. At Iran's request, the United States delivered a stiff protest. Yet Americans in Iran reported not withdrawals but Soviet reinforcements, and the movement of Soviet units from the north toward Tehran. Joseph C. Goodwin, the Associated Press correspondent in Tabriz, reported he could barely hear the Soviet foreign minister's announcement of a pullback over his shortwave radio because of the roar and rattle of heavy Soviet tanks past his window, down the road toward the Iranian heartland.[8]

While Truman, Byrnes, and other American leaders later claimed that Washington's strong warnings to Moscow and its efforts through the United Nations resulted in Stalin's eventual retreat, at least as much credit is due to Qavam. When the Iranian prime minister had visited Moscow for talks in early March, he was subjected to strong threats from Stalin and Stalin's top aides. Qavam replied that only a new Majlis could change the law to permit a Soviet oil concession, that elections were necessary to elect a new Majlis, and that elections could be held only if Soviet troops were withdrawn from Iranian soil. He used a conciliatory tone: If the Russians would drop their pressures, Qavam implied, he would meet most of their demands.

Byrnes promised to support Iran's sovereignty with military strength if necessary, but the United States did not completely trust Qavam. Was he playing a double game? Would he fill the role of Quisling, as had many formerly non-Communist politicians in Eastern Europe? Even Qavam's old colleague Hussein Ala, once again ambassador to the United States, was unsure of his intentions, as was the shah and the United States ambassador, George V. Allen. Qavam was running the country and although the shah was eager for more active involvement in the political crisis, he was left with little more to do than pose as a symbol of Iranian independence.[9]

The combination of American pressure and Qavam's deception finally worked. Believing in Qavam's submissiveness, the Soviets agreed to a deal with Tehran in mid-May. They would pull out their troops and the Azerbaijan problem would be declared an internal Iranian affair; in exchange, Qavam would submit an agreement to the Majlis within seven months giving the USSR majority ownership in a joint north Iranian oil company. Thus the Soviet Union would avenge its 1944 defeat and gain a firm foothold within the borders of its southern neighbor.

For several months Qavam played along. He asked the United States to take no further actions on Iran's earlier complaints and to cease efforts through the United Nations. Many Iranians joined the Tudeh Party, convinced that the Soviets were the wave of Iran's future. In August, Qavam appointed three Tudeh members and three pro-Tudeh politicians to his cabinet. A State Department report concluded: "Russia has already achieved such dominance over Iran that Iran seems to have lost its power to speak as a free agent." [10]

Despite appearances, Qavam had not sold out to the Soviets. Rather, he was stalling for time in order to organize his own political power. Qavam settled a revolt by some of the southern tribes—who hated the shah's authority but feared the Tudeh even more—in exchange for their electoral support. Meanwhile, Soviet Ambassador Ivan Sadchikoff was putting pressure on Qavam for the promised Majlis ratification of the oil-concession proposal. When the original September 24 deadline came and went, Sadchikoff delivered an ultimatum. Simultaneously, the still-autonomous Azerbaijan regime became more arrogant in its negotiations with Tehran. Members of Qavam's own cabinet, eager to curry favor with those who seemed certain to control Iran's future, passed on details of internal government deliberations to the Soviet embassy.

At this dramatic juncture Qavam proceeded to the next step in his plan—to neutralize the USSR's leverage against Iran. On September 30 he told Ambassador Allen that United States military supplies and financial credits were needed to reestablish Iran's independence. Allen agreed—only by strengthening Qavam could the prime minister be made to resist Soviet pressures. Despite the growing crisis, up to this point the United States had been reluctant to increase aid to Iran or to make any deeper commitment. Now both the military and the State Department saw the necessity of helping Iran.

Undersecretary of State Dean Acheson thought that only a concerted program of economic assistance might stop the existing unsettled situation or even a protracted Iranian civil war. Otherwise, Qavam might be at the USSR's mercy.

The Joint Chiefs of Staff, asked to certify that protection of Iran was in the United States national interest, replied in the affirmative on October 11. Iran was of strategic importance to the United States, both as a source of oil and as a defensive position to protect United States-controlled oil wells in Saudi Arabia. It might also serve as a territorial "cushion" in preventing any Soviet attack from overrunning the Middle East.

While in the past the United States had been willing to agree to some Soviet arrangement over north Iranian oil, American experts now concluded that northern Iran was an unlikely source of large-scale petroleum production. However, since the USSR "does not now derive sufficient oil from sources within her borders to support a major war," it was deemed likely that Moscow wanted to obtain oil fields in southern Iran, Iraq, and other parts of the region. Any cession of northern Iran or of Azerbaijan to de facto Soviet control would provide a possible first base for an extended Soviet advance. Consequently, the United States military urged limited assistance to the Iranian government to enable it to ensure internal stability.[11]

One week later, on October 18, the State Department agreed to give broad-based assurances to Qavam of United States support, including a commitment to an Export-Import Bank loan, some military aid for defensive weapons, an enlarged United States military advisory mission, and increased cultural exchanges.

Qavam had not waited for this reply. He had already organized the cabinet to exclude the Communists and their supporters. Two months later, in December, Iranian troops marched into Azerbaijan and Kurdistan to overthrow the two Soviet-backed regimes. The Azerbaijanis greeted the central government's return with great enthusiasm; the pro-Moscow leaders either fled over the border to the USSR or were executed. The Majlis refused the Soviet oil concession, with only two Tudeh deputies dissenting.

With careful timing, Qavam mobilized mass support for his

Tehran government and brought the shah into action. The Tudeh quickly collapsed. Ambassador Allen commented that American support for Iranian sovereignty had been an important factor in this victory. "Practically every Iranian," he said, knew that Soviet acceptance of this counteroffensive lay "primarily in the fact that [the] Soviets were finally convinced that the United States was not bluffing." [12]

However, Iranian and American leaders had by no means reached a complete understanding. The shah and the Tehran politicians now believed that the United States would provide them massive economic and military assistance. The 1947 Truman Doctrine, which gave such help to Turkey and Greece, and the Marshall Plan, which helped rebuild war-ripped Europe, tended to heighten such expectations.

American policymakers felt that the United States task was to safeguard Iran from Soviet pressure or takeover. Internal reform was thought necessary to prevent a domestic collapse or a Communist-led revolution. Steps toward democratic political institutions, toward press freedom, and toward land reform were seen as preconditions for greater American help.

There was also a second conflict. Iranian officials naturally thought that their country should be at the center of American concerns, while United States counterparts gave Iran a low priority compared with other allies in the Middle East and elsewhere. These mutual misconceptions, which haunted United States-Iranian relations over the next twenty-five years, were visible almost immediately after the dissipation of the Russian threat. The main contentions concerned Iran's development program and the level of United States military aid.

On the former issue, the Tehran leaders wanted economic modernization to advance at top speed. The World Bank and the State Department were more pessimistic about Iran's prospects. The vagueness of Iran's plans, the obvious lack of preparation for using foreign loans efficiently, and the enormous—and wildly fluctuating—demands for money discouraged bankers and potential aid donors.

Military relations went only slightly better. Although a small sales agreement was concluded in June, 1947, the first arms shipment did not arrive in Tehran until March, 1949. True, Ambassador Allen promised to support Iran against Soviet intimidation when the Majlis finally rejected the Soviet oil proposal in October, 1947, but this did not go beyond the American concept of a limited defensive alliance, a commitment that was not enough for the shah. Iran wanted its own American arms to use as it pleased, not just American pledges of protection in the event of Soviet aggression. After all, they argued, Greece and Turkey were receiving large amounts of equipment. The difficulty, of course, was that Washington thought Iran less stable and less reliable than either Turkey or Greece, an assessment that if put bluntly to the proud Iranians would surely have offended them.

In keeping with the Washington view, Undersecretary of State Robert Lovett wrote in December, 1947 that "U.S. military assistance should continue [to] be aimed at internal security, not national defense of Iran." Furthermore, according to Lovett, Iranians were "justifiably hesitant [to] obligate themselves financially to foreign Governments . . . because of [the] plausibility it would lend to Soviet-inspired charges of American dollar imperialism." Small amounts of economic aid to strengthen the social structure and central government were useful, but the United States should avoid stirring up unnecessary Soviet-Iranian friction.[13]

The shah's views could not have been more different. The Soviets might attack at any time, he told American officials, and Iran needed a strong army of 150,000 men. It would be a good idea to limit Iran's forces, replied John Jernegan, director of the State Department's Office of Greek, Turkish, and Iranian Affairs, because "it could be such a drain on the national economy as to increase the very poverty of the people, which His Majesty considered the greatest asset of Communism."[14]

The prophetic quality of this statement and others made by the State Department at this time is striking in light of what would happen in the 1970s. For example, American diplomats repeatedly warned that an oversize conscript army might disintegrate in the face of a real challenge, that overspending on modern arms distracted the shah from concentrating on social improvements, and that the appointment of corrupt men undermined the people's respect for their monarch. The shah was obsessed with weaponry too advanced for Iran to handle and was dangerously indecisive in making policy choices. Secretary of State Dean Acheson saw Iran as potentially another China, ripe for a Communist triumph.

America's role, as seen in this analysis, was to guarantee Iran's security against a direct Russian attack. This contingency, though unlikely, could never be countered by Iranian forces alone. Further, the principal threat to Iran was internal revolution. This, United States policymakers agreed, should be the shah's primary concern. Iran would be better off with a smaller and more efficient army to maintain internal security, while domestic reforms would remove the causes of discontent. The American military umbrella, rather than a large showy Iranian army, would provide the best deterrent to Moscow's ambitions.

Iran could solve many of its problems, the Truman administration argued, by proper use of its own resources, particularly oil revenues. The prospect of American aid would provide psychological support and could be used by Washington as leverage to encourage necessary reforms. While careful never to admit this publicly, American leaders thought that the amount of aid would have to remain at token levels.

The shah's experiences pushed him in another direction. Traumatized by his early observations of the Russians—their 1941 invasion and the dethronement of his father, their arrogant wartime treatment of Iran, their postwar refusal to withdraw, and their establishment of Kurdish and Azerbaijani puppet states—the shah wanted his own full-scale military deterrent.

He passionately demanded large tanks and jet planes as well as the biggest possible army. Ironically, he was acting as a proud Iranian nationalist, refusing to be dependent on any foreign power. During the 1970s, as soon as he had far larger petroleum revenues and geostrategic leverage on his side, the shah would have his way with the United States. In the intervening years, the shah consistently ignored the United States

military advisory mission and reinterpreted the positions expressed by the United States ambassador, State Department,
and Pentagon to suit his own desires. Despite United States
advice to the contrary, he was determined to take more power
into his own hands and to build up the Iranian army.

So much money was going for the pay, food, clothing, and
housing of this enlarged army, American advisors argued, that
little would be left over to maintain a combat force. As for the
shah's constant attempts to obtain the most up-to-date tanks
and jet planes, American Ambassador John Wiley commented,
"His thinking (in) this regard is strictly in never never
land." [15]

The American government's desire to press for democratiza-
tion was faced with several particularly Iranian paradoxes.
The shah's personal popularity was greatly enhanced by his
prime minister's successful blocking of Soviet intervention.
Now he was eager to do something about Iran's chaotic political and economic situation. Yet he was also aware that those
Iranians who were lavishing expressions of devotion on him
would be the first to denounce him as a dictator if he took any
steps that affected them personally.

Only the Majlis provided an alternative power center, but it
was almost completely paralyzed by its lack of party discipline and the corruption of its elections. Even more prob-
lematic was the fact that since the Majlis was controlled by
Iran's traditional landlord elite it was most hesitant to enact
any social reforms. The State Department was concerned that
the shah, in trying to tilt the political balance in his own direction, might open the door to a right-wing military dictatorship. The New York Times shared the concern that any return to "strong-man government" in Iran would "strengthen
the hand of the Communists by alienating a large element of
the population." [16]

The political impasse was partly broken after the February
4, 1949 assassination attempt on the shah. The would-be mur-
derer, disguised as a journalist, fired at point-blank range as
the monarch toured the Tehran University campus. Bravely
facing his assailant, who was an extremely poor marksman,

the shah escaped with only minor wounds; his bodyguard killed the attacker.

Though the Communists' power had declined sharply since the Azerbaijan crisis, a new opposition center had arisen around the Muslim terrorist organization, the Fedayeen-i-Islam,* under the direction of Ayatollah Sayyid Abu al-Qasim Kashani. Already some devout Muslims had concluded that the modernization program had gone too far. But the two anti-shah philosophies could sometimes attract the same adherents. The would-be assassin in February, 1949 had affinities for both the Tudeh and Islamic-fundamentalist groups, as a search of his papers revealed.

The government quickly moved to outlaw the Tudeh. There were many arrests and trials; martial law was declared after the discovery of an alleged revolutionary plot. These tense events coincided with an upswing of anti-Iranian Soviet propaganda, centered around the charge that the country was becoming a United States military base. There were a number of Soviet-Iranian border clashes.

While confronting these challenges, Iran also was hit with a crop failure and an economic depression. As mentioned above, Tehran's attempts to secure foreign loans had not met with much success. American critics suggested that Iran was exaggerating war damage and underestimating government receipts. Since the idea of peacetime foreign aid was still a new and somewhat suspect program for Congress and the American public and since most of the available funds were going through the Marshall Plan to help Western Europe, the prospects for increased assistance to Iran were dim.

As the banks had advised, the Iranian government hired a consulting firm to draw up a seven-year economic plan. Armed with this proposal and seeking both economic and military financing the shah pressed for an invitation to Washington. The shah's first visit to America, in November, 1949, was a complete public relations success. He addressed the United Nations, inaugurated an Iranian Studies Center at Co-

* This group is not to be confused with the later Marxist group, the Fedayeen-i-khalq.

lumbia University, and inspected West Point. However, his reception by the American press, which has often displayed a fascination with foreign royalty, was far more enthusiastic than was the reaction of the United States government.

The shah, editorialized *The New York Times,* was "not only a progressive ruler but also the head of a friendly nation which provided the lifeline of the grand alliance during the war and which has now become one of the principal bulwarks against Soviet imperialist expansion." Iran's successful resistance of Soviet pressure "was largely due to the youthful Shah's own cool-headed but adamant stand. . . ." Iran, the newspaper concluded, should receive a sympathetic hearing in Washington for its aid requests.[17]

Iran's domestic political conflict, explained a correspondent for *The New York Times* shortly thereafter, was between the "youthful reformist mentality of the Shah" and "the hesitant, conservative or downright reactionary stand of the thousand families" who controlled the parliament. "There is universal recognition that the corruption, nepotism and general incompetence characterizing the rule of the thousand families is the chief hindrance to the (development) plan's success." In short, the throne was supposedly seen by Iranians as "on the side of social progress" while the Majlis was "regarded as the stronghold of reaction."[18]

President Truman, Secretary of State Dean Acheson, United States generals, and State Department officials did not see the distinction in such stark terms. Acheson pointed out that Iran was the only country with a favorable dollar balance receiving grant aid. In addition, the $650 million economic plan was thought to be seriously threatened by the shah's drive for a larger military budget.

The shah was told that American resources were not unlimited and that Congress would never support large-scale aid to Iran. Instead, Iran should depend on oil revenues and bank loans. United States technical help would come through the Point Four program, but Iran must be patient: modernization would not take place overnight.

The shah, Acheson later said, was a "very impractical

young man . . . full of grandiose ideas; he fancied himself as a great military leader" but his belief that Iran's army could contain the Russians was "utterly fanciful and never had any basis at all." Even the 1949 development plan, Acheson thought, was too ambitious and beyond Iran's capacities.[19]

Perhaps most interesting was the shah's November 18, 1949 meeting with Acheson. The secretary of state's analysis foretold what actually happened in Iran a quarter-century later. An attempt to match Soviet military spending, he warned, would lead to such weakness that there might be a collapse without any military attack. "The best way to prevent war, which was after all our real objective, was not by military preparations but by so developing our free economic and social structures that the Russians would be deterred from attacking."

Acheson then referred the shah to the problems of Chiang Kai-shek, who was, at that time, being defeated by the Communists in China's civil war. He attributed Chiang's debacle to his failure to institute reforms and to his mistaken dependence on a large—but vulnerable—army. The shah rejected these arguments. China fell, he replied, because of that regime's corruption, a problem that did not exist in Iran. He wanted reforms, the shah continued, but Iran could not risk a military defeat. The substance of Acheson's position seemed to elude him.[20]

Once the shah failed to win his aid demands in the United States, it became even more evident that Iran would have to depend on its oil revenue for development funds. The country's growing economic and political problems made the ongoing negotiations with the AIOC for a more favorable petroleum revenue contract immediately critical. Thus was set the stage for the next turbulent period.

Even if the absence of American aid had not required it, the issue of the AIOC contract would still have become an explosive one in the opening months of the 1950s. Iranian resentment toward AIOC operations had been growing for decades. Economic grievances were, of course, central; in the early postwar years the British government and English stockholders had received three times as much from company profits as did the Iranian government. Even so, the Iranian-AIOC conflict was heavily political—due to its very size and importance the company came to symbolize foreign domination of Iranian affairs.

These issues posed special problems for an Anglo-American partnership, as the Iranian question had done during the war years. Many United States officials doubted, as one embassy report put it, British ability to realize "that, whether they like it or not, they are no longer merely in the oil business in Iran, but instead are involved in a play of social forces which, considering the outside threat of Communism, requires unselfish action and long-range vision."

In fact, the British Embassy had little control and often even little knowledge of AIOC's activities of intelligence, bribery, and political intrigue. The company acted "as a law unto itself" and seemed "more antagonistic than friendly toward any lasting economic development of the country." Washington rejected a British government proposal that American aid be used as leverage to secure Iranian ratification of the company's original offer. Washington, once again, was caught in the middle. It must avoid "the old Persian trick of playing one great power against the other" while, at the same time, the United States had to maintain Iranian goodwill and a policy independent of London's hard-line.[21]

During the 1948–51 negotiations the company offered only minor concessions. AIOC did not take sufficient account of the rising nationalist spirit taking hold not only in Iran but throughout much of the region. By the time AIOC faced this new trend by meeting Iran's more moderate requests, the Tehran government had been pressured by popular opinion into more far-reaching demands.

The United States government sympathized with many of the Iranian demands. Better to be flexible and encourage Iran's political stability and continued oil production, Washington told the British, than to provoke a counterproductive and bitter conflict. Many Truman administration policymakers, including Secretary of State Acheson and his Middle East ad-

visors, thought that the region's nationalists would provide a
strong bulwark against Communism. By blocking change, the
Americans believed, the British might force Iranian nationalists into an alliance with the Soviets. Of course, it was
British—not American—investments that were in jeopardy.
American interests in Iran were strategic, not economic. The
small United States military mission was already helping the
Iranian armed forces to set up training schools to teach the use
and maintenance of P–47 Thunderbolt fighters, C–47 trans-
ports, jeeps, and trucks.

At the beginning American optimism was strong. It was
widely believed that the oil negotiations could lead to a mutually acceptable and a mutually beneficial agreement. Only a
narrow margin separated British concessions from Iranian demands, Assistant Secretary of State for Near East Affairs
George McGhee told AIOC executives in January, 1950, and a
bit more flexibility would lead to a successful outcome. AIOC
officials claimed that they had already made such liberal concessions that soon the company would have "nothing in the
till." McGhee found this hard to believe, he said, since the
company's annual report indicated that profits were far from
trifling. Conditions were changing in the Middle East and
AIOC must adjust to the times. After all, American companies
in Latin America and the Persian Gulf were moving toward a
50/50 profit split with the local governments. Why would Iran
settle for less?[22]

As the talks dragged on and on, however, Washington's
own disputes with the shah also continued. The shah demanded more arms and the Americans criticized his leadership and the country's social structure. American diplomats
still believed in the shah's good intentions. For example, some
pointed out, he had, in February, 1950, transferred the royal
estates—the land seized by his father from Qajar nobles and
from other enemies—to the Imperial Organization for Social
Welfare for distribution to the peasants. Years later this program would form the core of his "White Revolution." But
while the thirty-year-old shah was thought to be sincerely
dedicated to social justice and to improving the living stan-

dards of his people, he was also seen as a dangerous combination of stubbornness and weakness. Perhaps, mused one United States ambassador, "he is a little too Westernized for an Oriental country."[23] Was he really capable of putting into motion a program of reform from above?

Good intentions were simply not enough for that crisis-ridden country, whose social and political structures had advanced little over those of the preceding centuries. The economy was still dominated by archaic feudalism and corruption; the ruling hierarchy was inefficient and immobile; the hunger and despair of the masses were an invitation to subversive activity and revolution. Acheson wondered whether Iran's government was so corrupt and incompetent that any equipment or money put into it would be thrown away in a losing cause—as in the case of China.

The search for charismatic, non-Communist reform leaders preoccupied United States foreign policy toward the Third World in the early 1950s. American hopes in Iran were focused first on General Ali Razmara and later on Muhammad Mossadegh. The United States' long, if imperfectly implemented, tradition of liberal anti-imperialism encouraged support for local complaints against the British, who were seen to be blocking the progress and peaceful change that were deemed necessary to creating a stable Iran. Washington sought instead to find and encourage forces that enjoyed popular support, as long as they were also anti-Communist.

The Iran crisis that began in 1950 posed a major test for this policy. The tension was between the belief that, on the positive side, liberal nationalists would prove to be more reliable friends, and, on the negative, the concern that they might set in motion forces that could lead inexorably to a Communist takeover. The ultimate test would be over whether these reformers could provide a stable government.

In February, 1950 the shah appointed Ali Mansur, a man with a less than pure reputation for integrity, as prime minister. It was not long before the shah abandoned plans for his antigraft campaign, which had been long awaited by the United States as an indicator of how much Iran was prepared to help itself. The highly touted seven-year plan was disrupted as leaders siphoned off money for personal pork-barrel projects. Ali Mansur even dared to send an emissary to the American ambassador's personal physician, who was also a Majlis member, to ask his price for supporting the government. "The time of collapse may not be far away," concluded a State Department report in April.[24]

The American view of the situation remained essentially consistent throughout this period. The major problem was the behavior of the Iranian leadership—its inability to break the traditional pattern of corruption, its failure to manage the economy, and its unwillingness to make needed reforms— failures that all invited disaster. If only strong leadership could be brought forward to organize and mobilize the country, United States policymakers reasoned, Iran, without much American aid, might finally be able to carry out a coherent development plan, particularly if an agreement was reached with AIOC.

Despite this theory, political considerations were forcing the United States into a more active role. Only by providing Iran aid and assistance through its immediate economic doldrums could Washington maintain any leverage in pushing for longer-range reforms. Further, Iranians had been led to expect American assistance, and the failure to provide it was already damaging United States prestige in the country.

The State Department took three steps to meet the challenge of this crisis. First, Ambassador Henry Grady, an experienced aid administrator, was transferred from Greece to Iran. A study mission was also dispatched to consider Export-Import Bank loans.

Second, Washington increased pressure on the AIOC and the British government to be more responsive to Iranian demands. The Iranian nationalists compared their escalating dispute with Great Britain to their earlier resistance efforts against Soviet demands for oil concessions in northern Iran. After all, Muhammad Mossadegh's 1944 bill prohibiting oil negotiations until the war ended (an act aimed at the Soviets) was coupled with calls for Iranian control of all oil production. The October, 1947 Majlis act rejecting any petroleum concession to Moscow had also called for opening a new round of talks with the AIOC.

Now the members of the Majlis even more strongly reflected the growing nationalist opposition to any petroleum arrangement that maintained the status quo. The 1949 Supplemental Agreement between the company and Iran could not hope to secure the Majlis's ratification. While McGhee and others in the Truman administration felt the contract offered Iran a big improvement, they realized that it still fell far short of what other oil-producing countries were being granted.

As the proposal languished in the Majlis throughout 1950, the State Department made monthly approaches to London, calling for further concessions and criticizing the company's "take it or leave it" approach. A 50/50 split on profits between American companies and petroleum-producing states was becoming standard and Acheson decried AIOC's "inflexibility" in refusing to bend. Washington was further angered by evidence of British attempts to forestall United States aid to Iran in order to force the Majlis to capitulate to AIOC's position.

Third, Washington sought to use its aid as leverage in eliminating the disreputable Mansur regime. Since Mansur was incapable of either making reforms or securing passage of a new oil contract, the State Department argued, he could hardly expect Washington to strengthen his position by providing him with economic help. Within Iran, proreform politicians used this stand to argue for Mansur's ouster.

General Ali Razmara, the hero of the reoccupation of Azerbaijan, seemed a much more attractive candidate for prime minister. To enhance his image as a practical and hard-hitting leader, Razmara promised to revive the anticorruption campaign and to limit the shah's power. In June, 1950, with no sign of resolution of Iran's economic and political crisis in sight, the shah gave Razmara the office.

There is no evidence that America supported Razmara's candidacy for prime minister, though Iranians seemed convinced of this point; Razmara and his friends, following traditional practices, may have themselves spread such rumors.

What may have further contributed to the impression of an American link to Razmara was the memory of an embassy limousine, American flags flying, parked outside Razmara's house during the years he was the Iranian military chief of staff. The limousine belonged to Deputy Chief of Mission Arthur L. Richards, who had been asked by Ambassador Wiley to discuss then-current problems with Razmara and who had taken to doing so every Thursday over tea.[25]

Despite American hopes, Razmara proved to be a disappointing politician, unable to delegate authority, develop programs, or mobilize popular support. Adding to Razmara's own personal shortcomings, the actions of the shah, of the United States, and of Great Britain all conspired against his success. And ultimately, whatever Razmara might have accomplished, great or small, would have posed the same problem for the shah as had the achievements of Qavam before him and those of Mossadegh and Ali Amini later. Any strong prime minister would inevitably seem to threaten the shah's political power and perhaps his very throne.

Thus the shah set about undermining Razmara, whose own political base was very shaky. The shah appointed old guard officials loyal to himself—bypassing Western-trained technocrats—and tried to centralize ultimate decision making in his own hands. He also tried to compete with Razmara for the support of the armed forces. An unwanted long-range consequence of this pattern was the narrowing of the shah's own popularity in the civilian bureaucracy. Over the years, his advisors and cabinet ministers were reduced to mere "yes men." Ultimately, the shah himself was a victim of the decline in the quality of his staff.

Although many Iranians saw Razmara as "Washington's man," the United States had little to do with his appointment, though it had pressed for Mansur's removal. Actually, the State Department was not at all pleased with Razmara's performance. They saw the prime minister as a neutralist who refused American loans, severely curtailed travel by embassy officials, and pressed for improved relations with the Soviets. At the same time, his criticisms of the upper class were watered down. During Razmara's administration, noted an embassy report, American influence in Iran reached a low point.[26]

In part this diminished influence was the result of nothing more complex than a breakdown in communication, as an attempt to establish a police intelligence network demonstrated. Both the shah and Razmara wanted to develop an Iranian version of the FBI and asked for advisors from that American agency. This was impossible, Washington replied, but perhaps private citizens—most likely retired employees—could be found who would work for Iran on a contract basis. Some qualified people were located but Tehran did not follow through and the arrangement was abandoned. Only seven years later SAVAK was founded with American assistance.

More often, problems were created by the differences between Iranian aid requests and limited American responses. Despite a May, 1950 mutual defense assistance agreement, United States actions were more symbolic than real. For example, the United States Embassy was raised to "Class One" status, the staff was enlarged, and Marine guards were deployed.

In contrast, Ambassador Wiley wrote in January, 1950, the Iranians set their country's strategic value so high, they felt the United States "was literally over a barrel and obliged to give Iran the sun, the moon and the stars." But Washington had no intention of providing "even a slice of the Milky Way." The shah's weakness "is that his ideas exceed the financial capacity of Iran for the maintenance and operation" of military equipment.[27]

A few months later, after the Communist invasion of South Korea, the shah used this new analogy. Iran might soon face the same fate, he told American diplomats, and with only light weapons his army would not be able to defend the country. But the American Embassy and military mission had already decided against equipping his air force with jet fighter planes. British companies were criticized for trying to foist on Iran munitions and machinery that were poorly adapted to Iranian conditions and capacities. Iranians "should not be tempted to waste their foreign exchange on equipment which cannot be used by them for some time to come."[28] The same problem would be created by American companies two decades later.

Similar differences of opinion took place over economic relations. "The Iranians built a dream world in which our part was to loan them $250 million," as one American embassy report put it, "and when we played our role only to the extent of making a $25 million loan, the Iranians thought we had let them down." A decline in American prestige followed. The Iranian slang phrase for a pledge that would not be kept became, in contemporary parlance, an "American promise."[29]

Bureaucracy and red tape in the American lending institutions, which might have been reduced by a more determined leadership, were another part of the problem. Equally significant was the United States preoccupation with the Korean War, which forced Iran's problems in 1950 onto a distant back-burner.

The International Bank for Reconstruction and Development and the Export-Import Bank did not take into account the political necessities underlying the aid request. By September, 1950 the United States could offer only a twenty-five-million-dollar loan from the former and a one-half-million-dollar Point Four assistance program. Razmara wanted four times as much and United States Ambassador Henry Grady, who tended to favor the Iranian requests, wrote in deep frustration: "The disappointment the people of Iran feel toward the indifferent and routine manner in which our Government has been fulfilling a definite promise is fully understandable."[30] Acheson, perhaps overly defeatist, thought no amount of money could help Razmara.

While Acheson may have been correct, given political trends in Iran, his policy seemed part of an unfortunate pattern of watching Iranian politicians go out onto a limb and then abandoning them there. McGhee was well aware that if something did go wrong in Tehran there was no conceivable way in which the United States could fully back up an earlier commitment. This was not Razmara's understanding. When he told American diplomats that the only way to implement the development program might be to imprison recalcitrant Majlis members and run the country with dictatorial powers, Washington did not respond with either agreement or discouragement to this obvious trial balloon. Without United States aid, the shah's support, or British concessions on the oil issue, Razmara could find no way out of his dilemma.

The highly emotional oil issue unquestionably dealt the fatal blow. The same day Razmara became prime minister the Majlis appointed a committee to investigate the Supplemental Agreement. Mossadegh, the committee's chairman, and a number of his supporters in the National Front then used the hearings as a forum to demand nationalization of AIOC's facilities and cancellation of its concession. On December 26, 1950, accepting the unpopularity of the proposed agreement, Razmara withdrew it.

Only then did the British company finally understand the need for yielding further ground. The public announcement of a Saudi Arabian contract with an American consortium providing for a 50/50 profit distribution spurred them to offer a similar arrangement to Iran. Razmara was reluctant to proceed with the whole matter but under pressure from the shah he agreed to go ahead. On March 7, 1951, however, before he could even announce this new proposal, he was assassinated by Khalil Tahmasibi, a member of the extremist Islamic Fedayeen-i Islam. For the British, the moment had passed. It was too late even for the 50/50 offer; in the following weeks the tide of opinion favoring outright nationalization swept everything before it. Iran was about to enter the turbulent Mossadegh era. On April 30, 1951, the Majlis completed passage of a law nationalizing the Anglo-Iranian Oil Company; the shah signed this measure on May 2.

While American handling of the Russian threat against Iran had been a great success, Washington had proved somewhat bumbling in the more delicate task of assisting Iranian modernization. Acheson had been right in understanding the limited impact the United States could have, but he had also underestimated what could be accomplished. The United States correctly identified the need for reform and the importance of the oil issue but was unable to develop a mechanism for solving these problems.

"We lacked decisiveness and vigor," Acheson later admitted, while the men in the field suffered from "thinking in terms of large financial resources." The limited available funds were not used—the Majlis did not even accept the Export-Import Bank offer. AIOC's acceptance of Razmara's reasonable demands might not have prevented the escalation of the conflict to the point of nationalization, but the chances for calming the situation—and AIOC's responsibility for missing such opportunities—were nonetheless real. This was Acheson's evaluation. But given the AIOC's obduracy, the failure to provide American aid only fueled the rising temperature of the petroleum conflict.

Along with the 50/50 split, Razmara had asked AIOC that Iran be given the right to inspect the company's books, that within Iran oil be marketed at cost rather than at world prices, and that the company increase its employment of Iranians at executive levels. Considering the economic and political disruption of the Mossadegh era, these changes would not have been much of a price to pay.[31]

The shah's memories of this period—though not entirely accurate—are equally interesting. His failure to obtain more aid was in part Iran's fault "because the Americans realized that we were not yet handling our internal affairs with the necessary firmness. I was determined to show America and the world that Iran would make good use of any additional aid that could be granted." This was one more experience that reaffirmed the shah's belief in the need for Iran's self-reliance and the necessity of a strong government under his control in Tehran. Yet he implies that the blame for failures in these areas also lay with the United States.[32]

The New York Times, in its editorial on the Razmara assassination, portrayed the murdered prime minister in the most glowing terms. He was "not only his nation's 'strong man,' who seemed best able to keep the divergent political elements together," but he was also devoted to the "urgently needed

social and economic reforms." The editorial illustrated a pattern of misperception common to both American journalists
and diplomats: the reinterpretation of Iranian political goals to
match American conceptions of progress and justice and the
relatively uncritical praise of those leaders identified with
such goals—an attitude that would later invest in the shah as
the master reformer far greater hope than reality warranted.
Razmara and the shah, the editorial concluded, had provided
what was perhaps the last chance "to transform Iran from a
backward and still feudal country into a modern state and society as the best defense against Communism." [33]

In sharp contrast to this stood the State Department's assessment of the shah's role. He was, the American Embassy concluded, "greatly responsible for destroying the promise of
achievement once inherent in Razmara and his government."
The shah was seen as a far weaker and more ambiguous figure
than the brave and determined reformer portrayed in the
American media. [34]

As would happen so often in United States-Iranian relations
from that point on, every actor would pin responsibility for
misunderstandings and disasters on all the others who were
involved. Yet The New York Times' urgent tone was far more
predictive than the United States government's relaxed handling of the situation. Iran was indeed on the verge of a revolutionary crisis.

3
A Revolution Is Overthrown
1951–53

In the early 1950s the British Embassy in Tehran was a gigantic compound, covering sixteen city blocks of lovingly landscaped ground. Nearby was the Russian Embassy, an only slightly less impressive expanse surrounded by a high brick wall. By contrast the American Embassy was tiny. Though just completed in 1952, it was so small that it was still necessary to rent additional office space elsewhere, so unimposing that it resembled a Midwestern secondary school. Appropriately, it was dubbed Henderson High, after Ambassador Loy Henderson.

But diplomatic architecture often tells more about long-past history than about current reality. Despite its still-modest embassy, the United States was already the principal world power and the major foreign influence in Iran. Iranian leaders had consciously used their "American card" to end forever the era of Anglo-Russian hegemony over their country.

Yet American objectives in Iran remained limited. Although on exceptional occasions Iran had been used—and might in the future be used—as a wartime supply route or as a front

54

line in repulsing Soviet expansionism, Washington preferred to keep aid and commitments at the lowest possible levels.

When William Warne arrived in Iran in November, 1951 to run the United States Point Four technical assistance program there were still hopes that such modest levels of involvement would be sufficient to accomplish America's limited goals in Iran. American advisors worked hard to raise wheat yields, to fight malaria, to train teachers, to build textile mills, and to develop a sanitary water system. Undoubtedly, such programs won the appreciation of those Iranians who were aware of them—a smaller number than one might think—but great powers do not live by expressions of goodwill alone. The development of an Iranian crisis of international proportions would soon force on the United States an agonizing reappraisal of its policy toward Iran.

The political events of the early 1950s are little more than ancient history to most Americans. To most Iranians, however, that period was the essential backdrop to their 1978–79 revolution and was the main rationale used to justify their seizure of the American Embassy in November, 1979. Without an understanding of this earlier era, then, it is impossible to understand the later fervor in Tehran's streets.

As Iran had been a major testing ground in the late 1940s— during the period of the American transition from wartime Big Three ally to Cold War combatant—so it would become in the early 1950s a similar testing ground as the United States moved from liberal to conservative Cold War policies. The Roosevelt and Truman administrations had tried often to foster non-Communist nationalist, liberal, and social-democratic movements. Since reform and economic development would undermine the appeal of Communism, they argued, the United States should encourage allied governments to be popular and representative.

Because the Truman and Eisenhower administrations were both within the Cold War consensus, the differences between them are often underestimated today. Given the political predispositions of Eisenhower's secretary of state, John Foster

Dulles, congressional and Republican party pressure, and an atmosphere heated by McCarthyism and by the stunningly rapid Communist victory in China, the trend was toward greater suspicion of Third World nationalism. Status quo stability and military pacts seemed to provide better security against Communist encroachment than did having one's allies in the midst of social upheaval.

With the change in administrations, the role of the Central Intelligence Agency also underwent major revision. Under Allen Dulles, the secretary of state's brother, the CIA gained greater access to the White House. Although pro- as well as anti-nationalist factions existed in the CIA (as in the State Department), the agency's tendency was increasingly toward associating nationalist movements with incipient Communism. Covert activities, including deep involvement in foreign coups, were enthusiastically undertaken. The overthrow of the Mossadegh government in Iran in August, 1953 was the first major operation of this sort. Accounted a great success in its time, it was model as well as impetus for much to follow.

The Cold War consensus stood on three levels of priority. Most important was the Soviet/Communist plane: Russian expansionism, whether through outright conquest and annexation or through the midwifing of new pro-Moscow Communist regimes, constituted threats to American interests that had to be prevented at all costs. Second, Western Europe was the most vital area to be protected in this containment strategy, and good relations with the governments of Western Europe were of high importance, particularly those with Britain and France. Of necessity, this objective tended to restrain Washington's enthusiasm for decolonization movements that had as their logical goal the dismemberment of its allies' empires. On the third level of priority were the aspirations of what is today called the "Third World." Within this last priority the commonly held main objective was the prevention of the spread of Soviet influence in these regions while avoiding any excessive conflict with America's main allies.

The policy debate here concerned not the end itself but only the best way to achieve it. All agreed on the need to oppose direct, overt Soviet or Communist aggression as in Iran in 1946 or in Korea in 1950. Beyond this there was the question of where and to what extent the United States should support the maintenance of European empires. In Indochina, where Communists clearly led the nationalist movement, the answer was a wholehearted pro-French stand; in many other places, traditional American anticolonialism preferred seeing the colony gain its independence.

Where countries were already independent and where Communist-led revolutions seemed possible, a different choice was to be made. Should the United States back all existing governments, even those that seemed to have lost popular support, against all opposition forces, even those that were not Communist dominated? Or was the answer to support active non-Communist reform movements in attempts to redress popular grievances before these grievances became fuel for full-scale revolutions? Here, while Truman and Acheson felt social change was inevitable—and thus should be encouraged in a manner consistent with American interests—Eisenhower and Dulles tended to see reform movements as disruptive and as likely to be captured by local Communists. The Iran experience marked the transition from a United States foreign policy based on the first perception to one based on the second.

Between March, 1951 and August, 1953 events in Iran were daily front-page news as well as a test of both viewpoints. The downfall of Mossadegh and the end of attempts to nationalize Iranian oil, brought about by a CIA-supported uprising, laid a basis for the later unpopularity within Iran of the shah and the United States. Having begun as the nationalists' ally in their struggle against outside control, the United States ultimately became identified by many Iranians as the new imperial force in the country, even by some among the shah's supporters.

Yet by no means was this turnaround due solely to decisions taken in the United States. America's split with Mossadegh and his National Front was caused largely by failures of the nationalists themselves. Both the Truman and Eisenhower administrations would have been happy to see Mossadegh succeed in reshaping Iran, provided only that his government remain friendly toward the United States; the choices ultimately taken were prompted by his inability to create a stable regime. Something had to break the impasse created by Mossadegh's inability either to defeat AIOC or to compromise with it. The country seemed headed toward a breakdown in which the Tudeh would be Iran's only cohesive political force, raising a spectre particularly disquieting to the Dulles State Department.

Muhammad Mossadegh was, undoubtedly, one of the most fascinating and unique personalities in twentieth-century politics. Born to a wealthy landlord family in 1881, Mossadegh (like his rival, the shah) had studied in Switzerland. He returned home in 1906 to work as a civil servant in education and in provincial government. More than once he had run afoul of Reza Shah and had been forced out of public life. As an increasingly influential Majlis member during World War II, he developed his concept of "negative equilibrium." Rather than appease the Great Powers by granting them equal concessions, Mossadegh argued that they should be kept in dynamic balance by being kept at arm's length. This plan, standing in contrast to the shah's alignment with the West, would be the foreign policy advocated years later by Ayatollah Ruhollah Khomeini's followers.

Yet it was Mossadegh's behavior as much as his political philosophy that unnerved contemporary American diplomats. In complete contrast to the stoic and subdued stereotype of a statesman, Mossadegh wore his emotions on his sleeve. It was his style to cry, faint, and moan. He would play the fragile old man—complaining of dizzy spells and illness—or he would be jovial and sprightly, depending on his moods and on the political requirements of the moment.

On one occasion, as Acheson later recounted, when the secretary of state met him at Washington's Union Station, Mossadegh emerged from the train hanging onto his son's arm and bent weakly over his walking stick. As soon as he saw Acheson, though, he freed himself, tossed his stick to an aide, and skipped down the platform like a teenager, with quick, almost birdlike movements.

Such performances were no mere exercises in eccentricity; Mossadegh was well adapted to the requirements of Iranian politics. To draw in large numbers of Iranians who had never before been politically active, Mossadegh had to emphasize the dramatic. His whole strategy was to embody Iran personally, its problems and its requirements. The highly emotional component in his nationalist cause took hold among urban Iranians especially; his charisma could never be matched by the shy and stilted shah.

Western opinion, often ignorant and condescending toward Iranian political culture, generally failed to understand the very pragmatic nature of Mossadegh's approach or the special flavor of Iranian statecraft. Lacking the power to achieve his desired total victory over external forces, however, Mossadegh was brought down finally by a fatal flaw: an inability to compromise. While Mossadegh's personality and political ideology were far from those of the Ayatollah Khomeini, both the movements they led and the tactics they employed had a good deal in common. Indeed, Western media descriptions of Mossadegh might be freely interchanged with their portrayals of Khomeini twenty-five years later.

For example, there was *Time Magazine's* lurid portrait of Mossadegh in its January, 1952 "Man-of-the-Year" story on him:

> In his plaintive, singsong voice he gabbled a defiant challenge that sprang out of a hatred and envy almost incomprehensible to the West. There were millions inside and outside of Iran whom Mossadegh symbolized and spoke for, and whose fanatical state of mind he had helped to create. They would rather see their own nations fall apart than continue their present relations with the West. . . . He is not in any sense pro-Russian, but he intends to stick to his policies even though he knows they might lead to control of Iran by the Kremlin.[1]

The lanky and rumpled prime minister was neither pro-Soviet nor pro-Communist: his nationalism was single-minded. Acheson saw him as being, aside from his anti-British sentiments, "a most conservative, rich, reactionary,

feudal-minded Persian."[2] But American leaders thought him
naive about the Tudeh's aims, a concern that worried them
more and more as time went on. For his part, Mossadegh
mistakenly thought he had unlimited time to solve the AIOC
conflict and that political momentum was on his side. In the
Qavam tradition, Mossadegh saw himself as the cat and the
Tudeh as the mouse: he could manipulate it however he chose
and destroy it whenever he desired. Such an unrealistic attitude horrified Americans and undermined Mossadegh's own
position at home.

In contrast, the shah saw himself (as did many American
observers) as a hardheaded political realist, carefully weighing every political issue and objective, each geographic and
economic factor, and steering Iran safely among them. He believed that economic and military modernization was a precondition for true national independence and that his opponents were naive, demagogic, and backward looking. There
was more than a little truth in this analysis, but the shah
failed to grasp one factor that doomed his paternalistic approach to failure—that is, that a subjective perception often
gains such power to move a nation that it becomes the primary force, smashing every other consideration.

The long-range strategies of the shah and of Mossadegh differed in that the latter saw independence as the necessary first
step from which all else would flow. Limiting foreign influence and expressing Iranian pride took priority over modernization. The shah saw national independence as a product of
modernization. Most of Mossadegh's supporters were by no
means antimodern—the movement's backbone was the urban
middle class, which had the most to gain by progress—but
they were ambivalent in later years about the shah's development programs. Beneficial as they may have been for some Iranians, these plans also strengthened the shah's autocracy, denying the middle class participation in governing the nation.

Yet much of the shah's criticism of the opposition's lack of
realism was also based on historical experience. Mossadegh
and his fellows had stirred passions they could not possibly

hope to satisfy. The Iranian prime minister had failed to leave himself maneuvering room; Mossadegh was afraid, Dean Acheson would tell an executive Senate hearing in 1952, that "someone is going to move out and be more of a nationalist than he is, and he has to be the most nationalistic. . . ." This was a perceptive appreciation of Mossadegh's dilemma. "If he were doing things which were sensible," Acheson commented, I think he would run greater dangers."[3] In fact, Mossadegh found himself unable to make necessary compromises for fear that his supporters might, perhaps literally, tear him to pieces. A similar tendency would overshadow the relatively moderate politicians in Ayatollah Khomeini's era.

British shortsighted intransigence in the face of Middle East winds of change also contributed to Mossadegh's downfall. Better to shut down the Iranian oil fields, argued London, than to accept nationalization. The British economy was weak enough; a sudden wave of takeovers abroad might wipe out the foreign investments on which it depended. After all, there *was* plenty of oil; so much so that companies had banded together to *limit* production lest oversupply drive down prices. And if they chose to, the Anglo-Iranian Oil Company and its supporting sisters could compensate for the Iranian close-down simply by increasing production in the Arab states. A worldwide oil deficit might even strengthen the company's case by intensifying American pressure on Iran to reach a settlement. In fact, the Iranian-AIOC conflict did force the United States Foreign Petroleum Supply Committee to organize defensively for the redirection of available supplies. Economic necessity and common political interests induced the United States government to support on practical grounds the British hard-line it was opposing on a diplomatic level.

Alas for Mossadegh, he did not possess similar leverage. Although Washington's assistance had grown from $500,000 in fiscal 1950 to $1.6 million in 1951, and to $23.4 million in 1952, American aid was simply not available to Iran in the amounts needed to sustain the nation's staggering economy.

On strictly economic bases, many members of Congress, including Senators William Fulbright and Owen Brewster, were
against doing more. Further, by threatening to turn to the
Soviets for support, Mossadegh assured the victory of the
anti-Mossadegh forces within the executive branch as well. In
June, 1953, President Eisenhower responded to Mossadegh's
urgent plea for increased aid by advising the premier that Iran
would have to find the additional funds by settling its differences with the British and renewing the flow of oil revenues.
Financing of Mossadegh, frozen at an annual rate of $22.1
million, would continue only to prevent Iran's complete collapse by assuring that military and bureaucratic salaries were
paid.

In light of British intransigence and Iranian domestic factors
preventing compromise, it is doubtful whether any reasonable
increase in American aid could have saved Mossadegh.
Though there was some American recognition of the dilemma
that tied Mossadegh's hands, his continued failure to resolve
the nationalization dispute, it was reasoned, portended chaos.
And chaos might lead to a Communist takeover.

John Foster Dulles, Acheson's successor as secretary of state
from 1953 to 1959, though not as monomaniacal about Soviet
expansionism as he has been portrayed, still opposed the re-
form-as-the-best-means-of-fighting Communism strategy. "I
recognize full well," he told an executive session of the Senate Foreign Relations Committee shortly after taking office,
"that there are plenty of social problems and unrest which
would exist if there were no such thing as Soviet Communism
in the world, but what makes it a very dangerous problem for
us is the fact that wherever those things exist, whether it is in
Indo-China or Siam or Morocco or Egypt or Arabia or Iran . . .
the forces of unrest are captured by the Soviet Communists. . . ." Under normal circumstances, he added, the United
States did not want to support dictators, "but in times like
these, in the unrest of the world today, and the divided spirit,
we know that we cannot make a transition without losing control of the whole situation."[4] This approach saw Mossadegh
as the stalking horse of a Communist takeover.

Mossadegh (and Egyptian President Gamal Abd al-Nasser for that matter) disagreed. The United States had made an error in China, Mossadegh had told Acheson, by backing Chiang Kai-shek who was reactionary and bound to fail. America was once again "backing the wrong side in Iran," the prime minister warned. One day it would also pay the price there.[5]

This extensive discussion of context and background is necessary for an understanding of the events and decisions of the all-important Mossadegh years. When the Majlis voted for nationalization in April, 1951 the intimidated shah appointed the movement's leader, Muhammad Mossadegh, as prime minister. Some 12,000 oil-field workers had already gone on strike against the AIOC, while the resurgent Communist Tudeh attacked Mossadegh and showed its strength with a May Day demonstration of 30,000 people.

This threatened instability and the quick breakdown in Anglo-Iranian negotiations brought a swift, though cautious, United States response. Washington supported Iran's right to nationalize, but called on both sides to work out their differences peacefully. Formally, United States policy was neutral and noninterventionist, but in practice it sought to mediate with a pronounced pro-Iran tilt. While American personnel would not be sent to help the Iranians produce, pump, and process oil, Mossadegh was assured of continued United States technical assistance.

One particular American fear was that the British might launch some ill-conceived military operation against Iran. The Labour government, which despite its socialist credentials took many of its cues from the AIOC directors, was under tremendous pressure from the Conservatives. When the Conservatives retook power the following year, Winston Churchill made no secret of his belief that a splutter of musketry would have solved the Iran problem, a viewpoint that horrified Acheson.

When McGhee presented his case for compromise to the AIOC board at a London luncheon he was told that the company had the best performance record in the Middle East and that only the British knew how to deal with the Iranians. Underlying this confidence were comforting but false British intelligence reports claiming that Mossadegh was not all that popular and would not long remain in office, particularly if faced with strong British resistance. American intelligence stated opposite conclusions: that Mossadegh was leading a national revolution and that intransigence would only make his political position stronger.

In turn, the British complained about American "harassment" and "unhelpful needling." Both sides tried to keep their differences quiet. Acheson was worried that excessive pressure on London, "in a matter which they feel very strong about . . . could further stiffen their attitude and make hope for successful negotiations with Iranians remote." Convincing Britain to accept nationalization in principle "has been delicate and difficult" and they might still change their minds once again. The problem was, of course, that when Washington failed to take a stronger public stand, the Iranians accused the United States of complete support for the British position.[6]

In contrast to the State Department, The New York Times was unsympathetic to Mossadegh and editorially furious over his policies. In an "orgy of nationalist feeling, always near the boiling point in a country that has long been a focus of Great Power disputes and exploitation," the Iranians "have flung discretion to the winds for the satisfaction of getting rid of the 'foreigners.' " Yet practical problems had been ignored in this "almost pathetic delirium." How would the Iranians pay for and maintain the installations? The Times did not propose either a British compromise or United States aid, either of which might have contributed to rational solutions to Iran's seemingly insolvable problems.[7]

But this was precisely President Truman's problem. While the AIOC would only offer a 50/50 split plus joint purchasing and marketing operations—in short, substantially what they had suggested to Razmara—the president tried to develop other options. In exchange for British willingness to recognize the nationalization decree, he wanted the Iranians to negotiate on implementation and compensation. Shortly after the nationalization decree, he approved NSC 107/2, which called for bringing United States influence to bear to gain a quick settlement, "making clear both our recognition of the rights of sovereign states to control their natural resources and the importance we attach to international contractual relationships." On June 1, Truman suggested the reopening of talks along these lines.[8]

At first, Mossadegh played his hand shrewdly, insisting that his government wanted to keep the oil flowing and blaming the British for disruptions in production. He criticized the Soviet Union more strongly than had Razmara, pledged to protect British nationals in Iran, and stressed his desire for close relations with the United States. Washington was displeased, however, by his rejection of a second AIOC initiative, an early sign of Mossadegh's own inflexibility.

Over the July 4th weekend of 1951, Acheson, McGhee, and other top policymakers met with British Ambassador Sir Oliver Franks at the home of Averell Harriman. Harriman was one of America's most distinguished statesmen, having served as ambassador to both London and Moscow. He had no special knowledge of Iran, although he had visited there during World War II and had met the shah.

Faced with news of preparations on Cyprus by Britain's Sixteenth Paratroop Brigade, Acheson warned Franks that America would not passively accept a British invasion of Iran. But what could the United States do to defuse the crisis? A suggestion was made that Harriman be sent to Iran as a special emissary, an idea that captured the immediate support of everyone except Harriman.

Nonetheless, a few weeks later he was off to Iran to be initiated into the remarkable intricacies of negotiating with Mossadegh. From the first moment Harriman and his translator Vernon Walters entered Mossadegh's unpretentious home, they were struck by the sharp change from the palaces in which the shah had feted them with caviar. The prime minister himself was abed, wearing a buttoned-up camel-hair jacket, his palms crossed directly below his neck. The whole atmosphere emphasized Mossadegh's frailty.[9]

Walters sat on the bed close to Mossadegh's ear, since the prime minister was somewhat deaf, while Harriman sat at the

foot of the bed. Mossadegh particularly emphasized his mistrust of the British. "You do not know how crafty they are.
You do not know how evil they are. You do not know how
they sully everything they touch." Harriman assured him that
he had fought two wars by their side and knew England's
good as well as bad side. Mossadegh also referred to the atmosphere of "terror, terror, terror" in which he lived. The conversation neatly defined the two forces blocking an agreement:
the British and Mossadegh's own extremists.

With little give from either of them, Mossadegh could not
promise much. "Today," wrote Walters in his memorandum
on one session, "Dr. Mossadegh and Mr. Harriman played the
same record on both sides for two hours." At the same time,
Mossadegh was very entertaining. After one particularly
marked anti-British tirade he referred to his grandson, the
apple of his eye, who was at school—in England.

A far greater gaffe, for which Mossadegh ultimately would
pay dearly, was his raising of the Communist threat. If Britain
or the United States did not help him solve his problems,
Mossadegh warned, there might be a Communist coup. This
was at a time when the growing Tudeh was organizing street
marches against Harriman's visit, using the slogan, "Harriman
is here to make another Korea in Persia." The Western press
was full of stories that "for want of a protector" Mossadegh's
regime might be tempted into a "cozy tête-a-tête with the
Soviet Union." [10]

Another key political force was Ayatollah Abd al-Qasem
Kashani. Kashani had long been a religious propagandist and
an anti-British activist. His father had been killed fighting the
British during World War I. Kashani himself had been arrested by the British during World War II, by Qavam during
the 1946–47 crisis, and by the shah after the 1949 assassination attempt against him. He held a position in Iran's religious
hierarchy similar to the one filled by Khomeini twenty-five
years later, but Kashani could not compete with the charismatic Mossadegh for popular support. His power was projected by assassination squads, like the one that had killed
Razmara. Kashani did not even stop at threatening Harriman's

life or at accusing Mossadegh of being pro-British. "If Mossadegh yields," he told Harriman, "his blood will flow like Razmara's."

Harriman knew an impasse when he saw one. On July 28 he flew to London to meet with the British cabinet. Despite his failure to make progress with Mossadegh, Harriman had become convinced that the Iranian national movement was genuine and popular, that armed interference would lead only to Soviet intervention, and that British intransigence might well create a more extreme, and pro-Soviet, regime. His arguments proved persuasive, for he returned to Tehran in August, 1951 with a British-AIOC negotiating team. Harriman confidently declared that "Persia would realize her national aspirations in the best possible way and at the same time benefit to the greatest possible extent from the important technical, transportation and marketing facilities of the international oil industry."

The British were willing to accept nationalization in exchange for compensation and if a British technical company—with a British general manager—was put in charge of production. Once again the talks broke down, this time over the second demand. Harriman thought himself robbed of a near victory over a minor point, but bitter diplomatic conflict over small questions often masks far more fundamental disagreements.

The Americans put much of the blame on the British, who leaked their positions to the press and unnecessarily antagonized the Iranians. At one point, British negotiator Richard Stokes went into a tirade, telling Hussein Ala that all Iranians were corrupt and that they could run neither a business nor their own government. Later, shown the overcrowded housing of some AIOC workers, Stokes commented, "Well, this is just the way all Iranians live." This "was unfortunately true," Harriman noted, but he wondered why a company making $300 million a year could not provide better conditions.

American press correspondents at this point were also kindly disposed toward Mossadegh. "The British diplomats who . . . long for return of good old days, often fall into fatal error. They fail to consider the revolutionary aspect of the Mossadegh regime," wrote one, referring to Mossadegh's broad-based, if poorly organized, support. "Because of his long advocacy of nationalization of petroleum, Dr. Mossadegh's following is nationwide," explained another, and one American official compared Mossadegh's status in Iran to that of Thomas Jefferson or Thomas Paine in the United States.[11]

Yet the crisis only deepened. AIOC's decision to close its Iranian refinery at the end of July had helped doom the Harriman mission; Iran's takeover of the installation in late September added to the acrimony. Now no one was making any money from Iranian oil. The British fruitlessly turned to the World Court and the United Nations. When Mossadegh came to the United States in October, 1951 to speak to the United Nations where he made a fine showing, Acheson and McGhee seized the opportunity to reopen talks.

While the Iranians and British still were close on paper, Acheson wrote, "It was like walking in a maze and every so often finding oneself at the beginning again." At one point Acheson thought an agreement had been reached, but the new Conservative government in London led by Winston Churchill took a hard line. Once again the Americans gave up. "You have never understood," Mossadegh explained, "that this is basically a political issue."

Indeed it was. The night before Mossadegh left Washington Walters went to see him at the Shoreham Hotel. "Dr. Mossadegh," he pleaded, "you have been here for a long time. High hopes have been raised that your visit would bring about some fruitful results and now you are returning to Iran empty-handed."

"Don't you realize," the prime minister answered, "that, returning to Iran empty-handed, I return in a much stronger position than if I returned with an agreement which I would have to sell to my fanatics?"

True as it was that Mossadegh could offer no pliancy in return, he still needed American aid. No oil revenues were coming in, due in part to British threats to take legal action against any buyers or shippers of the "stolen oil." Mossadegh was convinced that the United States would abandon any support for Britain in order to save Iran from Communism and from economic collapse. Meanwhile, the National Front introduced an austerity program to tighten Iran's belt. Yet, as *The New York Times* correspondent Michael Clark pointed out, Mossadegh "simply cannot afford to drive the people to desperation by cutting their pathetic standard of living. . . . The government cannot, to save itself, go on eating up the country's patrimony indefinitely." The regime's response was to expel Clark for "writing lies" and for "activities in favor" of the AIOC. "A foreign correspondent cannot play with the political and economic life of our country," commented Iran's foreign minister.[12]

Clark was writing no more than the truth: within Iran the situation was becoming more and more unruly. Rightists charged that Mossadegh was leading Iran toward Communism; leftists accused him of being a tool of American imperialism. National Front cadre attacked and wrecked opposition newspapers on both ends of the political spectrum. The British were convinced that this instability would lead to a more "reasonable" government; the Americans feared it might produce a Tudeh victory. Consequently, the United States continued the attempt to play "honest broker" between the two quarreling countries.

This was not an easy or honored task. Ambassador Grady expressed surprise when his aides told him that the United States exerted little influence in Iran. But as embassy counselor Arthur Richards explained in a memo to Grady, there was a difference between influence and public perceptions. "We are accused of interference whether we do anything or not." Similar memos were being written within the embassy by other officials. "We should be prepared to find increasing criticism of the United States for alleged interference in their internal affairs," noted John Stutesman. At the same time, his analysis went on, "we should be prepared to find politicians calling for our help and resenting non-interference on our part."[13] He too was right on both counts. Iranian attitudes had created a no-win situation.

For example, when Hussein Maki, leader of one of the most important National Front parties, was not invited by Mossadegh to join his delegation to the United States, rumors spread that his participation had been blocked by the Americans. Politicians continually visited the embassy, asking for help in removing Mossadegh or seeking office for themselves. Given the constant jealousies, political maneuvering, and personal ambitions of the National Front leaders—not to mention the intrigues of the court and opposition—Tehran was kept in a continual uproar.

The embassy's main function was the gathering of information. American diplomats met not only with the shah, Mossadegh, and other government officials, but also with a wide range of people on all sides of the political disputes. A series of discussions were even held with Ayatollah Kashani. Embassy staff members regularly undertook extensive travels around the country, sometimes using a Chevrolet station wagon, visiting towns, villages, and tribes, investigating economic, political, and social conditions. Consular officers even had their own sources inside the Tudeh, enabling them to report regularly on local Communist meetings.

This kind of research, an integral part of the diplomat's job, was often viewed with suspicion by Iranians. Under the shah's regime in later years the mission's flexibility was circumscribed until it became largely dependent on government and SAVAK channels for information. Yet to Ayatollah Khomeini and his followers, virtually all information-gathering activity was viewed as spying.

Mossadegh's attitude was not all that different. On one occasion, in late 1952, the Iranian authorities wanted to arrest a State Department employee as a spy after he interviewed people and inspected docks, railroads, factories, and public works. The man, who volunteered to stand trial to prove his innocence, was allowed to leave Iran. He was not, however, accused of being an American spy but of being a British agent! The Iranians' fears were really focused on British subversion and Iranian leaders often charged each other with working for London. Some claimed that a raid on the residence of AIOC's British manager supplied secret documents proving that Mossadegh's close advisor (and later foreign minister) Hussein Fatemi and the prime minister's son-in-law, Senator Ahmad Matin-Daftari, were traitors. In exchange, Mossadegh paid similar compliments. He even charged the British with instigating public servants to demand higher salaries.

Spy scares played a particular role during the January, 1952 elections. Just as the American Embassy became the main target in 1979, the British Embassy was labeled a spy center in 1952. Hussein Ala, now minister of court, told Grady's replacement, Ambassador Loy Henderson, that Iran held documents proving England's interference. When Henderson asked for proof, Ala merely replied that such trespasses were a matter of public knowledge. All British consulates were shut down shortly thereafter. Some Iranian militants also wanted to close all the American consulates; Kashani successfully demanded the banning of all foreign cultural institutions outside of Tehran. In this xenophobic atmosphere, the National Front won a solid victory at the polls.

Buoyed by this result, Mossadegh continued to chip away at the power of both the shah and the Majlis. He appealed over their heads to the people. The previous September, when opposition deputies briefly prevented a parliamentary quorum, Mossadegh told the crowd outside, "You are the ones who count. The Majlis is not truly representative of the nation." [14] He broke the tradition of holding weekly cabinet meetings in the shah's presence and refused to consult the monarch on political decisions.

The embassy, already disillusioned by the shah's behavior during Razmara's term of office, reported constantly on the shah's weakness. The "Shah will not willingly change from [his] habitual vacillation or drop his policy of awaiting [the] play [of] other forces which may painlessly depose [the] Mossadegh government without his intervention."[15] A similar passivity marked the shah's response to the revolution a quarter-century later.

Acheson, increasingly concerned about the deteriorating situation, asked whether the continuing oil crisis would drive Mossadegh into the USSR's arms or whether it might lead to a Communist-dominated regime in Tehran. If only the conflict could be settled, the secretary of state said, Mossadegh would move *for* reform and *against* the Tudeh; Acheson was confident of Mossadegh's anti-Communism. Or perhaps, he suggested, the existing state of affairs might continue for a long time without a breakdown of the country. He also wondered whether Mossadegh could rally public opinion and take unpopular austerity measures to avoid a fiscal collapse. Already, his regime was two weeks behind in paying the army.

Washington decided then to help Mossadegh one final time in the hope of finding some solution. During Mossadegh's visit to the White House in late 1951, the Iranian prime minister told Truman, "Mr. President, I am speaking from a very poor country—a country all desert—just sand, a few camels, a few sheep. . . ." "Yes," Acheson interrupted, "and with your oil, rather like Texas!" Acheson's point was that Iran needed aid only because it was failing to solve its problem with AIOC. The United States was willing to expand Point Four technical aid, but it refused to make a large loan to Iran.

As America tried to use assistance to hasten a settlement, Mossadegh sought his own leverage, using Iran's domestic unrest and the possibility of rapprochement with Moscow. In the spring of 1952, he began to negotiate with the Russians over the sale of Iranian oil and started to talk about the necessity of Tehran's neutrality in the Cold War. These threats won him a temporary victory. American military aid was continued on favorable terms, but he was again warned of the need to reach agreement with Britain before funds could be increased.

To cope with Iran's internal crisis, Mossadegh continued to expand his powers. In July, 1952 he demanded dictatorial power for six months and the War Ministry portfolio, giving him control over the armed forces. "Having brought his country to the verge of bankruptcy," charged the anti-Mossadegh *New York Times*, "Premier Mossadegh is now trying to take it further along the road to ruin. . . . What he proposed is in effect a legalized coup d'etat that smacks of Hitler's tactics." [16]

The shah finally put his foot down and, when Mossadegh resigned, he appointed Qavam as prime minister. Qavam explained that though he respected "the sacred tenets of Islam, I divorce religion from politics and will prevent the dissemination of superstitions and retrogressive ideas." [17] Neither the religious nor secular wings of the National Front had any intention of giving in so easily. Several days of fierce pro-Mossadegh rioting in late July, with the number of fatalities as high as two hundred and fifty, forced the shah to give way. One of the most active National Front organizers was the retired general, Fazlollah Zahedi, whose home was a meeting place for Mossadegh's supporters.

Mossadegh's resignation was rescinded and Kashani became president of the Majlis. The ayatollah arranged the release of Razmara's assassin. By October, Mossadegh felt strong enough to dissolve parliament entirely. In January, 1953 the prime minister's special powers were extended for an additional twelve months.

These tumultuous events led to an upswing in anti-American sentiment, as the Tudeh and allied radical factions in the National Front charged that a conspiracy involving Qavam and the American Embassy had been behind the shah's attempt to unseat Mossadegh. Mobs attacked American consulates and libraries; Washington had stabbed Mossadegh in the back, they claimed, because of its limited aid and alleged pro-British stand.

The New York Times could only protest editorially: "We know that our object is quite honestly to be helpful and humanitarian [and] in the process to strengthen Iran against chaos and communism. To do good, even against the wishes of the beneficiary, is still the right thing."[18] Mossadegh still tried to turn America's good intentions to his own benefit, but results were still lacking.

Both Mossadegh and the shah were badly shaken by the violence in July. During his first meeting with the prime minister after his return to power, Henderson found him to be almost incoherent. "As I listened to him I could not but be discouraged at the thought that a person so lacking in stability and clearly dominated by emotions and prejudices should represent the only bulwark left between Iran and Communism." For a time, Henderson wondered if Mossadegh might be mentally unbalanced, but the prime minister seemed to recover his equilibrium in the following weeks.[19]

The shah also seemed to be in bad shape. After his initial intervention, the shah's courage waned; visitors reported that he had aged visibly. The crisis continued and deepened with no end in sight.

The deteriorating situation set off a last effort by the lame-duck Truman administration, with British approval, in August, 1952.* Under this plan, Iran would submit the compensation question to the International Court of Justice and would use AIOC channels to market their oil. The United States would give Iran $10 million in emergency aid to tide them over until petroleum revenues became available. Mossadegh rejected this plan since it seemed to tie Iran to continuation of the AIOC monopoly. He expressed his gratitude for American efforts but, given the failure to make any progress, he broke off relations with Britain.

American analysts continued to decry British obstructionism and to fear that Iran might go Communist, but the need for Anglo-American collaboration elsewhere limited their options. The oil corporations also proved uncooperative. Mossadegh's negotiations with the independent Cities Service Company went nowhere and the bigger companies supported AIOC. They ignored a November State Department hint that it had no objection to their buying nationalized Iranian oil.

* President Truman declined to seek another term in the November, 1952 election.

In cabinet meetings, Acheson and Secretary of Defense Robert Lovett argued that stabilizing Iran was so important that a pending antitrust suit against American petroleum companies must be dropped to win their cooperation. Despite Justice Department opposition, President Truman terminated the grand jury investigation. Only Venezuela and the Middle East could supply the oil needed by America in any future war or by Europe under peacetime conditions, a trilateral State-Defense-Interior Department study showed the president. Since the Middle East was a politically explosive region, since oil was the principle source of those countries' wealth, and since the oil companies dealt with this vital resource, the report concluded, the "American oil operations are, for all practical purposes, instruments of our foreign policy toward these countries."[20]

Time was running out for the Truman administration. Acheson suggested in early November that the United States advance Iran $100 million against future petroleum deliveries. One or more American companies would be encouraged to purchase and market Iranian oil either alone or in conjunction with AIOC, with compensation for the British company to be negotiated afterward. AIOC refused to allow it.

Truman aide Paul Nitze was dispatched to talk to Anthony Eden. Iran was on the verge of explosion, Nitze told him, and the United States would no longer wait for AIOC to make concessions. If necessary the White House would act alone, bringing United States oil companies into the picture. Eden knew this was an empty threat—American oil giants had earlier closed ranks with AIOC. Fearful of setting a precedent endangering their own contracts, they were willing to destroy anyone, including powerful tanker owner Aristotle Onassis, who attempted to undercut AIOC by circumventing the boycott of Iranian oil. Besides, they were understandably skeptical about Mossadegh's willingness to accept an agreement on any compromise terms.

So failed Truman's last attempt to solve the Iranian oil conflict. The mercurial Mossadegh was by no means gloomy at this turn of events—he thought, mistakenly, that the incoming president, Dwight Eisenhower, would offer a better deal. He did not seem to understand that as time weakened the National Front's domestic base he would be less able than when he had been at the peak of popularity to put through a settlement. Mossadegh had waited too long.

He had sought to copy Qavam's skillful game of brinkmanship. But while Qavam had toyed with the Soviets and the Tudeh, at the decisive moment he employed the shah, the army, and, most important, United States support to keep Moscow at bay. Mossadegh lacked both the nerve and the institutional support that had carried his predecessor to success. Mossadegh desired complete United States support against the British but resented any American pressure on him to settle with London. The Tudeh exploited the American connection by charging that Mossadegh would give Iranian oil to the United States and that Washington wanted to convert Iran into a gigantic military base. Even Mossadegh's selection as "Man of the Year" by *Time Magazine* was used to demonstrate that he was an American puppet.

By mid-1952 many middle-class elements, frustrated by the continuing crisis, began to desert the National Front. At the same time, the Tudeh finally concluded that fighting against the broad national sentiment represented by Mossadegh had been an error. Though the Ayatollah Kashani was eager for rapprochement, the Tudeh's first offer of alliance was strongly rejected by the National Front's left wing. State Department analyses saw the shift in Tudeh tactics as a possible imitation of those employed by the Communists as a first step in the 1948 takeover of Czechoslovakia—entering the government coalition and gaining key cabinet posts. Despite Mossadegh's resistance to Tudeh overtures, Ambassador Henderson still believed him to be naive on the question of Communism.

Mossadegh certainly was naive about changes taking place in the United States government. Even before Eisenhower's inauguration in January, 1953, Mossadegh wrote him expressing hope for understanding and assistance from the new administration. "For almost two years," Mossadegh noted, "the Iranian people have suffered acute distress and much misery merely because a company inspired by covetousness and a desire for profit supported by the British government has been endeavoring to prevent them from obtaining their natural and elemental rights." The American government however "has pursued what appears to the Iranian people to be a policy of supporting the British Government and the AIOC." Mossadegh wanted sympathetic consideration of Iran's claims. "I hope," replied President Eisenhower, "our own future relationships will be completely free of any suspicion, but on the contrary will be characterized by confidence and trust inspired by frankness and friendliness."[21]

Despite these sentiments an incipient British coup effort against Mossadegh was already attempting to draw in the United States. Shortly before the 1952 presidential election, the British government invited Kermit Roosevelt of the Central Intelligence Agency to London and proposed that the CIA cooperate under the code name "Operation Ajax" in an operation to bring down Mossadegh. Allen Dulles, then CIA deputy director, decided to await Eisenhower's inauguration, since he knew that Acheson opposed any such action. Walter Bedell Smith, the CIA's director, was aware of these contacts but avoided involvement in them.[22]

Ambassador Henderson returned to Iran at the end of 1952 for two more months of negotiations with Mossadegh, meetings supposedly conducted with only an American Embassy Iranian staff member as translator. On at least one occasion, however, Henderson noticed while leaving the embassy the cane of Foreign Minister Hussein Fatemi resting on the second floor railing. Apparently, Mossadegh had asked his advisor to eavesdrop from an adjacent room.

During the talks, Mossadegh recorded each point of agreement in a small black book. Once, when Henderson reminded the prime minister of some previous point that had been settled, Mossadegh checked his notebook and answered that he could find no reference to this issue. Henderson realized then that this was not the original notebook and that these discussions were just one more exercise in futility.

The breakdown of these negotations only reinforced the

new administration's view that Mossadegh should be overthrown. On February 3, as soon as possible after Eisenhower's
inauguration, a British delegation came to Washington to
meet with Allen Dulles, now CIA director; Smith, now the
undersecretary of state; and Secretary of State John Foster
Dulles. London's representatives recommended Kermit
Roosevelt's appointment as the operation's field commander.
They decided to send him to Iran to investigate conditions
there, but both sides were optimistic that most of the army
and the people would support the shah in any showdown.

The outlook in Iran was not bright. After Mossadegh won
the extension of his emergency powers in January, the shah
threatened to go into exile, a traditional Persian method of
protest. The rumor of the shah's departure brought on a wave
of pro-shah rioting during which one mob stormed Mossadegh's house. The agile-when-necessary politician escaped
by climbing over the garden wall into the adjoining offices of
a United States aid mission. Although Ambassador Henderson helped restore calm by persuading the shah to stay on, his
growing direct relationship with the monarch—bypassing
Mossadegh—provoked concern within the National Front.

The American Embassy in Tehran was reporting that Mossadegh had near-total support from the Iranian population and
was not likely to fall. On the other hand, his goal of a republic
or the demotion of the shah to a mere figurehead was blocked
by the army's continuing loyalty to the shah and by the rallying of the opposition, including such former National Front
stalwarts as Maki and Kashani, around the court. Having been
able to achieve little of a positive nature, Henderson reported,
Mossadegh had made a wider and wider circle of enemies. He
"has thrown out [the] British; emasculated [the] Majlis; eliminated [the] Senate, forced all well known politicians out of
public life; deposed all prominent civilian and military
officials; sent various members [of the] royal family into
exile. . . ."[23]

Roosevelt saw the potential in mobilizing this opposition
and a trip to Iran confirmed his views. There he contacted two
Iranians with intelligence training and brought them back to

the United States for training and for lie-detector tests to ensure their reliability. So secret was this whole operation that Roosevelt was not allowed to use the standard CIA pseudonyms; he had to invent special ones for the occasion.

Henderson was also carrying out a hardening line in light of the deteriorating situation. There was much discussion as to whether Iran would collapse economically; its peasant-worked agricultural sector seemed able to endure, at least at a subsistence level, the growing urban anarchy, but the country had clearly reached a political dead end. When Secretary of State Dulles made plans for his May, 1953 Middle East visit, Henderson advised him to avoid Iran lest his presence be regarded as an American endorsement of the Mossadegh regime. During this time, when Dulles was attempting to assemble a "Northern Tier" military alliance to contain the Soviet Union, Iran was hardly a pillar of stability.

Both the American press and the American government were moving toward this conclusion. "It now seems clear," stated *The New York Times* in an April analysis, "that Britain with U.S. backing will stand on her last offer. Any new initiative must come from Iran, from Mossadegh or an eventual successor. Which it is to be may be decided within the next few weeks."[24] The CIA believed that the erosion of Mossadegh's base would make him dependent on the Tudeh and therefore dependent on the Soviets. The Soviets, well aware of this possibility, seemed to be working diligently to take advantage of the situation. American intelligence claimed to have information that the Tudeh planned to eliminate the shah and keep Mossadegh as a figurehead. This fear was reinforced by the appointment of Anatol Laurentiev—the man who had masterminded the Communist takeover of Czechoslovakia in 1948—as the new Soviet ambassador in Tehran.

Mossadegh's May 28th letter asking President Eisenhower to increase United States assistance and to help him avoid chaos represented the prime minister's last chance for survival. The president did not reply until June 29, after consultations with John Foster and Allen Dulles, Walter Bedell Smith, and, Ambassador Henderson, among others. Decisions taken in the intervening month would lead to Mossadegh's defeat.

Smith gave Eisenhower material from some of Henderson's gloomy cables. "Most Iranian politicians friendly to the West would welcome secret American intervention which would assist them in attaining their individual or group political ambitions," the ambassador had cabled. Americans were becoming increasingly unpopular as "deteriorating conditions of the country fan the embers of xenophobia. Only those sympathetic to the Soviet Union and to international communism have reason to be pleased at what is taking place in Iran."[25]

In his final months of power, Mossadegh even spent the army and civil service pension funds. It was necessary, said Secretary of State Dulles, to maintain some aid but it ought to be aimed at preventing total collapse rather than at helping Mossadegh solidify his rule. The forces of order had to be kept in operation until someone dependable could be found to govern.

Indeed, as Mossadegh realized, the army was the shah's last remaining card; consequently, the prime minister pressed the Majlis to give him direct control over the military. These and other demands tended to alienate many in Mossadegh's coalition. Kashani went over to the opposition; whole sectors of the National Front broke away; and dozens of deputies resigned when Mossadegh threatened to dissolve parliament by national referendum. The erosion of his own base forced the prime minister to rely increasingly on the Tudeh's support.

The Communists clearly had become the best-organized and most-disciplined force in the country. They had infiltrated many government departments, particularly the ministries of justice, education, and health. The American Embassy estimated their strength in Tehran at 8,000 to 10,000 activists, with an equal number in other cities and a great many nonmember supporters. The shah was the only other political force with a strong political base in the country. Yet little further consideration seems to have been given by the Eisenhower administration to the alternative of providing full United States support for Mossadegh and his non-Communist allies to reestablish order. That strategy had been attempted over the previous two years, American policymakers concluded, and had not produced success.

Given this situation, alongside the strong personal support of Eden and Churchill for covert action, the American government made its decision. The go-ahead was given at a meeting in Secretary of State Dulles's office on June 22, attended by Allen Dulles, Kermit Roosevelt, Ambassador Henderson, Secretary of Defense Charles Wilson, and a number of State Department officials. One of them, Robert Bowie, then director of the State Department's Policy Planning Staff, would be deputy director of the CIA at the time of the 1978 revolution. While some of the participants were a bit less enthusiastic than John Foster Dulles, Dulles had apparently already decided to implement the anti-Mossadegh operation. Consequently, on June 29, President Eisenhower refused Mossadegh's May 28th request; the United States would neither increase aid levels nor buy Iranian oil. The die was cast.[26]

Once the decision was made, only Henderson, Minister-Counselor Gordon Mattison, and Chief Political Officer Roy Melbourne, among the embassy officials, were informed of the plan, and none of them played an active role in its execution. They were pleased by the choice, but Henderson insisted that he should not return to Iran or talk to Mossadegh while the Anglo-American operation was under way. In the event of failure the ambassador might need to intervene with the prime minister. Other than Roosevelt's five-man team—which included the CIA man in Iran, his assistant, and two junior officers who helped with administrative duties—American personnel in Iran were not aware of what was going on; even the two knowledgeable diplomats remaining in the embassy did not seek details.[27]

Through early July, Mossadegh became increasingly desperate as news of Eisenhower's rebuff was leaked by his enemies. Therefore, the United States and Iranian governments agreed to release the correspondence. Meanwhile, the Tudeh seized every opportunity to step up its public activity; its demonstrations were now larger by far than those of the dispirited National Front. By acclaiming Mossadegh, whom they previously had condemned, Tudeh leaders were confident they would now earn for themselves a place in the government.

Kennett Love, correspondent of *The New York Times* and the only American journalist in Iran that summer, found the Tudeh to be surprisingly courteous but firm. "Do you think they can refuse our support much longer?" Tudeh leader Mustafa Lankorani asked him as the two stood on the speaker's platform in front of the Majlis building during a one-hundred-thousand-person Tudeh rally on July 21. As the crowd shouted anti-American slogans, he added, "You have seen for yourself how small they are and how big we are!" [28]

Appearances were deceiving. Kermit Roosevelt returned to Iran on July 13, and on August 1 had his first meeting with the shah. A car picked him up at midnight and drove him to the palace. Roosevelt lay down on the seat and covered himself with a blanket as guards waved his driver through the gates. The shah got into the car and Roosevelt explained his mission, which, he told the shah, was supported by Eisenhower and by British Prime Minister Winston Churchill. Up to that point the shah had known nothing of American plans. He had been impressed and depressed by Mossadegh's reception in the United States. Though he knew he had British support, the monarch was not convinced that this would be helpful, given the country's anti-British attitudes. The shah had awaited such an opportunity; he would participate in Roosevelt's plan.

The CIA provided $1 million in Iranian currency, which Roosevelt had stored in a large safe—a bulky cache since the largest banknotes then available—the 500-rial denomination—were worth only $7.50. Of this sum, $100,000 was given to the two Iranian agents to disburse among the athletic club thugs and the poor of the south Tehran slums. The shah would fly to a remote town on the Caspian Sea, leaving behind him two decrees: one dismissing Mossadegh; a second appointing Fazlollah Zahedi as prime minister.

Meanwhile, Mossadegh was trying to handle the growing

chaos by taking dictatorial powers. The referendum to dissolve the Majlis was held August 3, amid mounting Tudeh demonstrations supporting Mossadegh. Without a secret ballot and with rigged counting, the results were 99.9 percent in favor of the prime minister's initiative. Opposition deputies cabled the United Nations charging Mossadegh with violations of human rights. President Eisenhower also criticized the referendum. When Mossadegh declared the Majlis dissolved and lifted the parliamentary immunity of legislators, thirteen of them took refuge in the Majlis building.

Mossadegh also tried to consolidate Soviet assistance. He thanked Moscow for improving relations and proposed a joint Iranian-Soviet commission to resolve standing bilateral problems. The Iranian press hailed these moves, expressing the hope that they would force the United States to adopt a friendlier policy. On the contrary, such moves only further alarmed Washington.

The crisis was clearly reaching the point of no return. "Having already reduced the shah to a virtual prisoner," *The New York Times* editorialized on August 4, Mossadegh "is now trying to eliminate the last citadel of opposition to his ambition by crushing the final vestiges of parliamentary government." They thought he would succeed and that "Iran [would] pass under a dictatorship which the communists support as a precursor of their own tyranny." [29]

This was the moment when the shah played his final card. While Zahedi hid out on one of his family's rural estates, Colonel Nematollah Nasiri of the Imperial Palace Guard was entrusted with serving the shah's two decrees on Mossadegh. (Nasiri was later head of SAVAK, the shah's secret police, and was one of the first men executed by the anti-shah forces in 1979.) Another officer betrayed the plan, however, and Mossadegh's supporters arrested Nasiri as soon as he delivered the decrees.

Mossadegh's aides declared this to be a coup attempt and imprisoned a number of oppositionists, including some of the National Front's former leaders. A price was put on Zahedi's head, but Zahedi appealed to the military. He claimed to be

the rightful prime minister and charged Mossadegh with stag-
ing a coup by ignoring an imperial decree.

As president of the Retired Officers Association, Zahedi had
good contacts in the army. He also had some friends among
the nationalists now in opposition, since he had served as
minister of the interior in Mossadegh's first cabinet before his
own break with the National Front. Zahedi's son, Ardeshir,
was deputy administrator for the American aid program and
acted as his father's liaison with the CIA. At the time of the
1978–79 revolution, Ardeshir would be Iran's ambassador to
the United States.

All in all, only five Americans with a half-dozen Iranian
contacts had organized the entire uprising. Having finished
his part of the operation, Roosevelt relaxed at a friend's house
in Tehran to await results.Yet everything seemed to go wrong.
Rather than announcing Mossadegh's removal on the morning
of August 16, Tehran Radio broadcast news of an attempted
royalist coup and of Nasiri's arrest—without mentioning the
shah's decrees dismissing Mossadegh and appointing Zahedi
in his place. The United States Embassy was grim and worried; Ambassador Henderson, hearing the news from Beirut
where he was vacationing, rushed back to find Tehran in
chaos. Communist mobs with red flags tore down statues of
the shah and his father, pillaged shops, attacked the offices of
opposition groups, and threatened Americans.

In Isfahan, demonstrators marched outside the United States
consulate chanting, "Yankees, go home!" In Tehran, Tudeh
flying squads tore down the old street signs and renamed the
avenues "Stalin," "People's Democracy," and so on. The shah,
concluding all was lost, fled to Italy.

The following day the confusion continued. The Tudeh
warned the government to break with the United States; Mossadegh's aides hinted that the shah might be deposed, calling
him a traitor. More dissidents, including a dozen Majlis deputies, were arrested.

Finally, on August 18, Henderson met with Mossadegh and
demanded protection for American citizens in Iran. Mossadegh's police chief called out police and soldiers to stop the

Communist demonstrations. The Tudeh was forced off the streets by soldiers chanting, "Long live the Shah, Death to Mossadegh!" Up to this point, one of Roosevelt's aides had contacted a few military men, but now the shah's broad support in the army was graphically shown. Persuaded of the Tudeh's threat, more enlisted in Zahedi's cause. The tide was turning.

Early the next day, the men organized with $100,000 of CIA funds finally appeared, marching out of south Tehran into the city's center and gathering hundreds of recruits along the way. They destroyed the offices of a pro-Mossadegh newspaper and crashed through the gates of the prime minister's house, though Mossadegh himself escaped for a few hours. By noon they had taken the Foreign Office and other government buildings. The previous American pessimism—Smith had ordered the CIA operatives' withdrawal, thinking the plan had failed—was quickly reversed.

Riding in a taxi that morning, *The New York Times* correspondent Kennett Love saw shopkeepers running to slam down their protective iron gates. Having almost been killed by a Tudeh mob two days earlier, Love now instead heard shouts of "Long Live America!" This was a pro-shah mob. Love found himself in the midst of a cheering throng; people stopped cars and made drivers put the shah's picture on their windshields often using one-rial banknotes.[30]

Gangs with clubs, knives, and rocks controlled the streets, overturning Tudeh trucks and beating up anti-shah activists. Quick-witted entrepreneurs sauntered up and down Tehran's streets selling full-color pictures of the shah. One embassy political officer later recalled how his car, flying American flags for protection, was cheered along the entire nine-mile route from the embassy to his home in the northern suburbs. The CIA payments alone could not explain the rapidity of the movement's spread and the enthusiasm that greeted the shah's return to power. Roosevelt had been correct: there was still a reservoir of support for the shah among tens of thousands of Iranians either tired of the chaos of the Mossadegh regime or fearful of the Tudeh.

As Roosevelt congratulated Zahedi in Zahedi's basement hiding place the new prime minister's supporters burst in. A startled Roosevelt scrambled to hide behind the furnace while Zahedi was carried upstairs on the shoulders of his supporters. He was put onto a waiting tank, which then drove off slowly through applauding, waving crowds, past the American Embassy and through the center of Tehran. The mobs supporting the Communists had either changed sides or had left the streets, giving up without a fight.

American Embassy officials around Tehran had been busy that day phoning in reports from around the city and these were quickly forwarded to Washington. About noon, most had concluded that the shah had won but Roy Melbourne delayed any such claim until 2:00 P.M. He then went to Henderson adding, as a private opinion, that despite the CIA's role, these had been the most genuine demonstrations he had witnessed during two years in Iran. One proof was that earlier marches tapered off in the intensely hot Tehran afternoon, but these were continuing and growing. Henderson smiled and replied, "I agree with you, but we certainly can't tell that to the department!" as the reason for concluding that Mossadegh was finished.[31]

That evening, Ardeshir Zahedi visited Henderson to ask for suggestions. The ambassador recommended that Mossadegh not be harmed when and if found and that the new regime inform embassies and civil servants that this was no coup but merely a change in government. This technically was true, of course, since the shah had the constitutional right to dismiss Mossadegh. By refusing to accept the shah's decrees Mossadegh already had violated legality. Equally important, Mossadegh had squandered his legitimacy by moving to eliminate all restraints on his own power.

During the following days the new prime minister met daily with his American advisors. The immediate priority was to gain United States aid for the rebuilding process. Zahedi scarcely exaggerated when he wrote Eisenhower on August 26, "The treasury is empty; foreign exchange resources are exhausted; the national economy is deteriorated. Iran needs immediate financial aid to enable it to emerge from a state of economic and financial chaos." He made it clear that Iran intended to settle the oil conflict with Britain as soon as possible. This, after all, had been Washington's precondition for increased assistance to Mossadegh.[32]

Little time was wasted. The first infusion came from the $900,000 left in Roosevelt's safe. Henderson quickly promised to continue Point Four aid and to arrange a $45 million emergency grant. American press and official praise for the shah's return to power was extensive; although some reporters apparently were aware of CIA involvement in these events, the details remained unpublished for decades.

The New York Times vigorously supported the return of the shah: "While he has been a weak monarch on the whole, he was always true to the parliamentary institutions of his country; he was a moderating influence in the wild fanaticism exhibited by the nationalists under Mossadegh, and he was socially progressive. The Shah was almost alone in dividing up his vast estates and fostering agrarian reform." Iran's difficult social situation made matters "so dismal as to be almost horrifying." The rich ruling class of landowners and army officers were as a group "selfish, reactionary, short-sighted and incompetent. The tragic poverty of the masses is not exceeded anywhere in the world." Mossadegh had not been the man to deal with these problems according to the Times. He had "flirt(ed) with Russia," had destroyed the Majlis with the Tudeh's assistance, and was responsible for the growth of Communist strength in Iran. The only two alternatives seemed to have been the shah or the Communists, explained the editorial. The newspaper was hopeful that law, order, and constitutionality would be restored and that a new relationship with the West would produce a revival of the oil industry, setting the nation's economy back on the road to recovery.[33]

The course and outcome of the Iran crisis illustrate well the complexity of diplomatic decisions. In the long run the CIA's support for the shah's return would breed Iranian anti-Americanism and play a central role in shaping the attitudes of the post-shah regime. The idea expressed by Eisenhower on

several occasions thereafter that he had saved Iran from Communism, and even that Mossadegh's government had been a
"Communist-dominated regime"—Allen Dulles expressed
similar views—encouraged a tragic confusion between militant nationalism and Marxism-Leninism that plagued United
States policy elsewhere in the Third World.[34]

At the same time, it would be misleading to conclude that
the United States helped evict a popular nationalist government and replace it with an unpopular and antinationalist
one. By the autumn of 1953 Iran was at the end of its tether;
the Communists were growing in strength and the National
Front was disintegrating. Continuation of the status quo did
not seem a viable option, although the Eisenhower administration might have tried to work with rather than undercut
Mossadegh. After all, if Mossadegh had lost control of events
this might in part be attributed to the American decision to
freeze the level of economic assistance. There might have
been further efforts to find a settlement, despite earlier failures.

At the same time, however, Mossadegh's ill-fated decision
to use the Communist threat as a means of gaining American
support boomeranged. And given Acheson's many attempts to
work with Mossadegh and the lack of progress produced by
his various plans, Eisenhower's responses, aside from moral
considerations, were not necessarily illogical. By August,
1953 Mossadegh's regime was becoming a dictatorship—and a
tottering one at that—even without American intervention.

In the days after Mossadegh's removal, the shah and Zahedi
seemed as popular as the National Front leader had ever been.
No more eager than the National Front to give away any of
Iran's national rights they simply realized, in the face of Mossadegh's failure, that nationalization could not be achieved at
that time. Thereafter, without ever forgetting his ultimate
goal, the shah noved cautiously step by step to achieve the
same ends.

Equally, it cannot be said that the United States overthrew
Mossadegh and replaced him with the shah. The CIA merely
provided minimal financial and logistical aid for Iranians to

do so. Many of them were genuinely frightened by the prospects of a Tudeh takeover, were distressed by Mossadegh's steps toward dictatorship, and were disillusioned by his inability to maintain order. As Richard Cottam, an Iran scholar noted for his sympathy to the nationalist cause, points out, "Regardless of foreign participation, Mossadegh could not have been overthrown if significant elements of the population had not lost faith in his leadership." [35]

This is an important and often-neglected point that Allen Dulles did not seem fully to understand. Overthrowing Mossadegh had been like pushing on an already-opened door. Support from the general population and from a united military had been necessary for success. When the CIA attempted similar adventures elsewhere under less favorable conditions the result was often a farcical disaster.

Once having intervened, Washington, like Dr. Frankenstein, found definite limits to further control of its creation. By contributing to the elimination of the division of power among shah, prime minister, and Majlis that had existed since Reza Shah's fall, American policy so strengthened the shah as to make him impervious to foreign pressures. The middle class and the National Front, including many of Iran's most capable, honest, and forward-looking people, were removed from any real role in the decision-making process. Representative government—either in the electoral or in the charismatic-leader style—was ended. Contrary to popular Iranian belief, the developments of 1953 did not give the United States any long-term hold on the shah.

In the short run, the shah was soon to find that the emergency commitments of August, 1953 would not necessarily provide him with the level of United States economic and military assistance he had sought since 1947. When Anglo-Iranian negotiations resumed in Washington during October, the new Tehran regime discovered it would not be easy to pry open American purse strings or to weld closed the oil companies' loopholes. The proud shah's desire for an independent military and for international economic standing were reinforced by this experience.

Indeed, United States-Iranian relations seemed to devolve on the same basic contentions that had marked them in the late 1940s. The shah demanded more help in light of what he saw to be an insecure geostrategic position. The Americans continued to preach military restraint and the importance of social progress to produce internal peace. Chastened by the Mossadegh era, however, Washington would listen more closely to the shah in the future. Often in the following years the shah's Iran indeed seemed to be a lonely island of stability in a volatile and strategic region.

4
An Alliance Is Made
1954–68

The shah's assumption of governing power ended the political instability of the Mossadegh era, but did little to resolve the underlying problems of political legitimacy and cyclical economic crisis that had plagued Iran for so many decades. Painfully aware of this, American policymakers sought continually to minimize their commitments to Iran. Not until the mid-1960s would Iran's growing oil wealth, its changing strategic situation, its seemingly successful "White Revolution," and the shah's demonstrated ability to maintain order gradually convince American officials that more might be expected from the United States-Iranian relationship.

But in the intervening years, Washington's commitment continued to be essentially limited to Iran's protection from direct Soviet attack. Doubting the durability of Iran's domestic tranquility, Washington generally tried to avoid provoking Moscow into harassing the country, while American leaders continued to stress to the shah that only economic development and social reform would substantially improve his nation's security.

The idea, so often and widely promulgated after the

1978–79 revolution, that all Iranians detested the shah's regime from 1953 on is surely erroneous. Many former participants in the National Front, dismayed by Mossadegh's failures and demoralized by his defeat, went to work for the shah's government. While some of them gradually dropped out, trying to maintain a legal opposition movement, others rose to high positions, including cabinet and ambassadorial posts.

No bloodbath followed the shah's return to power. A few dozen of Mossadegh's closest civilian and military supporters were imprisoned and only one of them, Foreign Minister Hussein Fatemi, was executed. Mossadegh himself was tried in a military court on charges of rebelling against the shah, tolerating the rise of the Tudeh, undermining the army's loyalty to the shah, and illegally dissolving the Majlis. A central issue was Mossadegh's ignoring of the shah's decree removing him in August, 1953. After all, the shah had remained head of state throughout the entire Mossadegh era, his power overshadowed but still in place.

In his own defense, Mossadegh challenged the shah's power to dismiss him and the competence of the military court. He attributed his own fall to a British plot and, in a rousing summation speech, called on Iranians to continue the fight against foreign political influence. He was sentenced to three years imprisonment in January, 1954, but was released, along with a number of his imprisoned colleagues, in August, 1956. Mossadegh retired to his estate where, shortly thereafter, he was threatened by a gang of thugs, probably at the regime's instigation, and was forced to request government protection. These guards also doubled as a form of house arrest, continuing until his death in 1967.

The main force of repression was directed against the Tudeh. During the two years following the shah's return there were constant rumors of Communist revolutionary plots along with the arrests and executions of underground Tudeh members, many of them in the military. A secondary target was the Islamic fundamentalist group around Ayatollah Kashani, who himself was briefly arrested in January, 1956 in connection with the Razmara assassination. The shah was thus able to uproot the main two revolutionary movements that threatened the existing system and to stabilize his own rule.

The shah's emergence as a strong monarch was made possible by the fact that the events of August, 1953 brought no mere regression to the pre-Mossadegh status quo. All barriers to the shah's power were swept away in the new Iran, with both positive and negative implications for the country's development. Iran's parliamentary system had often been corrupt, inefficient, and antagonistic to reform; its demise made possible a revolution from above, allowing for a more efficient administration of the country and removing some of the class bottlenecks that had blocked efforts to broaden land ownership and reform tax structures. Yet at the same time, the Majlis had spread authority and had provided some representation to the middle and upper classes.

While the Majlis continued under the shah, it became a shadow of itself. Often the shah allowed a loyal opposition party headed by one of his friends; at other times he substituted a single party. In either event, parliament became a rubber stamp for the executive branch. Further, although elections in Iran had never been particularly honest, the benefits of such practices had been spread among several groups; now corrupt polling practices, rigged to favor the shah's candidates at the expense of the urban middle class, alienated the politically active strata as well. Each round of fixed elections, those of 1954 and of 1960, for example, convinced more elements of the impossibility of peaceful parliamentary opposition.

The prime minister's office was also subjected to the shah's will—the prime minister had always been the shah's appointee; now he became, in effect, the shah's executive assistant. In contrast to the National Front's concept of a constitutional monarch, a position held onto by the moderate opposition even during much of the tumultuous 1978–79 revolution, the shah increasingly became the sole ruler. His removal of Zahedi in April, 1955 showed that he would brook no partner: the shah had the power to hire or fire his prime ministers at will.

Without the restraining hands of the parliament and of a

strong prime ministership, Iran now moved toward a one-man dictatorship in which the shah relied for his political survival on the passivity of the peasantry and on the energy of the armed forces and of SAVAK (the State Organization for Intelligence and Security), the secret police organization. This system allowed Iran to move faster, but it also removed some of the brakes that might have kept it from derailing.

Determined to modernize Iran and to win American support and aid in the process, the shah made his plans to lay a foundation for the country's military and economic strength. In terms of improving his own image, he was more successful in the American press initially than in the inner councils of the United States government. Yet ultimately his strategy was successful both in the United States and on an international level. Even the Russians, whose hostility toward Tehran continued for a decade after the shah's return, were finally moved toward some attempts at reconciliation, as evidenced by the shah's 1956 state visit to Moscow and by their return of Tudeh fugitives to the shah's punishment.

Domestically, the first task was the restoration of Iran's economic equilibrium. The Iranian economy "will have nowhere to go but up from the rock bottom state of near bankruptcy it achieved in 1953," reported The New York Times shortly after the shah's triumph. The question, however, was whether the new regime would use renewed American aid "to create the basis of a healthy economy or, as in the past, simply as a perennial transfusion for an unhealthy one."[1] In fact, the emergency United States aid program would seek merely to do the latter; the new oil agreement was to lay the foundation for the former, though it would take a decade to bring results.

Despite Eisenhower's quick reaction to the first plea of Prime Minister Fazlollah Zahedi for increased aid, the original $45 million granted was augmented in March, 1954 only by a mere $6 million more. Zahedi quickly realized that this doling out of funds was being used as leverage to force a quick settlement of the oil dispute. Only in November, 1954, when the first oil tanker left port, did loans and gifts reach sizeable proportions. Between August, 1953 and the end of 1956, the

United States gave $200 million in economic and $200 million in military assistance.

In those surprisingly innocent days, this assistance program created something of a scandal. Both the General Accounting Office and the House of Representatives International Operations Committee found management of the operation to be shocking and slipshod. It was, argued the congressional report, "neither technical assistance nor economic development, but an *ad hoc* method of keeping the Iranian economy afloat." That was the whole point, argued the State Department, to help Iran "through one of the most difficult periods in her history when economic and political disaster threatened to push Iran behind the Iron Curtain."[2]

Especially important in putting Iran back on its feet was the oil agreement the United States helped negotiate between Tehran and the petroleum corporations. Two foreign-owned management/operating companies would carry out the exploration and refining of Iranian oil under a contract with the National Iranian Oil Company (NIOC) and would sell the product to a new consortium. The old AIOC monopoly was replaced on the purchasing end by a partnership with interest divided in the following proportions: 40 percent for AIOC, 14 percent for Shell Oil, 8 percent to each of five American giants, and 6 percent to the French Compagnie Française des Pétroles.

The Justice Department was forced to retreat from its complaint that such a combination violated antitrust laws—national security was a higher priority—but American independent companies were later cut in for a small share. Iran held only two of seven seats on the technical companies' boards, and while Iran's national company (NIOC) had title to the oil, its powers were sharply limited. Still, it was a far cry from the old days when Iranians were not even allowed to see the company's books, and Iran's financial share, 12½ percent of the posted price, was a significant increase. The consortium agreement also promised a regular rise in the volume of production.

After three years of intensive effort, said *The New York*

Times in greeting the agreement, "one of the bitterest disputes that has afflicted the post-war Middle East," had been settled. It was a major victory for American diplomacy and "laid the basis for a viable Iranian economy." [3] The shah was not as jubilant, but this new arrangement did considerably boost export levels—and hence Iran's income—in the following years.

Although the 1954 settlement was certainly a step backward from Mossadegh's design for an all-Iranian oil industry, the gradualist strategy produced real results. Ironically, this arrangement was never discussed in the United States Congress, which later succumbed to protectionist fears that cheap Iranian oil would flood the country. In 1956, oil-import quotas were passed in attempts to protect domestic producers and encourage development of domestic reserves. This policy was part of an era when the United States was the world's largest oil producer and when oil companies feared that an oil glut would send prices crashing. Of course, from the standpoint of the 1970s and 1980s, when the dominant feature of the petroleum factor in international politics became the product's short supply, manipulated by Middle East oil-producing states, much United States policy during the 1950s and 1960s seems strange.

Iran progressed nonetheless. By 1957 NIOC was negotiating deals with independent companies to develop areas outside the consortium concession. In the mid-1960s, Iran began partnerships with diverse companies on a 75/25 profit division, with the lion's share going to Iran. NIOC increased its know-how over the years and opened direct sales to Third World countries, eventually constructing its own refinery and new pipelines. When oil-producing nations united to form the Organization of Petroleum Exporting Countries (OPEC) in 1960, Iran was a charter member.

Slowly, the increased flow of American aid—$611 million in economic aid and a somewhat smaller figure in military aid between 1953 and 1961—and the rapid growth of oil revenues—from $90 million in 1955 to $482 million in 1964—provided a firm grounding for the shah's plans.

Nevertheless, the shah was not satisfied. The United States had given twice as much aid to Yugoslavia, three times as much to Turkey, and four times as much to Taiwan as it had to Iran, he complained in his memoirs. The shah constantly pressed Eisenhower for more aid and for a stronger United States commitment.

Iran's new pro-West orientation complemented this aim. "We have witnessed how aggressors have wantonly occupied neutral countries in defiance of international law and their own undertakings," declared Prime Minister Zahedi in July, 1954. The State Department was pleased but cautious as Iran moved toward open adherence to the Western camp. While Iran might play an important role in regional defense, it told President Eisenhower, modernization of the army should not become "an undue burden on the national economy." American military aid should also be limited lest Iran's army become an undue burden on the United States economy as well as on its own.[4]

Dulles heeded this advice. When Great Britain, Turkey, Pakistan, and Iraq moved toward a collective-security agreement—the Baghdad Pact—in 1955, the American secretary of state tried to keep Iran from joining. "It's too soon after their troubles," he commented, but he was also concerned about the upcoming Geneva summit conference. Soviet assumptions that America had encouraged Tehran to become a member might wreck the meeting. Before Dulles could act, however, Tehran announced its decision to sign the treaty.[5] The shah had outflanked his American friends. It would not be the last time he would do so.

Especially after the 1956 Suez conflict, in which Britain, France, and Israel attacked Egypt in an attempt to bring down the charismatic Gamal Abd al–Nasser, the shah continued to hammer away on his old themes. He wrote Eisenhower that "in this age of atomic warfare, the occurrence of regular armed conflicts with conventional weapons is not to be ruled out as a thing of the past." Aggression could be prevented only "if countries occupying key positions are well prepared and their military as well as financial and economic needs supplied." Americans did not always understand, the shah concluded, that Iranian military weakness might endanger not only Iran but the entire region.[6]

Eisenhower and Dulles, in contrast, agreed with the views of their predecessors in regard to Iran's true military capability. Iran could never really build a strong enough military force to check the USSR. Instead, Tehran should rely on American guarantees. After all, if the Soviets invaded Iran it would quickly lead to a much wider war that would, of necessity, involve the United States. Rather than engage in an unwinnable arms race with Moscow, the shah ought to build a smaller force capable of maintaining order and of preventing internal Communist subversion. Most important, he might better devote his attentions to developing Iran, since poverty and frustration were the surest breeding grounds of revolution.

Yet the shah was also responding to new political events in the Arab world to his south and west. The explosion of coups, revolutions, wars, and civil strife, which marked Arab politics of the 1950s and 1960s, naturally made Iranian leaders nervous. For the shah, such disquieting events included Nasser's rise to Arab leadership, Egypt and Syria's alliance with the Russians, Nasserist attempts to overthrow Jordan's King Hussein, and the 1958 civil war in Lebanon. The Middle East reverberated with the sounds of crashing thrones. The July, 1958 military coup in next-door Iraq, where the Hashemite royal family was massacred and a pro-Moscow regime installed, brought the royal nightmare too close to home.

While the shah's demands for military aid continued, the potential enemy changed. Instead of a full-scale Soviet invasion, the shah became preoccupied with a possible Iraqi attack and with the expected spread of revolution across the Persian Gulf. Radical Arabs might arm and help opposition forces within Iran.

Consequently, the shah strongly urged an activist and interventionist American foreign policy against those Arabs he saw acting as Soviet surrogates. He pressed for full United States membership in the Baghdad Pact, supported the 1957 Eisenhower Doctrine (which promised to aid Middle East states facing Communist-backed aggression), and endorsed the 1958 American troop landings to help end the Lebanese civil war.

American response to these blandishments was cautious. The shah was the most faithful of allies, he never tired of telling Washington. Although in an exposed position, he had resisted both the Soviets' threats and their overtures. Still, Dulles believed that America's retaliatory strength was the greatest barrier to any Soviet advance. If sixteen full-strength divisions were needed to defend Iranian territory, as American generals estimated, only ten of these need come from Iran itself. American power would make up the difference.[7] Moreover, Iran's political and economic structures were too fragile to be of much help beyond the country's own borders.

Apparently unaware of the reasons for the reservations of the United States government, American press coverage of Iran praised the shah for ignoring Soviet attempts to lure him out of the Baghdad Pact. "Iran is the calmest country in the troubled Middle East today," reported The New York Times in December, 1956. "Partly responsible for this is a highly successful campaign against subversive elements." The Tudeh, in fact, had been shattered and the Muslim fundamentalists seemed to have lost influence. The American Embassy explained this stability in one word—prosperity. Yet this was largely a result of American willingness to cover the government's annual budget deficits. Iran's elite had done little to help themselves.[8]

The shah personally enjoyed a good press, though in the late 1950s effusive articles were often matched by more worried analyses, obviously drawing on American government sources. Some reporters were almost ecstatic about what they found. "Iran today is experiencing a gilded convalescence under a mild despotism" that the shah "and his advisors believe necessary for recovery," wrote a correspondent for The New York Times in April, 1957. This combination had produced "internal order, a pro-Western foreign policy and a modest start in the profound economic and social reforms considered essential for long-term stability."

Menaced for centuries by Russian dreams of expansion, "Iran has a life and death interest in . . . collective security" and disliked Arabs "who by ill-considered adventure if not design would unlock the door for the Soviet Union." While relatively soft on the shah's methods, this and other articles explained well the roots of his foreign policy. Further, despite a strong element of wishful thinking, many commentaries did not stint on the real internal problems facing Iran.

Thus, this report continued, the "slowness" of Iran's rulers "in moving against corruption and inefficiency and . . . a feudal landholding system" clouded Iran's future. Admittedly, the 80 percent of the population that lived in villages as virtual serfs of the one thousand wealthiest landowning families cared little about security considerations. "Centuries of neglect and exploitation have left them disease-racked, ignorant and illiterate." The rising middle class, the only force that might break the landowners' power, was "frustrated and leaderless," denied the right to political activity or influence. Inflation, land speculation, and the juxtaposition of conspicuous consumption and abject poverty made the Iranian situation a "race between reform and revolution." [9]

Nor was the Iranian view of America's help and suggestions for reform all favorable. Although in 1956 Iran hosted the largest United States aid mission in the world—with three hundred employees—local people seemed almost unaware of its real achievements. Such Western innovations as wolf whistles, blue jeans, and feature films (though men and women attended separate showings) that appeared in Tehran were seen by many as cultural contaminants; Muslim activists were already protesting and calling for an end to the country's "Americanization." Noted one survey, Iranians only saw America "as some great gift store where prices may be high, but everything is cleaner, better packed and of higher quality than anywhere else." [10]

Aid and oil revenues had not been used very productively. By 1957 Washington was growing tired of financing Tehran's budget deficits. A prime cause of the imbalance was the regime's inability to tax the wealthy, landed aristocracy; it was far easier to raise money by taxing sugar and other staples of the peasant and working-class diet. The situation was even more frustrating because of the shah's belief that his diplomatic allegiance to the West and his vulnerable position in relation to the Soviet Union obligated the United States to pick up Iran's tab.

Growing American concern was reflected in a January, 1958 article by correspondent Sam Pope Brewer, which included a rare look at the complaints of the surviving National Front opposition. "Iran is in a state of discontent that is dangerous to her internal security and to the stability of the Middle East," he wrote, describing charges of corruption within the shah's own family and repression against oppositionists. "The shah," he concluded, "has been increasingly authoritarian. The fear is that this might drive the non-Communist opposition into the arms of the Soviet Union." [11]

Yet the shah's analysis of Washington's continuing obligation to him was essentially accurate. As the Middle East situation became increasingly unstable, American policymakers had to counter the possibility of an additional crisis in Iran. The military coup in neighboring Iraq in July, 1958 resulted in that country's apparent alliance with the USSR. Secret Soviet arms shipments to Baghdad in the following months doubled Iraq's armed forces. At the same time, Moscow launched another campaign to entice Iran out of the Baghdad Pact, offering in exchange a long-term nonaggression pact. A Soviet-sponsored clandestine radio station, the National Voice of Iran, took to the air to denounce the shah. Washington's Iran specialists saw the Soviets as making a major effort to undermine the shah and to stir up trouble within Iran, particularly among the Kurdish minority there.

Soviet Premier Nikita Khrushchev told Iranian Ambassador Masud Ansari in the autumn of 1959 that a neutral Iran could obtain "ten times" as much American aid, as well as Soviet assistance. Unless the Iranians changed their ways, he warned, Moscow might invoke a forty-year-old treaty with

Iran—repeatedly disclaimed by Tehran—permitting Soviet military action against foreign bases on Iranian soil. Some Iranian leaders were badly shaken by these threats.[12]

In the face of this situation, quick American action was necessary. For the first time, the American ambassador in Tehran hailed that country as a "valued ally" of the United States. President Eisenhower promised to accelerate the supply of military equipment and training assistance. In March, 1959, a bilateral United States-Iranian defense pact was signed. This accord—and contemporary parallel agreements with Pakistan and Turkey—declared support for Iran's independence and integrity, continued military and economic aid, and rapid reinforcement in the event of aggression against Iran. A visit by Eisenhower in December was aimed at further reassuring the shah.[13]

Fundamentally, however, the White House's perceptions of the situation had not changed. Since any direct Soviet attack through Afghanistan or Iraq was still considered unlikely there was resistance to any large-scale, costly military buildup for Iran. Indeed, Eisenhower was more concerned about the weakness of the shah's domestic base. Secretary of State Christian Herter warned that the deterioration of Iran's economy—inflationary pressure and a worsening balance of payments—was caused by the shah's many military projects. He suggested that the United States might reduce military and economic aid to pressure Iran into decreasing public expenditures and to reevaluate its own military spending. This policy would later be adopted under President Kennedy.[14]

Given Washington's hesitations, the shah's complaints continued to escalate throughout 1960. The Iranian forces were short 30,000 men, he wrote Eisenhower, and his air force needed bombers to counter the military buildup in Iraq and Afghanistan. Eisenhower calmly replied to these criticisms of the 1959 plan (whose defensive purposes were reflected in its name, Operation Counterbalance) that Congress would not approve the levels of aid the shah wanted and that such measures would damage Iran's economy.[15]

With the regional situation becoming more and more frightening, the shah's nervousness was understandable. Nasser broke relations with Iran in 1960 because of Tehran's continued diplomatic ties to Israel. Arab nationalists launched all-out propaganda attacks against Iran. Persian settlers in the Arab sheikdoms of the Gulf were denounced as part of a plot to steal these lands from the Arabs. Iraq, Syria, and other Arab states supported a "liberation movement" claiming Iran's oil-rich southwestern province of Khuzistan (which they called "Arabistan") for the Arab world. Cairo also courted the Gulf Arabs still under British colonial rule while Iraq threatened to take over Kuwait.

American leaders' genuine concern over these external threats to Iran was fully matched by their continued belief that internal problems posed the major danger to the country's stability. These shortcomings, principally the politically unrepresentative nature of the regime and the country's unsound economic structure, seemed to culminate in the crisis of the early 1960s. When in the spring of 1960 pressure from the International Monetary Fund and the United States government forced some reining in of the runaway economy, the application of spending brakes increased unemployment and added to urban dissatisfaction. Additionally, enraged by rigged elections in August, 1960, the opposition took to the streets for the first time in years. Many were predicting a crisis—even a revolution—in Iran, though the shah would survive for another two decades in power.

In retrospect, Iranians, after the 1978–79 revolution, would strongly criticize American policy toward the shah during the 1950s. America, they charged, had brought the shah back to power in August, 1953, trained the SAVAK, and supplied the military and economic aid that perpetuated his rule. Tehran's police patrols even rode in jeeps marked with the United States aid insignia—clasped hands imposed on the American and Iranian national shields. Although Americans were blamed for not forcing the shah to change his ways, attempts to force reforms also constituted interference, which the Iranians claimed to resent. "The United States spent billions of dollars in Iran and saved Iran from the chains of the USSR,"

one Iranian civil servant told an American scholar, Marvin
Zonis, "but the people hate them. My opinion is the same as
almost the entire nation. The United States imposed prime
ministers on the king [shah] and the people; prime ministers
with programs prepared in Washington with little knowledge
of Iranian conditions."[16]

American policymakers during those years were not unaware of these complaints, but on three points their perceptions of the political situation differed from those of both the
contemporary and later opposition. First, the opposition in the
late 1950s and early 1960s believed that it was in Washington's power to force the shah to change his ways. Short of
threatening a coup against him, which would not only have
run directly contrary to America's aim of stabilizing the
regional situation but would also have been inconsistent with
the nonintervention posture Iranians demanded of the United
States, Washington did make attempts to press for reforms.
Yet the shah's critics repeatedly overestimated American influence in Tehran. "People do not understand why the Americans permit the corruption and inefficiency they see," said
one of them in January, 1960. Another commented, "Tell the
Government it must stamp out the influence-peddlers and enforce the law or there will be no more help from Washington."
Ironically, in terms of later developments, some anti-shah activists had no qualms about demanding American intervention in Iran's internal affairs—as long as it was in support of
their own side in the battle.[17]

Second, while the Iranian dissidents were almost exclusively concerned—and understandably so—with the Iranian
internal situation, the United States had broader interests and
worries. When asked whether an end to American aid would
result in Iran's collapse and a Soviet takeover, one Iranian
critic of the shah responded that at least in a Communist police state something would be done for the people, while
"under this police state, there is no freedom and nothing is
done for the people."[18] From Washington's point of view,
though, its fifteen-year involvement with Iran had been
mainly premised on avoiding a Communist takeover as its top

priority. American policymakers argued that the Iranians were better off under a non-Communist regime and that Iran's independence made possible some eventual improvement. But American priorities were also concerned with preventing an expansion of Soviet power and a collapse of the political systems in the region.

Third, and perhaps most important, Washington thought it saw a way to institute reforms, avoid revolution, strengthen Iran, and satisfy the dissidents all at the same time. The main criticism of the shah, after all, addressed itself to the slowness of the reform process. Part of this was due not to the bureaucratic inefficiency of the shah's government itself—for Iran had been governed similarly for centuries—but to changes in the expectations of the people. As one Iranian put it, "Forty years ago influence and privilege were part of the acknowledged system. Now people have heard of something better and they are demanding to have it." [19]

The main Iranian criticism of American policy, reported *The New York Times* in January, 1960, involved "the feeling that the United States is not trying hard enough to get the work of reform done." [20] If only Washington applied enough pressure on the shah to speed up land reform and other changes all would be well. Accelerating the pace of modernization would create a stronger and more stable Iran sooner. Essentially, this was the same view that characterized American policy toward Iran since 1946. By the time the Kennedy administration came into office, however, the State Department was more determined than ever to press for an early completion of Iran's revolution from above. If the shah wanted to finish Iran's ark before the flood, there seemed precious few years left.

While the shah had created a tame two-party system in 1957, he found it difficult to keep under control. Some leaders of the loyal opposition began to call for free elections in the summer of 1960 and condemned the fixing of past parliamentary ballots. These forces found a leader in Dr. Ali Amini, whom the shah appointed prime minister in May, 1961 in order to calm the widespread dissent. Amini was to be another in that line of strong politicians—Qavam, Razmara, Mossadegh, and Zahedi—curbed by the shah when they seemed to challenge his preeminence.

Amini, a member of one of Iran's leading landowning families, had studied law at the University of Paris and had served as a minister in the cabinets of Razmara, Mossadegh, Zahedi, and Hussein Ala. Having broken with Mossadegh in July, 1952, Amini was regarded as a traitor by the National Front, particularly after he joined Zahedi as minister of finance and directed his oil negotiations and campaign for American aid. The shah distrusted him as a potential new rival and when Zahedi fell, Amini was made ambassador to Washington in 1955. Amini was recalled, however, three years later on the shah's suspicion that he had been involved in a half-baked coup attempt.

As ambassador, Amini apparently made a good personal impression on then-Senator John Kennedy. Although the shah's later claim that Amini was appointed prime minister due to American pressures seems untrue, there was no question that Amini was popular and well liked in the United States. Starkly stating the choice Iran faced, Amini warned: "Divide your lands or face revolution—or death." This provided, editorialized the *Times*, "the best prospect in years—and perhaps the last—of progress in one of the sickest of the world's sick nations."[21] Many American diplomats agreed.

It was not that Amini's theoretical views were so different from those of the shah, who had also long favored a redistribution of Iran's land, but that Amini wanted a more systematic and far-reaching change. The shah was suspicious: Amini had, after all, been an activist in the National Front, which stood for limiting the shah's power. Nor was the shah willing to follow Amini's proposals for comprehensive economic planning and a strong anticorruption drive. For Amini, the land reform was only a first step; for the shah, in practice, it was an end in itself. The shah's failure to follow through was to be a key element in his own regime's downfall.

A second miscalculation made by the press and by later administrations was that the reforms would end middle-class grievances. Increasingly Iran's new skilled urban strata advocated the cessation of American aid to the shah's regime. The shah's mechanisms of political control were still far less complete than they became in later years. "Nowhere in the world, in all probability, is so much free-swinging comment and criticism hurled at the Government and chief of state" as in Iran, wrote Harrison Salisbury in December, 1961. There was widespread "cynicism and skepticism over the Shah and his policies." Many Iranians thought the shah's commitment to the United States was "too firm." "Their repugnance to communism is matched only by boiling frustration at their inability to exercise the powers and formulate the policies that they feel are the just due of their new-born strength."[22] The White Revolution, the oil boom, and the continuing growth of the middle class only further whet these appetites and frustrations. In 1978 they would be expressed in their full fury.

American attempts to bring about reform in 1962–63 were nonetheless good faith efforts to address these problems. Ironically, a passing remark by Khrushchev in 1961 helped put the issue high on Kennedy's list of priorities. Iran, the Russian leader told him, was a typical unstable pro-West country about to experience political upheaval. The USSR would not be involved, he continued, but would be blamed anyway, damaging United States-Soviet relations. Kennedy requested a full State Department report as quickly as possible. It should be noted that the Eisenhower administration had probably passed along similar warnings to the incoming president.

Kennedy's March, 1962 plan sought to shift the shah's preoccupation from military security to economic progress, even if it became necessary to limit American military aid as leverage. The unwieldy army would be reduced from 240,000 to 150,000 men over two or three years and would be geared, in the words of the American proposal, "to military realities rather than to the political glamor value of advanced weaponry." To gain the shah's agreement, the United States would reissue security guarantees, promise large contributions to any sound economic plan, and develop a five-year military-modernization schedule.[23]

In a series of meetings through the year, the shah ac-
quiesced to Washington's pressures, though he was hardly
pleased. To go along, however, the shah felt it necessary that
he make some important changes. On the foreign front he
needed to improve relations with his neighbors. As it then
stood, he had no friends among the Arabs to his west; the Soviets to the north remained belligerent; and to his east Afghanistan and Pakistan, while not at odds with Iran were in
conflict both with each other and with India.

Therefore the shah moved dramatically toward rapprochement with Moscow, a step he had considered as early
as the 1959 talks following the coup in Iraq. Fortunately, the
USSR had greatly reduced its price for friendship. Its condition—that Tehran pledge to forbid any United States missile
bases on Iran's soil—was hardly onerous, since the deploy-
ment of Polaris submarines lessened considerably the need for
such facilities.

Not only did the Soviets cease propaganda attacks on receipt of the shah's commitment, but they actually switched to
a campaign of praise and detente. By the mid-1960s large
amounts of Soviet economic aid, including some light military equipment, were flowing into Iran. The USSR also became a valuable market for Persian natural gas.

Through this same period the shah had been moving to
strengthen his domestic control. General Teimur Bakhtiar, the
powerful head of SAVAK, was removed from power in 1961
after he had organized demonstrations against Amini's reform
programs. There was, however, a deeper reason for his dismissal. Some three years earlier, Bakhtiar had visited the
United States and met with Kermit Roosevelt and Allen Dulles. To their horror Bakhtiar told them that he wanted to take
over political power from the shah. Dulles replied that he
would receive no American support for any such action.

Allen Dulles then called his brother, warning him not to
allow Bakhtiar to say anything of his plans. John Foster Dulles
kept up a verbal barrage from Bakhtiar's entrance until he was
able to usher him out. The CIA informed the shah of Bakhtiar's disloyalty and the shah bided his time until he could

remove the SAVAK chief.[24] Some time later, after Bakhtiar had gone into exile in Iran's enemy neighbor, Iraq, his own SAVAK managed to assassinate him.

In July, 1962, the shah removed Amini, who seemed a second potential threat. Amini blamed his downfall on a shortage of American financial aid, though his real problem may have been Washington's inability to protect him against the shah. It was then that the shah proceeded to create his own reform program from above, his "White Revolution."

These land reform decrees set off large demonstrations led by Muslim clerics, including Ruhollah Khomeini, between October and December, 1962. One clash at the Fayziyeh School in Qom ended with the killing of a number of religious scholars, further embittering clerical opposition to the shah. During a second round in June, 1963, three days of antigovernment riots in Tehran were crushed with as many as 3,000 dissidents killed. A sharp SAVAK crackdown followed.

Today this battle is a source of pride for Iran's Islamic rulers, who say they opposed the shah's program only because such changes, if successful, would have strengthened his regime. But to admit that the provocation for their fiercest fight was the breakup of estates and a threatened erosion of landlord power hardly augments the Iranian clergy's populist credentials. It might be said in defense of the Muslim clergy that the mullah's objection was to the government redistribution of *waqf* land, land whose revenue was intended for religious and charitable purposes. But any rationalization or justification for violent resistance to land reform in a country of so poor a peasantry must remain less than totally convincing.

On the other hand, the fallout of these riots was to have fatal consequences for the shah and for the Americans as well. The real underlying cause of the clerics' success in their agitation was the regime's lack of a popular base, its illegitimacy in the eyes of so many Iranians because of the events of 1953, and the growing dissatisfaction of the urban middle class. In the American media, however, the "reactionary" revolt only validated the shah's reform credentials. By defeating these backward forces, reporters said, he had opened the door for the kind of political and economic progress that Americans had advocated for years. The depiction of the shah as a progressive ruler would be continued in the American media for over a decade. When conflict first erupted in 1978 it was misinterpreted to be a repeat of the 1962–63 confrontation.

"The Shah of Iran," wrote Max Frankel in January, 1963, "is rapidly altering his country's political and economic life with a reform program of revolutionary proportions." A forthcoming referendum on the White Revolution would give the shah constitutional power "in many respects comparable to those recently assumed by President De Gaulle in France." The shah seemed to have been transformed into "the unaccustomed role of a Western-style politician."

Following the shah's victory in the vote (the first in Iranian history in which women participated), The New York Times called the success a triumph for "a revolution in which Iran's ruler has aligned himself directly with the workers and peasants against conservatives and traditionalists." Although the Times did report that the shah's opponents could run only as independents and were forbidden to organize or hold rallies, it nevertheless found the election "the fairest and most representative election Iran has ever had." One Times editorial stated: "The great mass of the Iranian people are doubtless behind the Shah in his bold new reform efforts" and it held high expectations for "the coming elections to restore parliamentary rule." [25] There is reason to hope, said another Times editorial of that period, "that Iran will gradually come to see better days. The people who voted so solidly for the Government-supported candidates must have thought so." [26]

Richard Cottam, an Iranian specialist and former State Department official, tried to explain that the election was neither free nor a victory for democracy: "Have we now all become so enamored of economic determinism to expect this one act to produce a happy non-communist political stability?" As the American press saw it the answer seemed to be in the affirmative. [27]

One man who was decidedly not reconciled to the shah's

rule was a leading activist in the movement against the shah and his White Revolution, Ruhollah Khomeini. One June, 1963 morning, at 3 A.M., several dozen SAVAK paratroopers surrounded his modest residence in Qom, arrested him, and took him off to Tehran. During the drive, the car stopped to allow him to pray on the road. He was held in Tehran for two months, then returned to Qom to be kept under house arrest.

Khomeini was firmly convinced that only America support and aid enabled the shah to stay in power and he focused much of his wrath on the United States. For example, during an updating of the old bilateral military agreements, Washington sought to include a standard clause giving United States military advisors immunity from prosecution under Iranian law. Mossadegh had agreed to such a provision, but the aroused anti-shah opposition now interpreted any such regulation as a reminder of the hated extraterritoriality statutes of the colonial era.

The Majlis's approval was attacked by Khomeini in the most unrestrained language. The decree, he said, placed "the Iranian people under American bondage . . . because America is the land of the dollar and because the Iranian Government needs dollars." Appearances seemed to support this allegation. Only a few days after passing the immunity law, the Majlis approved another bill arranging a $200 million United States loan for military purchases.

In one speech in Qom, Khomeini virtually declared war on the shah. He refused to recognize the government or courts, he said, and would deny any law that allowed, in his words, any American servant or cook to terrorize pious religious leaders. "Iran has lost her greatness. The might of the army has trampled" on the people, Khomeini concluded. Finally, in November, 1964, he was exiled to Turkey. Shortly thereafter, he moved to Iraq, lecturing on theology in the Shi'a holy city of Najaf.[28]

The shah appeared to have won a total victory. President Kennedy, Secretary of State Dean Rusk, and the specialists at the CIA and State Department were relatively satisfied by the shah's initial steps toward reform. The monarch had, after all, accelerated the land-distribution program, provided additional benefits for urban workers, made his army smaller and more efficient, and eased Iran's relationship with Moscow. Interim economic and agricultural problems could be worked out. The hostility of urban intellectuals, landlords, and religious leaders would not just disappear, but their disunity and the army's loyalty would probably assure stability. Even with his shortcomings, American policymakers agreed, the shah seemed the only man who could provide Iran with political continuity.

Still, the enthusiasm for the shah of American policymakers did not equal that of the news media. There were those in government who were very aware of the likelihood that the shah would not follow through on this promising start. The CIA, for example, concluded that planning for the White Revolution was weak and that long-term economic development remained a low priority for the shah. Twenty-five percent of Iran's budget still went for military spending. Most important, while land reform seemed to engender some peasant enthusiasm, it could succeed only if cooperatives were properly organized. Otherwise, poor peasants on their small allotments could never hope to finance their own planting and marketing. Under such circumstances, a CIA report predicted, Iranian agriculture would regress. And this is exactly what did happen.[29]

A Bureau of the Budget study was even more critical. The shah's approach was quite different from the comprehensive development plan that most Americans believed they were supporting. While economic stagnation would lead to greater urban discontent, the confusion in the land-reform program might reduce farm production. Without the necessary economic and administrative underpinning that the shah's plan had neglected, the report continued, the shah could not build a political base within the peasantry; he would become increasingly dependent on the military. The "reversion to a U.S. role as friendly advisor to a regime whose policies are characterized by short-term expediency and neglect of the fundamental course necessary to the increasing well-being of its people" would be a high-risk proposition.[30]

While the Bureau of the Budget thought the State Department too passive, even United States Ambassador Julius Holmes warned Secretary Rusk that Iran lacked the infrastructure as well as the managerial and technical personnel required for rapid economic development. Projects faced endless delays while Iranian government departments bickered among themselves. The need for an investment program was simply not recognized. In 1963, long before the financial avalanche created by the oil price boom, the country's economic situation was already getting out of control.[31]

By 1963 American-trained Iranian economists and planners were being fired or ignored; consequently, American advice had little effect on the shah's regime. American diplomats in Tehran were also aware of America's increasing unpopularity among young Iranians—earned through a sort of guilt by association. Students in the universities, which were rapidly expanding, were especially frustrated by poor living conditions, overcrowding, and indefinite prospects for future employment. The most popular teachers, like Mehdi Bazargan in the School of Engineering, were opponents of the government. While President Kennedy was personally respected, the United States was seen as the main prop of the shah.

A 1963 West German poll showed that 33 percent of young Iranians asked saw America as "aggressive" (compared with only 19 percent who so labeled the USSR); 85 percent believed that American aid worked "to make the rich richer"; only 8 percent thought American aid "improves the standard of living of the many." Fully 50 percent thought the United States "is too much on the side of having things remain as they are."[32]

The Iranian government's mishandling of the immunity bill further damaged the American image in Iran. Even the pro-shah New Iran Party split on the vote in the Majlis, with opponents calling those who had supported the bill "traitors." The shah was insensitive to this dissent, calling the close vote the result of a subversive plot. The more likely cause was the gov-

ernment's failure to explain the routine legislation's real purpose. Meanwhile, Khomeini's vitriol spread like wildfire
through the bazaars, and bootlegged tapes of his latest
speeches enjoyed large audiences. His exile lent him the aura
of martyrdom and likely contributed to the elevation of his
status among the clergy. Most significant, the embassy reported that the clergy was reaching out to make alliances with
nationalist politicians.

Originally, government officials had assured the Americans
that there would be no problem with the immunity bill. After
it ran into trouble, however, they argued that the United
States, with its wide intelligence system, should have predicted the results that did follow. Consequently, according to
Iranians, the Americans were at fault for accepting Iranian
evaluations and pledges. Such belief in American omnipo-
tence boded ill for the future.

So much depended on the shah's ability to lead, yet American leaders had had ample experience of what a tender reed
this could be. Lean, handsome, and only beginning to approach middle age, the shah had undergone one of the most
remarkable on-the-job training programs in history. Skiing
trips to Switzerland contributed to his robust health and with
his dark, soulful eyes and determined expression, it was understandable that the shah was seen by foreign admirers as the
embodiment of the Iranian nation.

In many ways, though, he remained the painfully shy and
inarticulate young man who had first mounted the throne,
British and Russian bayonets at his back. His speeches were
stilted and uninspiring. Despite strenuous attempts of syco-
phants to build a cult of personality around him, the shah
lacked the charisma of a Nasser or a Mossadegh—he was a
ruler, not a leader. By surrounding himself with yes-men, the
shah had also winnowed out any political figure who might
teach him unpleasant truths. Playing off bureaucrats and departments in an atmosphere of suspicion and fear, the shah
could not hope to produce a respected or efficient government.

For the shah, nationalism was the road to Iran's renewed greatness, stirred to life by military might and imperial splendor. He was no unyielding reactionary: in the areas of economic development and modernization his motto seemed to be, The sooner, the better. As early as 1965 he was promising that within twenty years the Iranian standard of living would be the highest in the world. His dreams and ambitions for his people were on the grandest of scales.

Yet unlike the new-style dictators springing up all over the Third World, he was unable to cultivate even the illusion of mass participation. Nor was he able to fully utilize the modern techniques of a single-party state to create an ideological conformity. He tried to build skyscrapers of modernism while devoting little time or planning to the political foundations they required. His impatient attentions seemed always to return too quickly to military affairs and foreign policy.

Given these limitations, the chances that the shah would become a great domestic reformer and a constitutional monarch were slim; but the chances that if only he would hold onto power at home he might become a dominant regional figure on a strategic-military level were correspondingly great. Kennedy's assassination in November, 1963 and his replacement by Lyndon Johnson, who was preoccupied by the Vietnam War and by the problems of his own "Great Society" program at home, marked an end to American pressure on the shah for reform. In the mid-1960s this resulted in a return to the traditional United States policy of limiting arms aid. By the end of Johnson's term, however, the shah was to be accepted on his own terms: Iran would try to become the great power of the Persian Gulf.

At first, the shah was bitter about Washington's continued reluctance to increase aid: "Is it because we have been successful in creating a country that is developing and has begun a social revolution that we are no longer important?" Sarcastically he asked, "Why do the Americans think I am making trouble . . . when I have done the things they said they wanted?" In other words, having fulfilled his end of the bargain in instituting domestic reform, he expected that the United States would provide him the arms he wanted without further ado.[33]

There definitely had been strings attached to the 1964 United States-Iran Military Sales Agreement. This four-year plan provided for up to $50 million a year (increased to $100 million after two years) for weaponry, beginning with M–60 tanks. But these sales would be approved only after an annual review of Iran's economic development and social programs. Washington wanted to check closely into whether military purchases would interfere with economic and social progress. Tehran did not like this approach; it was deemed unwarranted interference in internal affairs.

The shah was also unhappy over other aspects of America's Middle East policy. When the United States recognized the pro-Nasser government in North Yemen's civil war, the shah sided with the royalist opposition, an ironic twist since Nasser was at that time blasting Iran as an "American colony."

In reality, there were many significant political differences between Washington and Tehran: America's focus was on Soviet activities; the shah was more concerned about Iraqi and Egyptian ambitions. When Johnson cut off military aid and spare parts to Pakistan, an old ally, in its 1965 war with India, the shah bitterly commented, "Now we know that the United States would not come to aid us if we are attacked."[34] Circumventing American regulations, the shah bought several dozen United States-built F–86s and spare parts from Canada and sent them to Pakistan. Washington did not protest.

When the shah met President Johnson in July, 1964 their main topic was Nasser. The shah's traditional distrust of the Arabs was combined with his knowledge that Nasser had overthrown the Egyptian monarchy and had been friendly with Mossadegh. Cairo's 1960 break with Iran, ostensibly over Tehran's continued diplomatic relations with Israel, was taken as a personal insult by the shah. Nor could the Arab threats to Khuzistan, whose oil provided 75 percent of Iran's export earnings, and to the Persian Gulf, through which the petroleum was shipped, be taken lightly.

Conscious of Iran's own Kurdish problem, which might be exploited by the Arabs, the shah began to aid Iraqi Kurds against the Baghdad regime, and when Egyptian troops arrived in Iraq for maneuvers, the shah suggested to the United States and other allies that something must be done to stop Nasser before he took over Iraq and the Gulf. The shah also complained that United States food aid to Egypt helped finance Nasser's ambitions, that Iran's defenses were inadequate, and that he needed United States aid to strengthen his forces in Khuzistan, which Arab leaders had started to call Arabistan. Washington recognized the validity of some of these complaints—e.g., Egyptian-backed Iranian Arabs had begun subversion and sabotage operations against the Khuzistan oil pipelines—but its response did not satisfy Tehran. The shah decided he would have to act on his own; his resentment of Washington's position was intensified in 1965 by American attempts to discourage him from building up his Gulf fleet.

On the domestic scene, the ongoing White Revolution and the co-optation or suppression of internal opposition made the shah more self-confident than he had ever been. The economic situation at home steadily improved. Sources of foreign aid were diversified by the shah's successful visit to the USSR in June, 1965. The shah and the controlled Iranian press were outspokenly critical of some American policies, particularly Washington's attempts to limit Iranian arms purchases. If necessary, the shah warned, Iran would seek new markets for its oil and new sources for its arms. Unless the United States sold him the modern F–4D fighter plane, he told American negotiators, he might turn to Moscow for equivalent equipment. Such leverage was one factor in his success in obtaining the aircraft.

The shah also sought to block any official American contacts with his opponents. Ambassador Armin Meyer recalls that shortly after his arrival in Tehran in 1965 he encountered a woman on one social occasion who had the same name as a former prime minister. Learning that she was a relative, Meyer mentioned that he would like to meet this politician some day. But the former prime minister was not in the shah's good graces, and a few days later the Iranian ambassador in Washington called on the undersecretary of state to protest Meyer's behavior. Meyer told the State Department, which promised to support him on the matter, that the conversation was only tea-party small talk.

When Meyer next met with the shah, reference was made to this affair. Meyer explained the facts and suggested the importance of keeping in touch with the opposition. The shah was not persuaded. In Iran's culture, the monarch said, opposition elements assess amicable treatment as a sign of weakness.[35]

The shah's new independence was predicated on the changing realities in the international petroleum market. America was becoming more and more dependent on oil imports, particularly from the Middle East, and oil-exporting states were becoming more conscious of their ability to increase their financial share from that trade. The Middle East war of June, 1967 led to a world oil scare, with some talk of an Arab oil embargo against Israel's friends. The shah felt he should be rewarded for his continued, reliable supply of oil to the West.

In 1966 he had successfully pressured the oil consortium into increasing production rates in Iran—and hence his government's revenues. He demanded another increase in early 1968 and, when the oil companies balked, afraid of creating a glutted oil market, the State Department entered the picture. The corporations were asked to go along with the shah and to compensate for increased Iranian output by holding down the production of Iran's Arab competitors. The basis of the request was national security. Undersecretary of State Eugene Rostow urged them "not to antagonize the shah" lest he join some future oil shutoff against the United States. This step was also needed, Rostow told the complaining company executives, to counter the USSR's gains in influence in Iran.[36]

This placed the oil companies in a difficult position. As far as the major corporations were concerned, too much oil was already being produced. The shah was determined, however, to obtain the revenues he needed for his Fourth Development plan. If the consortium production would not generate the required revenues, he warned, he would seize the oil fields. Although continuing to argue over production levels, the consortium came up with more money. This was one of the first steps contributing to the revolution in the pricing and control of oil that was to culminate in 1973.

Meanwhile, increases in Iran's exports, in its Gross National Product, and in its industrial production led to the conclusion that Iran had reached the developmental "take-off" point. American aid was virtually terminated at the end of 1967, after having supplied Iran with nearly $1 billion during the preceeding fourteen years. While the United States aid program in Iran had once been regarded as one of the "more inefficient and corrupted of American overseas aid efforts," concluded The New York Times, Washington now pointed to Iran as "one of their more notable success stories."[37]

These accomplishments and the shah's new Soviet connection encouraged greater American arms sales to Iran. Already the shah's army was equipped with M–1 rifles, 106–mm artillery, M–47 tanks, 3.5–mm antitank rocket launchers, F–86 fighters, and C–47 transport planes. This was still not enough, though, in view of the shah's attempts to keep up with Iraq and Egypt. He wanted more and better equipment: a comprehensive radar system to watch out for Soviet attacks, a ground-to-air missile network to protect his Gulf coast, supersonic aircraft, and even long-range surface-to-surface missiles to deter his Arab enemies.

The State Department justified the sale of F–4D fighter planes on the grounds that the USSR had long since sent advanced fighters and bombers to Iran and Egypt. "We've been painfully careful in this area not to get out in front with our arms sales," Rostow wrote President Johnson in November, 1966. "But the Communist nations have put in some $2.3 billion in arms, and there comes a time when we can't refuse to sell the legitimate means of defense." Since Moscow had provided its allies with Mig–21s, Rostow wrote Senator William Fulbright, chairman of the Senate Foreign Relations Committee, America had to decide "whether we should leave our friends without the means they feel they need to defend themselves or attempt through modest sales to help them achieve at least minimum defense capability."[38]

Fulbright was not convinced. "I believe we are doing a great disservice to Iran by selling them these arms," he told a congressional hearing.[39] Given Iran's poverty, it should have other priorities.

A number of Defense Department analysts agreed with Fulbright's viewpoint. Every year the department's International Security Agency (ISA) was responsible for requesting a "threat assessment" from the Joint Chiefs of Staff in order to justify arms sales abroad. After 1966 ISA argued that Soviet-Iranian relations had improved to the point that there was no immediate threat along their mutual border. Their bilateral trade and their natural gas deals, plus the fact that relatively second-rate Soviet units faced the border were cited as factors in this conclusion.

Actually, ISA officials felt that the Iranians were spending too much money on arms, a position that this agency would take repeatedly until the shah's fall. The State Department consistently disagreed. Year after year, until the Nixon administration ended the debate in 1969, the White House supported the State Department position.

There were numerous signs of the shah's new strategic orientation. In March, 1965 he decided to focus military planning on the Gulf, and the following February he ordered formation of a new Third Corps, including paratroop units, to be based at Shiraz. In February, 1967, more Iranian army units and bases were shifted from the Russian border in the north to the Persian Gulf. As Nasser's influence reached its full height the shah's nervousness rose to corresponding levels. Nasser had installed a congenial regime in North Yemen while Nasserist rebels in the British colony of South Yemen seemed near victory. Syria had its most radical government ever, calling for guerrilla wars of liberation throughout the Middle East. Iraq was friendly toward Egypt and unfriendly toward Iran. The Russians were supplying all three of the large Arab states with modern equipment. There were few friendly faces for Iran or for the United States in the presidential palaces of the Middle East.

Then a dramatic event signaled a turning point in the

shah's victory over the vestiges of the Kennedy policy of arms restraint. During May, 1967 Nasser moved his troops into the eastern Sinai, openly threatening war with Israel and the closing of the Gulf of Aqaba. Even King Hussein of Jordan joined the Egypt-Syria alliance. Upon the demand of Nasser, the United Nations meekly removed its peacekeeping force from the Egypt-Israel border. The world held its breath.

Suddenly, Israel replied to its neighbors' pressure with six thunderous days of battle. Israeli troops drove through the Sinai up to the Suez Canal, destroying the Egyptian air force and army wherever it found them. Jordan was swept out of the West Bank and Syrian forces were knocked out of their strategic positions on the towering Golan Heights. The power balance was decisively shaken. New attitudes were born about the political value of a strong military to small nations.

The shah's prophecies about the region's instability seemed fulfilled, but the pattern of events also indicated new opportunities for American policy in the Middle East. In November, the shah was promised two full squadrons of new Phantom F–5s and more equipment on an easy-credit loan plan. Methods were developed to circumvent congressional controls. For example, the Defense Department used a revolving fund to finance purchases through the Export-Import Bank. The 1968 Foreign Military Sales Act and later amendments were designed to prevent such measures, but the executive branch found new ways around the legislature. Objections to the arms buildup by the Agency for International Development, which ran United States foreign-aid programs, were also ignored.

There were still a few voices that warned of the danger in abandoning or even lessening the Kennedy-era pressures for internal reform. Even though the shah seemed to be clearly in the saddle for the forseeable future, and indeed had created an unchallengeable domestic position, he was not without his critics at home either. "The Shah's regime is regarded as an unpopular dictatorship not only by its opponents, but far more significantly, by its proponents as well," wrote American Embassy political counselor Martin Herz in 1964. Even high-ranking members of the shah's regime were unwilling to defend the government's repression.

"There is real danger that if a revolutionary change were to occur, the pent-up grievances . . . are more likely to explode into demagoguery, extremism, revenge-seeking and a search for new enemies," Herz continued. Foremost of these enemies would undoubtedly be the United States, which was widely seen as the shah's main backer. The shah was already convinced that it was a mistake to yield to foreign advice by "giving even a little leeway to the opposition." Perhaps he was right, Herz admitted: "The shah is riding a tiger from which he cannot safely dismount."[40]

Yet, this prophetic view was also a minority one. Assistant Secretary of State Lucius Battle expressed the dominant analysis when he told a congressional hearing: "The success the Shah has achieved has been phenomenal and has aroused the envy of others who would prefer to see what the Shah calls his 'White Revolution' change color. Our economic assistance, now shifting from grant to credit sales, has assisted Iran in maintaining the security and stability which were prerequisites for economic and social development."[41]

These years, then, helped establish an American image of Iran on three points. First, social and economic changes were needed in Iran; the faster they were carried out, the better Washington liked it. The shah was not likely to be criticized for moving too quickly since American policymakers were conditioned to equate a rapid pace with success.

Second, while lip service continued to be given to the broad nature of dissatisfaction among Iran's urban population, the non-Communist opposition was seen as primarily reactionary, perceived by Americans as being motivated solely by Islamic fundamentalism. Journalists and policymakers believed that as modernization continued these forces would lose their power to move the Iranian people. Thus liberal criticism of the shah in the United States was undercut by this identification of his enemies as reactionaries.

Finally, the shah seemed firmly in control at home. Increasingly, the main threat to Iran was perceived as foreign in nature and the shah's ability to become a major actor on the international scene began to be accepted as reality. In the uncertain world of Middle East politics in the latter 1960s, Iran appeared as an island of stability in a region filled with turmoil.

These misperceptions, it should be repeated, were accepted far more fully within the American press than they were in the United States government by 1968. However, developments during the next few years would intensify them on both fronts.

As for Iran, American participation in the events of 1953 in no way made the shah a United States puppet. Washington and Tehran held two different views of Iran's internal and international needs, which, though often running parallel, just as often put the two capitals in conflict. A study of a series of United States-Iranian conflicts before and after 1953 concluded that Iran won the disputes in only four out of fifteen cases in the earlier period, compared to five out of seven (a 71 percent success rate) during the later era.[42] After 1968, strategic requirements would move Washington's objectives for Iran and its neighborhood closer and closer to those of the shah.

5
An Imperial Dream
1969–74

When President Richard Nixon and National Security Advisor (later Secretary of State) Henry Kissinger took office in 1969 they inaugurated a turning point in United States policy toward Iran. From its traditional peripheral position, Iran emerged as the key pillar of support for American interests in an increasingly important part of the world. This change did not represent, however, a victory for American over Iranian concerns; rather it marked the triumph of the shah's own long-held view of a proper role for himself over twenty years of State Department reservations.

When the shift came it was in response to strategic, political, and economic developments in the Persian Gulf. Within Iran's neighborhood was developed the world's greatest concentration of petroleum production. Great Britain, the colonial power controlling much of the Gulf's Arab shore, seemed unwilling to defend it and the United States was unable to do so. The shah nominated himself for the role.

Washington also came to accept the shah's assessment that the principal threat to regional stability was no longer the USSR but local radical forces against whom Iran's army might be the logical defender. Iran, formerly a mere trip-wire for triggering American retaliation against Soviet aggression, could become an actual bulwark against the Soviet surrogates in the area. The shah was eager to assume responsibility for this task; his mounting oil wealth enabled him to do so.

Although Iran's transformation into a regionally dominant power was made possible by the 1969 Nixon Doctrine and by certain May, 1972 Nixon promises to supply the shah the necessary weapons and technical aid, the beginnings of the shift in roles went back to the Johnson administration. In 1966 the State Department was warning that Iran's budget deficits came from excessive expenditures on military hardware. The shah, said one report, "is blaming us for high prices, even though it is not our idea that he should have all the most expensive equipment." Raymond Hare, assistant secretary of state for Near East and South Asian affairs, argued later that year that Iran's weapons purchases were behind the shah's demands for higher petroleum prices.[1]

But American officials began to change their view of Iran's military demands as soon as they heard of Britain's plans to withdraw its military forces and political authority from the Gulf. They judged that independence for Kuwait, Oman, Bahrein, Qatar, and the other sheikdoms would produce unstable regimes, a conclusion shared by the shah. Radical Iraq, Nasser's Egypt, and Soviet-backed local Marxists, they feared, would rush in to fill the Gulf's power vacuum.

The United States, heavily committed to an increasingly costly and unpopular Vietnam War, could not take up this new burden; nor did it seem likely that the American people would accept such a task even after the war ended. There was also a recognition of the fact that sensitive Arab nationalists would surely resent the replacement of Britain with another Western power, particularly one so closely allied with Israel. A strong United States military presence would also suggest a renewal of past European colonialism.

Given the limited number of options, few officials could argue that Iranian military forces might not best fill the gap. When some State Department Arab affairs specialists pointed to traditional Arab mistrust of Iran—an attitude symbolized by the use among Arabs of the name Arab Gulf rather than Persian Gulf—this potential problem was partially solved by the designation of a "two-pillar" policy; Saudi Arabia as well as Iran would be responsible for maintaining regional security. But considering that country's relative backwardness, the Saudi role could not have been expected to be more than symbolic. Any real strength would have to come from Iran.

Undersecretary of State Eugene Rostow also had doubts and proposed an alternative plan. In January, 1968 Rostow publicly suggested that a broader security grouping, including Turkey, Pakistan, and Kuwait, as well as Iran and Saudi Arabia, fill the power vacuum. Predictably, Iraq, Egypt, and Syria attacked this scheme as a danger to Arabism and as a revival of the old Baghdad Pact. When Turkey, Pakistan, and Kuwait expressed reluctance to embark on any such effort it left dependence on Iran the only considered possibility.

The stakes were high. About 75 percent of the non-Communist world's oil reserves, 66 percent of global reserves, and 33 percent of current petroleum production were located in the countries bordering the Persian Gulf. These countries provided half of Western Europe's and almost all of Japan's requirements. Every thirteen minutes a tanker passed through the narrow Straits of Hormuz, a choke-point that a small naval or terrorist force might easily block.

There was no measure of subservience to Washington implied in the shah's eagerness to become the Gulf's guardian. That body of water was Iran's main trade and oil-export lifeline. Any hostile fleet in the Gulf or at the Straits of Hormuz might threaten his country's long, exposed coastline. Therefore, the shah wanted both superpowers to stay away, leaving security to the local states. He even opposed the presence of a small United States base in Bahrein, lest it be offered as a precedent for Soviet counterparts elsewhere in the Gulf.

In fact, the shah's intention was to use American arms in order to free himself as much as possible from any dependence on American protection. "What would happen if Iraq were to attack us tomorrow?" he asked in a June, 1969 newspaper interview. Recalling the 1965 India-Pakistan war, he continued: "When Pakistan was forced to call a cease-fire line well inside Pakistan's territory only a few miles from Lahore, what did CENTO do? What did the United States, with whom Pakistan had a bilateral treaty, do? We cannot rely on others for our defense; that is why we are building up our forces."[2]

Another threat, he noted a few months later, "comes from weak governments, weak countries, corrupt countries, where the element of subversion will have free ground for their activities." "Internal struggles and strife" within the "medieval" systems on the Arab side of the Gulf would also endanger the area's peace.[3] Iran's duty as the region's principal power would be to defeat any foreign attack on it or on others and to help fellow conservative regimes against domestic revolutions.

Both tasks necessitated cooperation between Iran and its Arab neighbors and the shah made sincere efforts in this direction. He dropped Iran's long-standing claim to Bahrein and visited Saudi Arabia in November, 1968. In 1970 Iran renewed relations with Cairo, chastened by its disastrous defeat at Israel's hands, and improved its ties to Pakistan, India, and Afghanistan. The shah also successfully courted the People's Republic of China, which likewise feared Soviet encirclement.

Iran settled other territorial disputes with Saudi Arabia, including the prickly question of offshore boundaries. The shah entertained Arab rulers on hunting trips and invited them to tour Iran. He gave economic assistance to some of the poorer sheikdoms. For their part Arab oil producers worked closely with Iran in common efforts to raise petroleum prices.

Yet the success or failure of these attempts at accommodation were never allowed to alter the shah's ambitions. "Iran is prepared to cooperate with any and all littoral states," the government's 1969–70 official yearbook announced, "but if they are unwilling, Iran is equally prepared to act on its own."[4]

The greatest friction continued to be with Iraq. In April, 1969 the Baghdad government suddenly claimed the entire Shatt al-Arab River, which formed the Iran-Iraq border, as an

integral part of its territory. Unless Iran recognized this seizure, Iraq warned, it would bar Iranian ships by force. When
Iran denounced the now-violated thirty-year-old bilateral
treaty providing for joint administration of the river, Iraq responded by expelling tens of thousands of Iranian nationals.
For a time the two countries were in a virtual state of war.

Two months later, the "Nixon Doctrine" was issued on
Guam. Intended to signal a new American policy toward
Southeast Asia, this declaration also provided the basis for the
two-pillar strategy in the Gulf. Disillusioned by the problems
of direct military involvement in Vietnam, the United States
was shifting to an indirect projection of power through speci-
fied Third World allies. America would continue to supply a
shield against direct Soviet aggression; in any other contingency a threatened nation would have to provide for its own
armed defense, using United States military and economic aid
where required. The United States would become the arsenal
rather than the policeman of the non-Communist world.

This was precisely the relationship preferred by the shah;
but if Iran were to do its part in the Gulf, he argued, it would
need a vast amount of weaponry. Washington agreed. From
1950 to 1970 Iran had received $1.8 billion in United States
military-grant aid. In the following six years, American arms
sales totaled $12.1 billion, of which 80 percent was for equip-
ment. By comparison, 80 percent of the dollar value of United
States sales to Saudi Arabia during the same period went for
construction and support services.[5]

The shah, of course, had been preoccupied with obtaining
military equipment since the late 1940s. He regularly read the
armaments trade magazines and "knew more about new
weaponry developments than most of our people who went
there to talk to him," as one Defense Department official later
commented. He concentrated all important decisions in his
own hands, including the planning of future purchases, and
his attention was focused more and more on military issues
than on economic or social domestic problems.

Since the shah wanted to maximize Iran's military buying,
officials in his government and armed forces, many of whom

were soliciting bribes from arms companies, had no incentive to reject any opportunities to obtain additional planes, tanks, and ships. The corporations they were dealing with also had an interest in selling the maximum possible amount of equipment. Consequently, a great deal of Iran's money was wasted. Military expenditures outstripped Iran's skilled labor pool and eventually even outran petroleum revenues.

The arms-transfer program became a remarkable mess. Radar and other materiel costing hundreds of millions of dollars were ordered prematurely and had to be stored or left unused. Top Iranian officers, including the navy commander and the admiral charged with negotiations for the massive Chah Bahar harbor-drydock complex, were jailed for embezzling millions of dollars. The CIA and the United States air force fought for control of Iran's electrical intelligence system; the air force and navy competed on the sale of fighter planes.

The Iranian military had no cohesive system for requisitioning needed parts. Harbors were clogged with delivery ships. Training pilots barely had time to master one aircraft before being forced to start over again on the arrival of the next, more advanced system. This chaos was not necessarily innate in the two-pillar policy. Rather, it resulted from the shah's having gained the upper hand in the United States-Iranian relationship, a transformation that would later be completed by President Nixon's May, 1972 promise to allow him to buy from Americans anything he wanted short of nuclear weapons.

Nixon was an old friend of the shah from the Eisenhower administration days, their acquaintance and mutual confidence renewed by the American's 1968 pre-election visit to Tehran and by the shah's October, 1969 trip to Washington. Between these two visits, a March, 1969 Defense Department memorandum once again raised reservations about arms sales—particularly because of the possible security compromise of new technology and the danger of placing so much reliance on one man—but a State Department policy review, ordered by Kissinger, disagreed.

Under the direction of Assistant Secretary of State for Near

East and South Asian Affairs Joseph Sisco, the State Department once again triumphed over the Defense Department. Indeed even the annual review of the arms program was phased out. While defense secretaries continued to worry, none would dare challenge Kissinger, who had the ear of both Nixon and his successor, Gerald Ford. Kissinger's later appointment as secretary of state in September, 1973 would further solidify the pro-shah lobby within the government.

Kissinger's conception was that the shah should "fill the vacuum left by British withdrawal, now menaced by Soviet intrusion and radical momentum." Best of all, "this was achievable without any American resources since the shah was willing to pay for the equipment out of his oil revenues."[6] There was, however, one catch: the more equipment Iran ordered, the more oil revenue was required to pay for it.

Iran had enjoyed some success in the 1960s in pressuring oil companies for production increases. A second money-raising possibility, proposed by the shah on his 1969 visit, was to barter oil for arms. The United States would buy more oil than it really needed at prevailing prices and use the surplus to build a strategic reserve. President Nixon rejected this suggestion; in later years, as petroleum costs climbed, more than one high official would look back with regret on this as a missed opportunity.

Tehran's remaining option was to raise the price of oil. In turn, it became an unspoken American policy to use arms sales to help balance the United States' rising oil-import bill. Some observers believed the result was an inflationary leap-frogging in which petroleum prices and arms prices pushed each other ever upwards.

Of course, military expenses made up only one factor in the shah's decision to maximize oil prices. Nevertheless, the results were dramatic. Iran produced 1.7 million barrels-a-day (b/d) and received $482 million in 1964. By 1973, 5.9 million b/d earned $4.4 billion. After OPEC's price increases took full effect in 1974, 6 million b/d, virtually the same as the preceding year, returned $21.4 billion. The shah could afford to buy almost anything—or so it seemed at the time.

October, 1951: Premier Muhammad Mossadegh being carried by admiring Iranians after he had reiterated his determined stand on the nationalization of the Anglo-Iranian Oil Company. (UPI)

August 16, 1953: Mossadegh's Day: Noisy demonstrators massed in Tehran's Parliament Square, after Mossadegh, then still de facto premier, prematurely announced the smashing of a pro-shah coup d'etat. (Wide World Photos)

August 19, 1953: The Shah's Day: Royalist demonstrators ride on a truck through the streets of Tehran during the uprising that ousted Mossadegh and restored Shah Muhammad Reza Pahlevi to power. (Wide World Photos)

1967: Coronation photograph of Farah Diba and Shah Muhammad Reza Pahlevi. (SIPA Press)

October 11, 1978: The exiled Ayatollah Khomeini, in his garden at Ponchartrain, near Paris. (UPI)

December 10, 1978: On the first of two Ashura holy days, a crowd of between 2 and 4 million Iranians march through central Tehran, calling for the shah's downfall and the installation of a new Islamic government. In the background is the Shayabad monument, built by the shah to celebrate a new Iran. (Michel Setboun/SIPA Press)

November, 1978: The Tehran Bazaar, the day before it was closed by the police, who reportedly fired on a group of demonstrators. (Alain Keler/Sygma)

1979: Women receiving arms training as part of the Islamic leaders' plan to create a reserve militia of 20 million Iranians to defend the accomplishments of the revolution. (SIPA Press from Black Star)

November 6, 1979: The American Embassy in Tehran after it was seized by Islamic students demanding the extradition of the shah from the United States. (P. Ledru/Sygma)

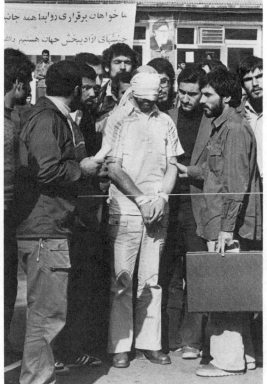

November 8, 1979: An American hostage being displayed by students of the Islamic Revolutionary Committee before crowds of shouting Iranians. (P. Ledru/Sygma)

December 9, 1979: Supporters of rival Ayatollah Shariat-Madari meet with Khomeini supporters in Tabriz. (Magnum)

March 8, 1980: Iranian President Bani-Sadr in front of a poster of the
Ayatollah Khomeini. (Kalari/Sygma)

Iran's dependence on oil also had its negative side. The shah was well aware that unless new reserves were found it would be impossible to maintain such levels of production in the 1980s. The temporary decline of the petroleum market in 1976–77, because of the West's business slowdown, fueled an Iranian recession. At the same time, the shah's concern over his one-product economy—oil provided over 80 percent of foreign exchange—pushed him into a crash industrialization program whose problems paralleled those of his military-modernization drive.

Up to 1969, the oil companies had been strong enough to hold production and prices in line; in response, Iran and other oil-producing states formed the Organization of Petroleum-Exporting Countries (OPEC). Although the shah was not the most extreme price-hawk, he was no more subservient to the United States on oil matters than on strategic and political issues. "I cannot build the future of my country on promises," he said in May, 1969. "I say this is our oil—pump it. If not, we pump it ourselves." [7]

In December, 1970 Iran sponsored an OPEC proposal threatening a halt in production unless the share of the host countries was increased. The private companies, shaken by the challenge, asked former Undersecretary of State William Rogers to send Undersecretary of State John Irwin to Tehran with a warning: the shah's relations with the United States would be damaged if oil deliveries were cut off. But Irwin, accepting the shah's assurance that OPEC's quarrel was only with the companies, endorsed the shah's proposal that separate Persian Gulf price agreements would insulate the area from increases by Mediterranean producers.

This led to the February, 1971 Tehran Agreement, in which the companies granted large price increases to producing countries in exchange for their promise to keep the prices stable. Six months later, however, OPEC countries returned with more demands. Libya and Iraq nationalized most of their oil production in 1972 and Iran took over its consortium the following year. These events laid the basis for OPEC's tripling of prices at the end of 1973, breaking forever the market power of the "Seven Sisters" oil companies.* During this whole era, the United States government put a higher priority on good relations with Iran than on attempts to stop or delay this process.

Meanwhile, Iran still was able to maintain a generally favorable image in the United States. The American press accepted the two-pillar strategy, celebrated the shah's White Revolution, and praised Iran's economic progress. Writing in 1970, *The New York Times* correspondent in Tehran found a new feeling of hope and pride as well as "new office buildings, supermarkets, freeways, and modern factories." The White Revolution was seen as "a sweeping program of reforms aimed at turning a primitive, peasant society into an industrialized nation." True, there was "no real democracy in Iran. The press is controlled, criticism of the Shah is forbidden and his power is absolute. Yet his personal popularity has soared with the White Revolution." A later article claimed that growth and stability seemed enough for many Iranians, even without any democracy.[8]

Military progress was also impressive. The International Institute for Strategic Studies in London commented that the Iranian air force was "more than a match for the combined Arab air forces in the Gulf area," that the navy was far superior to any potential Arab rivals, and that Iran enjoyed a clear military advantage over Iraq. "Already Iran's military power is being taken into account" in world affairs, exulted the shah.[9]

Britain's withdrawal from the region prompted the shah to accelerate his buildup. He announced that Iran's navy would be greatly expanded in order to patrol the Indian Ocean as well as the Persian Gulf. Iranian troops were sent to fight a Marxist insurgency in Oman. A lavish celebration at Per-

---

* During the 1973 Arab-Israeli war, Arab oil producers attempted to use their petroleum as a political weapon against the United States and several smaller Western friends of Israel. The embargo of October, 1973–March, 1974 involved both production cutbacks and a refusal to sell oil to specific consuming states. Ironically, some of the most radical Arab states—Iraq and Algeria, for example—took advantage of the situation to sell larger amounts under the table. But Iran did not participate in the embargo at all, and its output increased, helping supply its own allies, including the United States.

sepolis in March, 1971 of the twenty-five hundredth anniversary of the original Iranian empire was intended to mark contemporary Iran's graduation into the ranks of the Great Powers. Yet the shah's wasteful expenditures on imported food, crockery, and luxuries for the pageant—in a country where annual per-capita income still was only $350—brought mixed reviews.

In an analysis of Iran's prospects that month, *Washington Post* correspondent Jonathan Randal found the small terrorist opposition groups to be of little threat. More serious was the widespread corruption, including "voluntary silent business partnerships and other means of creaming off unearned income prevalent in the royal circle and among their close friends." Although Iran was one of the few underdeveloped countries "whose problems are the consequences of its own success," the shah's full-speed-ahead program strained a vulnerable economy; future difficulties "may lie less in politics than economics."[10]

The first act of Iran's new imperial era was the seizure of three strategic islands that guarded the Hormuz Straits—Abu Musa, and the Greater and Lesser Tunbs—all three previously the property of Arab sheikdoms. This step was implemented with British, and possibly with American, consent. On one island, Arab police resisted the Iranian troops; there were casualties on both sides.

After the takeover, Iran offered compensation to the former owners, but the sheik of Sharjah, who accepted, was later assassinated in reprisal by local opponents. Libya used the Iranian occupation as an excuse for expropriating British Petroleum; Iraq broke relations with Britain and Iran. The overall effect was to strain Arab-Iranian relations.

This unmistakable sign of Iran's intention to police the Gulf was followed by another: a $2 billion order for helicopter gunships, F–5E and F–4 fighter planes, and C–130 transport planes. This was the biggest single deal concluded to date by the Pentagon, but the context of events in and around the Gulf toward the end of 1971 and the beginning of 1972 seemed to justify such measures. This included the completion of Britain's withdrawal, the partition of Iran's neighbor Pakistan after another losing war against India, the emergence of a Marxist South Yemen, the ominous terrorist attack on an oil tanker in the Red Sea, the South Yemen-backed guerrilla war in Oman's Dhofar province, the growing Soviet naval activity in the Red Sea, and an Iraqi-Soviet friendship treaty. The shah began to add more of everything to his shopping list: ships, helicopters, tanks, hovercraft, late-model Phantoms, and the construction of a string of bases along the Gulf.

President Nixon reacted with a series of decisions culminating in his May, 1972 visit to Tehran. There he promised the shah that detente did not imply any division of the world into American and Soviet spheres of influence—the shah well remembered the 1907 Anglo-Russian agreement—and that old friends like Iran would not be neglected. Most important, the president promised to sell Iran any nonnuclear weapon it wanted in unlimited quantities. The United States also agreed to the shah's two other demands in this connection: America would provide technicians to train the Iranian military in the use and maintenance of this equipment, and would join Iran in supporting the Kurdish nationalist insurgency against Iraq.

Earlier, there had been a number of Defense Department objections to any open-ended commitment. The Pentagon had advised against selling laser-guided bombs to Iran and opposed any firm offer to sell the F–14 or F–15 because they were still in early stages of development. By the time they could be delivered, they argued, it might no longer be in the American interest to supply them to Iran. Defense Secretary Melvin Laird had been reluctant to send technical assistance teams. Questions were also raised about security; advanced weaponry secrets might leak from Iran to the Soviet Union.

But Nixon's choice foreclosed such concerns. Policy was now a matter for implementation, not debate; the Defense Department review process was to be a rubber stamp. Even if Iran bought the wrong equipment or items it would never use, there was now no incentive for American officials to oppose such sales. No one had considered the possible conflict between the goal of keeping the shah happy so that he would remain a firm American ally and that of objectively strengthening Iran's military forces and political stability.

Everyone in the bureaucracies—the State Department, the CIA, the Defense Department, and the United States military—knew that news contradicting the White House line would not be welcome. Under such circumstances reports would be returned for rewriting and the individual's career might be unfavorably affected. Internal government analysis over Iran became an exercise in the mobilization of wishful thinking.

In Tehran, "it was a salesman's dream for a while," said General Ellis Williamson, chief of the United States Military Assistance Advisory Group (MAAG) there from 1971 to 1973. About thirty-five corporate visitors a week dropped in at MAAG headquarters, and this was only a portion of the total. General Hassan Toufanian, Iran's vice-minister of defense in charge of military procurement, complained about this deluge. Other countries trying to sell weaponry to Iran, he told Williamson, had only one producer per item. To obtain a clear deal with reliable prices and delivery dates, Toufanian went on, he met with only that nation's defense minister, ambassador, and the relevant industrialist. But the Americans rigidly separated government and business—the ambassador and MAAG were ordered to remain neutral among competing companies and to stay away from attending company presentations to the Iranians. The shah, Toufanian explained, preferred government-to-government dealings.[11]

The shah also said he wanted to eliminate Iranian "influence peddlers" who engineered deals for Western companies through contacts and bribery of military and government officials. These agents, ran the official Iranian position, were swindling both sides—American companies because their claims of influence were phony and the Iranian people because these fraudulent fees were unfairly passed on through price increases. But the companies knew all too well that the right agent often made the difference between successful and broken deals, a fact also well understood in the State Department.

Even the best-intentioned Iranian government officials ob-

viously had difficulty judging the claims of competing companies on the benefits of different weapons systems. Both American salesmen and Iranian bureaucrats often underestimated
the extent of maintenance problems and the cost of training
Iranians to keep up a given type of equipment. Price increases
and the problems of meeting promised delivery dates caused
additional confusion.

This led to significant tension. Iranians felt cheated when
they could not operate the advanced technology ordered, but
were insulted by any American suggestions that they should
go slower. By the time of the 1978–79 revolution this resentment had helped produce the widespread Iranian conviction
that the Americans had defrauded them. Ayatollah Khomeini
and others maintained that the Americans had grabbed Iran's
oil money and left them in exchange useless American hardware, or, at the very least, material designed to serve United
States purposes rather than Iranian interests.

The United States decision to send as many advisors as necessary also had important ramifications outside weaponry
maintenance. The presence of these Americans stoked traditional Iranian xenophobia. Back in 1952, Ambassador Loy
Henderson had warned of the need for United States military
and technical personnel to maintain a low profile: "The more
attention that is attracted to the activities of these American
nationals the more susceptible the Iranian people in general
are likely to be to appeals to throw the Americans out of the
country." No matter how sincere individual Americans were
in their desire to help Iran, Henderson explained, local sensitivity to foreign influence and mistrust of non-Muslims would
produce more suspicion than gratitude.[12]

During the first three years of the Nixon administration,
Defense Secretary Melvin Laird and the MAAG had resisted
sending the number of technicians requested by the shah, in
part because of war requirements in Vietnam. The acceleration
of the shah's military-expansion program, however, greatly
increased the need for instructors and advisors. But it was
hard for Iran to keep up its own commitments: villagers barely
acquainted with automobiles were becoming mechanics for

armored personnel carriers, tanks, and supersonic aircraft. The Iranian air force had excellent pilots but few good electricians. Ironically, air force technicians—who had experienced the greatest of cultural leaps—furnished a reservoir of revolutionaries in the military for Ayatollah Khomeini's forces.

By July, 1976 there were 24,000 Americans working in Iran, with their number increasing at a remarkable rate. While the State Department issued soothing statements predicting this growth would level off soon, officials privately commented that without more and more American personnel the whole Iranian military would grind to a halt. American advisors and Iranian counterparts generally worked well together, but the relatively higher living standards of the Americans and the false—though emotionally powerful—belief that they were taking jobs away from Iranians ultimately heightened anti-American feelings. Reza Barahani, an anti-shah writer, later explained how "I simply had every bad notion of the Americans before" coming to the United States because the only Americans Iranians ever saw were "working for" the shah.[13]

This was hardly surprising since most American technicians and their families lived lives well isolated from Iranians. They bought their goods at PXs, lived in special subsidized housing, sent their children to their own schools, and socialized primarily with each other. Bell Helicopter alone had 1,700 employees working on a forty-five acre Isfahan base. Company inducements for them and their 6,000 dependents included tripled salaries, promotions, and tax breaks. But their skills were indispensable for Iran's military: Bell helicopters needed eight to ten hours of maintenance for every hour of flight. Few of these Americans spoke Farsi and, given their physical and cultural isolation, most had ideas about Iran not much different from those held by fellow Americans back home. Understanding Iran, after all, was not their job. But by the same token their on-the-spot presence did little to raise the level of knowledge of the American government about the Iranian political scene.

The third element in the United States-Iranian agreement was

American support for the Kurdish revolt in Iraq. The Kurds, a non-Arab people divided among the rugged border lands of Iraq, Turkey, and Iran, had striven for decades to gain some measure of autonomy. In these efforts, various Kurdish political groups had sought support from widely divergent sources. They alternately cooperated with and fought against the Iraqi central government as Iraq's Kurdish policy shifted over time.

Since Iraq was attempting to undermine the central government in Tehran through support of Iran's Arab minority, Tehran sought to trouble Baghdad by aiding its two million rebellious Kurds. Of course, the Kurds were seen as mere pawns in the Iranian-Iraqi conflict. The Iranian government never thought that the Kurds might actually win their war and had little desire for them to do so—their victory would encourage hope for independence or autonomy among Iran's own two million Kurds.

Both the State Department and the CIA had serious reservations about American participation in this game; Kissinger did not discuss the matter with the National Security Council staff. The Forty Committee, responsible for ruling on covert operations, was not informed until a month after operations had begun. Former Treasury Secretary John Connally was sent as messenger to inform the shah of the start of arms deliveries to the Kurds; eventually, the CIA supplied tens of millions of dollars worth of Soviet and Chinese weapons captured in Vietnam and elsewhere. Kurdish leader Mustafa Barzani presumed that this logistic support also meant American political backing for his cause.

Kurdish successes on the battlefield were undermined, however, by diplomatic developments. In March, 1975 Jordan, Egypt, and Algeria finally succeeded in negotiating an Iraqi-Iranian agreement that settled the border dispute and pledged both sides to stop supporting each other's enemies. The shah abandoned the Kurds to their fate, sealing his border with Iraq, and Washington went along with his decision. Cut off from their rear base, the Kurds were forced to surrender or become refugees.

Fulfillment of the shah's three conditions guaranteed his

willingness to cooperate with America's new policy, although he needed little incentive to seek military primacy in the region. Iran was the "most determined and best equipped state in the Gulf to assert leadership," Assistant Secretary of Defense James Noyes declared. The shah himself explained that he was buying modern arms to become so self-reliant that he would never have to pick up the telephone to call President Nixon.[14] The combination seemed perfect.

The events of 1973 reinforced the White House's belief in the correctness of its strategy. The October, 1973 war between Israel and its Arab neighbors and the dramatic emergence of the energy crisis reminded Americans of the Middle East's fragility as well as its political and economic importance. Yet that year's petroleum revolution also foretold the further concessions the United States would have to make to ensure the shah's continued support of American policy and interests.

In January, 1973, on the tenth anniversary of the White Revolution, the shah announced his decision to take control of oil production from the consortium, transferring management to the NIOC. "We may say that the Nationalization Act has been implemented in its fullest sense after a lapse of 23 years, thus realizing our long-cherished national objective," rejoiced Prime Minister Amir Abbas Hoveyda. The shah had succeeded in implementing Mossadegh's failed dream.

Worried that this action might further upset the already reeling international petroleum system, the Treasury Department proposed a strong White House message asking the shah to rescind his action and to hold down prices. The shah returned a blistering reply: nobody would tell him what to do. Another United States protest, following steep OPEC price increases later that year, generated a similar response.

Both sides well understood that growing American vulnerability over oil had increased the shah's leverage against Washington. In 1970 the United States became a net importer of oil; three years later 23 percent of these tanker-loads originated in countries bordering the Gulf. By 1976, 42 percent of United States consumption came from overseas, 38 percent of imports were from the Gulf. American dependence on foreign oil passed 50 percent in the winter of 1977. Iran, the world's second largest petroleum exporter and America's number three supplier, provided an increasingly large portion of these needs.

The Arab oil embargo, beginning in October, 1973, graphically illustrated the political potential of this shift in the international balance of power. Yet the shah's continued supplying of America throughout the crisis, despite Arab pressure on him, seemed to confirm the correctness of United States policy toward Tehran. The shah found other ways to mend his fences with the Arabs: calling for Israel's withdrawal from the territories occupied in 1967, airlifting medical supplies to Jordan, providing logistical aid to Saudi Arabia, and permitting overflight of Soviet supply planes. At the same time, he backed Kissinger's peace mission and sought to promote an Arab-Israeli settlement. Iran's cordial relations with Israel had long been a plus in the eyes of Congress; now, like the great world leader he thought himself, the shah was trying to build good relations with both sides in the conflict.

But the shah was far less evenhanded in his defense of OPEC's actions. The West, he argued, was wasting oil and was making OPEC the scapegoat for its own problems, and for the "excessive profits" of the oil companies. When President Gerald Ford called for price reductions, the shah suggested that industrialized nations might first cut their own prices for exported goods; perhaps products might be indexed for stability. Yet he also warned that Iran would not be intimidated: "No one can dictate to us. No one can wave a finger at us, because we will wave a finger back." [15]

Earlier, Nixon and Kissinger, who had become secretary of state in September, 1973, rejected suggestions by Treasury Secretary William Simon and others to use arms sales as leverage against Iran's oil policy. After all, they argued, the shah was paying for the arms and other suppliers, particularly European ones, were eager to grab this business. Besides, the special strategic relationship was too valuable to endanger.

Western states simply would have to make up for their balance-of-payments deficits by selling more to Iran and other OPEC members. Military deals took up a large part of the slack, but consumer goods, food, and industrial equipment were also exported in growing quantities. An American trade center in Tehran and a United States-Iranian joint economic commission were organized to facilitate commerce. By 1975, American companies had ventured over $1 billion there.

Despite these efforts, the oil shock also stimulated domestic criticism against Washington's Iran policy. State Department officials already were beginning to leak concerns over a Gulf arms race or war; the general public was unhappy at Iran's seeming ingratitude. The shah defended his arms program with the same vigor with which he supported the quadrupling of oil prices. The October, 1973 Arab-Israeli war provided a timely example of the shah's concerns: "Wasn't Israel and the rest of the world surprised by the huge amount of weapons that were poured on her and which almost crippled her?" he asked. "I'm not taking any chances." [16]

Assistant Secretary of State Joseph Sisco concurred with Iran's concern. The shah had plenty to worry about, he explained: a long border with the USSR; Moscow's tightening alliances with Syria, Iraq, South Yemen, and Somalia; Iraq's threat against Kuwait; South Yemen's subversion in Dhofar; the Soviet-Indian friendship treaty; and the upswing of Soviet naval activity in the Persian Gulf and Indian Ocean.[17] Privately, the State Department added Iraq's clandestine anti-shah radio stations and the Baluchi guerrillas in Pakistan, as well as Baghdad's aid to Arab separatists and urban terrorists within Iran.

Congressman Lee Hamilton, chairman of the House of Representatives Committee on Foreign Affairs' Middle East subcommittee, still thought the United States response disproportionate. "You do not need a sledge hammer to crack a nut," he complained. "Since 1965, our sales of arms and services to Iran and Saudi Arabia are roughly six times estimates of Soviet activity in the Persian Gulf area." He implied that the volume of sales was being based more on the desire to soak up petrodollars than on Iran's reasonable needs and he was particularly worried about possible Iranian-Saudi friction.[18]

Sisco disagreed. Arms sales were not knee-jerk reactions to

the energy crisis or to minor border incidents, but were meant to allow allies to defend themselves without United States intervention. "An Iran and Saudi Arabia which not only are but feel themselves to be secure," Sisco explained, "are essential prerequisites to a policy based on their roles of assuming primary responsibility for maintenance of stability in the area." [19] In the narrow sense Sisco was quite correct. The fear of Saudi-Iranian conflict was exaggerated; Saudi Arabia complained about Iran's growing power and ambitions from time to time and noted the shah's hawkishness on oil prices, but relations between them were never angry. Similarly, the need to retrieve the dollars America was paying for petroleum was only a secondary motivation for the huge arms-sales program.

But American officials, preoccupied with the international implications of the United States-Iranian relationship, remained poorly informed on Iran's rising domestic difficulties. In retrospect, it seems so clear that the shah's almost unlimited appetite for security tended to undermine the very stability he sought, but as long as the problems manifested themselves only domestically, they went unnoticed by American policymakers. For example, the desire for the superficial signs of modernization led the shah's advisors to welcome rural migration to the cities and even to end government investment in the countryside's fifty thousand villages. The political consequences were disastrous. Those who stayed home were embittered because the shah's regime had not helped them; those who moved to cities, disoriented by their sudden entry into the twentieth century and unable to find jobs or hope in that strange new world, gradually turned to their religious leaders for guidance. The result would be seen in the mass anti-shah demonstrations of 1978.

As early as 1973, Iran specialists, most notably Professor Marvin Zonis of the University of Chicago and Professor Richard Cottam of the University of Pittsburgh, were trying to draw attention to the troubles on that country's horizon. While acknowledging Iran's economic successes, they also pointed to the growing gap between rich and poor, the endemic corruption, and SAVAK's repression, all of which were alienating millions of Iranians from their shah.

Certainly between 1967 and 1970 alone, Iranian ownership of radios per 1,000 people had increased from 110 to 200, of autos from 9 to 16, and of telephones from 7 to 10. The number of primary-school pupils had doubled, those in secondary school had quadrupled, and university populations had tripled. Despite this real material progress, Zonis explained, outsiders were misreading the realities of Iran. "One can visit the Hilton, La Residence, the Key Club, the Dargand, the Imperial Country Club or one of the staggeringly large number of boutiques in Tehran and not realize he is in one of the poorest nations in the world."[20] More than a few Western visitors, including journalists, seemed to make precisely this mistake.

Cottam discussed the frustration even of government bureaucrats at the red tape, corruption, and overconcentration of power in the shah's hands that made it so difficult to deal with the country's crises. Iranians generally believed that a few wealthy agents and corrupt officials were reaping all the benefits from foreign purchases and that the demands of these few for consumer goods were burdening everyone else with inflation. "I know of no more successful public relations operation than the Iranian Government's," said Cottam, but an investigation would reveal "scandals that would make Watergate look like nothing."

Iran was still a poor country. Over 75 percent of rural families earned less than $66 a month and malnutrition was widespread among them. Food prices alone rose 10.2 percent from 1971 to 1972; by 1975 the overall inflation rate had almost doubled. Urban migration did not result in new jobs: although Iran's gross national product doubled between 1962 and 1971, employment increased by only 23 percent—this in a country with a high birth rate. Oil production, Iran's largest money-earning industry, required relatively few workers. Worse, its large profits made it easy for Iran's wealthy class to import consumer goods and even to buy food abroad rather than produce it at home with Iranian labor.

There was also a whole set of political problems. "As countless historical cases exemplify," said Zonis, "state power cannot be built except on the base of an advanced, committed,
and involved population." This did not necessarily imply democracy, as Soviet experience demonstrated, but it did involve finding ways to mobilize and motivate people, including broad acceptance of a regime's nationalist legitimacy. The
shah never succeeded in this task, particularly because so
many Iranians saw him for better or worse as an American
agent. Unless his authority "can dissociate itself more completely from our Government," Zonis concluded, "it will be
troubled by widespread doubts as to its policies and loyalties."[21]

Doubts about the wisdom of America's Iran policy quickly
spread from the academics to the journalists. European correspondents were the first to see the flies in the ointment. In
1973 Le Monde's Eric Rouleau was already writing about the
full range of Iran's internal problems: The housing crisis in
poor urban areas, where "rents have doubled in three years"; a
bureaucracy that was "in many cases incompetent or corrupt";
inflation and a greater dependence on food imports; and the
huge unemployed sector that kept wage levels low. Tehran,
whose modernization was so often used as a metaphor for
Iran's state of affairs, consumed 50 percent of the country's
available services and products though it held only 10 percent
of the population. Its Westernized northern and central neigh-
borhoods, Rouleau wrote, "are islands of prosperity in a sea of
poverty." Other Iranians were turning to alcohol and narcotics
in disturbing numbers.

"Some observers are amazed that the absence of safety
valves, like independent trade unions, a representative parliament and genuine opposition parties, has not led to mass
outbursts," Rouleau concluded. This was because Iran's
"economic progress has been really beneficial—even modestly—for some sections of the population, and this in turn
has given rise to hopes in other strata." Another reason was
the "very backward and politically immature" peasantry,

whose recent migrants also made up most of the urban working class.[22]

The following year some American newspapers began to report these problems, although this more critical approach did not become fully evident until 1975 and 1976. Moreover, the continued lack of any visible opposition within Iran and the accelerating economic boom still promoted optimism over the shah's future prospects. Thus, Lewis Simons's May, 1974 *Washington Post* series discussed Iran's new oil wealth, the luxury and development visible in Tehran, and the confidence of Iranian government officials in their dramatic economic plans. At the same time, it cited American specialists as predicting mounting discontent if the shah proved unable to keep his promises.

Notwithstanding any good intentions about these promises, there were simply not enough teachers and schools to implement the projected free education, not enough facilities for improved health care; there was not even enough milk for a school milk program. The shah's belief in quick, easy development was everywhere evident; said his chief planner, "We have no real limit on money. None." But the barriers to success also seemed endless. There was the overconcentration of power and wealth, wild inflation, luxury-centered consumption, debilitating corruption, the military's priority over civilian needs, the lack of trained technicians, the general wishful thinking that substituted for truthful evaluation among those who ran the country, and the rising food-import bill.

Nor did Simons fail to mention a "police-state" atmosphere, the shah's growing isolation from the people, and his increasing inability to obtain accurate information from his sycophantic advisors. "Nevertheless," Simons concluded, "the great majority of Iranians all but worship him. . . . There's no denying that Iran's gains in the last decade have been impressive. . . ." Further, given Iran's strategic importance, the United States government did not "worry about restrictions on Iranians' personal freedom, although they concede their existence." As one American diplomat put it, "The govern-

ment is stable, that's far more than you can say about any of
the others in this part of the world."[23]

A more optimistic correspondent of The New York Times
continued to see the shah as a genuinely popular reformer
seeking to foster increased political participation by the general population. Similarly, Business Week warned of dangers
but sang of the dazzling prospects. A generally upbeat Newsweek story explained the shah's goal as trying to "raise Iran's
standard of living fast enough to prevent his subjects from
. . . organizing a revolution of their own against him."[24]

Nevertheless, the foci of media coverage of the Iranian dilemma remained the international rather than the domestic
aspects of the shah's policies. There were reports that State
Department officials were beginning to say privately that the
arms-transfer program had "achieved a magnitude people
didn't anticipate" without adequate "consideration of the
long-term consequences"; Congressman Hamilton was quoted
as calling United States policy toward Iran "a high-risk kind
of venture." In August, 1974 the Washington Post, warning
of the shah's regional ambitions, asked if American interests
dictated support for "what can only be described as Iranian
imperialism?" It advocated a congressional investigation of
United States arms policy. Over the following months, many
other voices chimed in with challenging questions.[25]

Although there were more than a few conservatives worried
that the shah's appetite for military hardware might escalate
the Persian-Arab conflict, most critics of United States policy
toward Iran tended to be liberals. On the other hand, many of
the Iranian Embassy's best friends in Washington were also
liberals, usually senators and reporters who had been won
over by the image of the shah as reformer. To further compli-
cate the problem, the issue of a proper attitude toward Iran became caught up in the struggle between Congress and the
White House for control of foreign policy that marked Washington political life during the mid-1970s.

The case against the administration's way of handling relations with Iran rested on several different arguments. Critics
of the shah deemed his regime to be repressive, unpopular,

and lacking even minimal domestic support. Nations so governed were thought to be inherently unstable and, particularly when they were autocratic monarchies, doomed by the irreversible tide of history. It was only a matter of time before the Pahlevi chapter of the age of royalty was closed; all appearances to the contrary were believed deceptive. For ten years I have been predicting the shah's overthrow, more than one specialist commented, and I see no reason to change my prediction.

Further, by putting so much American prestige on one man, who might die or be assassinated, this view continued, the White House was taking an extraordinarily dangerous risk. And what a man he was: arrogant, ambitious, and likely to create a local arms race, if not an outright war. Iran was already strong enough militarily to handle any conceivable threat to its sovereignty, except those so massive that they would naturally trigger direct United States intervention; the continued excessive buildup of the shah's military might was promoting rather than defusing regional tension and instability.

In addition, critics continued, the administration had greatly overestimated the Cold War implications of the area's problems. The Soviets did not seem interested in escalating Great Power rivalry in the Persian Gulf, nor were they likely to attack Iran in the near future. An Iraqi offensive against Iran seemed equally farfetched. It may have been that Washington had reversed the causality of interrelated events and that it was America's arming of Iran that was encouraging Moscow to give Iraq more advanced weapons. Diplomatic mediation may have been the best way to ease friction in the region; the successful conclusion of an Iraqi-Iranian treaty in 1975 seemed to reinforce this argument.

Finally, the critics still assumed that Washington could exert a fair measure of leverage over the shah. The United States might press him over oil supplies and prices, urge him to make more domestic reforms, or persuade him to slow down his military expansion. Different groups of critics emphasized different aspects of these arguments but, all in all,

most would have favored the more limited and cautious policy toward the shah that had been employed in the years prior
to 1968.

Defenders of the two-pillar policy replied that United
States-Soviet detente did not extend to the confrontations in
the Gulf, that Iraqis and other radicals were trying to subvert
the region, and that the shah's arms were acting as deterrent
to open war. Since America was unwilling or unable to be the
region's policeman, Washington could hardly deny the shah
the means for his own self-defense.

After all, they reposted, when compared to other rulers in
his neighborhood, the shah was popular, progressive, and
stable; modern Iranian history did not hold much hope for the
creation of a successful democrncy there. Most took his presence for granted. If the shah did fall from power or die, they
believed that the geostrategic factors shaping the shah's policy
would continue to operate and would keep any new leader
friendly toward the United States. After all, the Russians and
Iraqis would still be on Iran's borders and any new ruler
would still need American help and technology to cope with
the tasks of defense and development.

Supporters of the Nixon-Kissinger policy toward Iran also
minimized the extent of American leverage over the shah. If
Washington tried to pressure him he would simply turn elsewhere to buy arms and to sell oil. But no matter who might
succeed the shah, they argued, there was no sense in alienating
him while he ruled, nor in undermining a strategy that
seemed to be working. The continued incumbency of that policy's architects in the White House resolved the debate in
favor of those who supported a continued free hand for the
shah.

Both American sides, however, agreed on several important
points. All concurred that the faster the shah carried out his
promised reforms, the more quickly Iran would be able to
modernize. And the more quickly Iran modernized, the more
stable his government would become. This consensus came
out of the 1950s-1960s view that poverty and frustration bred
revolution. Economic progress above all would defuse the

time-bomb of Iranian backwardness. The shah, all agreed, rightly believed himself engaged in a race against time: the questions were merely over the details of the best course and pace to be followed by him.

Modernization theory, as developed by Western political scientists of the day, sharply differentiated between the social forces at work in "traditional" and in "modern" societies. As a culture became more developed, ran this line of analysis, traditional institutions would fade; religion, for example, would lose its hold on the people. The idea that certain innovations—like improved systems of communication and urban migration—might strengthen the hold of the older framework, even revitalize it, was outside the scope of this evaluation. Speed of change, in and of itself, with the loss of equilibrium and the dislocation it produced, was generally not perceived as capable of generating "backward-directed" revolutions.

At the same time, even those who most strenuously documented Iran's severe internal problems did not envision the near-future emergence of any cohesive opposition. On the contrary, Iran's oil prosperity seemed to be undercutting any urge to express dissent, while SAVAK was preventing any manifestation of it. The shah appeared to be more popular than he had ever been before. Indeed, no real anti-shah movement was visible until it appeared in full force during the 1978 demonstrations. What so caught Washington and the American press by surprise was that the dissatisfaction boiling beneath the surface had been as much the product of spiritual and psychological dissatisfaction as of materialistic or political deprivation.

A third problem derived ironically from the failure of prior criticism. Some time before the shah's fall, a diplomat asked the director of the State Department's Office of Iranian Affairs whether the shah was likely to remain in power. The official simply waved his hand at a row of pictures showing the shah meeting every United States president from Roosevelt on. "Well," he replied drily. "He's been there this long." The shah's downfall had so often been predicted and his survival so often observed that warnings about his imminent downfall had gradually lost credibility. There were some who were not dazzled by the emperor's new clothes, including a few of the Nixon Doctrine's strongest advocates. But who could forget the many previous experts who had ended up sounding like Chicken Little when the sky had not fallen?

Finally, the shah maintained his reputation as a well-intentioned reformer. If he was an autocrat, he seemed to be more in the tradition of Peter the Great than of Ivan the Terrible. Nor was the shah in any way indifferent to the potential benefit in Washington of his image as a progressive. His attempts to maintain that accreditation generated both substantive policy initiatives and public relations efforts.

Iran's emphasis on education can be placed in the former category. The shah built new universities to promote the rapid expansion of Iran's student population, seeking aid from fifty American colleges for this purpose. Yet the speed of his drive for modernization dictated that many young people be sent abroad for study; by mid-1977 there were an estimated 60,000 Iranians attending American universities. The financial contributions and tuition payments for these Iranian students, at a time when American university enrollments were falling, created additional inducements for academic communities to accept them in large numbers. The Iranian government also gave millions of dollars in direct grants to a wide variety of technical schools, colleges, and universities.

Harvard received a $400,000 grant to plan a postgraduate university in northern Iran; Columbia gained $361,000 for an international medical complex and for aiding a new Iranian social-welfare school. An $11 million educational exchange program linked Georgetown and Ferdowsi Universities. Many of these projects, cut short by Iran's budget deficits and by the shah's downfall, were never fully implemented.

One unforseen or, at least, poorly understood consequence of quickly educating so large a number of students was the remarkable brain drain it produced. Between 1950 and 1968, a total of 325,731 students completed studies in other countries while only 22,681 of them returned to Iran. Others who had

studied in Iran went overseas to further personal professional
or financial goals. A decade after gaining degrees, 160 out of
315 physicians who had graduated from the University of
Tehran Medical School in June, 1966 were permanent residents in the United States.[26]

The shah's image as a progressive was also furthered by a
host of direct public relations efforts, including the spon-
sorship of pro-shah books and advertisements. The New York
advertising agency of Ruder & Finn received a $507,000 con-
tract to promote Iran's image; one of its executives, Marion
Javits, wife of the New York senator who was a Foreign Relations Committee member, was paid $67,500 a year to conduct
a pro-Iran information campaign. After newspaper coverage
suggested a possible conflict of interest in this arrangement,
the Iranian government shifted its account to another firm.
The well-connected former undersecretary of state, William
Rogers, became the lawyer for the American operations of the
Pahlevi Foundation, an ostensibly charitable fund that served
as one of the royal family's main financial bases.

But the most active force in these endeavors was the Iranian
Embassy in Washington. Under the direction of Ambassador
Ardeshir Zahedi its staff increased by 250 percent between
1973 and 1979. Zahedi, a gregarious and suave man whose
social activities were an integral part of his work, was well
acquainted with the American people. He had made his first
visit to the United States in 1943, at the age of fifteen, and
later worked his way through an American college. Back in
Iran, he worked as a liaison officer with the American aid mission and in 1953 was go-between for the CIA and his father,
Fazlollah Zahedi, during the planning of the 1953 anti-Mossadegh operation. Despite his father's removal by the shah two
years later, and more than one period of his own in personal
disfavor, the young Zahedi remained loyal to the shah.

The Iranian Embassy, one of Washington's most inefficient,
was as much under Zahedi's personal control as the Iranian
government was under the shah's. It did not function in the
normal fashion; rather Zahedi communicated directly with the
shah, ignoring Foreign Ministry channels. He built around

him a group of loyalists in competition with his rival, long-time Prime Minister Abbas Amir Hoveyda. When Zahedi was foreign minister he clashed with Hoveyda over the size of his department's budget. Hoveyda deemed himself personally insulted in the argument and convinced the shah to oust Zahedi. Only the empress's intervention made possible Zahedi's return to a position of authority.

Determined to avoid any such humiliation in the future, Zahedi even eliminated SAVAK's presence from the embassy lest it threaten his control. His sole master was the monarch himself, as witnessed by the floor-to-ceiling pictures of the shah and empress in the embassy reception room.

Even within Washington's already bustling, social scene, Zahedi became famous for his lavish parties and generous gifts to political and media luminaries. In one month, he might give three formal dinner-dances, each for seventy-five guests, two or three buffet dinners for three hundred, and one or two receptions for fifty, besides countless business lunches, late-night suppers, and pool-side barbecues. Entry into Iran's impressive Massachusetts Avenue chancery building became one of Washington's most sought-after indices of social success.

But Zahedi's frequent society-page appearances and his playboy image cloaked a well-organized lobbying effort. Zahedi believed that he could more easily influence politicians, reporters, and columnists through personal friendship and gifts of gold or diamond jewelry, caviar, flowers, champagne, and rugs. Middle East rulers commonly put a high value on the American media's power. Egyptian President Anwar al-Sadat has called Walter Cronkite, "one of the people who rule the United States," and Morocco's King Hassan II dramatically explains that the tools of mass communication, rather than missiles or atom bombs, are "the most dangerous weapons today."[27]

Zahedi's object was not to win one or two favorable articles, but to place his own image of Iran into the minds of influential Americans so that they would perceive it as a modern, progressive, and successful country, taking its place in the ranks of world powers. Moving with an already powerful current, he largely succeeded in this effort. Yet this achievement eventually backfired. American reporters and politicians were hard-pressed to explain in 1978 why, if Iran were so successful, so many people had gone into the streets to overthrow the shah. Consequently, this overestimate of the shah's support and the underestimate of the opposition's appeal lulled Washington into passivity until it was too late to take action.

Persistent rumors have hinted at the existence of Iranian political operations equal to or greater than South Korea's notorious influence-buying campaign and that the shah contributed large amounts to Richard Nixon's 1968 presidential campaign. After the shah's fall, Shahriar Rouhani, the Khomeini-appointed successor to Zahedi, accused the Iranian Embassy of "cash payments, bribes, provision of luxury overseas travel accommodations, prostitution, and blackmail of American officials and public figures." No proof has been offered to back up any of these allegations.[28]

Obviously, Zahedi's prolific gift-giving was intended to win friends for Iran. Over 1,000 presents were delivered each Christmas, including 150 cans of caviar, 90 bottles of Dom Perignon champagne, and 600 to 700 books. This probably did not change any sympathies directly, for the White House and Congress were already friendly toward the shah. But given the importance to Iran of continued and unfettered United States military supplies, neither Zahedi nor his monarch wanted to take any chances. Further, Zahedi wanted to maintain his own informal and independent sources of information in Congress to augment and to verify the news he received through State Department channels. He had particularly close relations with Senators Charles Percy, Jacob Javits, Barry Goldwater, Birch Bayh, Lloyd Bentsen, and Abraham Ribicoff, among others. As for any possible illegal or unethical activities, extensive investigations and interviews have failed to turn up a single authenticated case.

While Zahedi's success very much relied on the indifference or sympathy of most Americans toward Iran, anti-shah Iranians within the United States often damaged their own

154   PAVED WITH GOOD INTENTIONS

cause. They gained some press coverage from protests during the shah's visits, letters to newspapers, and paid advertisements, but they failed to spark any real opposition. The virulent anti-American rhetoric and New Left alliances of the Iranian Student Association cut them off from mainstream American opinion and sometimes produced a pro-shah backlash. The most active factions were outspokenly Marxist; there was little foreshadowing of the Islamic fervor that would dominate the movement after the ascendancy as absolute leader of Ayatollah Khomeini.

Given all these factors, United States-Iranian relations generally continued on a smooth footing. By 1975, despite rising public criticism, the bilateral tie remained a "very special one," as Sisco's successor, Alfred Atherton, put it, and "had probably never been better," as Kissinger appraised it.[29] Nevertheless, there were still misgivings and muffled voices of dissent even in the highest circles of the administration.

On February 21, 1976, United States Ambassador Richard Helms gave the shah a message from President Gerald Ford. "I have let it be known to the senior officials of my administration who deal with these issues that they should keep constantly in mind the very great importance which I attach to the special relationship that we enjoy with Iran," Ford wrote. "The collaboration between our two countries is firmly based on common interests, which are not changed by the recurring ups and downs of economic and financial affairs which may affect both our countries."[30]

Such a communication was necessary precisely because economic and financial affairs had created friction on both sides. Iran's participation in the recurring rounds of OPEC price increases had angered many Americans. At various times, Defense Secretaries James Schlesinger and Donald Rumsfeld, Treasury Secretary William Simon, and others pointed out the link between arms deliveries and oil prices. Schlesinger sought to raise research and development charges to Iran for the F–14 after the 1973 price rises while in 1976 Simon advocated restricting or terminating some food and arms sales to obtain added leverage. The White House turned down each of these proposals.

Others, despite the public relations campaigns of Ambassador Zahedi and the new chic of the royal family, apparently maintained a relatively low opinion of the shah himself. General George Brown, then chairman of the Joint Chiefs of Staff, spoke disparagingly of the shah's visions of a revived Persian Empire. In February, 1974, Simon called the shah a "nut," in a widely publicized speech. The treasury secretary's subsequent protestation that he had only referred to the shah's extreme enthusiasm probably did little to assuage Tehran's anger.

Rising United States dependence on Middle East oil, which increased from 6.6 percent of total energy needs in 1975 to 12.4 percent in 1976, made good relations with a stable Middle East all the more necessary. By 1976, Iran was supplying 8 to 9 percent of those imports. Paying for all this oil required more and more sales of military and civilian goods to the OPEC countries. The shah's new status led him to lecture American businessmen to become "more aggressive and dynamic," while telling Westerners to work harder. Iran would provide the example: "In 10 years' time," he said, "we shall be what you are today."[31]

Commercial prospects for both sides certainly did seem excellent in the mid-1970s. A March, 1975 United States-Iranian trade agreement called for $15 billion in commerce over the next five years, one-third of it in petroleum. In exchange, the United States would provide eight nuclear power stations and their fuel, prefabricated housing, hospitals, ports, electrical equipment, fertilizers, pesticides, farm machinery, superhighways, and a vocational training center. An even more optimistic 1976 trade protocol projected $52 billion in trade over the next five years.

But practice did not match projections. By 1974 Iran's economy had been seriously strained from inflation, breakdowns in planning, a contraction of oil markets, and by the rate of development itself. The 1975 budget had been planned to be three times larger than its predecessor, allocating 28 percent for defense and 24 percent for economic development. But revenues did not meet expectations.

The measures taken to contain this crisis only undermined the shah's political base. The 1975 "antiprofiteering" campaign led to the fining of 10,000 merchants, the arrest of 7,500 others, and the closing of over 600 shops. The alienated bazaar tradesmen were thereby made more receptive to the anti-shah speeches of Ayatollah Khomeini. According to the shah himself, the decision that brought down his throne was taken at this time. To effect another saving it was decided to end the traditional government subsidies to Muslim mullahs. The beginning of the merchant-clergy alliance emerged when businessmen stepped in to make up the mosques' new deficit.

These two groups were also united in their belief that a small strata of new rich, whose success was based on corrupt court connections, were monopolizing Iran's oil wealth. The shah did little to curb the ascendancy or the arrogance of this new class, which lived by high-level corruption. One visiting American was surprised to see a number of deserted, partly completed construction projects. The reason, he was told, was that the contractor's ability to win government contracts had not depended on any ability to fulfill them. His few employees simply went from one site to the other, doing a little here and a little there.

The very day in February, 1976 when the United States Treasury reported a sharp decline in Iran's investible surplus—from $10.7 billion in 1974 to a projected $4.5 billion in 1976—Empress Farah was returning from Europe with a planeload of three tons of French rose marble for the royal family's new swimming pool. The next day, the Tehran government announced a $2.4 billion budget deficit for the coming year despite $20 billion in oil revenues. Rising military costs were named as the cause for the shortfall.

When the shah warned that he would have less money to spend for purchases from the United States, the *Washington Post* greeted this possibility with optimism. The "mindless American policy of supplying our most advanced military technology to Iran is increasingly likely to get both countries

AN IMPERIAL DREAM 1969–74   157

into trouble," it announced in a February, 1976 editorial, and
Iran's need to economize offered an escape from "a network of
commitments that are becoming steadily more dangerous and
onerous. . . . As long as economic requirements have to take
second place to military ambitions that require Grumman
Tomcats at $18 million apiece, the outlook for stable growth
[in Iran] is obscure." [32]

   If the shah had to choose between arms and economic development, however, his decision would not be in doubt. Indeed, in 1975 and 1976 an increasing volume of criticism of
the administration's Iran policy addressed itself to exactly this
reality. It was one of two main issues eroding Washington's
earlier consensus of confidence in the shah. Dismay over the
seemingly out of control arms-sales program was the first. The
second was the increasing American embarrassment and re-
pulsion over revelations of repression in Iran.

6
Arms and the Shah
1975–76

The single most important link in the United States-Iranian alliance during the last decade of the shah's rule was Washington's massive arms-sales program. During the 1970s, Iran became the largest buyer of military equipment in the developing world; roughly 27 percent of its government spending went for defense, and this budget quadrupled in size between 1973–74 and 1976–77. Over one-third of United States foreign military purchases during that period were made by Iran. Inflation made this program steadily more expensive: a Spruance-class destroyer selling for about $200 million in 1974 cost about $350 million two years later.[1]

The shah's philosophy was to buy the best equipment in the greatest quantities at the fastest possible rate. This meant the most up-to-date systems: hovercraft with surface-to-surface missiles, mine-laying helicopters, small aircraft carriers with vertical takeoff (V/STOL) planes for anti-submarine warfare. Some of this equipment was bought from Britain, France, Italy, and even the USSR, but the overwhelming majority, particularly for the air force, was ordered from the United States.

158

"If one understands the Iranian government's perception of the threats it faces and the interests it seeks to defend," wrote Iranian military expert Shahram Chubin, "its weapons acquisitions are not difficult to comprehend."[2] The country's wild terrain and long, exposed borders dictated a large troop airlift capacity, a stronger air-defense system, supersonic interceptors equal to Soviet and Iraqi first-line planes, and a navy able to defend not only Iran's shores but free access to the Persian Gulf as well. Iran's goal of coproducing the most advanced equipment—for which its industrial base was clearly inadequate—was justified as part of a drive for the greatest possible degree of self-reliance.

"What is the use of having an advanced industry in a country which could be brought to its knees [by outsiders]," asked the shah, rejecting as irrelevant any guns-versus-butter debate. Internal development was worthless without defense: "There is no economic power without military power."[3]

While there was a strong factual basis for Iran's strategic worries, the arguments for the breakneck pace and massive size of the buildup were not as compelling. Was it really necessary to exhaust so totally the country's skilled labor pool, its resources, and its income on military spending? The program's excessive speed and its early investment in new weaponry meant that Iran would bear a large part of the increased per unit costs associated with underwriting the research and development phase of all new technology.

The short answer lies partly in the psychology of the shah and partly in the glorious prospects raised by OPEC's great victory in petroleum pricing. Oil seemed to be a genie of unlimited bounty, capable of fulfilling not only Iran's wishes but also those of Iran's oil-producing neighbors, friendly and unfriendly. Chubin claimed that Iran's defense spending was not out of line with that of other Middle East countries and represented no greater a percentage of Gross National Product than did the military budgets of Iraq, Israel, Jordan, Saudi Arabia, Syria, and Egypt.[4] Yet whereas the participation of these countries in the Arab-Israeli conflict provided strong, domestic support for high military spending, Iranian public opinion did not understand why so much of their oil income was being spent for war equipment.*

The shah considered stability on the Arab side of the Gulf, and in Pakistan and Afghanistan, to be of prime importance for Iran's interests. He worried about Soviet support for Iraq, about Moscow's moves toward creating an Indian Ocean fleet, and about its entrenchment in South Yemen and Somalia. American policymakers shared the same concerns. Although the shah did not have complete confidence in the United States, his alignment with Washington was vital if he were to defend himself against the giant on his northern border and the forces of revolution supported by it.

In Washington's analysis, Iran's orientation was a natural result of geopolitical realities—unlikely to change no matter what regime came to power. While this was perhaps a correct analysis of objective power factors, it underestimated the importance of ideological and emotional factors. Iranians believed, rightly or wrongly, that the shah's foreign policy did not serve Iranian interest; that it served only to perpetuate his own regime and United States influence in Iran. The shah's strategy was aimed at guaranteeing Iran's independence, but his opponents managed to convince most Iranians that it led only to dependence on America.

Ironically, though, the entire United States strategy was based on greater dependence on the shah. True, after 1968, the United States aerospace industry underwent a contraction due to post-Vietnam cutbacks in government spending, anti-inflationary measures, and a temporary decline in the civil air transport market. The need to counterbalance the outflow of American dollars for foreign oil also increased pressures for sales abroad. Between 1970 and 1975 American military exports increased from $1 billion to $10 billion a year, primarily to Saudi Arabia and Iran.[5]

But American policy was motivated by strategic rather than economic factors. These latter considerations may help ex-

* It might also be noted that Saudi Arabia and Iraq had higher per capita oil incomes than did Iran, while the other countries mentioned received large amounts of foreign aid.

plain how the arms-sales program got out of hand, yet have little to do with the origins and nature of the two-pillar approach. At the same time, some of the economic benefits of the policy may even have been illusory. While foreign sales sometimes reduced costs for the United States military, the stretching of delivery times forced increased maintenance expenses on existing systems and inflationary overruns on the awaited replacements. A Congressional Budget Office study on Iran's order of 80 F–14s, for example, showed an initial United States Navy saving of $60 million in production expenses, while additional closing costs and slower procurement added $120 million to their bill.[6]

The decision to sell the shah anything he wanted threw open all the doors to the candy store. The shah had no idea of self-restraint; his pliant officials, moved by their own aggrandizing impulses, were eager to go along. Defense Department officials, particularly those from the air force and navy, were given every incentive to maximize sales and to override any objections by referring to the needs of national security and military strategy. The State Department and the CIA were given every incentive to avoid criticism or even pessimistic reports. The arms companies, of course, wanted to do as much business as possible. The result was predictable; what is surprising was that so many within the United States government did raise objections and that the system, albeit belatedly, finally tried to rein in the policy.

Most damaging was the contribution of the arms-sale process to two vicious circles. First, the companies promoted specific weapons in Tehran even before they had been approved or ordered by the United States military. Consequently, the Iranians were constantly finding new things to order that the United States was committed to sell them. Thus, the pace of orders went faster and faster as competing vendors tried to leapfrog each other by offering newer and fancier weaponry. Second, Iran's high expenses for military imports sharpened its appetite for revenues. The subsequent increases in oil prices contributed to inflation in the West, which, in turn, pushed up once again the cost of arms. Obviously, the shah's appetite for military hardware was by no means the sole cause of OPEC price-rise demands, but it was a factor in destabilizing the economic and commercial status quo.

In theory, the sales procedure was for the Iranian government to ask the MAAG to quote prices on a given item. When an order was made, the MAAG relayed it to the Defense Department which, in turn, farmed it out to ISA's Near East and South Asia region. They would discuss this with their counterparts in the State Department's area bureau and would make a recommendation. The secretary of state had the final decision, though he became involved only with particularly large and controversial deals. In practice, the May, 1972 White House decision had approved in advance virtually every order that came from Tehran. Finally, the Defense Security Assistance Agency carried out the actual arrangements for payment and delivery.

Understandably, the companies did not wait passively for the Iranians to discover their wares. Their problems, however, were both unusual and complex ones; these businesses needed guidance through the labyrinth of Iranian bureaucracy. Grumman Aircraft Corporation President Joseph Gavin explained the problem to a Senate investigating committee: "Imagine . . . that you, unable to speak English, represent a foreign manufacturer trying to sell an aircraft to the U.S. Navy. You would probably know who is the Secretary of Defense, the Secretary of the Navy, and the Chief of Naval Operations, although you might well be uncertain about the separate roles and responsibilities of each of them.

"You would soon find your way to the Naval Air Systems Command," he continued, "but at that point you would be confronted with literally hundreds of specialists, both military and civilian, each with complicated titles and complex relations to each other and each very busy with his own problems." This was the American position in Iran: "We knew nothing of Iranian laws, traditions and customs," while competing companies had already retained Iranian sales representatives. So each American firm hired its own agents.[7]

When Martin Hoffmann, a special assistant to Defense Secretary James Schlesinger, visited Iran in the fall of 1974 he found that this system was not working to everyone's satisfaction. No American laws were actually being broken, but there were a number of potential problems. For example, arms manufacturers were pushing their products without Defense Department clearance and without checking with the MAAG. No classified specifications seem to have been compromised, but the United States government had no idea who was telling the Iranians what, whether the shah was being steered toward certain systems, and what impact such actions might have. Iran's purchasing decisions often turned on which companies had the better salesmen, or worse, the sharper agents.

Hassan Toufanian, vice-minister of war in charge of Iran's arms-purchasing program, was equally dissatisfied. Some companies were misrepresenting their products, he told Hoffmann, claiming that the prices quoted sometimes did not include surcharged research and development costs. He asked for greater Pentagon controls on the companies.

The shah particularly objected to paying any agents' commissions on equipment purchased through the United States government. When Senate investigators disclosed that Northrop paid $2.1 million for the F–5 sales and Grumman put up $24 million in such fees on the F–14 deal—both amounts added to Iran's bill—the shah forced both companies to make restitution. Grumman settled for payment in spare parts, but this arrangement was cancelled after the shah's ouster.

Defense Department officials thought cynically of these Iranian complaints as mere varnish on the regime's corruption. Everyone knew that large amounts of baksheesh were changing hands; in two specific deals Textron paid $2.9 million and Northrop $700,000 which ended up in the pockets of Iranian officers and royal family members. Yet Toufanian's statements might better have been taken as attempts to get Washington's help in saving Iran from the effects of its own system.

On the other hand, the American side was not entirely free from any conflict-of-interest taint. Many American officials in the arms-sales program later turned up working for private companies involved in those transactions. Three months after retiring as chairman of the Joint Chiefs of Staff, Admiral Thomas Moorer visited Tehran as a consultant for Stanwick International Corporation, a firm managing Iranian ship repairs. After his retirement in 1972, General Hamilton Howe, considered the father of air cavalry doctrine, was hired by Bell Helicopter to help direct its sales program. As part of the company's campaign, he first lectured Iranian army commanders on military tactics, then showed them a film demonstrating the merits of Bell's Huey Cobra helicopter.

Other companies recruited former MAAG commanders: Major General Harvey Jablonsky returned to Iran to push Northrop's telecommunications system; Air Force MAAG chief Major General Harold L. Price went to Philco-Ford, selling aircraft warning systems and telephone cables, and Navy MAAG chief Captain R. S. Harward went first to TRACOR, supplying sensors and aircraft equipment, and later moved to Rockwell International, one of the largest contractors for Iran. None of this was illegal, but it did strengthen the bond between the military and their suppliers—which many Defense Department civilians already thought too close. In the eyes of Iranians, American officers and the salesmen must have become indistinguishable.

By far the most serious and controversial case was that of Richard R. Hallock, Schlesinger's personal representative in Iran between 1973 and 1975. Hallock, a self-made mystery man and a former Schlesinger colleague at the RAND Corporation, was supposed to be a watchdog and investigator on the arms program's functioning.

Hallock did not waste much time. He quickly proposed sharp cuts in the billion-dollar Iranian air defense electronics program and was able to build close relations with the shah. He made such a good impression that Intrec, his consulting company, signed a multi-million dollar contract with the Iranian government in July, 1974 to advise it on research, planning, and training. The programs he advocated to the shah, however, were not necessarily those backed by the MAAG and the Defense Department. There were also rumors that Intrec had among its clients a number of companies seeking Iran's business, including Northrop, E Systems, and Teledyne-Ryan. This seemed to put Hallock in the enviable position of advising the shah on what to buy, advising the United States government on what to recommend to him, helping the arms-supply companies close the deals, and overseeing the program under which all these transactions were being made. Although Hallock's associates denied any conflict of interest, blaming the innuendos on jealous corporations whose proposals Hallock had opposed, the Defense Department's Criminal Division launched an investigation and his connection with the United States government was terminated.

Lower-ranking Americans got along passably well. While the Defense Department sent Technical Assistance Field Teams (TAFTs) to give on-the-job training, the vast majority of American advisors in Iran were provided by the contracting companies. According to official figures, there were 16,700 Americans in Iran by 1975, of which 1,355 were military staff, including 201 in the world's largest United States MAAG, and some 600 assigned to the rotating TAFTs. In addition, there were 2,000 civilian Defense Department employees, along with 3,200 Americans and 1,400 third-country nationals working for United States defense industry employers.[8]

Advisory services cost Iran $5.5 million in fiscal 1974, climbing to $94 million within two years. By then, Iran was paying for all the TAFTs and some of the MAAG expenses. Friction between individual Americans and Iranians was generally limited, though some Bell instructors were censured or even dismissed for drinking, fighting, and racing motorcycles near mosques. For their part, American pilots complained about the low quality of the Iranian trainees and about the loose safety regulations. After the assassination of two MAAG colonels in May, 1975, senior officers had armed guards, escort cars, and some carried weapons themselves.

While doubtlessly true that many American military men pressed too hard for quick modernization of the Iranian armed forces, sometimes becoming virtual salesmen for advanced weapons, such over-enthusiasm was most often due to their determination to achieve their mission of creating a credible military force out of the Iranian armed services. When discovered, such zealots were cautioned toward restraint. The goal was not, they were told by superiors, to remake the Iranian military into a mirror image of its American counterpart. Few had many illusions on that score; the Iranian army did not have a high reputation. Poor performance and even poorer leadership were the norm: in the Oman fighting Iranian junior officers and senior noncommissioned officers had enjoyed the lowest casualty rates.

The sheer complexity of modern warfare, so different from the straightforward infantry tactics of Reza Shah's day, compounded many of Iran's military problems. As early as 1970, Grumman began attempts to sell its forthcoming F–14 to Iran. Distressed by Soviet overflights and Iraq's new MIG–23s, superior to Iran's Phantoms, the shah was receptive to Grumman's approach and began his own lobbying effort within the United States government. The Defense Department questioned whether the sale was in the interests of either the United States or regional security, but President Nixon went along with Tehran and promised the plane to the shah in May, 1972.

So complicated was the F–14 that even the United States Navy had difficulty operating it. As another example of Iran's appetite for the most advanced equipment, the model of Spruance-class destroyer ordered by Iran was even more sophisticated than the kind bought by the United States Navy. These systems required a high level of technical capability, well-educated technicians, and modern management procedures, all of which Iran lacked. To provide the needed personnel, one United States study concluded, the Iranian military might need virtually the country's entire high school graduating class each year.

Those aware of the difficulties lying behind the glowing press releases, particularly those among Defense Department logistical specialists and ISA analysts, were critical of the existing United States policy. On the other side, the military services and the Defense Security Assistance Agency generally supported the program. Military intelligence, which emphasized the Soviet buildup of Iraqi forces, was also in the latter camp.

More often than not, the secretary of defense, especially during the Schlesinger years, leaned toward the doubters. Yet the Schlesinger-Kissinger relation was already tenuous enough without the introduction of an additional issue of contention. Besides, since Kissinger always had the president's ear and since he also controlled the State Department—supported there by Undersecretary Sisco, an architect of the policy—dissent was deemed useless. Kissinger's well-known ferocity in bureaucratic battles and his primacy in policymaking discouraged open debate.

Of course, the Washington bureaucracy always had its own means of passive resistance, able to outlast any political appointee. Critics leaked information to Congress and the newspapers, dragged their feet on specific projects, and wrote memos complaining about the dangers. Yet those opposed to the policy remained a small minority. Most of those involved in its implementation still believed it was going rather well; criticism, external and internal, only made them defensive.

On occasion, the main area of complaint—the possible leak of American technological secrets to Moscow—forestalled the sale of some specific item to Iran. Such a case involved a "smart-bomb" system not used in Vietnam. Another major project was deliberately misplaced in the files until the Iranian government lost interest. Although there were never any known security leaks of American classified information, one Iranian general was executed as a Soviet spy shortly before the revolution. It seems quite possible that once the shah fell Moscow's agents quickly gained access to the sophisticated planes, electronic gear, and other material left behind.

The strategic importance of certain specific projects overrode general security concerns. Thus, the Defense Department ended up supporting the sale of the AWACs aircraft-borne radar warning system because the competing ground-based system would have been far more costly and would have involved more American technicians on the scene. But this proposal served other interests of the American armed services as well. AWACs sales to Iran would bring per unit costs low enough to convince European allies to buy them, which, in turn, might further drop unit cost enough to persuade Congress to acquire the system for American use.

Another dimension was the potential support such systems might provide to American defense requirements. In the event of a larger war, Iranian AWACs units could guide American fighter planes defending the Middle East against Soviet attacks. Even so, the sale of AWACs barely avoided being blocked by congressional opposition in 1977. The high priority the shah placed on obtaining the system disposed the Carter White House to follow through on the project, but the revolution came about before a single plane could be delivered.

A similar multi-use criterion influenced development of the top secret IBEX project, designed to put a $500 million surveillance system on Iran's borders and to expand the number of CIA monitoring stations from two to eleven. Rockwell International won the contract in 1975, but stories of influence buying and of American skepticism over the practicality of the system led to Iranian complaints that their country was being used as a technical dumping ground. In August, 1976, three American advisors working on the project were murdered by terrorists. Eventually, IBEX was abandoned.

The presence of the monitoring installations, designed to eavesdrop on Soviet missile ranges and bases in the southern USSR, was one of the most important services the shah offered his allies. These installations provided vital intelligence, necessary for any strategic-arms-limitations agreement and were often cited as one reason why Washington ought to avoid ever antagonizing the shah.

These special stations originated in a rather curious fashion. In the early 1950s, the American consul in Tabriz held an advanced degree in physics and his hobby was electronics. Tinkering with his own receiving equipment, he intercepted a strange, continuous sound. After checking, he concluded that this was produced by missiles in flight. He obtained more sophisticated apparatus and soon it became apparant that he had become the first foreigner to detect the Soviet missile test center at Kapusin Yar.

While concerned about security leaks, a regional arms race, and the shah's ambitions, not even the strongest critics of existing policy ever suggested that the shah's government might fall. The National Intelligence Estimates and the reports from the State Department, the CIA, military intelligence, and the MAAG all discounted the likelihood of any domestic upheaval. When Israel's representative in Tehran, Uri Lubrani, suggested to American visitors as early as 1974 that the shah's regime might be entering its final days, the United States Embassy ridiculed the notion.

Yet while Iran itself was thought to be in reasonably good shape, by mid-1975 the United States-Iranian arms-sales relationship was increasingly seen as a serious mess. A January, 1975 General Accounting Office (GAO) study warned that the advisory program was draining off critical military skills needed by United States forces. A RAND Corporation critique pointed out that there was no joint Iranian planning; all services reported separately to the shah. A later GAO report concluded that the Defense Department apparatus for monitoring contractor performance was often inadequate and needed major improvements. If this were not corrected, "The Government of Iran will not develop the desired defense capabilities and our relations . . . could suffer avoidable strain."[9] One participant called the situation a "managerial nightmare."

Other reports found the Iranian armed forces to be years away from being a credible military organization. They pointed to difficulties in motivating the conscript force and to its poor technical level. There were, as well, problems in training and in securing good officers and skilled technicians. The shah's own regulations, designed to prevent the military from posing any political threat to him, also weakened its capacity to perform its mission.

The policy shortcomings being discovered by some in the executive branch were also becoming visible to those on the outside. Mounting congressional criticism of the administration's arms-sale programs led to a provision in the Foreign Assistance Act of 1974 that gave Congress up to thirty days to block a major arms deal. Senator Henry Jackson asked Secretary of State Kissinger for a reassessment of his Iran policy after the March, 1975 Iran-Iraq agreement seemed to reduce the Iraqi threat to Iran that had been an often-cited justification for the pace and quantity of arms sales. Senator Edward Kennedy called for a six-month suspension of weapons transfers to the Persian Gulf countries, questioning whether the president's strategy really increased United States influence in the region. Representative Les Aspin of Wisconsin tried to stop the sale of six destroyers. Other proposals called for taking into account the human rights policies of arms customers, for more public disclosure of military transfers, and for increased congressional oversight.

Defense officials made a number of attempts to straighten out the program. Air Force General Robert Huyser, commander of United States forces in Europe who was also responsible for Middle East MAAGs and logistical planning, traveled to Tehran several times to advise the Iranian government. Seeking to wean Tehran, the United States refused to do contingency planning for the Iranians. Meanwhile, General Howard Fish, director of the Defense Security Assistance Agency, tried to tighten his agency's operations.

The main effort was made by Defense Secretary Schlesinger. After severing ties with Hallock, he dispatched Eric von Marbod to Iran in September, 1975 as his new personal representative. There, von Marbod attempted with some success to convince the Iranians to cancel several unrealistic projects. At about the same time, Schlesinger sent C. Glenn Blitgen, another Defense Department civilian, to study Iran's military absorptive capacity and the arms-sales program's internal management. Blitgen, too, concluded that things were moving too fast.

This second mission led to a Defense Department report for President Ford late in 1975 requesting a reconsideration of United States policy toward Iran. Top personnel in the State

Department and the National Security Council, who were happy with the existing policy, managed to water down the re-evaluation, first by broadening it into a study of American policy toward the entire Persian Gulf and then by guiding it into an almost verbatim restatement of past principles. Many of those involved believe that it was Kissinger who was responsible for so slowing down this project that it was never really finished during Ford's remaining months as president. But the backstairs debate influenced the Carter White House when it took office in January, 1977.

Some Iranian leaders were also becoming increasingly nervous over the level of arms purchases, primarily because of the rising costs of equipment and Iran's lagging oil income. Already, falling petroleum revenues had forced the deferral of some of the shah's planned roads, airports, docks, and communications facilities, among other things. The idea that Iran's spending might outrun its skyrocketing profits had seemed impossible in 1974, but the shah's spendthrift ways had managed to force the country into deficit once the income rise leveled off.

One major error was Iran's overestimate of future Western oil consumption; OPEC's high oil bills, along with other problems, had produced an economic downturn in the industrialized world. To try to raise oil shipments, Toufanian again suggested a straight oil-for-arms trade, but again Washington replied that the United States was not in the oil buying and selling business.

When Toufanian met with Secretary of Defense Donald Rumsfeld, Schlesinger's successor, in January, 1976 he demanded that the price of arms be lowered and that the United States help Iran sell more oil; otherwise, he threatened, Iran would seek new suppliers and new allies. The shah gave similar warnings, demanding oil companies pay more per barrel to make up for the lower quantity of Iran's production they were using. In response, Defense Department personnel were instructed not to push further weapons sales. If Toufanian wanted to cancel any existing deals they should quickly agree to do so.

172 PAVED WITH GOOD INTENTIONS

As the year went on, tempers quickened on both sides. In another discussion, Toufanian defended sharp increases in Iran's oil prices by holding up a helicopter door handle priced at $11.62. "This costs us one barrel of oil," he fumed. He also claimed that it cost Iran 10,000 barrels of oil a year to support a single American warehouseman or mechanic.[10]

The disillusionment was by no means one-sided. When Toufanian complained that one system had gone up 50 percent in price between 1973 and 1976, General Fish replied, "Yeah, but the price of oil has tripled." An angry Schlesinger had declared earlier, "We are going to make them pay through the nose, just as they are making us pay them through the nose for oil."[11] By the mid-1970s each side was blaming the other for the cycle of mutual price increases.

Another conflict developed around mutual charges of corruption. Shortly after Toufanian's visit, the shah sent Rumsfeld a six-page letter charging top Pentagon officials with "malfeasance" and "crude deceptions" in hiding deficiencies in the weapons sold Iran. He told visitors that he was fed up with "the chicanery of Pentagon officials and their military and civilian representatives here. . . ."[12]

Who was the more culpable, the one who demanded or the one who paid a bribe? The shah did little to end the taking, in which members of the royal family were often involved. True, Admiral Ramzi Attaei, commander of the Iranian navy, was sentenced to five years imprisonment for embezzlement in 1976—the scope of the crime indicated by the $4 million fine he was also required to pay—and nineteen Iranian army engineers were also convicted. But Commerce Minister Fereidun Mahdavi was removed when his anticorruption campaign aimed too high.

Prime Minister Hoveyda attacked the foreign companies for their behavior and the foreign press for its criticism; he insisted that all charges were being investigated and accused some companies of pocketing money they claimed to have paid as bribes. "All this is a sad reflection on the standards of conduct that we have come to expect from the international business community," he said. "We are constantly being lectured to about our various shortcomings and yet it seems that those who preach to us themselves suffer from a laxity of moral tone."[13] Ironically, the shah arrested Hoveyda as a scapegoat for corruption shortly before his own fall; the former prime minister was one of the first men executed by the victorious Khomeini forces.

These cross accusations produced more and more disenchantment between the two partners. Typical of the state of congressional, press, and public criticism was a February, 1976 editorial in The New York Times warning that the United States was making a "profound mistake" by selling so much weaponry in the Persian Gulf; local governments were making an equally profound mistake by squandering their wealth on military display.[14]

Such doubts made the shah even more insecure about American support and more strident in his replies. If the United States ever cut off the flow of weapons to him, he assured Americans, Iran "can hurt you as badly if not more so than you can hurt us." Washington's only options, the shah said, were arms sales or regional instability. His old fear of Washington's unreliability returned: "I am afraid that today America's credibility is not too high. You look rather like a crippled giant." Yet he would not remain passive in such an event, the shah promised. "We have ten other markets to provide us with what we need. There are people just waiting for that moment."[15] When the United States refused to sell him nuclear reactors, he simply turned to France.

The hardest blow to administration policy was struck by a devastating Senate Foreign Relations Committee staff report on arms sales that was released in August, 1976, during the final months of the Ford administration. The study concluded that Iran would probably not be able to engage in major combat operations over the next five to ten years "without sustained U.S. support." The price of Iran's regional superpower status had become the possibility that America might be dragged into a local war, at a time and place of the shah's choosing.

By subverting ordinary review procedures, the report continued, President Nixon's 1972 decision had "created a bonanza for U.S. weapons manufacturers, the procurement branches of the three U.S. services and the Defense Security Assistance Agency." Up to 1975 there had been no close supervision of arms salesmen, an excess of interservice rivalry, and a failure to inform the Iranians of the complexities of training, logistics, and maintenance required for their new equipment. Though both Iran and the Defense Department were praised for finally beginning needed reforms, only recently had there been any appreciation of the management problems involved. The program was still not under control.

Nor was that all. The presence of so many Americans in Iran created socioeconomic problems there and might lead to serious anti-Americanism "if there were to be a change in government," a possibility that could not be ruled out. The American commitment to support the equipment it sold might become a trap, with thousands of Americans held in Iran as "hostages" to guarantee United States backing for Tehran's policies. Already, there were 24,000 Americans there, including 4,000 military personnel and the employees of forty companies implementing military contracts. By 1980, it was estimated, there might be as many as 50,000 to 60,000 United States citizens in Iran.

The staff report did not advocate any sharp reversal, noting, "The United States cannot abandon, substantially diminish, or even redirect its arms programs without precipitating a major crisis in U.S.-Iranian relations." But it did call for a far more responsible execution of American policy.[16]

This far-ranging critique was widely quoted and discussed. Secretary of State Kissinger, who was scheduled to hold important talks with the shah just days after the report's release, gave the administration's response, arguing that the United States could not assume all responsibility around the world—it had to value and support friends like Iran. Those who did not want heavier direct commitments abroad could achieve this end only through greater indirect commitments. The pace of arms sales, he told a Tehran press conference, would continue through 1980.

The shah was less calm; for him the American headlines seemed to fulfill his worst nightmares. Iran, he proudly announced, would not change its plans: "We are a sovereign country looking after our defense. . . . We are the only judge of what we need." He asked, "Can the United States, can the non-Communist world, afford to lose Iran? Do you have any choice? What will you do if Iran is in danger of collapse?" The answer, he thought, was clear: "If you do not pursue a policy of standing by your own friends, who are spending their own money and are ready to spend their own blood, the alternative is nuclear Holocaust or more Vietnams." [17]

Certainly, the Ford administration had no thought of lessening support for the shah. Kissinger's announcement in late August of plans to sell Iran 160 F–16s for $3.4 billion, with delivery between 1979 and 1983, was intended as a sign of that continuity; the attempt of several senators, including Gaylord Nelson and William Proxmire, to block this deal was equally a sign of the emerging mood in Congress.

The affair of the F–18L light bomber at the end of 1976 only further confirmed the critics in their objections. Northrop was trying to persuade the United States government to buy that plane, still on the drawing board. Without breaking any laws, the company circumvented controls on monitoring arms sales abroad by taking its case directly to Iran. As a government official explained: "They get Iran all hot to buy this plane and then if the [Pentagon review] is negative, we've got a diplomatic problem on our hands." [18]

After Northrop President Thomas Jones met with the shah, Toufanian ordered 250 F–18Ls plus equipment and services, a $2.5 billion value. According to some sources, Northrop helped prepare Toufanian's letter and may have given Iran the impression that the Pentagon agreed. But Rumsfeld barred any such arrangement pending United States government approval of the plane's export. The Defense Department, which had not yet decided whether it wanted the F–18L, was not going to finance its development merely because Iran wanted it.

The staff report and other investigations were clearly turn-

ing the tide against the arms-sales program. The Senate
Foreign Relations Committee now asked that no more major
sales be submitted for approval until after a complete review
of all United States transfers to the Gulf. Even Fred Iklé, the
Ford administration's conservative director of the Arms Control and Disarmament Agency, warned that supplying additional fighter planes to Persian Gulf countries would be "destabilizing."[19] Ford's successor would even more seriously
and skeptically reconsider the strategy adopted in 1972.

While the United States-Iranian military relationship was
perhaps the issue that received the most attention in these
years, revelations about the shah's repressive policies had an
important psychological effect in the debate over American
policy. "The shah of Iran retains his benevolent image despite
the highest rate of death penalties in the world, no valid system of civilian courts and a history of torture which is beyond
belief," said Amnesty International's 1974–75 report. Yet the
Iranian government's policy here was complex and subtle, by
usual police-state standards.

For example, the widely quoted figure of 25,000 to 100,000
political prisoners often attributed to Amnesty International
was actually cited from opposition sources; Amnesty International estimated the real number at "several thousands."
Thus, while repression was ferocious—with "routine" torture
of political prisoners during interrogation and imprisonment—the number directly affected seems less than claimed
by the post-shah regime. Further, when an international commission went to Tehran in early 1980 to hear directly from the
victims of torture and repression, many of the injuries displayed were inflicted not in the former government's prisons
but in the fighting during the revolution.

On a global list of countries holding political prisoners Iran
ranked behind Cuba, Ethiopia, East Germany, Pakistan, Oman,
Syria, and others. William Butler of the International Commission of Jurists, whose 1976 mission concluded that there was
abundant evidence of systematic psychological and physical
torture, said the shah was "way down the list of tyrants. He
would not even make the A-list." Western estimates suggest

that the shah's regime killed around 10,000 people in over thirty years of rule, about half of them during the 1978 revolution. Amnesty International estimated about 300 executions from 1972 on, though there must have been hundreds more never officially announced. Nevertheless, even if these figures are doubled, they fall far short of the 300,000 deaths in Uganda, millions in Cambodia, and around 6,000 in one year in neighboring Afghanistan. The records of many Third World and most Communist states are no better than that of Iran under the shah.[20]

Still, from the viewpoint of Iranians living under the shah's regime, all this had an abstract ring. The shah's Iran was a police state, though its treatment of prisoners was based heavily on Iranian historical practices. Those convicted of ordinary crimes were treated as badly as were the political prisoners. Unfortunately, prison reform does not seem to have any higher priority with the post-shah government than it had for the royal regime.

The intensity of anti-shah hatred after the revolution can be explained by three particular features of Iranian repression. First, prisoners were subjected to horrendous torture, equal to the worst ever devised. Jailers regularly used beatings, shock treatments, electric drills, and other instruments that sometimes left prisoners crippled or insane. It is still not clear whether the CIA was involved in training SAVAK on torture techniques, though such things were not so alien to Iranian traditions that instruction seems to have been needed.

Second, SAVAK deliberately spread fear of its methods and exaggeration of its power as a mechanism for maintaining control. Prisoners were often released only if they, or members of their family, agreed to become informers. Further, given the importance of the extended family in Iran, every time one person was killed or arrested the government made one hundred bitter enemies from among his relatives. Since most Iranians, particularly in urban areas, had kin who had suffered the depredations of SAVAK, its methods became their most emotionally expressed complaint.

Finally, and perhaps most important, SAVAK's victims

were not merely a small group of active dissidents or a politically conscious minority. The existing system meant that the entire population was subjected to a constant, all-pervasive terror. While most secret police operations concentrate on finding their government's most active enemies SAVAK went out of its way to punish those suspected of the most petty offenses. The broad nature of SAVAK's intimidation and the surety of its blow was a constant psychological humiliation for almost every Iranian. The result was a deep desire for vengeance on the part of the shah's subjects.

Some of those who would lead the anti-shah revolution were direct victims of SAVAK. Ayatollah Khomeini's oldest son, Mustafa, killed under mysterious circumstances, was probably assassinated by its agents. Ayatollah Hussein Ali Montazeri, one of the most fiery of Khomeini's advisors, was reportedly tortured by SAVAK, which also beat up his eighty-five-year-old father. The shah did face a real terrorist problem throughout the 1970s, but SAVAK, in response, terrorized the entire population.

At the same time, while the shah must take responsibility for SAVAK's actions, it operated, like so many secret police agencies, as a law unto itself. General Bakhtiar's attempt to take power provided the shah with one cautionary example, but other SAVAK leaders also had their own independent power bases. Government officials in favor with the court might fall afoul of SAVAK and lose their positions. Ambassador Zahedi refused to even allow them into his embassy because of some of his past experiences. Ultimately, SAVAK's last commander would betray the shah and help to deliver the country to Ayatollah Khomeini.

The all-pervasive, constant intimidation has been recorded many times. Teachers for Tehran's United States-run Iran-America Society were told by embassy officials to assume that there was at least one SAVAK informer in every classroom; the same rule applied in Iranian universities. One instructor reported that despite this warning he occasionally mentioned the shah "just to get a reaction." "It's amazing," he declared, "they are so paralyzed with fear at the mere mention of his name that they don't even bat an eyelash."[21] American advisors, cautioned to be careful, generally referred to the shah and empress by humorous code names.

General Nematollah Nasiri, a former military academy classmate of the shah whose loyalty had been so decisively demonstrated in 1953, commanded SAVAK, holding the rank of deputy prime minister. General Hussein Fardost, an old classmate of the shah at the Le Rosey School in Switzerland (also attended by American Ambassador Richard Helms) and one of the monarch's closest friends, headed the Special Intelligence Bureau, which kept tabs on SAVAK. The number of full-time SAVAK employees was relatively small—slightly over 3,000—though the number of paid informers, including journalists, students, waiters, drivers, and businessmen, might have easily numbered twenty times as many.

SAVAK also tried to keep an eye on American critics. When Senator Edward Kennedy visited Iran in 1975, uninvited SAVAK agents crashed his meeting with journalists at the Tehran Hilton. An aide to Senator Gaylord Nelson, who had come to gather information on Iran's military buildup, was briefed by an Iranian editor at an embassy luncheon who later turned out to be a SAVAK agent.

When embassy press attaché Max McCarthy asked several Iranians in casual conversation the rationale behind Iran's military purchases, word soon reached the shah, who expressed his displeasure at one of his regular sessions with the CIA station chief. Some weeks later, Nasiri summoned the CIA man and a top assistant and read them a detailed account of the attaché's conversations.[22]

SAVAK's Anti-Sabotage Committee, located in an alley off Foroughi Street in downtown Tehran, had carte blanche to investigate and arrest almost anyone in the country. For example, in April, 1973, during a break in the trial of several persons accused of plotting against the royal family, two *Kayhan* reporters, Massoud Alai'i and Mustafa Bashi, greeted one of the defendants, their former colleague Khosrow Golesorkhi.

They were immediately arrested. Alai'i was released after he wrote an article denouncing the plot; Bashi was kept in jail four months.

Whatever the actual number of informers, their omnipresence was a basic article of Iranian belief. One veteran East Tehran resident said he personally knew forty full-time agents within a square kilometer of his home; an Iranian journalist said that each of Tehran's twenty-nine police precincts had its own intelligence section where a SAVAK team administered a network of informers. SAVAK's Internal Security Department ran its own separate system as well.

In October, 1976 the shah told CBS's "Sixty Minutes" what Iranian students had long claimed—that SAVAK also operated in the United States. There were about fifteen to twenty officials working mostly out of Iranian consulates, perhaps fifty to one hundred full-time informers, plus a number of others on retainer. Students involved in political activity were threatened with loss of scholarships and persecution at home unless they cooperated by reporting on their peers.

SAVAK also exchanged information with the CIA. In fact, since CIA operatives in Iran concentrated on gathering material about the Soviets and since they were careful not to offend the shah, the United States was almost completely dependent on SAVAK for intelligence on developments in Iran itself. At times, President Nixon and Secretary of State Kissinger expressed displeasure at the CIA's heavy reliance on liaison with local intelligence agencies in various countries, but this system was still in place at the time of the 1978–79 revolution.

Like many authoritarian leaders, the shah had great difficulty in understanding the internal workings of a free country. He constantly mistook American permissiveness toward the anti-shah political activities of Iranian students or exiles as United States government support for them. This led to frequent complaints from Iran's Foreign Ministry: Why, they asked, would Washington allow such attacks on a friendly country? The shah was particularly eager to avoid any demonstrations during his trips to the United States; he interpreted the violent Washington march during his December, 1977

White House visit as an intended signal of Carter administration disfavor toward him.

A particular target of Tehran's ire was the *Iran Free Press*, an outspoken anti-shah newspaper published in Virginia by Nasser Afshar, a naturalized American citizen. On numerous occasions, Iran's Foreign Ministry requested information on Afshar, which was supplied, and requested that the publication be shut down. The State Department replied that while the paper might well be irresponsible and inaccurate, no legal steps could be taken against it.

Some time in 1975 or 1976, SAVAK decided to assassinate Afshar. They requested a complete file on the editor from the CIA, without apprising them of their final intentions. The Agency went to the FBI, obtained a file on Afshar and turned it over to SAVAK. In the meantime, the CIA obtained word that SAVAK had been training a non-Iranian assassin, though it did not know for what purpose. Some months later, the man in question contacted the CIA, told them that he had been ordered to carry out the murder, but had refused to go through with it.

On a more mundane level, the CIA exchanged information with SAVAK on Iranian students, justified by Tehran's real problem with terrorists. A very large number of the students, of course, chose to stay in the United States after graduation, more often for personal and professional than for political reasons. The CIA also trained SAVAK, up to the time of the shah's fall, in such areas as surveillance techniques, agent handling, and intelligence-gathering methods.

Within Iran itself, the CIA and the American Embassy played only the most marginal of roles. Far from being a "nest of spies," the embassy was, due to its extreme caution in avoiding any offense to the shah, poorly informed. Thus, there was little reporting on human-rights violations until 1975, when Amnesty International, the International Commission of Jurists, and the United States media brought the subject to public attention.

Embassy staffers were somewhat beleaguered. Any Iranian they spoke to might be a SAVAK agent and their remarks might quickly reach even the shah himself; they suspected that their mail was opened by Iranian censors. The shah's regime was so eager to control all information that it even requested in May, 1976 the closure of the United States Armed Forces Radio and Television Network because its Iranian listeners—estimated at 200,000—knew it to be an objective source of news. American personnel were told not to divulge to any American correspondent information that the Iranian government did not want disclosed.

Outside of university unrest and urban terrorists, whose activities were covered in intelligence reports, no structured internal opposition existed; consequently, the embassy cannot be faulted for failing to find active dissidents. But this was not the issue: the real problem was the failure to penetrate the shah's public relations facade, to gather information from unofficial sources, to transmit the serious discontent that was spreading among the people, and to describe the serious problems facing them.

These shortcomings were due in part to the tight control exercised by the Iranian government and in part to self-imposed limits. The United States did not want to offend such a sensitive and important ally; the State Department hierarchy was determined to discourage critical views of existing policy.

The best of American diplomatic and intelligence reporting often reflects the shrewd analysis of a full-time specialist who studies a specific subject from a wide range of sources. Even with the right person in the job, it is still very difficult to make accurate predictions of future developments. Further, the best kinds of information generally come from open discussion with one's counterparts in official and unofficial meetings; in situations where different political factions are trying to elicit United States sympathy or support, these factions themselves test the validity of conflicting opinions. Neither of these conditions existed in the American considerations of an Iranian policy. The tendency was, instead, to depend solely on the country's elite for data; Iranian officials were discouraged from being open with their United States counterparts. Further, the concentration of American personnel in the capital city also limited the information to which Americans could have access regarding the real situation in the rest of the country.

Foreign Service Officers often wear a set of political, bureaucratic, and cultural blinders. They are accustomed to serving existing policy. Promotion is enhanced by the ability to get along with the ambassador and with the conventional wisdom. Many American diplomats move in narrow and relatively Westernized circles, with only a superficial understanding of the language, history, and ideology of the country in which they serve. Although there are many honorable exceptions, those who would be critical of existing policy must also filter their reports through an ambassador whose standing in Washington may depend on his ability to get along with the host regime. He has an incentive to reassure Washington that all is going well and that American policy is being effectively implemented.*

After information is collected it must be interpreted. Despite Iran's importance, however, the State Department had few officers familiar with that country. Among the reasons for this is one that is absurdly simple: because personnel are frequently moved around (two- to three-year tours of duty are common) it made little sense from a career point of view to specialize in so distinctive a country. It had long been the accepted wisdom among careerists that generalists had far better prospects for promotion than those who established themselves in narrow areas of expertise. It is no wonder then that there was no shortage of Arabists, who could broaden their foreign service experience by serving in any one or more of two dozen different countries; in contrast, a knowledge of Farsi would be useful only in one.

As an explanation of the department's lack of adequate understanding, Iran's rise to importance had been so rapid that there had not been time to reverse employee trends and de-

---

* It is fascinating to compare the structural problems of the American Embassy in Tehran with those of its counterpart in Saigon during the collapse of South Vietnam. The inside account of Frank Snepp, Decent Interval (New York, 1977), provides many parallels.

velop a better-prepared group of Iran experts. Further, any Iran specialist who offended the shah's government, and was declared persona non grata and ineligible to return to Iran, would have had his value to the department sharply curtailed.

At any rate, the State Department Middle East regional bureau tended to focus on Arab issues, particularly the Arab-Israeli conflict and on the unstable patterns of Arab politics. Iran policy was considered a success precisely because that country seemed, to use the then-current phrase, an island of stability in a tumultuous area.

At last, one comes to the level of persuasion. Once data has been analyzed it must be explained to the real decision-makers, those at the top of the State Department, the National Security Council and, most important, the staff and resident of the White House. These people generally have little or no experience in dealing with the Middle East and rarely have studied the region. As one veteran of the process put it after two decades of such efforts: "If you can't get them to understand the difference between Sunni and Shi'a Islam, you can hardly go on to more subtle points."

Policymakers usually approach problems with a predetermined view of the situation—the "conception" in intelligence jargon—often hallowed by long years of continuity in a foreign political system or conflict. The conception of the shah's Iran was that of a strong, emerging state, a close ally, and a regional pillar. Leaders can develop a strong vested interests in a given interpretation of events and, as human beings, like to believe that their policies are enjoying success. In short, they prefer to hear only good news about the correctness of policies they themselves had instituted.

In the United States government there is a high value placed on bureaucratic discipline, a virtue of which Henry Kissinger was an outspoken admirer. To tame the bureaucracy, he believed, was a precondition to successful diplomacy. The irony is that once tamed, the bureaucracy will reinforce the prevailing views at the top. For better or worse, it can also create a surprising degree of conformity in the administrations that follow.

Since all three levels suffered from shortcomings in dealing with Iran, the government's inability to keep up with developments there is not surprising. The Iranian Embassy in Washington worked its spell on elements in Congress and on the mass media. The restrictions placed on the American Embassy in Tehran sometimes made it hard to learn seemingly simple things.

The most devastating error may have been the failure to discover the shah's cancer. There were rumors in Tehran, for example those denied by Iranian government spokesmen in September, 1975, that the shah was drawn and thin because of a lingering and grave malady. But these stirred no great curiosity in Washington: embassy reports portrayed the shah as fit and healthy. Consequently, the American government spent the first nine months of 1978 waiting for some strong response to the revolution from a man broken in both body and spirit.

The embassy also tried—and failed—in its effort to find out how many political prisoners there actually were in Iran. In the end, they simply accepted the official Iranian figures, which high-ranking American officials used repeatedly in testimony and speeches.

Such political and information considerations explain Atherton's warm defense of Iran's human rights record in September, 1976 congressional hearings.[23] Modernization was a difficult process, he began, and yet the shah's White Revolution had achieved great things. Land titles had been distributed to 2.6 million people, women's rights had been furthered, and Iran now boasted a Literacy Corps, a Health Corps, rural development teams, profit-sharing schemes, and subsidies to stabilize prices. The shah had destroyed reactionary vested interests—tribal chiefs and large landowners—who stood in the way of progress.

Referring to the two main terrorist groups, the only visible opposition at the time, he commented that "their principle motivation appears to be the destruction of the current society and its leaders; these groups have not promoted constructive alternatives." Although Atherton did not say so at the time, it was known that they were trained by some of the Palestine Liberation Organization's constituent groups.

In view of the Iranian government's military court system,

he continued, "it is difficult to discount the many persistent reports" of torture. He did not condone cases of "harsh methods" but many of these reports were two to three years old and, most recently, "all concerned terrorists." An embassy investigation showed, he maintained, "that many of those alleged to have been tortured had been killed or wounded in armed exchanges with the security forces or suffered wounds during the clandestine preparation of explosives."

Under the strictest definition of political prisoners, Atherton went on, Iran held only 100 to 150. Most of the total of 2,800 to 3,500 jailed for offenses against the state had been convicted of specific acts of violence. The United States did not make official representations to Iran on human rights questions for the reason that the administration of the judicial and penal system "is above all a matter of internal Iranian responsibility, and that one sovereign country should not interfere lightly in another's domestic affairs."

Assistant Secretary of State Atherton concluded at the congressional hearing: "I believe that the advances which have been made in improving the human rights of the broad majority of Iran's population under considerable adversity far outweigh such abuses as have occurred in an attempt to control the violent challenges to the government."

It cannot be doubted that in making such statements American officials were trying to avoid any offense to the shah. Realpolitik dictated that he was the ruler of Iran and would, the White House thought, remain so for the forseeable future. Washington needed and would continue to need his friendship and favor in protecting America's regional interests. Yet such statements were no mere cynical instruments of statecraft; as far as one can tell, the vast majority of American policymakers sincerely—and mistakenly—believed them to be true.

Ambassador Helms was also a strong advocate of the continuing correctness of the two-pillar policy. As he put it in a February, 1976 speech at Iran's National Defense University: "Because of the the tremendous amounts of oil that are shipped out of the Gulf. . . . It is no overstatement to say that the Persian Gulf is a life line for all the world." This route must be kept open and safe; the United States saw Iranians "as a stabilizing influence in the region" who were "able to defend themselves against outside threats and to play a role commensurate with their interests." Certainly rapidly modernizing Iran was going through an inevitable period of difficulties, policymakers told each other, but in a few years the country would settle down and assimilate all the benefits of its progress.

Helms not only believed in Iran's strategic importance, but also respected the shah's leverage vis-à-vis the United States. The shah's acceptance of United States listening posts in northern Iran to gather information on Soviet missile launches—an important resource in verification requirements for the SALT treaty—as well as his purchases of arms on a cash basis and his regional leadership role made him a figure who could not be easily influenced by the United States.

The appointment of Helms as ambassador to Iran seems to have been a spur-of-the-moment decision. When President Nixon found it expedient to fire the director because of his refusal to use the agency to bail Nixon out of Watergate, he offered Helms an embassy appointment as consolation. Helms suggested Iran as a major post, which, unlike the big European embassies, was not run directly from Washington.[24]

Nonetheless, the presence of the former head of the CIA in the American Embassy in Iran was a symbol of the bilateral relationship's importance. One often-told story has it that a Soviet ambassador once asked Hoveyda, "Why do the Americans send you their Number 1 spy?" The Iranian prime minister looked him straight in the eye and answered, "Because they are our friends. They do not send us their number 10 man." The story, likely apocryphal, illustrates the point that the shah appreciated the appointment of such a seemingly powerful man, with direct lines to the White House; the shah's successors saw it as one more item of proof that the real role of the American Embassy was to act as nerve center for American domination and interference in Iran.

By the end of 1976, however, the United States-Iranian relationship was undergoing a serious challenge within the United States. In part, this took place within the broader context of the soul-searching that followed the Vietnam War and the Watergate scandal. As a *Washington Post* editorial put it, many found Nixon's legacy on Iran, "an implicit commitment that Americans cannot accept—and yet cannot easily reject. Condemning this kind of high-handed and irresponsible statecraft is simple enough. But working out a remedy is going to be as difficult as it is urgent." [25]

President Ford's opponent, Democratic candidate Jimmy Carter, raised another criticism in their October 6 debate. The United States had become, "contrary to our long-standing beliefs and principles—the arms merchant of the whole world." Ford replied that Carter did not understand the need for arms sales: Iran, with Iraq and the USSR as neighbors, needed those weapons to protect its security. [26]

Within the administration, the growing criticisms set off defensive reactions. Some few were convinced that the time had come to get out the truth about existing problems; most saw the criticism as an impugning of their own work. Maybe the complaints about arms transfers and the shah's behavior were true, they said, but following the existing policy was vital to American security. Firm in this belief, they tried to make reports more palatable to Congress and to the public, obscuring some bothersome facts.

Obviously, the shah himself preferred Ford's re-election. The incumbents were well known to him as supporters of his own objectives. Carter, with his talk of human rights and arms-sales cutbacks, introduced a worrisome factor.

The architects of the two-pillar policy, on the other hand, were generally more secure in the belief that the policy would continue no matter who won the election. Their position, they believed, was based on objective facts. The shah was strong in authority if not in personality; Iran was successfully modernizing, economically and militarily. Even if the shah were to disappear, Iran's policy was not likely to change—the Iranian military was the ultimate guarantor of the pro-American alignment. They had long worked with Americans, been trained by

Americans, used American weapons and needed American spare parts to continue to maintain their arsenal. The Soviets, Iraqis, and other hostile forces would still stand at their borders to remind them of their need for a strong friend.

In short, although the domestic assault on administration policy increased rather than abated, many—probably most—government officials, members of Congress, and reporters still accepted substantially the misleading image built up by the shah. Even those who railed against the amounts of arms sales or against repression still thought that they were dealing with a fully-clothed emperor. It was the very confidence the shah had generated among his allies that was to contribute to his downfall.

7
The Pillar Crumbles
1977–78

In January, 1977, President Jimmy Carter, a politician outspoken on human rights and arms exports—the two most controversial issues in United States-Iranian relations—entered the White House. Despite expectations, his administration did not inaugurate a sudden sharp break with its predecessors' practices.

Three factors helped determine the direction of Carter administration policy on Iran. First was the tremendous momentum of previous American commitments regarding regional strategy and arms sales. Most of the career officials kept over from the previous regime supported the two-pillar and Nixon Doctrine approaches and even those few within the administration who were critical of standing policy differed with the majority mainly on tactical grounds. After all, unless they were willing to accept a much-enlarged direct projection of American power into the region, they were faced with the same reality of United States dependence on Iran that had motivated the policy in the first place. Further, American political and military strategy was somewhat like a large and unwieldy ship that required considerable time to be turned about. In 1977, the Carter administration was dealing with arms deliveries planned for 1981 and beyond—schedules had already been set for the president's entire first term. In addition, as long as the policy seemed to be working—that is, that it had not broken down into crisis—it was bureaucratically difficult to push through any revisions.

Second, the Carter administration was slow to recognize the signs when the policy did go into crisis—the White House did not seem to understand the seriousness of the situation until November, 1978, after ten months of riots and demonstrations in Iran—because its own image of that country was based on perceptions it had inherited from its predecessors. Few among the new officials challenged the belief that the shah was a relatively successful modernizer, albeit a somewhat ruthless one, and was quite capable of maintaining order at home. Indeed, critics within the new administration much more often expressed concern that the shah was becoming too powerful rather than that he might lose power. His influence on oil prices, his huge arsenal, and his regional ambitions all psychologically prepared the Carter White House for problems that might be brought about by an excessively strong shah—not an excessively weak one.

In the inner-government debate over arms sales, those urging restraint based their argument on President Carter's injunction that the United States not be the first to introduce new kinds or quantities of weaponry into the region. Supporters of the standing policy thought the Gulf so important and so unstable that the shah had to be given the equipment he demanded in order to defend it. Critics questioned Iran's human rights record; defenders claimed the shah had made much progress on that front. Those favoring cutbacks expressed fears of a regional arms race; those favoring high levels of arms sales pointed to Iraq's own buildup and to Soviet gains in the Horn of Africa, South Yemen, and Afghanistan as justifying a strengthening of the shah's forces.

In these debates advocates of large-scale arms sales to Iran almost always won. Their trump argument was that denial of weapons would be not only a risky vote of no-confidence in the shah's leadership at a time America needed Iran's help but also futile, since the shah would merely buy what he wanted elsewhere. Both sides of the debate focused on the international aspects of United States-Iranian relations and not on Iran's domestic problems. The critics of existing policy could barely win official recognition of the powerful argument that Iran was experiencing difficulty absorbing weaponry already delivered.[1]

Third, the American response to Iran's problems both before and during the revolution were conditioned by the administration's international vision. Coming to power in the aftermath of the Vietnam War, Carter and his advisors were reluctant to commit the United States to helping repress overseas political unrest, particularly in conflicts and in situations where military involvement might become necessary. To some extent, in the case of Iran, this reluctance represented a logical continuation of the Nixon Doctrine. If the shah was strong enough to preserve order in the region, with American help generally being limited to aid and advice, he certainly ought to be expected to maintain order at home.

Yet the Carter White House deemed revolutions against dictators part of the natural process of history. In such situations they placed more emphasis on maintaining a posture capable of adjustment to changing political circumstances than on active counterinsurgency. They also doubted that the United States would ever again be able to manage international events to the extent it once had.

A review of the handling of human rights and arms-sales questions vis-à-vis Iran in 1977 reveals some of the inner ambiguities of the Carter policy. As early as September, 1976, the shah, concerned about American congressional and media attacks on his image, invited the International Commission of Jurists (ICJ), Amnesty International (AI), and the International Red Cross (IRC) to suggest ways of improving the human rights situation in Iran. These agencies held a number of meetings with Iranian officials; IRC representatives toured Iranian prisons.

It is not clear whether their recommendations had any long-standing effect on the treatment of Iranian prisoners, but several respected outside observers suggested that progress had been made. Iranian expert James Bill called 1977 "the year of liberalization"; Richard Cottam reported that the shah was improving prison conditions and had ended torture.*

At the same time, as these and other sources reported, arrests continued. The influential Ayatollah Mahmud Teleghani, for example, was sentenced to ten years imprisonment. While no American pressure was actually applied on the shah, Washington did discuss two specific issues with Iranian officials, urging that innocent people should not be arrested and that prisoners should not be tortured. These appeals were distinguished from any call for a broader liberalization of the political system, which was not made. There was a big difference, of course, between requests that prisoners not be beaten and demands that Iran be transformed into a democracy. Complaints after the revolution by the shah and his defenders that Washington forced him to become too soft, and thus encouraged the upheaval, seem, simply, to have no basis in fact. The human rights issue did provide one political dividend for the American Embassy in Tehran. In attempts to hear from the other side contacts were renewed for the first time in years with opposition leaders, particularly some in the National Front, who would play important roles during the revolution.

Despite these limited efforts, the United States government spent more time defending the shah's human rights record than it did criticizing it. The State Department hierarchy saw the human rights issue as a nuisance that might create frictions in United States-Iranian relations, which it was their job to protect. In preparing their annual reports and hearings on human rights, they fought among themselves more over their portrayal of Iran than over that of any other country in the

---

*Currently available information throws considerable doubt on whether such progress was made. Some sources claim that the only prisoners IRC visitors were allowed to speak with were guards in convicts' clothing. On the other hand, the total number of political prisoners seems to have been closer to the lower official estimates than to the huge figures cited by the opposition and widely accepted by Americans after the shah's fall.

world. Most of the time, the State Department regional specialists emerged victorious.

The congressionally-mandated State Department human rights report prepared in late 1977 rationalized Iran's performance by reference to the forced pace of economic and social modernization and to the threat posed by terrorism. Though arbitrary imprisonment and unfair trials continued, the report said, the penal code was fairly enlightened and there were now fewer allegations of torture. They estimated that there were 3,300 to 3,700 political prisoners, but that the number had been reduced by the shah's amnesties.

"Roughly two-thirds of the Iranian Government's total spending in the period 1973–78 can be classified as outlay for economic development and social welfare programs," the study concluded. "We believe the Iranian Government is committed to prison reform and that prison conditions have indeed improved." In short, the Iranian government was said to be doing a good job in meeting human needs and to be genuinely trying to improve its performance on human rights.[2]

The State Department's report of the following year, prepared in the midst of the revolution, was only marginally more critical. It agreed that the development of political institutions had lagged behind economic modernization and that in the past "violations of human rights by security forces were fairly common-place," but this had begun to change in recent years. Torture in prisons "apparently ended" in early 1977 and substantial numbers of political prisoners were released. Early in 1978 the government announced reforms, including civil court trials for political offenders, greater choice of counsel, and increased judicial protection for the individual. True, during the fighting there were numerous instances of harsh and often brutal treatment, but they might have been produced by an erosion of SAVAK discipline, it was claimed.[3]

In contrast, a study by the respected Congressional Research Service released in July, 1978 was far more critical. It spoke of the need to weigh "the benefits of modernization . . . against present limitations on individual freedoms and civil rights."

The White Revolution achieved "considerable success" in the former field but also "engendered an intolerance toward political dissent and has led to an increasing reliance upon the armed forces and security organizations to control opposition elements."[4] Military expenditures had competed with funding for economic development. Growth was unbalanced, waste extensive, projected goals were not met, housing was in short supply and inflation was a continuing problem.

Contrary to retrospective impressions, the State Department hardly went out of its way to criticize Iran. Even when repressive techniques were cited, they were counterposed to the successful modernization efforts underway. But it was the nature of modernization itself—its methods and impact on the lives of Iranians—that caused as much or possibly even more opposition to the shah than did human rights violations. Iranians therefore turned toward the alternative, negative view of modernization offered by Khomeini's camp. American policymakers and journalists, with a naive belief in the force of economic development in politics, had great difficulty understanding the roots of this response, even after the revolution.

As the revolution approached, the shah's nervousness about the administration's intentions was matched by the opposition's hopefulness. Particularly expectant were those elements of the National Front that had been friendly toward the United States. In May, 1977, fifty-four Iranian lawyers signed a declaration protesting legal revisions they felt undermined the judiciary's independence. The following month, National Front leaders, including Karim Sanjabi and Shahpour Bakhtiar, issued an open letter calling for an end to the dictatorship and for implementation of the 1906 constitution. These appeals received no open encouragement from Washington yet even some of the religious opposition seems to have had hopes for American sympathy. "We didn't expect Carter to defend the shah," Ayatollah Hussein Montazeri later recalled, "for he is a religious man who has raised the slogan of defending human rights. How can Carter, the devout Christian, defend the Shah?"[5]

If Washington's human rights policy had sent some confusing signals, its arms-sales policy continued to be one of clear support for the shah. Despite Tehran's cutbacks in purchases, the shah continued to obtain about one-third of all United States foreign military sales. In a two-and-a-half hour meeting with the shah in May, 1977— the month in which President Carter articulated his new policy of limiting military exports—Secretary of State Cyrus Vance promised that the United States would remain Iran's main arms supplier. The idea of linking such sales to human rights reform was not even discussed; Vance denied any intention to seek such leverage.

During the Carter administration's first few months it did attempt to distance itself from most of the prior Kissinger-Ford policies. As one senior White House official put it, "The shah has to learn this isn't the Nixon-Kissinger administration any more." In May, 1977 Carter's arms-export guidelines mandated that all sales be demonstrably in the national interest, that a quantitative ceiling be placed on them, that the government more closely supervise companies, and that the United States not be the first to introduce new weapons into a region.

Thus, the new president tacitly abandoned the 1972 United States-Iranian understanding and returned to the normal arms-sales-review process for the first time in a decade. During those early months, Carter himself sometimes studied specific proposals in great detail. Congressional review provisions had also been strengthened, stretching the time for consideration of administration requests. Pressures on the bureaucracy to approve all new sales, such as the White House had applied in prior years, were removed. But the emphasis remained on gradual change rather than on dramatic reversals.

In practice, the changed attitude had little practical effect on sales to Iran. One exception involved several navy frigates. In early 1978, to circumvent its own quota, the administration had to arrange to have the ships built in West Germany and Holland while the United States provided only the armament. In another instance, the F–18 was not sold to Iran because the American military did not want to build it for itself. Orders for

F–16s and AWACs were delayed by internal debates and congressional criticism.

The administration's original resolution was eroded by the natural processes of the presidency. New chief executives, along with their staffs and appointees, come into office with large-scale ideas for changing everything, only to settle down into old patterns as existing power groups and national interests assert themselves. Both outside criticisms and internal doubts about the dangers of excessive idealism also played a part with the Carter administration, as did the loyalties of career officials toward policies they had been implementing for years.

Although there was more freedom of debate within the Carter administration than there had been during the Nixon and Ford years, the advocates of change usually lost on the Iran issue. National Security Advisor Zbigniew Brzezinski and Ambassador William Sullivan were strongly against exerting any pressure on the shah. Other key people, such as Assistant Secretary of State for Middle East and South Asian Affairs Alfred Atherton and the director of the Office of Iranian Affairs Henry Precht, who had just returned from service in the Tehran embassy, also supported the established policy.

Iran's declining oil revenues, however, continued to force some cutbacks in purchases. In February, 1977, faced with such deficits, the shah trimmed $2 billion from his defense budget, while also reducing spending on foreign aid and internal development. Contributing to the shah's new willingness to go along with military cutbacks were his military's increasing absorption problems: Iran was one year behind on training support personnel and establishing facilities for the F–14; millions of dollars worth of radar equipment rusted in warehouses.

The biggest dispute over arms sales took place not between Iran and the Departments of State or Defense but between the White House and Congress. This concerned the sale of seven AWACs (Airborne Warning and Control system) early-warning radar planes, modified Boeing 707s full of elaborate radar, communications, and jamming equipment. These units, each carrying a crew of seventeen and costing $125 million apiece, had radar systems capable of looking down on a two hundred-nautical-mile radius of air space. If the Soviets were to obtain its secrets they would counter American cruise missiles; consequently, preserving the security of AWACs was of the greatest importance. CIA Director Admiral Stansfield Turner had serious reservations over the sale, as did a number of senators.

In reply, the White House and Defense Department pointed out that Iran had already received other advanced equipment without security mishap. Since Iran had no air-defense system the shah had put a high priority on obtaining one. The alternative to AWACs—a ground-based chain of radar installations—would have been far more expensive and would have required more technicians to maintain than the four hundred needed for the AWACs.

Selling AWACs to Iran would also bring down the per unit cost low enough for these systems to be attractive to Western European NATO members. These purchases, in turn, would bring the price down to a level at which Congress might be willing to allocate funds for the United States military to have the system. Nevertheless, when the proposal was sent to Congress in the spring of 1977 there was widespread opposition. In July, the House International Relations Committee voted nineteen to seventeen to block it; its Senate counterpart seemed likely to do the same. With summer adjournment coming up President Carter decided to withdraw the request temporarily rather than face rejection by Congress.

During recess, two compromises were worked out. The Senate Foreign Relations Committee asked for and received assurances from the president that the sale would "stabilize the Middle East regional military balance." On the security issue the president promised to remove encipherment gear and other especially sensitive equipment, to institute continuous monitoring of Iranian security precautions, and to cancel the deal if these were inadequate. The sale was then ratified.[6]

Iran needed and deserved AWACs, Secretary Vance said, because the shah was a major oil supplier for the United States and a protector of regional stability: "To preserve our mutual confidence Iran must know that the United States will help it to meet its legitimate defense requirements." Critics disagreed. A *Washington Post* editorial called the sale "an embarrassment to Mr. Carter's professed intention to reduce the American role as the leading arms merchant in the world." Twenty-two senators had tried to block the AWACs transaction but had lacked the required votes.[7]

Given Iran's extensive and vulnerable borders, a comprehensive air-defense system seemed a reasonably nonlethal, innately defensive type of equipment for the United States properly to provide. The strenuous opposition and controversy in Washington shows just how far congressional reservations had come over the arms-transfer program. Undeniably, in hindsight the security argument seems compelling, but fortunately, since delivery was scheduled for 1981, none of these planes were in Iran at the time of the revolution.

The second White House-Congress agreement assisting passage of the AWACs proposal was an administration promise to restudy the weapons-sales program. Some Defense Department experts felt real progress had been made since the crisis days of 1975 and 1976. Iran, they argued, was becoming self-sufficient in some areas of maintenance and in recruitment of technicians. Admittedly, contractor performance was uneven and Iranian forces continued to suffer from command and logistical problems, they added, but in a few years, say by 1985, Tehran would possess a competent and powerful military.

Thus, the classified State/Defense study yielded few surprises. It spoke about absorption problems with a candor not found in preceding years, but the old optimism still dominated. Also repeated was the list of geopolitical problems said to necessitate the buildup: the Soviet and Iraqi threats and Iran's importance in maintaining regional stability.

Others within the government, however, stressed still-unresolved difficulties. A Pentagon study requested by Defense Secretary Harold Brown reported in November that contractor competition was a continuing barrier to smooth operations. For them, "the stakes are so high and the temptation so great," the report concluded, "that they will continue in the future to pay agents' fees which can be shared by the Iranian officials." It called for additional restraints.[8]

In its contribution to the report for Congress, the State Department's Policy Planning Staff also dissented from the general optimism. It found a large and growing potential for political and social instability in Iran, to which weapons-absorption problems were adding. A strong Iran, their survey added, required more than a well-armed Iran—it also necessitated domestic tranquility. This view did not prevail.

Thus, the arms-sale program continued despite further congressional criticism, including Senate Majority Leader Robert Byrd's November call for a moratorium. An exchange of visits between President Carter and the shah in November, and December, 1977 was set up to reinforce mutual confidence and understanding between the two governments. There were many questions on the shah's mind. He wanted to know how the changing state of United States-Soviet relations might affect his interests and wanted reassurance that America was not entering a post-Vietnam stage of isolationism. Regional events also engaged his attention. There was Soviet intervention in the Horn of Africa and the disorder in neighboring Afghanistan that would lead to a Marxist coup in April 1978. Reports of declining Soviet oil production raised the possibility that Moscow might seek direct or indirect control over petroleum-producing sections of the Middle East.

This twelfth visit of the shah to Washington might have been successful in its private talks but was a fiasco on the public level. In Washington, 4,000 anti-shah students outside the White House attacked 1,500 pro-shah demonstrators —some of whom were subsidized by the Iranian Embassy —with clubs, leading to 124 injuries among marchers and police. Tear gas drifted over the White House's south lawn during the arrival ceremony, causing Carter to blink and wipe his eyes and the shah to dab at his face with a handkerchief. The protesters shouted, "Down with the fascist Shah" and "Down with U.S. imperialism." The occasion provoked student demonstrations in Tehran; fifty-six lawyers, writers, professors, and judges, mostly associated with the National Front, signed an open letter calling for disbandment of SAVAK and for free elections.

Despite these storm warnings, the shah was happy about his meetings with Carter. They discussed new Iranian arms orders and, to please his host as well as to stabilize his falling oil sales, the shah promised to oppose petroleum price increases at the next OPEC meeting. To reassure the shah, the president praised Iran as having "blossomed forth under enlightened leadership" and as having become "a very stabilizing force in the world at large" to which the United States was bound "with unbreakable ties" and an "unshakable" military alliance. Congress had to be consulted on future arms sales, the president added, but the shah needn't worry—already $12 billion in military equipment was in the pipeline, moving toward delivery in the coming years.[9]

Yet the signs of crisis within Iran continued. Even before the shah's Washington visit, Hoveyda resigned as prime minister in the face of increasing economic difficulties, shortages of consumer goods, and five-hour daily blackouts. Riot police put down demonstrations in November; lawyers who had signed protest letters were blacklisted. As in the early 1960s, the National Front hoped to win United States support and thought that Carter's human rights policy might protect their public statements. Bakhtiar greeted the president's arrival in December: "We have always supported Mr. Carter's campaign for human rights," he said, adding that he hoped the issue would be raised with the shah.[10]

But as far as could be heard publicly, Carter had only praise for Iran's ruler: "Iran is an island of stability in one of the more troubled areas of the world," the president said in one speech. "This is a great tribute to you, Your Majesty, and to your leadership and to the respect, admiration and love which your people give to you."[11] This might have been meant as no more than polite talk to an ally but it was still disappointing to the moderate Iranian opposition.

Nor was it all no more than diplomatic flattery. As 1978 began, the overwhelming majority of United States government officials and analysts believed that Iran would continue to be a strong ally. Information to the contrary was ignored. A later investigation by Congress concluded that "consumers did not demand analysis of the Shah's stability. Large arms transfers and other major policies in the region were pursued without the benefit of in-depth analysis of the Iranian political scene."[12] This was so, the study continued, because "long-standing U.S. attitudes toward the Shah inhibited intelligence collection, dampened policymakers' appetite for analysis of the Shah's position, and deafened policymakers to the warning implicit in available current intelligence." Analysts were not encouraged to challenge conventional wisdom, which many accepted anyway, either out of habit or out of conviction. Dissenting views were weeded out as briefings and position papers wended their way up the chain of command.

Such processes were by no means new in 1977. Before Jesse Leaf, at the time the CIA's chief Iran analyst, resigned in 1973, he wrote a report critical of the shah's policies as "sowing the seed for popular dissidence."[13] This conclusion was deleted because, a superior told him, it did not reflect overall United States policy toward Iran. The point missed by that official, of course, was that CIA findings should not have reflected United States policy but rather real conditions. This confusion in goals has continually vitiated the value of American intelligence agencies. Policymakers have held little interest in evaluations that have not confirmed the validity and efficacy of their own past decisions. "Until recently you couldn't give away intelligence on Iran," one specialist explained. Besides, CIA operatives in Iran were under as many restrictions in the collection of information as was the embassy. During the two years before the revolution the agency had few contacts with the religious opposition.

The idea of omnipotent intelligence agencies has been over-drawn by both the friends and critics of those institutions. It is a high-risk profession, trying to predict results of the interaction of a large variety of factors in situations where the outcome is subject to influence by whatever new players choose to thrust themselves into the game. The force of one man's personality can alter the outcome of the most apparently predictable event. A high percentage of the data gathered and the rumors intercepted are inaccurate. Much of the best work is done through the mundane use of publicly available sources: newspaper articles, statistics, radio broadcasts, and scholarly research. Often, despite the best efforts, drastic mistakes are made. Few analysts of the early thirties, for example, thought Hitler would be able to take power in Germany.[14]

Over time, observers of international affairs tend to take for granted the predictability and rationality of events. In his book on the CIA, Thomas Powers defines the two main clues used to understand a country's future behavior as "past behavior" and the belief that "no nation will run a risk without substantial chance of success in achieving a commensurate gain."[15] Obviously, these were not reliable guides to events in Iran in 1978 and thereafter.

Still, the religious opposition in Iran had been quiescent for fifteen years; Iran had undergone a seemingly great economic boom; and the shah's armed forces—standing at 350,000 men in mid-1977, 220,000 of them in the army—seemed adequate to deal with any internal challenge. CIA director Admiral Stansfield Turner later said that he knew of "no other intelligence service that predicted trouble in Iran" and that "even Ayatollah Khomeini didn't realize how well his force was moving along."[16]

The shah himself was baffled by the speed and popularity of the revolution—a sign of his isolation, which was itself one cause of the problem. "Driving through the city of Meshed in an open car only four months before the situation became desperate," he later said, "I was acclaimed by 300,000 people. Just after the troubles in Tabriz [in February, 1978] my prime minister went there and had an overwhelming reception. I can recall nothing in the history of the world—not even the French revolution—to compare with what happened subsequently."[17] Bereft of his closest advisor, Minister of Court Assadollah Alam who had died about a year before the revolution, and dependent on the inept and self-serving intelligence of SAVAK, the shah was told and shown only what his courtiers thought he wished to hear and see.

Most important, French doctors who examined the shah in early 1978 told him that he was fatally ill with cancer and that problems involving irrigation of the brain could slow his reactions and decision-making ability. This prognosis, which never became known to the United States government, made him listless and fatalistic, contributing to his personal collapse in the face of the revolution. This alone does not explain the difference between the shah's image and his performance. Even without this burden he was a weak and indecisive man.

Accepting the shah's self-evaluation of himself as commanding the loyalty of his people and of his seemingly successful past performance, however, the American government thought he was better qualified than any American to judge and deal with his country's domestic uprising. Given the amount of power centralized in his hands and the limited capability for United States involvement it was hard to see any option. After all, policymakers said, the shah had been on the throne thirty-seven years and had weathered many crises. He had created the Iranian government virtually single-handedly, possessed great wealth, excellent international connections, and the best-equipped, best-trained, most loyal army in the region. For years he had given Washington lectures on how to conduct policy. The man charged with the responsibility of protecting the entire region should surely be able to maintain his own regime on an even keel. All that was necessary were verbal assurances of Washington's support.

There had been much talk in Washington of what might happen if the shah were to die, but no one considered the possibility that he might remain very much alive, holding all the reins of authority, and yet incapable of exercising his power in any coherent manner. This was the crisis the United States would face in 1978. When Kermit Roosevelt, who well knew of the shah's weaknesses during the 1953 imbroglio, tried to explain the monarch's shortcomings to the Carter administration his advice fell on deaf ears.

Nevertheless, it would be foolishly simplistic to see the revolution as a mere response to a ruler's weakness. The progressive breakdown of Iran's economic and social system, plus the

long-standing resentment over repression and other government policies, merged with the ineffectual response from the
throne to create contempt for the shah's authority. The final
element was the emergence of a charismatic figure capable of
competing with the shah for public loyalty—even among the
peasants and conscript soldiers—Ayatollah Ruhollah Khomeini.[18]

The shah's wavering reactions could also be attributed to
the peculiar pattern of the revolution itself. Each wave of rioting was followed by a period of calm, encouraging Tehran
and Washington in their wishful thinking that the movement
was simply running its course before dying out. Actually, the
demonstrations followed the cycle of Shi'a mourning: every
forty days marches were held to honor those killed in the
previous round. During periods of high activity, as in early
September and early November, the shah would tend to favor
a harder line; when things seemed calmer, as in late August
and early October, he switched to a softer strategy.

The shah must have remembered his success in riding out
the 1962–63 upheaval over the White Revolution and, earlier,
in co-opting opposition elements after Mossadegh's fall. On
these two occasions, he had cracked down hard and then proceeded to separate moderates from radicals, winning over
some of the former, eliminating the latter. That strategy would
fail this time, first because the charismatic Khomeini was able
to keep the moderates in line and second because the fence
sitters gradually became convinced that the shah would fall.
On the earlier occasions, the hopelessness of dissent had led
the protestors to surrender. This time, the hopelessness of the
shah's position caused those in the middle to cast their lot
with the revolution.

Concern over American reactions might have affected the
shah's behavior, but only to a minor extent. After all, his
forces were not inhibited from regularly killing demonstrators
or from arresting opposition leaders. Iranian prisons were
filled to overflowing in the first half of 1978, until torture
chambers were converted into holding cells and beatings were
done in hallways. For the first ten months or so of the crisis

the Carter administration refrained from public or private criticism of the shah.

On January 9, 1978 only eight days after President Carter's departure from Iran, came an event marking the revolution's beginning. When theology students in the holy city of Qom demonstrated against the publication of an article by Minister of Information Darius Homayoun attacking the exiled Khomeini, police fired on the crowd, killing or wounding a number of people. On February 18, two days of rioting hit Tabriz, a city traditionally associated with Iranian constitutionalism. This time hundreds were killed or injured. The shah tried a conciliatory line, blaming provincial officials and removing the unpopular military governor. Troops were withdrawn; life seemed to return to normal; and even some dissidents thought the shah had won.

Such beliefs were short-lived. Another wave of protests broke out in Tabriz on March 29; the army had to deploy tanks against demonstrations in Tehran on May 11. For the first time chants of "Down with the shah!" were heard in the capital's main streets. When marches were blocked religious leaders called an effective general strike. On May 31, 2,500 students rioted at Tehran University. In July it was Meshed's turn. The biggest outbreak of violence began in Isfahan on August 11. Within twenty-four hours, Isfahan, Shiraz, Ahvaz, and Tabriz were all under dusk-to-dawn curfews.

The shah vowed that these troubles would not change his policies. Both massive arms purchases and his "liberalization" program would continue, the shah said: if reforms had helped ignite the flames, he claimed, they might also help douse them. As for relations with the Carter administration, he noted, "between governments we've never had it so good." He confidently exclaimed, "Nobody can overthrow me. I have the support of 700,000 troops, all the workers, and most of the people. I have the power." [19]

American correspondents echoed these sentiments. In an April story headlined, "SHAH MAINTAINS FIRM CONTROL DESPITE NEW WAVE OF PROTESTS," *Washington Post* correspondent William Branigan wrote, "Most diplomatic observers and dissidents agree that the shah has more than enough resources to crush any serious challenge to his regime." Jonathan Randal found the shah "firmly in control of Iran" in late May, though many Iranians were beginning to worry. Most reporters interpreted the Muslim clergy's leadership to mean that the opposition's main complaints were with land reform, liquor stores, and movies. Failure to perceive the diverse makeup of the opposition and the revolution's deeper roots made it impossible for American journalists or their readers to understand the revolt's breadth.[20] Yet during the spring and early summer even many of the shah's enemies thought his defeat to be unlikely.

One of the few pessimists in Iranian ruling circles was General Nasir Moghadam, a younger officer with good contacts and even friendships among the dissidents. In April, according to some sources, he sent the shah a thirty-page report, bypassing SAVAK by using his personal connections to the royal family. Moghadam warned that revolution was inevitable unless real reforms were made. Even the United States would abandon the shah if he showed himself incapable of dealing with the disorders, he wrote. The shah bided his time but finally appointed Moghadam head of SAVAK on June 6.

On August 20, in the midst of the holy month of Ramadan, a film theatre fire in Abadan killed 377 people. This was the sixth such conflagration in twelve days—the others had been set by fundamentalist extremists to oppose the showing of "sinful" movies. But in a country with an almost unlimited belief in conspiracy the word quickly spread that SAVAK had set the fire and locked the doors, trapping many women and children inside. Even within the country's prisons it became the main topic of conversation.

While the accusation is questionable the incident did illustrate the regime's incompetence. It took a nearby police station half an hour to call the fire department and the first trucks on the scene arrived with faulty equipment. At any rate, most Iranians saw the incident as a bloodthirsty massacre. Antigovernment agitation intensified.

Meanwhile, in Washington officials were equally slow in

seeing the seriousness of the crisis. Many of the Middle East specialists were tied up with the complexities of the Camp David peace negotiations between Egypt and Israel; congressional foreign relations committees were involved with proposed arms sales to Arab states. Brzezinski was working on normalizing relations with Peking, and Vance was laboring on the strategic arms limitation treaty (SALT–2) as well as Camp David. Consequently, monitoring Iran was relegated to Henry Precht at the State Department, to Robert Murray at the Pentagon, and to Gary Sick at the National Security Council (NSC). All three were several levels removed from the White House.

Within the bureaucracy there was still strong resistance to any suggestion that the shah might be slipping out of power. One official vehemently objected when a colleague qualified his description of the shah's regime as "one of the most stable" with the interjection "perhaps." Similar reactions met the warnings of academic specialists at a March, 1978 State Department seminar. Professor James Bill's paper, "Monarchy in Collapse," predicted that as violence escalated, more and more groups would coalesce in opposition to the shah's regime: "As this occurs," the paper concluded, "the Shah will have lost the will and capacity to use his traditional tactics of political control. Unless something is done to break this wildly spinning vicious circle, the future of the current actions in the Iranian political drama can only be a grim one. And the American future in Iran can in no way be considered bright." [21]

This tendency toward foot-dragging was also visible in two inner-government struggles that began in March. The first was over the National Intelligence Estimate (NIE), a periodic evaluation written under the supervision of the CIA director. During discussions on this document's next edition, the Defense Intelligence Agency (DIA) and the CIA were optimistic, but the State Department Bureau of Intelligence and Research, represented by George Griffen, felt that Iran's domestic problems belied such an upbeat assessment. Unable to bridge the gap, they finally agreed to lay aside the uncompleted NIE in mid-September.

A second conflict brought on a battle between a loose alliance of the Policy Planning Staff and the State Department Bureau of Political-Military Affairs on the one side and the regional bureau, represented by Deputy Assistant Secretary for Near East and South Asian Affairs Sidney Sober and Henry Precht on the other. The former wanted to study the arms-transfer system, with Policy Planning emphasizing absorption difficulties and stability, and the Political-Military people arguing that too much time and money were being spent on advanced technology rather than on building combat-ready forces. Some officials were concerned that equipment was being delivered too fast. One CIA analyst went along on the absorption problem until superiors ordered him to desist. But Brzezinski, Vance, and Brown killed the proposal to further investigate the military-sales program.

The daily intelligence reporting to the White House also suffered from shortsightedness. It was good on narration of current events but poor on analysis. Often, the CIA and State Department summaries were just even with or behind those of *The New York Times* and *Washington Post*. Only in August did they report that the shah was losing his grip and that Iran's social fabric was unraveling. During work on the uncompleted NIE (the sixty-page "Iran in the 1980s"), the CIA had argued that no drastic change was likely for Iran's political behavior in the near future. A twenty-three page study, "Iran After the Shah," concluded that "Iran is not in a revolutionary or even a 'prerevolutionary' situation."

A particular failing was the lack of insight into the opposition's goals or into its widespread popularity. The Defense Intelligence Agency (DIA) produced five appraisals of Iran in the first nine months of 1978, each of which underestimated the extent and possible consequences of the disturbances. As late as September 28, DIA's prognosis was that the shah would remain actively in power over the next ten years.

Assistant Secretary of State for Near East and South Asian

Affairs Harold Saunders testified in June, 1978: "We believe a large majority of Iranians thoroughly approve of the very substantial improvements that have been made in living standards and economic and social opportunities during the past three decades." Such statements were, of course, part of a strategy of support for the shah, but they also indicated Washington's naiveté regarding events in Iran.[22]

The embassy in Tehran was also slow to understand developments. Ambassador William Sullivan spent most of July and August on vacation; at all times he discouraged pessimistic reports. As early as May the shah had started obtaining through Ambassador Zahedi in Washington pledges of support from Brzezinski. But Americans were saying in Washington what embassy officials were saying in Tehran. We will back you, but Iran is your country and you are its rulers. You must make your own decisions. Given the shah's history of sensitivity to foreign domination this seemed the proper prescription. The problem now, however, was that the shah found it difficult to make any decisions in those early months of crisis.

Finally, on August 5, he promised free parliamentary elections for the following year. The Abadan fire on August 20 and the increased antigovernment agitation stirred him to further action. He removed Jamshid Amouzegar, Hoveyda's successor, and appointed as prime minister Jaafar Sharif-Emami, a man with a pious reputation who had been premier a decade earlier, but who was now old and ineffectual. His position as head of the Pahlevi Foundation, whose activities were rightly the focus of many suspicions about royal corruption, scarcely seemed likely to endear him to the demonstrators.

Behind the scenes, however, General Moghadam, the head of SAVAK, had worked toward this compromise. His contacts in the religious opposition had suggested Sharif-Emami, a man they thought had the shah's confidence but one with whom they could work. At this point, Khomeini had still not emerged as the rebels' unquestioned leader and many within the clergy were willing to settle for far less than an Islamic revolution; none had yet called for the shah's overthrow. What they wanted, as Ayatollah Kazem Shariat-Madari frequently claimed, was a return to the 1906 constitution in which the clergy, landowners, and the business community had been able, through their influence in a powerful Majlis, to participate in the governing of the country.

Indeed, many bazaar merchants and religious figures, as well as the National Front moderates, feared an all-out showdown with the government, whose military might seemed awesome. But at each step the shah gave them less than they sought while still not loosing the full power of his military. By late December, when he was finally willing to yield real power to an opposition figure, it was too late; their demands had escalated.

Sharif-Emami tried hard to bring about a reconciliation during his weeks in office. The Tehran media was allowed to admit for the first time that all was not perfect in Iran. "Why shouldn't we write about strikes?" the prime minister asked. "The people themselves know what is going on. . . . If our radio doesn't broadcast it, the BBC will."[23] Even opposition comments were occasionally permitted to be braodcast.

Some government officials resigned; others began to speak out. For example, Tehran city council member Muhammad Reza Taqizadegh talked about the capital's social gap:

> North Tehran's problem is having flowers along highways and high-rise parking lots, while South Tehran's problem is having a drinking water tank and drying North Tehran's sewage. Whereas North Tehran can be compared with the best of the world's cities, South Tehran has problems which, at times, do not even exist in the most backward Iranian villages.

In the northern section, 80 percent of the one million residents owned their own residences; in the south only 20 percent of the four million people owned their homes and even much of this was substandard.[24] Out of these southern slums came many of the anti-shah demonstrators.

The speed of events, and the uneven government reaction to them, made life in Iran unpredictable during these last

months of the shah's regime. As *Kayhan* put it: "Developments are taking place so rapidly that even those who are directly involved in them have no time for reflection and assessment." [25] This was particularly true of the shah himself.

His disorientation was amply witnessed in a late August interview with the West German magazine *Stern*. When asked
about the opposition's goals the shah compared them with the
Baader-Meinhof terrorist gang. Questioned on the revolt's
cause he replied: "There are people everywhere who are easily instigated. They hear a few words and immediately they
are electrified and stop thinking." He insisted that convening
parliament and holding new elections would settle the conflict.

"Corruption has grown constantly worse" over the last three
years, said the interviewer. Garbagemen, customs inspectors,
and others worked only when bribed. "Are you aware of
this?"

"Do you really have to bribe people?" asked the shah.

"Yes, daily," said the journalist. Otherwise, garbage would
pile up in front of the house. "Believe me, your Majesty, ev-
erybody among the people knows that this is so."

"Then," concluded the incredulous monarch, "we will have
to talk with the people about it. Perhaps the wages are too
low, too. But the salaries we are paying are not so bad after
all." [26]

This growing isolation from reality was revealed even more
markedly in the shah's private conversations. United States
Ambassador Sullivan and British Ambassador Sir Anthony
Parsons were repeatedly invited to hear his long, rambling so-
liloquies expressing his doubt, impotence, and frustration. He
had tried everything, the king mourned and nothing had
worked—neither repression nor liberalization. The anguish
erased his facade of self-confidence and assurance but it did
not help him understand the nature of the challenge. To him,
the enemy was always the left or, at best, "Islamic Marxists."
Both ambassadors listened, offering comfort but not advice,
simply assuring him—in Sullivan's case—that "the United
States always honors its obligations." [27]

Fulfilling his assigned function, Sharif-Emami began talks with opposition religious figures on August 31. But Shariat-Madari rejected these initiatives, which would have left the shah's power virtually intact. The government, he demanded, must return to the 1906 constitution, which provided for a strong parliament and a limited monarchy. Sharif-Emami refused to be discouraged: "There are no insoluble problems as far as the present government is concerned."[28] Sullivan wanted to negotiate with the opposition himself, though he agreed with the shah's position that minimal changes would suffice and he remained confident of the shah's survival. Washington, preoccupied with other matters, did not give clearance.

Shariat-Madari also had another demand: Khomeini's return to Iran. Having been exiled and largely ignored for fifteen years, Khomeini—whose promotion to the rank of ayatollah had been engineered by Shariat-Madari to protect him from execution in 1963—now had the attraction of a figure unsullied by any collaboration whatsoever with the shah's regime. His scowling countenance was becoming a symbol of the resistance movement's tenacity. Soon, demonstrators in Tehran were pelting soldiers with flowers and trying to win them over. "Iran is our country!" they chanted over and over again, "Khomeini is our leader!"

In response, the Iranian government made a serious error. Khomeini, they decided, was too close to home in Iraq; they pressured that country to expel him. Most important, they wanted to keep the ayatollah out of any Islamic country where he would have a natural constituency and might rally support. Kuwait refused him entry on a technicality. Khomeini went to France, from where he could easily communicate with Iranians through cassettes smuggled into the country, long-distance telephone, through messengers, and, ironically, most easily through the international news media.

Other events were setting the stage for Khomeini's dramatic ascendance as the opposition's leader. First came an incident that reinforced the hostility of the antigovernment forces and further narrowed the possibility of compromise. For some time the generals, disdainful of Sharif-Emami's liaisons with the opposition, had asked the shah for permission to crack down on the dissidents. On September 5, Ambassador Zahedi arrived in Tehran with a view of American policy mainly developed through his conversations with Brzezinski. This concept gave full backing to a hard-line stand, though it was based on Brzezinski's personal views rather than on official American stands. The following day, the shah agreed to ban demonstrations. The first test would be a large rally scheduled for the early hours of September 7.

At six o'clock that morning, marchers converged at Tehran's central Jaleh Square. Most of them were probably unaware of the imposition of martial law a few hours earlier. Soldiers demanded that they disperse and when they replied with brickbats the army opened fire. The exact number of casualties on "Black Friday" is still disputed but reliable sources agree that somewhere between 700 and 2,000 people were gunned down.

The events at Jaleh Square began to stir foreign understanding of the seriousness of the crisis. The Soviets took the hint and started up their National Voice of Iran (NVOI) radio station, located in Baku but pretending it was independent and operating from inside Iran. Its daily broadcasts supported Khomeini and tried to spread anti-Americanism in Iran, often employing the most blatant lies. In the midst of the Camp David conference, Israeli and Egyptian observers also began to note the situation. The day after the Jaleh Square shootings, President Anwar al-Sadat called the shah and extended his support.

Perhaps at Sadat's request, President Carter also telephoned the shah. He expressed his regret over the bloodshed and his backing for Iran's ruler. He hoped that the disturbances would end and suggested that liberalization be continued. This meant, in the shah's lexicon, some anticorruption moves and continued progress toward elections. The whole thing was handled in an offhand way; a routine press release was issued by the White House.

If it was true, as the shah's confidants later claimed, that the monarch was disappointed in the conversation, it is hard to see what more he expected.* Certainly the announcement of Carter's statement of support over Radio Tehran immediately following the Jaleh Square massacre led Iranians to believe that the United States supported or even—as it later became distorted in Iranian popular belief—had ordered the shootings. Thus, a leaflet distributed by the Confederation of Iranian Students in the United States during October claimed that thousands had been murdered "all with the direction of CIA and the U.S. government." President Carter, the leaflet added, "the so-called defender of human rights," called the shah "and approved of his recent killings."

Among some of the better-informed American officials, including Precht, Jaleh Square finally began to change their view of events in Iran. However, this turnabout was a slow process and no one pressed such doubts on his superiors; nor did anyone yet voice the idea that the shah might indeed fall. The optimism of former deputy chief of mission in Tehran Jack Miklos and of Precht in their secret briefing to the Senate Foreign Relations Committee on September 15 was so blasé that it angered several senators. The senators had a similar reaction to the testimony of Robert Bowie, director of the CIA's National Foreign Assessment section, on September 27.

Work on the National Intelligence Estimate was abandoned until the situation clarified. "Who ever took religion seriously anyway!" complained one CIA man during the last discussion. But CIA reports to the White House continued to take the shah's crackdown at face value. Indeed, Carter's intelligence sources had it both ways—the CIA stressing the army's ability to handle the crisis; the State Department seeing as the critical issue whether or not the shah's regime could convince oppo-

* The shah's supporters later claimed that a clearly worded cable, urging full-scale repression of the opposition and signed by President Carter himself, would have saved their government. Brzezinski's indirect, verbal assurances and the White House's public statements were deemed insufficient. It is hard to believe—to say the least—that only the lack of such a document prevented the shah's regime from taking effective action to protect itself, but this view does illustrate that pro-shah Iranians rated American influence as highly as did their opponents.

nents that it was serious about moving toward political freedom and social justice.

Only in late September did a working group on Iran emerge
under Deputy Secretary of State Warren Christopher (in
charge of the department while Vance was at Camp David).
They spent most of their sessions debating whether more public statements supporting the shah would prove helpful or
harmful to his interests and to Washington's.

For his part, Sharif-Emami had not given up. He was still
convinced of the possibility of distinguishing between the
"logical and sensible" opposition with whom dialogue could
be held—particularly Shariat-Madari—and those with whom
there was nothing to discuss—namely Khomeini.[29] But the opposition would not allow itself to be split so easily. Shariat-
Madari said he would no longer cooperate with the prime
minister and warned that if government policy were not modified there would be a revolution.

Each day's events in Iran made it easier to believe this.

8
Days of Reckoning
1978–79

During September, 1978 Prime Minister Sharif-Emami continued his attempts at reconciliation but the shah's support of
these efforts was uneven. He switched back and forth, applying military power and offering concessions, doing each in
turn halfheartedly. Not until the year's closing days did he finally conclude that far-reaching compromises were necessary,
but by then the situation had reached the point where it was
clear even to the shah that he could not have both peace and
his kingdom.

By September outside observers and middle-class Iranians
understood that the country was beginning to break down.
One strike after another had erupted over wage and political issues: in public transit, railroads, the postal and air-transport
services, textile factories, radio and television stations, and
even among the civil servants themselves. There were buying
panics and widespread hoarding of goods. The economy was
at dead stop. Within the three months after the Jaleh Square
massacre, later reports estimated, wealthy Iranians had sent
$500 million out of the country.

Others also saw the writing on the wall. The shrewd Ali

Amini, living in Paris and weighing a comeback in political life as a transitional prime minister, now called for the shah's abdication.[1] At the end of August, the Socialist International, headed by former West German Prime Minister Willy Brandt, denounced the shah and called on the United States to withdraw support.

The turmoil also forced cancellation of Iran's plans to purchase 70 F–14s for $2 billion, ordered only a few weeks earlier. But Washington was reluctant to stop arms transfers lest this reflect a lack of confidence in the shah. "Our continuing willingness to meet Iran's legitimate defense needs will be a clear expression of our firm support for that key country and the overall stability of the regime," said Undersecretary of State Lucy Wilson Benson.[2] Thus, though Washington had turned down Iran's request for 31 F–4G fighter-bombers at the end of August, this decision had not been meant to set a pattern. Not until November would it finally become clear to Washington that the shah had exhausted his last options. Then, a somewhat disorganized attempt would be made to mediate a smooth transition to a post-shah regime that would not be unfriendly to America.

Unable to give ground on the opposition's main political demands, Sharif-Emami acted where he could. The government conceded billions of dollars in wage settlements; the prime minister closed theatres and gambling halls and promised a return to the Islamic calendar. The shah did not attempt to change Sharif-Emami's strategy immediately. Although the army wanted censorship reimposed, after a two-week walkout in October by the staffs of *Ettelaat* and *Kayhan* Sharif-Emami gave the newspapers the right to publish freely. An amnesty released prisoners and even offered a pardon to Khomeini if he would moderate his stand. Hoveyda was removed as minister of court in preparation for his role as the scapegoat on corruption. On October 6, Sharif-Emami opened parliament, announcing, "Unrest will not interrupt the implementation of the general policy concerning the expansion of democratic liberties in our country."[3] Yet even the long-captive Majlis began to protest the shooting of demonstrators and government policies.

Gradually, however, the shah began to doubt whether this line was going to produce any results. Perhaps his sentiment was reinforced by Zahedi's second visit home, on October 9, carrying another message of support from Brzezinski. In meetings with the ambassador the shah started talking about a different kind of government response, a hard-line approach he repeatedly referred to as the "iron fist." In some ways, he seemed almost pleased that Sharif-Emami's plan had failed and he openly expressed contempt for his prime minister. This would only prove to the people, the shah said, that there was no alternative to the iron fist. He believed he had unlimited time, not realizing that every day of chaos further undermined any remaining hope that he might save his throne.

Still, the shah was no mere bloodthirsty villain. He genuinely felt responsibility as a symbol of the national identity and, in his own words, as head of the Iranian family. His reign had been based on a nationalistic goal of building Iran into a mighty and respected nation. Such sentiments forbade him from setting off a public bloodbath in his own country, among his own people; he did not want to be regarded in the world's eyes as another Idi Amin.

Even in October, much of the opposition did not believe it possible to dethrone the shah, excepting only after a full-scale, bloody civil war. The moderates, thinking that the United States would never let the shah fall, placed a high value on winning American support for their efforts. They would walk into the American Embassy in Tehran daily to talk about the situation and to present their plans for a solution. They signaled that with more government concessions, including an end to martial law and a move toward constitutional monarchy, a satisfactory deal might be worked out. A key question involved who would control the government during the period of preparation for new, free elections.

Yet the regime's strategy remained one of separating radicals from moderates, crushing the former, and giving the latter as little as possible. Only in December—when it was too late—did the shah understand the error of this plan; that the opposition, including the moderates, were gradually escalating their demands. The emergence of Khomeini as leader signaled the ascendancy to power of the most intransigent element in the movement as a whole.

When Khomeini sought refuge in France, that country's government asked whether the shah had any objection—he did not. So Khomeini moved into a simple bungalow in the garden of an expatriate Iranian's house. There, in the suburb of Nauphle-le-Chateau about twenty-five miles outside of Paris, was created a place of pilgrimage for Iranian dissidents and for journalists, all eager to see the elderly clergyman. Khomeini lived ascetically, in his black turban, brown collarless coat over a collarless green tunic, his feet clad in blue plastic sandals. Telephones rang, bringing news of more demonstrations in Iran. The walls were decorated with posters: "35 million Muslims have said 'no' to the shah," said one. A second showed a shantytown with the caption, "This is the shah's modernization." A third displayed pictures of people killed at Jaleh Square. Khomeini's aides, who themselves were becoming household names, tirelessly jockeyed for position. And everyone gave countless interviews to the press, radio, and television. The French government did nothing to quiet them, thinking of its gains in influence if their guests were to come to power in oil-rich Iran.

But Khomeini's public visibility was not matched by any private willingness to negotiate. On his arrival in France, the CIA rented a villa near his home. American Embassy political officers began to meet occasionally with one of his advisors, Ibrahim Yazdi, though these encounters generally consisted of Yazdi's monologues on his group's moderation. Other embassy officials stayed up late into the night translating for their counterparts in Tehran the dozens of speeches and interviews given by Khomeini and his entourage each day.

The rise to dominance of Khomeini and his hard-line politics was a gradual process. The National Front leaders, accustomed to making their own decisions, followed an independent line. Karim Sanjabi, for example, warned that if the shah opted for military repression he would "drag Iran to extinction." The only way out was a peaceful transition toward democracy; under such conditions the monarchy could continue. "What is important to us," he said, "is the sincere restoration of democracy and the integral implementation of our constitutional law." [4]

Shariat-Madari, while advocating a central role for Islam, spoke in similar terms, denying that the religious leaders were "reactionary and against progress. . . . We want science and technology, educated men and women, doctors and surgeons." But, he warned, political differences between opposition and rulers were becoming so great that Iran's independence might be endangered. He hinted at supporting the National Front as an interim government to prepare elections. [5] Many Muslim clerics, bazaar merchants, and urban professionals felt the same way: they wanted order restored, bloodshed ended, and the danger of dictatorship—whether military, Marxist, or Islamic fundamentalist—avoided.

Some of them even tried to explain to Khomeini privately that his extreme views were dangerous and might lead to a military takeover, but the ayatollah was becoming so strong that none dared differ with him publicly. Like Lenin, Khomeini steeled the opposition on a maximalist line. There can be no compromise, he proclaimed. The monarchy must be destroyed and the shah must be punished. Only a revolution and a return to fundamentalist Islam could cleanse the country. The opportunity must be seized immediately, or it would pass forever.

Mehdi Bazargan, Khomeini's advisor and his choice for prime minister, argued for a step-by-step approach. "I was convinced," Bazargan later said, "that there was only one way of freeing ourselves from the shah—to persuade America to abandon him gradually so that he grew weaker and weaker as the people grew stronger and stronger." He was sure that Iranians having "always been under the thumb of some despot or other" were "used to being obedient, and every time they rebelled suddenly and with force, it was a failure."

When William Butler of the International Commission of Jurists told him several times of the American fear that the shah's fall would lead to anarchy and Soviet intervention Bazargan replied that he did not want a sudden revolution either. "The people are not ready to cope with freedom," he told Khomeini in Paris; "they must be accustomed to it by teaching them to develop politically, by seizing power in small steps— first education, then the press, then the magistracy, then the economy and then the army—otherwise we will fall into chaos and perhaps we will find ourselves with another tyrant."

"No gradualism, no waiting," Khomeini replied. "We must not lose a day, not a minute. The people demand an immediate revolution. Now or never." There was almost an argument but, Bazargan recounted, Khomeini seemed so sure and unshakable that he gave way. "Very well," Bazargan conceded, "let us try. Let us carry out the revolution." [6]

Khomeini warned National Front leaders that they would be banished from the movement if they negotiated with the shah; moderates admitted that nothing could be done without Khomeini. The ayatollah vetoed Ali Amini, who had met with Shariat-Madari to explore the possibility of his forming a government, and demanded an escalation of the struggle to oust the shah. Like their mentor Mossadegh, the National Front leaders knew the dangers of allowing themselves to be outflanked in militancy. When oil workers went on strike October 31 at Khomeini's call, it was an ample illustration of his popularity among the masses.

A few Americans, like Richard Cottam, were so critical of the shah's regime that they welcomed Khomeini. The ayatollah's statements, he claimed, "are strongly in favor of land reform, welfare reform and an improved role for women in society." Some sought "a puritanical Islamic society," Cottam wrote, "but the thrust of the religious opposition is centrist and reformist." [7] No one in the United States government held this position—many preferred the shah; others hoped and believed that the moderate, non-clerical elements would emerge victorious.

The Carter administration remained unshaken in its strong public support for the shah. At the end of October the president told the crown prince, "our friendship and our alliance with Iran is one of our important bases on which our entire foreign policy depends," and he referred to the shah's "progressive administration." State Department spokesman Hodding Carter praised the shah's "political liberalization and economic reform. The Iranian government is capable of managing the present difficulties," he said, "although continuing violence and strikes pose serious problems."[8]

By early November, however, officials were becoming more pessimistic. Brzezinski in particular began to argue that the shah's overthrow was a dangerous possibility. The first meeting of a Special Coordinating Committee on the problem took place on November 2, chaired by Brzezinski, with Cyrus Vance and Stansfield Turner in attendance. Energy Secretary Schlesinger later came to about half a dozen sessions. Operating immediately below it was a working group headed by NSC staffer David Aaron, which started operations November 21. In light of Vance's constant absences, Brzezinski became for six weeks or so the leading figure in formulating American strategy—and he came down for strong support of the shah.

The combination of events—Khomeini's call for civil war, the concerns expressed to the American Embassy by Iranian officers, and a Joint Chiefs of Staff warning that the shah might fall—showed the need for action. Brzezinski and Schlesinger believed not only that Iran's own strategic importance must be taken into account but that the monarch's collapse would also make Iraq and other pro-Soviet elements primary in the Persian Gulf. The destruction of the shah's regime might also lead other Middle East monarchies to question the value of reliance on and alliance with the United States. Given these thoughts, Schlesinger began to press for sending American warships and Marines into the Indian Ocean.

Clearly, a decisive moment had come. "The situation was really boiling yesterday, but it's gotten worse today," said a top American official on November 5. "It's completely out of control. The next 24 to 48 hours are crucial and could be decisive. The shah's present government appears to be a lost cause. . . ." Another commented, "We're at the point where something major has to be done; the same business as usual won't work."[9]

The shah said similar things in a telephone call to Brzezinski that day and the national security advisor replied, on the highest authority, that the United States would back him to the hilt. The State Department, skeptical of the benefits of military rule, prepared a cable calling instead for a broad, coalition government, but Brzezinski quashed this move.

Thus, after three days of particularly serious rioting in Tehran—including the burning of all movie theatres, many banks, and the British Embassy—and after his consultation with Brzezinski, the shah appointed a martial law government. The man he chose to head it, General Gholamreza Azhari, was aged and seriously ill with a heart condition. But he was also a father figure for the armed forces, perhaps the only man acceptable to all of the mutually jealous generals. He was thoroughly loyal to the shah and not ambitious in his own right. Azhari also had the advantage of some service abroad, having once worked on the CENTO staff. The new prime minister quickly adopted a hard line against demonstrators while continuing to promise elections once order was restored.

When Khomeini heard of these new developments he said, "This is the end of the shah" and called for putting the monarch on trial after his defeat. If the "present method of political struggle doesn't work," he added, civil war would result. The ayatollah also gave one of the first hints of what his new state would look like. The shah, he complained, had given away Iran's resources to America, the Soviets, and the Europeans: "We want all these foreign influences and pressures out of the country."[10]

Keeping its promise, the United States administration again strongly endorsed Tehran's choice. The shah had "no alternative," officials said, after opposition leaders refused to enter a coalition and it became clear that Sharif-Emami could not restore order.[11] As a further sign of American support, President

Carter authorized shipment of 25,000 tear-gas cannisters as well as police batons, protective vests, and other riot-control equipment to the Iranian army. The human rights office at the State Department had earlier managed to block this sale for several months. While the State Department went along with the policy its emphasis was somewhat different from Brzezinski's, stressing that the restoration of order was a necessary prelude to the elections scheduled for June, 1979. But their skepticism was growing: "The military government is about the last card the shah has to play," said one policymaker. "He doesn't know what to do next, and neither do we. It will be a miracle if he is still around to hold the elections he has promised." [12]

The shah, however, had not altogether abandoned his conciliatory option. "The revolution of the Iranian people cannot fail to have my support," he said in a nationwide radio speech on November 5. "Unfortunately, side by side with this revolution, the plots and abuses of others have created riots and anarchy" and had endangered the country's independence. Though Ambassador Sullivan thought the speech had gone well, the divide and co-opt strategy could work only if elements of the opposition could be intimidated or enticed into splitting. To bring about the former condition was Azhari's job. Iran's economy and society, the prime minister said, were being "destroyed as a result of riot-mongering of enemy and colonial lackeys." Only when these were defeated would he "make way for a government which will have the freedom to carry out . . . a 100 percent national election." [13]

To appease the opposition, Azhari arrested Hoveyda and Nasiri as scapegoats for past corruption and repression respectively; to frighten the dissidents, he arrested National Front leaders Dariush Foruhar and Karim Sanjabi on November 11 for holding a press conference in which they declared the shah's government illegal. On November 28, with the Shi'a holy month of Ashura coming up, he forbade public gatherings except in the mosques.

Was the Iranian military capable of implementing an "ironfist" strategy? Perhaps, but the odds were against it. First,

despite its impressive statistics the army was weak from
within because the shah, for political reasons, had kept the
officer class divided. The core of the armed forces was unquestionably loyal, a fidelity based both on their condition of
privilege and on their ideological training. Every morning
soldiers pledged allegiance to God, shah, and fatherland.
Officers received from $2,000 a month for lieutenants to
$70,000 a year for generals. They were given modern housing,
servants, vacation quarters, and special discount stores. Pri-
vates on long-term enlistments received $400 a month.

But much of the rank and file were conscripts, many only
recently drafted from villages and campuses. They were only
paid $1 a day and while they formed only 20 percent of the
military they made up 40 percent to 50 percent of the infantry.
Possibly they would have been good soldiers against a foreign
foe—though they had not fought all that well in Oman—but
even the best troops cannot indefinitely be maintained in a
state of discipline and high morale if ordered to fire on their
own people. This had been shown in Pakistan the preceding
year, when the army, unwilling to continue shooting Islamic
demonstrators, joined them to overthrow President Zulfiqar
Ali Bhutto in July, 1977. Now, Khomeini was calling on Iranian soldiers to desert. By the end of November, if not before,
draftees were listening to the opposition's appeals and reas-
sessing their loyalties.

Yet with officers it was not a question of loyalty alone. Their
personal dedication to the throne was reinforced by a strong
psychological dependence on the shah. He had determined
who would be promoted, how the military would be organized, and what arms would be ordered. By long condition-
ing, the officers were trained to act at the time and in the manner dictated by their king. Contributing to this paralytic
loyalty was the fact that the officers were divided by jealousies
and suspicions. When, several years earlier, Admiral Ahmad
Madani had dared suggest that more power devolve on the
commanders of the three military branches, he was forced
into retirement. Not until after the revolution, when he threw
in his lot with Khomeini, did Madani again command the

navy. So it was that when the shah collapsed, his officer corps collapsed with him.

If the army had its draftees to worry about, the air force had its "homafars," technical specialists whose military rank, between officers and sergeants, was similar to that of warrant officers in the United States. But although these men wore uniforms they were not really in the military. Rather, they had signed ten-year contracts to obtain training as senior mechanics, communications and computer experts, and to fill other key positions. Many of them, however, had been forced to stay in the service after their contracts expired in 1977 or 1978. Even though their pay was equivalent to that of colonels and majors their status was far lower and they knew that with their technical training they could make more money in civilian life. When the crunch came, they would go over to Khomeini in large numbers.

The leadership of the air force was very pro-shah; most of Iran's purchases had been devoted to its equipment. Air force commander General Amir Hussein Rabi'i was perhaps the most able officer in the top circles of the armed forces. Just before Azhari's appointment, Rabi'i went to the shah insisting on action. Otherwise, Rabi'i warned, he could no longer guarantee the air force's loyalty. For the senior generals, the idea that the shah might give up any of his power was frightening. They did not like his seemingly conciliatory November 5th speech and could not understand his passivity, though rumors of the shah's cancer were already circulating widely in Tehran.

The generals wanted a tough reaction to the civil disturbances but did not feel properly equipped to deal with them; they wanted riot-control equipment. Many of the deaths that had occurred could have been avoided, they said. If they had had tear gas they would not have had to rely on bullets. Rabi'i, Toufanian, navy commander Admiral Habib Alahi, the hardline army leader General Gholam Ali Oveissi, SAVAK head Moghadam, and the dashing paratroop commander General Manuchehr Khosrodad, met frequently to try to map some course of independent action. Individually they visited the

American Embassy: "You Americans must make him do something!" they demanded, but they themselves did nothing. Their psychological dependence on the shah's direction was too great.

Throughout November and December Rabi'i turned his national air force staff meetings, held once or twice a month with officers from every base in the country, into virtual pep rallies for the shah. But the doubts of the generals gradually spread to the colonels and majors. By December, some of the long-loyal men even began to talk quietly of replacing the shah. Yet still they did nothing on their own, although Moghadam and Fardost might already have been thinking of changing sides, a step they took the following February.

The shah also knew that the martial law of the Azhari government was not working. He even began to tell his ambassadorial listeners that he had deliberately chosen an ineffectual general to prove that this option too could not succeed. On one occasion, Azhari called to ask the shah's permission to go on a picnic in the nearby mountains. The shah agreed, explaining to his guests in an aside that it didn't matter what happened to the prime minister. In December, Azhari spent ten days away from his desk due to his heart problem; eventually, he was evacuated to the United States for a major operation.

Azhari, unlike Sharif-Emami, had no plan. "Nations are like a man when he gets angry," he told one interviewer; "he needs time to smoke a cigarette, drink a cup of coffee, listen to some music. We are trying to win that time, and think that they are slowly coming back to work." [14] But the demonstrations would not go away—time was on the side of the opposition.

By this point the shah was well aware of his limited life expectancy and he must have given some serious thought to his son's succession. As far as can be determined, however, he felt he could hold on until elections were held and the situation stabilized. The American Embassy felt an agreement would be possible if the shah offered more to the opposition. Among Iranians, former Prime Minister Ali Amini suggested at the end of November that it might still be possible to establish a new government on the basis of the 1906 constitution. A cabinet of technocrats could be quickly empowered to schedule and regulate free elections.[15] The shah continued to insist on his own terms.

Meanwhile, the White House was awakening fully to the dangers of the crisis. No less than four visitors went to Tehran in late November to investigate: Treasury Secretary Michael Blumenthal; Robert Bowie, head of the CIA's analysis division; General E. F. Tighe, director of the DIA; and Senate Majority Leader Robert Byrd. Specialists were also sent from the State Department's regional bureau and Intelligence and Research branch. Byrd apparently reported that the shah was unlikely to take strong action and was unlikely to survive the disorders. The others probably reached similar conclusions. Additional personnel were also sent to reinforce the embassy staff.

Given the realization that valuable time had been lost, Carter blamed the intelligence services for not warning him earlier. On November 11, the president declared himself "not satisfied" with their performance on Iran. Although the NIE had never actually been completed, it was widely cited as an example of the inaccuracy of intelligence evaluations.

An additional sign of the internationalization of Iran's civil strife was Soviet Premier Leonid Brezhnev's sudden warning on November 19 against any United States military intervention to preserve the shah in power. Despite their support of clandestine antigovernment radio stations, the Soviets had, up to this point, maintained cordial relations with the shah's regime, but now this Brezhnev pronouncement strongly suggested that Moscow had concluded that the Iranian monarchy was doomed. The White House responded to the Soviet threat by saying that the United States had no intention of becoming involved.

Within Iran itself, many American residents seemed inclined to pull out. In the first few days of December, bloody street battles heightened the uncertainties of everyday life while rumors and anonymous leaflets hinted at violence against individual Americans. The American Embassy was reluctant to authorize a mass evacuation since this would undercut confidence in the shah, but the exodus started anyway. By mid-December Washington agreed to supply transport planes. "For the merchant in the bazaar, the dry cleaner, the people of my neighborhood," said an American teacher in Isfahan, "I am identified, however wrongly, with the repression imposed by Tehran. Every time the President says something favorable to the Shah, he makes it physically more dangerous for Americans in Isfahan." [16]

These events moved Washington to urge upon the shah the acceptance of a constitutional monarchy with a broader-based government; publicly, Carter tempered his words of support. While there had been abuses, the president said, "the trend has been . . . toward democratic principles and social liberalization." The message was that this should continue in the form of free elections and the decentralization of power. Carter concluded, "We personally prefer that the shah maintain a major role but that is a decision for the Iranian people to make." Later, in questioning, he repeated this in a slightly different form. Would the shah survive? "I don't know. I hope so. This is something in the hands of the Iranian people. . . ." Here was the first publicly expressed doubt that the shah would retain power. He might still do so, Carter was also suggesting, if he changed the policy he had been pursuing. [17]

As the White House was going through an agonizing reappraisal of the shah's situation, working-level officials in the State Department were urging the administration to separate itself from the sinking ruler. As a December 14 editorial in The New York Times put it: "The United States cannot be expected to leave all its stake piled on one throne. There must be avenues of retreat, one of which leads toward making the Shah a constitutional monarch acceptable to a broad coalition." Such hopes related more to the lost possibilities of August and September past than they did to the worsening conditions of mid-December. Yet Carter held no brief for Khomeini, whom he attacked for his fiery speeches, which, the president deplored, "encourage bloodbaths and violence." [18]

Was the iron fist an acceptable option at this point? Not to a president whose main aim was precisely to avoid bloodbaths and violence. A credible ban on demonstrations required that anyone who marched would have to be arrested or shot. New Jaleh Squares would have been inevitable; civil war would have been a high probability. Would a United States commitment to support the shah down this road have meant sending American troops if necessary? So soon after the end of the Vietnam War this was unthinkable. Would the United States even be willing to provide supplies for such an extended struggle when a prolonged period of instability was precisely what Washington was trying to avoid? The region would remain unsettled for years to come; the leftist forces might take leadership of the opposition and the Soviets might finally be afforded their pretext for intervention. Even if the anti-shah forces were not as eager for martyrdom as their rhetoric implied they were, the breakdown of order had gone too far for a simple show of force to have restored the status quo ante.

Rather than passively await the results of the shah's endeavors, the United States might have chosen a second option: to commit American prestige and influence in negotiations for a reform government with moderate opposition participation. In September or October such a plan might have achieved success, but its long-term prospects would still have faced a serious challenge from the radicals. At that time, however, Washington, the generals, and the shah himself were not yet prepared to make such concessions.

By November, when moderate opposition figures streamed into the American embassy to propose such a solution, there was no effective coordination between Washington and Ambassador Sullivan to put America's weight behind any of these plans. Already, Khomeini's hard line was fettering those in Iran who were inclined toward compromise. In the United States, the conflict between those who wished to give the shah unlimited support, like Brzezinski, and those in the State Department who were already concluding that the shah could not survive without concessions had still not been resolved.

While Carter's statements in mid-December indicated the

beginnings of movement toward the latter solution, political changes in Iran pointed in a similar direction. The release of National Front leaders Sanjabi and Foruhar on December 6 had led almost immediately to the resumption of talks between the two sides. Sanjabi, a mild-mannered and often indecisive seventy-three-year-old lawyer, wasted little time in declaring the continued demonstrations a "spontaneous referendum" for the shah's ouster.

While a coalition government was impossible, he warned, "unless there is far more substantial change concerning the monarchy," this requirement could be satisfied by establishing a constitutional monarchy under the shah's son. He also carefully expressed friendship toward the military and fear of what chaos might bring:

> We in the National Front want to maintain the army, we need a strong army, and we don't want to do anything to discourage the army. . . . We have never called for desertions or tried to create indiscipline. But inevitably, it is happening, and if it continues, it could become very dangerous.[19]

Impressed with these arguments, the shah sent for Sanjabi and the two men met for the first time since Mossadegh's fall. They talked for one hour and Sanjabi, according to his account, told the shah that he had to leave the country. The shah refused—no one else had his authority, he claimed. Instead he asked Sanjabi to participate in a national coalition government, an invitation Sanjabi rejected, saying there could be no coalition with the present regime. Their talks ended.[20]

The shah tried another National Front leader, Gholam Hussein Sadighi, who had been interior minister under Mossadegh. Sadighi proposed that the shah's powers be turned over to a Regency Council, which would govern in his stead. Again the shah refused.[21]

The minimal demands of the moderate politicians were based on both political and historical criteria. To accept the premiership under the shah, without first having secured some change in the distribution of power, would discredit them in the eyes of other oppositionists. Nor did they place a low estimate on the monarch's skill at political infighting. Once order was restored, they reasoned, he might quickly dispose of them. The past examples of Fazlollah Zahedi and Ali Amini, two seemingly entrenched prime ministers who had been so easily removed by the shah, as well as that of Mossadegh himself, provided ample warning. A fully legitimate and institutionalized change of power was also necessary to satisfy the armed forces, which otherwise would not alter its loyalties.

Khomeini's supporters not only opposed such a rapprochement, they dreaded it. Nor did they perceive any adjustment on the part of the United States in its support for the shah. The ayatollah asked some visiting Americans why Carter backed "a regime to which the Iranian people are unanimously opposed." He told another interviewer, "Every time Carter supports the shah, the people are massacred by the shah the next day," a somewhat scrambled reference to the Jaleh Square incident and Carter's after-the-fact expression of support for the shah. SAVAK violence was used against peaceful demonstrations, Khomeini said, "After all that, Carter says we are irresponsible." Americans would soon learn to their chagrin that no amount of reassurance could assuage his suspicions or change his conspiratorial view of events.[22]

Perhaps the clearest expression of the Khomeinist point of view at that time was presented by one of his advisors, Abol-Hassan Bani-Sadr. The revolution, Bani-Sadr wrote, was the result of economic, political, social, and cultural problems created by the shah's policies. Therefore, the crisis "cannot be resolved by a compromise that allows continuation of the very regime that has created the crisis in the first place."[23]

This conclusion, Bani-Sadr continued, was also tactically necessary. For twenty-five years the shah had tried to convince the urban middle class and other opposition elements "to accept a compromise based on the centralization of power under executive control and the evolution of Iran within the framework of American strategies." Such a plan had often worked: "Out of their greed for power and titles, or by reason of their misplaced faith that compromise would open the way to reform, some members of the opposition sided with the regime." Here was being sounded an obvious warning from the men in Nauple-le-Chateau to Amini, Sanjabi, Bazargan, and others participating in or advocating negotiations with the regime. The step-by-step approach of "gradual liberalization" and "a weakening of the shah's regime until it can be eradicated is rejected." For "the supporters of this course of action," noted Bani-Sadr, seem to be unaware that if the regime believed the first step *could* lead to the second, it would not itself propose this solution."

Finally, there was a clear expression of their determination that the new order be an Islamic republic under Khomeini's leadership. The only thing the opposition possessed of transcendent power, Bani-Sadr concluded, was the people's esteem for Khomeini. Any compromise would "disrupt this relationship" and serve as "a disastrous decoy." Those who accepted it "would be discredited, their followers disillusioned and the general uprising would disintegrate." There could not even be a "continuation of the shah's regime without the shah."

Inherent in this analysis were two points that would assume increasing importance in the months to come. First, the revolution was being steered toward the point of maximum militancy. Only by hewing to this course, which Khomeinists believed in for its own sake, as well as for its practical value, could the revolution triumph over the existing system. As in Mossadegh's day, compromise would be publicly equated with treason, even if such rigidity endangered the success of the entire anti-shah movement.

Second, hostility toward the United States was not something marginal for the Khomeinists but stood at the center of their thinking. A major feature of the shah's regime, both the ayatollah and Bani-Sadr argued, was its "subservience" to the United States and its collaboration with Washington. This precept established the anti-American orientation of the Iranian revolution: any friendliness toward the United States would be prima facie evidence of betrayal. Anyone exhibiting such softness would be deemed unfit for leadership.

America's eternal hostility to the revolution and its tire-
lessness in attempting to reverse it were thus established as a
matter of faith.

There were, of course, many oppositionists, some even
among the clergy, who did not see the United States as a permanent foe of the revolution. But Khomeini's ascendancy
meant that their attempts to preserve Iranian-American friendship would have to be conducted in secret, if at all. Such actions, even when they were clearly designed to produce or to
consolidate the victory of the anti-shah forces, would later
make them suspect.

Ironically, this ideology took hold at a time when the debate
in Washington was going against those advocating a hard
line. Brzezinski still believed that the shah could be maintained in power and, failing this, that the nature of the American commitment might make it more beneficial for the United
States to go down fighting with him. Any appearance of having abandoned the shah, he argued, would only undermine
other American alliances in the region. The national security
advisor's concerns were highlighted in his December 20,
1978 "arc of crisis" speech discussing the spreading instability in the area. With "fragile social and political structures in
a region of vital importance to us threatened with fragmenta-
tion. . . . the resulting political chaos could well be filled by
elements hostile to our values and sympathetic with our ad-
versaries. This could face the West as a whole with a challenge of significant proportions."[24]

Yet, while sharing these same fears most of those within the
administration were moving toward support of a different tack
to deal with the envisioned problems. Given the impasse in
the internal debate, Treasury Secretary Blumenthal suggested
bringing in George Ball, a former undersecretary of state who
had opposed the Vietnam War, later returning to his law practice and to an active career as a foreign policy commentator.
After a couple of weeks of study, including extensive reading
of earlier diplomatic cables, Ball recommended that the
United States encourage the shah toward a broadly based civilian government, one in which he would surrender most of

his power to a regency council. This had to be done before the upheaval made impossible all chances for the monarchy's survival. The recommendation was similar to that being put forward by Sanjabi and his colleagues.

According to Ball's plan, presented at an hour-long meeting with the president and Brzezinski on December 13, a council of notables would be created to insulate the new government from the shah. The problem was that the nominees on Ball's list were so disparate—ranging from Khomeini's clerical representative in Tehran, Ayatollah Muhammad Beheshti, to hard-line pro-shah loyalists—that the American Embassy in Tehran saw the plan as unworkable. Either President Carter rejected it on the spot at the December 13 meeting or Ambassador Sullivan's reservations killed the idea. At any rate, Carter's statements at the time—that the fate of the shah's rule was in the hands of the Iranian people—seemed to indicate his own growing doubts about the shah's survival.

By mid-December, then, the United States still did not have any coherent Iran policy nor was there even a system of coordination between the different policymaking groups. The president did not step in to settle the debates that grew hotter daily, and so there was no rallying around one position. Consequently, each step was dictated partly by chance, partly by the relative strength of various personalities in the administration, and very much by whatever turn events might be taking at the moment in Iran.

Schlesinger favored an all-out effort to keep the shah in power and to further this goal he urged the president to send a special representative to Tehran. This man, he suggested, might best be Brzezinski, whose views were directed toward this same goal. The visit would assure the shah of strong American backing for an iron-fist policy. Brzezinski agreed with the idea in general but worried that his presence would show too high a profile; instead, he suggested sending Schlesinger.

The discussion of Schlesinger's proposal took it far from where either Schlesinger or Brzezinski had intended. Vance, who had played only a small role up to that point, finally intervened. The shah could not survive, he told the president, and would have to be urged to leave the country. The king could not rule and, as long as he was there, neither could anyone else. On the other hand, Vance said, the transitional government finally selected by the shah to replace him might survive if the American envoy provided some assistance. Rather than dispatching a political representative, therefore, it was decided to send General Robert Huyser, who could concentrate on holding the Iranian military together during the difficult period to come. The key decisions were made by Vance and President Carter at Camp David during the Christmas-New Year's vacation period.

While rejecting the hard-line Schlesinger-Brzezinski suggestions, the president also opposed the proposal of Ambassador Sullivan, whose optimism about a successful working-out of the problem through diplomacy was shared by some State Department officials. They had called for attempts to foster a dialogue between the military and Khomeini, believing that these discussions might smooth the transition by bringing the armed forces in at an early stage. If senior officers gave up their positions, they argued, their younger replacements might be able to make peace with the revolutionaries. It is hard to believe, however, that the victorious militants would have accepted this as proof that the soldiers were not their enemies, and even Sullivan abandoned this earlier optimistic appraisal of the situation soon thereafter.

The Carter-Vance decision was rooted in a new development in Tehran. The shah had finally recognized the deteriorating situation and, giving in to the dissidents' demands of earlier months, found an opposition figure willing to serve as prime minister. A few days after Sanjabi's refusal, the shah summoned Shahpour Bakhtiar, a sixty-two-year-old scion of the powerful Bakhtiari tribe, a Sorbonne graduate, and a deputy minister in the Mossadegh government. During their first meeting, Bakhtiar showed his boldness by telling the shah that Khomeini had no program but was simply a symbol for the opposition. During a second discussion the shah asked Bakhtiar if he would become prime minister. Bakhtiar's conditions included press freedom, the release of political prisoners, and the dissolution of SAVAK, a free hand in running Iran, and the shah's departure from the country. The shah asked for two or three days to think about the last demand and finally, around December 27, he acceded. By this point, the United States was also pressing him in that direction.

This historic decision was made as Iran lurched into chaos. On December 25, American Embassy guards had to fire tear gas to ward off student demonstrators. Soviet broadcasts continually interpreted the revolution as being against American domination and provocatively linked the embassy and the CIA as the twin agents of United States imperialism attempting to defeat it. December 27 was a day of gunfire and lawlessness. Trucks and cars burned in the streets, which echoed to the sounds of sirens and gunshots, of auto horns and of exploding tear-gas grenades. Stores shut down as merchants carried off their stocks to hide them. Power was cut and oil was rationed as the petroleum workers' strike lowered production almost to zero—the country had only one week's reserves left at a time when night temperatures hovered around freezing. Sanjabi led a march of 10,000 as a funeral procession for a demonstrator killed the preceding day. Nervous troops opened fire on the peaceful march, and, after thirty minutes of wild shooting, several mourners and one of their own officers lay dead. Crowds chanted: "Carter gives the guns, the shah kills the people."

Thus was begun the "big push," an all-out attempt to bring down the shah. The strikes would end, said organizers, only when the shah left the country. Foreign oil technicians pulled out and the United States lost the 900,000 barrels a day, about 5 percent of its daily consumption, that Iran had been supplying. Schools were closed, garbage collection was discontinued, public transport was at a standstill.

At this obviously critical juncture, on December 29, Bakhtiar's appointment was announced. Immediately, the National Front expelled him—they would have no further talk of compromise. Yet even at this point die-hard supporters of the shah tried to block any transition. While Bakhtiar announced on December 30 that the shah would leave Iran, the shah's spokesman denied this. Ardeshir Zahedi insisted that Bakhtiar had been misquoted. For several days a behind-the-scenes battle raged over whether the shah would depart Iran. The first week in January marked the last stand of the shah's loyalists, led by Zahedi and by Army Commander Oveissi but Bakhtiar, with American support, made his statement stick. Although the shah would not leave for another ten days there was no longer any turning back.

While he waited for the shah's departure, Bakhtiar moved quickly to court popularity with the public and the military. He would prosecute corrupt officials, the new prime minister said, "hanging those convicted of the most flagrant violations." All top officeholders must be dismissed and replaced by those not identified with the old regime; the shah himself must pledge not to try to regain power. Bakhtiar also defended the importance of a smooth and legitimate transition: "If the shah fell now, the military would split into several factions, coup would follow coup and Iran would drift into chaos or civil war."[25]

With Azhari's resignation, it was also necessary to select a new chief of staff for the armed forces. Bakhtiar wanted to consult several people but, before he knew it, the shah, still in Iran, presented him with a *fait accompli*, the appointment of General Abbas Karim Gharabaghi.

Bakhtiar claims that Gharabaghi's name was suggested to the shah by General Fardost and therein lies a possible clue to this strange event. For Gharabaghi was indeed a curious choice for either man, certainly for the shah, to have made. An Azerbaijani who spoke Farsi with a strong Turkish accent, Gharabaghi was an outsider in the military establishment and did not enjoy a good reputation among other officers. Surely he was not someone who would back the shah's case against Bakhtiar's; nor was he likely to unite the military behind him. Why did Fardost press this man on the shah? Given the fact that both Fardost and Gharabaghi would later make their own deal with Khomeini and that both would not be harmed while their colleagues fled or were shot, the implication is strong that the shah's oldest friend had already betrayed him.

Pro-shah forces in exile would later claim that Moghadam had sent one of his aides to Paris in November, 1978 to contact the Khomeinist forces. Did plans for a betrayal go back that far? Moghadam and Fardost had both warned the shah earlier over the seriousness of the crisis. Did they use their foresight to switch sides before it was too late?

Whether or not there had been covert treason before Bakhtiar's appointment, by early January, Gharabaghi and Moghadam were meeting with opposition representatives Bazargan and Beheshti. These conferences would lead to Bakhtiar's fall in mid-February when the military abandoned him. On the other hand, pro-shah forces, including Zahedi and General Khosradad, attempted two abortive pro-shah coups during Bakhtiar's forty-plus days in office. Other friends of the shah, Oveissi and General Mulawi, commander of the Tehran police, left the country on January 8.

Meanwhile, adjusting to the new situation, President Carter tried two approaches to Ayatollah Khomeini to win his support for the Bakhtiar government, or at least for a negotiated settlement. In early January, Carter sent Khomeini a message saying that it was in everyone's interest to avoid an explosion and further bloodshed, adding that the shah would leave shortly and would not return. Khomeini replied that any monarchical regime was unacceptable: Carter must "remove" the shah and not support Bakhtiar.[26]

Another effort was aimed at arranging a meeting between an American representative, Theodore Eliot, inspector-general of the Foreign Service, and Khomeini. Sullivan and Vance both agreed with the idea and informed the shah, who had no objection. But Brzezinski vetoed the plan. Sullivan recounts that the shah reacted with stunned incredulity when informed of the cancellation. "How can you expect to have any influence with these people if you won't meet with them?" he asked.[27]

Khomeini did not entirely neglect his public relations with

the West. By back channels, his aides constantly argued their moderation. He himself seemed to hold out olive branches to the United States, suggesting that the two countries might start with a clean slate. "It would be a mistake for the American government to fear the shah's departure," he said on January 1. "If the United States behaves correctly, does not interfere in our affairs and withdraws the advisors who are intervening in our country, we will respect it in return," he added a week later.[28] But Washington did not understand the full implication of that statement until much later.

These hints that good Iranian-United States relations might survive the revolution, though they played on American hopes, were exceptional. Carter was, the ayatollah said elsewhere, an enemy of Iran for supporting the shah; the United States was "an accessory and has backed the massacre of our people by the shah's ignoble regime. It is now up to the American people to exert pressure on their government." Khomeini told another interviewer: "The United States obviously wants to have all countries under its influence, but we cannot accept such domination and our people are tired of it. Following our people's example, other countries will free themselves from the clutches of colonialism."[29]

Nor could there be any compromise with Bakhtiar's regime, which Khomeini labeled as "illegal" and one that "the people are resolved to fight until an Islamic government is installed. Any other regime would clash with the people." Bazargan, still treading cautiously, noted shortly after Bakhtiar's appointment, "It is obvious that only a return to a certain measure of democracy could mollify all these extremists. However, poor Bakhtiar has no margin for maneuver on this tightrope."[30]

Bazargan and Bakhtiar met at least once during this period and agreed that they had more in common as individuals than either did with Khomeini. Still Bazargan's loyalty to Khomeini was not shaken. He had always been more religiously oriented than his National Front colleagues. Born of a Tabriz mercantile family that had emigrated to Tehran, Bazargan had won a scholarship from Reza Shah in the late 1920s and had studied engineering in France. Joining the National Front, he was undersecretary for education and managing director of the NIOC during the Mossadegh regime. He had been jailed four times for opposition activity afterward. When Khomeini named a shadow government on January 13, Bazargan was chosen as his prime minister.

Against great odds, Bakhtiar strove to forge his own independent position, breaking with the shah's old policies. "Henceforth," he said at one of his first press conferences, "we shall not endeavor to become what you describe as the gendarme of the Persian Gulf."[31] He also criticized the shah for destroying Iran's economy despite gigantic oil revenues:

> An empty treasury, financial indigence, the bankruptcy of the private sector, general strikes, strikes by government organizations, rebellion by the younger generation, the anger of lecturers and teachers, the frustrations of students and pupils, plot and machinations by foreigners and their agents to further disrupt the situation and, above all, a nation in mourning—these constitute the inheritance received by your obedient servant from previous governments.[32]

The shah himself warned that Bakhtiar would not long survive his own departure, that the religious leaders or the army would oust him. Yet unwilling as he was to go—trying until almost the last minute to confine his exile to some resort area on Iran's Caspian or Gulf shores—the shah was finally forced to leave. The United States declared its support of Bakhtiar and Sullivan came to the palace to discuss the date and time of the shah's departure.

And so, finally, on January 16 the shah left for Egypt, taking with him a casket of Iranian soil. The word abdication was scrupulously avoided in all releases by both the shah's supporters and Bakhtiar's. Back in early 1953, in the middle of a government crisis, he had announced that he was leaving the country; on August 16 of that same year he had actually gone. Both times the Iranian people had turned on his opponents in thunderous pro-shah demonstrations. Now at the airport he told Bakhtiar, almost wistfully, that things would become so bad that the people would call him back after four or five months. But this was not 1953 and the prime minister did not believe that even the shah thought history would repeat itself. General Gharabaghi promised that there would be no military coup after the shah left: the army would support any legal government.

The original plan of exile was for the shah to come eventually to the United States and to stay indefinitely at the California estate of his millionaire friend Walter Annenberg. Initially there was no objection raised by the Carter administration, but when the Bakhtiar government ran into its own troubles and it appeared that the United States would have to deal with an Iranian government controlled by Khomeini, the administration changed its mind and made clear to the shah that he would have to find another sanctuary.

On the day the shah left Iran the people took to the streets, chanting, "The shah is gone! Now it's the Americans' turn." Even in wealthy north Tehran they took to the streets by the thousands to voice their joy. Lights were ablaze, automobiles loaded with people moved down the streets honking their horns, their windshield wipers—carrying pictures of Khomeini—swishing in rhythm. Young people made "V for victory" signs; mullahs were carried on the shoulders of crowds; others displayed banknotes with the shah's portrait cut out of them.[33] In many ways it was like the wild outpouring that had greeted the shah's restoration a quarter-century earlier, except that this time it was his departure not his return being celebrated.

The Iranian Embassy in Washington was the last stronghold for the shah's loyalists. There had been some debate there over Zahedi's policy of financing pro-shah demonstrations during the monarch's November, 1977 visit to the United States but generally the offices functioned smoothly. In the fall of 1978, however, the three code clerks went over to Khomeini and by the time the shah left Tehran, the diplomats had split into three factions. A small group, led by the military attachés, continued to support the shah; an equally small number —backed by Iranian students—vocally boosted Khomeini.

Many of the latter had previously been outspoken advocates of the shah. The majority of the two hundred officials and workers decided that as professional diplomats they should obey whatever government ruled their country, which meant, in January, 1979, that of Bakhtiar.

When Prime Minister Bakhtiar ordered that the shah's picture be taken down, the chargé d'affaires (Zahedi was in Morocco with the shah) obeyed, but pro-shah dissidents telephoned Zahedi, who countermanded that instruction. One night, the hard-liners broke into a warehouse where the pictures were being stored and put them back up. When employees came to work the next morning, the portraits were all in their accustomed places. Once again they were taken down and the chargé fired those responsible for their return. Zahedi, returning to Washington, attempted to remove the moderates. When the pro-Khomeini forces took over in Tehran and gained control of the Washington embassy, though, they fired virtually everyone, including the pro-Khomeini converts.

In his own office, Bakhtiar covered over the shah's portrait with an Iranian flag and put up a picture of Mossadegh. Could the Bakhtiar government long survive in the squeeze between mullahs and military? The White House thought so; the State Department ridiculed the idea. Everyone in Washington agreed on the need to keep Iran's military united, but the embassy and the State Department doubted that Bakhtiar could provide a stable government; the revolution's complete triumph, they believed, could not be long delayed.

The best that could be hoped for, they thought, was that the moderates would come to the fore and that Khomeini would retire to Qom to teach theology. Obviously, the special relationship Washington had enjoyed with the shah's Iran would not be restored, but the previous close alliance might still be replaced by an amiable, if more distant, link coupled with some cooperation in their mutual interests. After all, Iran would still face the long-standing geopolitical challenges that had so concerned the shah. As for economic relations, Senator Frank Church, chairman of the Senate Foreign Relations Committee, suggested that "any government in Iran that comes to power will have to sell its oil and the only place to sell its oil is in the Western world."[34]

Bakhtiar, of course, tried to carry out his own negotiations with Khomeini. He sent Jamaleddin Tehrani, head of the Regency Council, to Paris on January 16. When this failed, the prime minister called Beheshti and volunteered to go himself. At first Khomeini agreed to meet him, but changed his mind a few hours later; he would talk to Bakhtiar only if the prime minister resigned. Bakhtiar had little more success with the military. They promised to support him, but Bakhtiar knew only what Moghadam and Gharabaghi chose to tell him.

The task of expressing the United States desire to have the military remain united behind Bakhtiar was left to General Robert Huyser, whose mission was the outcome of the frantic White House policy debate of late December. Huyser knew little of Iranian politics, but he had a good reputation and a warm friendship with the key Iranian generals. His superior, General Alexander Haig, later maintained that he, Haig, had opposed the mission: the Iranian military was disintegrating and could be saved only if given the task of restoring order. Nor was Huyser delighted with his mission, although he did do his best to fulfill it.

Sullivan, for his part, was no more happy to see Huyser in Tehran than the general was to be there. The ambassador told Washington that the Iranian military needed guarantees and that these could be provided only through some sort of agreement with Khomeini. The White House agreed and behind Carter's secret message to Paris and his attempt to arrange a meeting with the ayatollah was his interest in obtaining such an arrangement. As mentioned above, nothing came of either effort.

The view that the shah was doomed had been reinforced at the Guadaloupé summit in early January, when Carter met with British Prime Minister James Callaghan, West German Chancellor Helmut Schmidt, and French President Valery Giscard d'Estaing. All three European leaders agreed that the shah was finished and Giscard d'Estaing, who spoke last, was particularly strong on this point. If the shah remained, he said, Iran would face civil war. Many people would be killed and the Communists would gain a great deal of influence. Ultimately, American military advisors on the scene would become involved in the fighting and this might form a pretext for Soviet intervention. What Europe needed, he continued, was Iranian oil and stability in the region. Khomeini had been living in France and, the French president suggested, might not be so unreasonable. Washington should reconcile itself to the political change.

So when Huyser arrived in Tehran, about the time Bakhtiar was being officially made prime minister on January 3, he represented not only the United States but also, in effect, the entire Western alliance. One of Huyser's most effective cards in winning the generals' acquiescence for the shah's exile were the minutes from that meeting of the allies. When Sullivan went to the shah to work out the details of his departure, Huyser went with him. It was at this meeting that the shah first learned of the general's presence in Iran.

Washington was more immediately concerned with the dangers of a military coup than with the equally dangerous possibility of the army disintegrating, but Huyser's job was to ensure that the military remained loyal to Bakhtiar and that it contributed to a smooth transition to whatever broadly based opposition regime finally came to power. He was also to assess the state of the Iranian armed forces: Were they united? Who were the key leaders? According to some sources, Huyser was also to hold the armed forces together for possible military action if necessary in Bakhtiar's defense. His reports about the military were optimistic. They were 85 percent loyal, he concluded, and they would probably fight if Bakhtiar gave the word to restore order. Every evening Huyser reported directly by telephone to the Chairman of the Joint Chiefs of Staff in Washington, General David Jones. Defense Secretary Brown or Deputy Secretary Charles Duncan usually listened in.

In his earliest meetings with the generals, Huyser explained why it was the view of the United States and its European allies that the shah's personal rule must end. Working mostly out of the United States MAAG office in the headquarters of

Iran's joint chiefs of staff, Huyser met with the generals daily and talked to Gharabaghi every morning. Admiral Alahi usually translated, but General Rabi'i, Huyser's closest friend among the Iranians, often helped. Among other things, Huyser pledged that the United States would supply Iran's armed forces with the fuel it needed to function. Shortly thereafter, a tanker arrived with 200,000 barrels of oil.

The generals also had their own requests. They wanted the United States to guarantee that Khomeini would not be allowed to return to Iran and they wanted an end to BBC broadcasts and to the distribution of Khomeini's inflammatory statements. Huyser could do nothing on these demands but he did refer them to Washington. Huyser also promised that America would back decisive action by the military if there were attacks on their installations or on the Bakhtiar government. Like Bakhtiar, however, Huyser was largely dependent on the top half-dozen officers for information; they could hardly be expected to reveal to this foreigner that their troops were no longer dependable or that they were thinking of making their own deal with Khomeini, though Huyser later claimed to have been suspicious of Gharabaghi's intentions. Still, as long as Huyser was in Tehran it seemed unlikely that they would go back on their word.

Sullivan's view of events was much more realistic. As if compensating for his excessive optimism of the previous year, the ambassador now reported, contradicting Huyser, that Iran's political structures were breaking apart. His personal attitude toward Bakhtiar verged on contempt. The troops simply did not support him, the embassy told Washington, and many leading figures as well as officers were preparing to join their Swiss bank accounts in exile. The White House preferred to believe Huyser, and Sullivan, long viewed by many as a holdover from the Kissinger era, was criticized as being defeatist and perhaps even disloyal to the Carter White House.

Recognizing the prevailing trend, Sullivan settled for urging Bakhtiar to meet with Bazargan, Beheshti, and Nasir Minachi, opposition leaders he characterized as reasonable men to whom one could talk. By mid-January, embassy

officers were conducting their own informal survey, testing
the possibility of bringing together Bakhtiar, the Khomeinists,
and the Iranian military on a political formula to restore calm
and to keep non-Communist forces in control of Iran. The
Khomeini forces, sensing their imminent victory, concentrated on subverting the military.

Once Khomeini judged conditions ready, he announced that
he would now return to Iran. Bakhtiar did not dare move to
block him, but he warned the Khomeinist forces not to violate
the law. Otherwise, Iran "would probably return to a black
period of dictatorship and possibly even of feudalism." Khomeini was welcome to come back, Bakhtiar announced, but he
would "not permit the affairs of the state to be governed other
than by and through the power of the central government." [35]

Yet if Bakhtiar held the office, Khomeini held the power. On
February 1 the ayatollah landed in a chartered Air France
plane at Mehrebad Airport, from which the shah had left two
weeks earlier. Seats on the flight had been sold to reporters to
help finance the trip. Hundreds of thousands of people poured
out to see him. His aides, National Front leaders, and
prestigious mullahs met him; Koranic verses were recited; and
Khomeini made a brief speech.

No soldiers could be seen anywhere but, as a last symbol of
the power of the old order, television coverage was suddenly interrupted and was replaced by a portrait of the shah, an occurrence attributed to "technical difficulties"; radio coverage was
also cut off in the middle of the event and replaced by recorded music. Still, the rally was a complete success. Thousands of banners lined the route, welcoming home Iran's new
leader.

Khomeini wasted no time in announcing he would not negotiate with Bakhtiar. Ghotbzadeh gave previews of the ayatollah's policies. The army, he said, "is overequipped and
trained by the Americans, does not serve the nation's defense
but the regime and Washington's designs in the region." Its
structure must be drastically changed and its armament
reduced.

As for foreign policy, he continued, the superpowers to the

north and south had convinced past Iranian politicians that the country could survive only by giving way to them. Yet complete dependence on one had never defended Iran against the others and worse, during periods of detente, the two foreign states had agreed to share influence in Iran. Khomeini's supporters did not take seriously any Communist threat because the Iranian people would accept only an Islamic ideology. "The only means of liberating Iran is to remove it from the hands of the superpowers," Ghotbzadeh concluded.[36]

Khomeini was still not secure about the irreversibility of his victory; this constant fear would play a central role in motivating the revolution's hysterical anti-Americanism and the future kidnapping of United States diplomats. The shah might return at any moment with American aid, producing for a second time the political miracle that had been pulled off in August, 1953. In Washington's view, the shah was gone forever, but no words or expressions of goodwill could convince Khomeini of American sincerity.

"We will not let the United States bring the shah back," Khomeini said shortly after his return. "This is what the shah wants. Wake up. Watch out. They want the country to go back to what it was previously." Soviet-directed radio broadcasts sought to spread this paranoia. "Embassy employees and 25,000 imperialist agents" were working to reinstate the monarchy, the programs lied. "We urge our fellow citizens to be alert and pay full attention to the activities of the U.S. Embassy." But such efforts did not so much inflame the populace as they reflected the prevailing mood in the country.

Government analysts in Washington preferred to look on the bright side. Khomeini's statements, one said, were necessary political rhetoric. "As unpalatable as it was for us, he would have weakened his position by doing anything else." They had not yet learned to take Khomeini's ideology seriously and literally. The hope continued, as one policymaker put it, that the ayatollah would be an "ultimate, moral arbiter" rather than a political power.[37]

Bakhtiar fought back bravely, if overoptimistically. "For 50

years, never has the army been so obedient to a prime minister," he claimed on February 2. In reality, the army was disintegrating, with thousands of desertions. SAVAK was also falling apart, as agents were either murdered or fled their posts in
the countryside and provincial towns. "If I do not resist there
will be a new dictatorship far worse and (more) horrendous
than the previous dictatorship," he stated on Tehran radio two
days later. "Power must emanate from the strength of law.
Club-wielding, mob rule and hue and cry do not constitute
power or strength. Power must be coupled with the faculty
of reasoning and thought."[38] He tried to distance himself
from the United States. Seven billion out of twelve billion
dollars in pending contracts with American arms suppliers
were cancelled. He also announced Iran's withdrawal from
CENTO.

On the other hand, Bazargan, Khomeini's shadow prime
minister, was careful not to attack the United States and he
implied that friendly relations would continue. "In establishing an era of equal relations with the United States," he told
a Greek newspaper in early February, "I do not see why we
should not buy weapons from it."[39]

Bazargan, who had prudently spent his first day following
his appointment by Khomeini hiding at his daughter's small
apartment, also named his own cabinet. There were signs that
the urban middle class was pleased by Khomeini's choice of
such a well-known moderate. New homafar demonstrations
at air bases on February 3 provided signs that the military
might also be about to change sides. Yet Huyser gave President Carter an optimistic report on February 5. Bakhtiar's government was now even better off, the general implied, because
of its handling of Khomeini's return. But if the White House
continued to believe in Bakhtiar's chances, there were few in
Tehran who had any such illusions. "Unless they blow it by
provoking the hardline officers," said one embassy official,
"the religious movement essentially has won. There is a good
chance their victory could be orderly, with any vestiges of the
Bakhtiar government fading away."[40]

The pace of demonstrations and strikes increased. The

Majlis ceased to function and, on February 9, Sanjabi called for Bakhtiar's resignation. The opposition's arrangements with Fardost, Gharabaghi, and Moghadam were completed and even Rabi'i joined in the still-secret decision to withdraw military support from Bakhtiar. On the morning of February 11 it was all over. Gharabaghi was due in Bakhtiar's office at nine o'clock for a routine meeting. He did not come. Bakhtiar called him up at eleven and the chief of staff told him that the army had decided to declare itself neutral.

"At that moment I realized it was finished," Bakhtiar later recounted. "And then machine-gun fire began to open up all around the prime ministrial office." He walked calmly down the back stairs, boarded a helicopter, and was taken into hiding. Some time later, early one morning, he took a commercial airliner from Mehrebad airport in disguise. He went into exile in France.[41]

This, then was the epilogue for twenty-five hundred years of monarchy in Iran. The revolution had triumphed; the main pillar of American policy in the Persian Gulf had collapsed. The future for both America and Iran was suddenly unpredictable. But to understand Iran's new order and its new foreign policy it is necessary to consider in more detail the motives for the revolution and the world view of its leaders.

9
Charismatic Disorder
1979

In the months after the revolution, a host of theories began to circulate among pro- and anti-shah Iranians, as well as among Americans, as to why the shah had fallen and what the United States would do now that he was gone. Within Tehran, from the very first days after the revolution, radical factions were interpreting American initiatives toward the new Islamic regime as sinister plots.

Committed to the position that America saw its interests as inexorably tied to those of the shah and that therefore it could never accept the shah's removal from power, they believed that, as in 1953, Washington would plot a counterrevolution. Very nearly every difficulty facing the new Islamic government was attributed to such machinations; anyone showing the least sign of softness toward the United States was to be discredited. The Ayatollah Khomeini repeatedly described America as a satanic force and as the new Iran's number one enemy.

From the beginning, this view was based on misinformation regarding attitudes in Washington. The Carter administration quickly accepted the shah's departure and certainly made no attempt to reverse the events that had brought him down. On the contrary, Washington's aim was to cut its losses and salvage whatever could be saved of the old relationship; the hope was that conciliation would elicit future Iranian cooperation, particularly against any expansion of Soviet influence in the area. This policy position was determined by strategic considerations the administration hoped would shape Iranian policy under the new regime, as they had under the shah.

Events subsequently demonstrated the fundamental misreading of the revolution involved in such thinking. The importance of the Khomeinist ideology was underestimated: the speeches of Iranian leaders were treated as mere rhetoric. The eventual triumph of "objective" geographic and economic factors were, mistakenly, taken for granted, as was the inevitability of a Tehran government directed by pragmatists attempting to achieve traditional political goals.

At the opposite end of the conspiracy-explanation spectrum were the theories of many former Iranian government officials and a group of American critics of the White House. Not only did the United States have no plan to return the shah to power, they argued, but Washington had been responsible for his removal in the first place. The collapse was caused by a conspiracy, according to pro-shah relations; some American analysts attributed it to presidential incompetence. Still others were willing to ascribe any adverse turn of events to some deep immorality in American foreign policy.

Indeed, it was quickly clear in the debate following the shah's fall that there were two possible American scapegoats: the Nixon and Ford administrations—for creating the close relationship with Iran—or the Carter administration—for presiding over its disappearance. Arguments in support of any of these positions, however, were subject to a distorting influence—the astonishment aroused by the event itself. How could this earthquake have happened? Why had the highly touted Iranian military collapsed so easily? Why had the reportedly dynamic and masterful shah fallen so quickly into confusion and passivity? These and other questions were asked by an incredulous American public. If there were contradictions here then someone must surely be at fault for failing to avoid such an easily preventable disaster.

Since most pro-shah Iranians were not likely to suggest that the failure lay with their own performance, and since those Americans who had taken part in establishing the special ties between the United States and Iran would not call attention to their own errors of performance and judgment, the blows fell on the Carter administration. Obviously, they agreed, it had been too harsh on the human rights question, too miserly with arms sales, and too slow and too soft in responding to the revolutionary crisis.

There is, however, yet another possible approach: *All* sides have tended to exaggerate the importance of American actions and decisions on events in Iran. In studying the history of the two nations' relations one is most impressed with Washington's difficulties in influencing Iranian affairs. Even the seeming exception—the overthrow of Mossadegh in 1953—is not so clear as it seems on first impression. American intervention in Iran in that year was the result of an unusual—and unrepeated—set of circumstances. The fact that Washington was seeking to undermine an already shaky regime—that the CIA was pushing open an unlatched door—explains why the 1953 operation was so simple and successful.

It is not necessary to ascribe the success of the Iranian revolution to some failure of American foreign policy. This misunderstanding has been created by the confusion that exists over the Iranian political situation. Those who assumed that the shah had been a pillar of strength and that his policies had been relatively successful at home found it hard to comprehend the nature of the revolt against him. But, on the contrary, if the shah's strength had been partly illusory and if his policies had caused disruption and dissatisfaction among Iranians then the uprising's appeal becomes understandable. The dislocation was not between a true image and irrational events but between a false image and a commensurate outcome.

During the first ten months of the revolution, when Washington never pressed the shah for concessions, the opposition was open to compromise. By the time the administration finally began to get more actively involved, in December, 1978, the shah was ready to give way but the antiregime forces had by then become intransigent. While the shah was not receptive to American pressures during the early period, neither would all-out support have guaranteed his regime's survival. The situation would have been the reverse of that which prevailed in 1953. At that time, the United States aligned itself with those trying to overthrow an ineffectual, collapsing regime that had brought great hardship to Iran; in 1978 it was the shah who headed the similarly faltering and even more unpopular regime.

Khomeini, too, overestimated the extent and potential of American influence in Iran but his view—whatever its basis in fact—became a major material force that captured the minds of Iranians and stirred their revolutionary passions. Twentieth-century revolutions have sprung far more often from nationalist-inspired hatred of outsiders than from class grievances. The Iranian revolution succeeded by mobilizing millions of Iranians against an America equated with satan and against a shah successfully portrayed as un-Islamic. Within this framework the behavior of Khomeini and other Iranian leaders was quite rational: they did not care what effect their actions had on Washington, they were concerned only with the reverberations in Tehran and around their own country. Indeed, the more reckless they were in contemptuous disregard for how the United States might respond to their insults, the more heroic and popular they became to their own followers.

But the mere presence of political dynamite does not always bring an explosion—there must be a fuse and it must be set off. What were the causes that turned a potential revolution into a rout of the region's most solidly entrenched regime? Former Secretary of State Henry Kissinger ascribes the events almost exclusively to American failings, presumably those arising after he left office. The transformation of "inchoate unrest into a revolution," he said, was caused by American weakness and by a clumsy tactical handling of the crisis by the Carter administration.

"To my mind," explains Kissinger, "the combination of Soviet actions in Ethiopia, the South Yemen, Afghanistan, plus
the general perception of an American geopolitical decline,
had the consequence of demoralizing those whose stock in
trade was cooperation with the United States, undermining
their resolution towards potential revolutionaries." The shah
did not resist the opposition more forcefully "because he must
have had doubts about our real intentions." The liberalization
strategy, forced on the shah by Washington, was mistaken, he
adds, since an ongoing revolution cannot be moderated by
concessions. These can come only when order is restored.

"Whether we like it or not," he concludes, "the shah was
considered our close ally in that area for 37 years. He left office under the visible urging of the United States." Other local
rulers, he suggested, would fear similar treatment by America
and seek alliances elsewhere.[1]

This analysis seems to ignore the fact that the idea of a
weakened America, especially in its resolve, was not new to
the shah: as early as 1958 it had been a major factor in his
drive for military self-sufficiency. Nor was it clear that United
States losses elsewhere had any major effect on the shah's
response to the rebellion—this understates the primacy of domestic Iranian forces operating in 1978. Moreover, during the
first ten months of the crisis, the White House had nothing but
private and public praise for the shah and his policies. The
mild expressions of doubt and the urgings toward "liberalization" and coalition took place very late in the game, after it
had already become clear that the shah's strategy was failing.
Further, even these statements were so phrased as to be en-
dorsements of the shah's own promises of free elections and
the establishment of a broader government.

Yet the idea of White House responsibility for the shah's
collapse was an irresistible one, especially among those who
sought the presidency. As early as January, 1979, Republican
candidate George Bush accused the president of "pulling the
rug out from under the shah." His "on-again, off-again statements . . . did much to hasten his departure," because the administration's policy of "splendid oscillation" severed the

links between the United States and its allies.[2] The onset of the hostage crisis helped to temporarily still such criticism.

Others, for equally political reasons, blamed the Kissinger-Nixon strategy of building up the shah as a regional great power. George Ball emphasized the "pervasive corruption" in Iran and Nixon's "disastrous encouragement to the shah to overload his country with inappropriate military hardware." This "costly burden" resulted in financial pressures that caused unemployment, disaffection, and an encouragement of the shah's megalomania.

Rejecting the Kissinger analysis, Ball wrote, "The reason the shah did not stand and fight was that his whole country was solidly against him and his army was beginning to disintegrate under the pressure of competing loyalties." "It is fatuous," he concluded, "to think that we could have kept a hated absolute monarch in power by encouraging the progressive use of military force. This was, after all, an internal revolt. What would Mr. Kissinger have done? Sent the Sixth Fleet steaming up the Gulf?"

This view can also be challenged. The Nixon Doctrine strategy was a response to existing limitations on American resources and to anticipated domestic opposition toward direct United States military interventions in defense of its allies. The shah's fascination with arms was not an American creation; nor would Washington's refusal to sell him arms have necessarily prevented his overloading his country with inappropriate military hardware purchased from other sources.

As for the immediate White House response to the revolution, many unpopular dictators have kept themselves in power through ruthless repression. While the shah's cause was hopeless by the time Ball appeared on the scene in November, 1978, there were times earlier in the year when different American actions might have contributed toward a different outcome. An understanding of the sad course of United States-Iranian relations must utilize aspects of both analyses.

A third and less satisfactory set of explanations was offered by pro-shah Iranians, including the monarch himself. The shah has blamed his downfall on a conspiracy, hinting that

American oil companies aimed to do him in as part of a scheme to raise petroleum prices. Khomeini, he added, was too uneducated to have planned the revolution; Khomeini's aides, Yazdi and Ghotbzadeh, had spent several years in the United States. Therefore, the shah implies, it was all a CIA plot.

Other Iranians have carried the idea further. They assume that the CIA clearly foresaw the future. Hence its refusal to halt the revolution is sufficient evidence of its complicity. The CIA and British intelligence, popular myths explain, smuggled in thousands of Khomeini cassettes and used the BBC to spread such a volume of anti-shah propaganda that the latter became known as the "Voice of Khomeini."

Hushang Nahavandi, a former minister of education and a respected university administrator, has developed this theory in some detail. "The Americans certainly supported Khomeini's movement and helped it to set up an anti-communist hardline Islamic regime in this part of the world." Carter, Nahavandi explained, realized that a crisis was coming and prompted the shah toward political reform while supporting "the emergence of an Islamic regime that would stand against any communist tide resulting from the imbalance in the country's social structure." Thus, Huyser's mission was "to prevent a pro-shah military coup like that of 1953 in which the opposition would be crushed and its revolution suppressed."[3]

Perhaps the most systematic analysis of the revolution made in the pro-shah media appeared in the magazine *Khandaniha* in December, 1978; the article reveals the flavor of this view, which has much in common with Khomeinist logic. Behind the upheaval, it explained "are non-Iranian hands skillfully, sometimes hastily, moving their unsuspecting and gullible puppets." "As always," external factors were primary in shaping that process.

The anti-shah demonstrations during the shah's November, 1977 Washington visit, "perhaps even encouraged by CIA officials," showed that the Democratic administration was intent on weakening the shah. After the Marxist coup in Afghanistan, the article continued, the United States wanted to force

Iran to break its ties with the Soviets. "Naturally, because of Islam's incompatibility with Communism, the USA would not object if the contemplated replacement government is a 100 percent Islamic theocracy." To achieve this, "it was necessary to create unrest and turmoil with Iran. Hence, experienced CIA operatives set to work."

A second reason for the revolution was the shah's activism in OPEC, according to this view. The oil cartel and the CIA were determined to remove the shah even—this in contradiction to the editors' first point—if they had to strengthen Communist influence in Iran. Even corruption was part of the foreigners' diabolical scheme.[4] These themes of conspiracy and of American responsibility for events within Iran thus characterized the CIA as scapegoat for the domestic difficulties of both shah and post-shah governments.

There are at least three problems with this analysis. First, it presumes both an all-powerful United States and the careful planning of all events. To Iranians, the idea that the CIA did not know what was going on in Iran or that America enjoyed only very limited influence over the shah was preposterous. Nor does the absence of hard evidence discourage belief in even the wildest theories. Rather, such an absence of evidence may be taken as confirmation of the all-pervasive nature of the conspiracy.

Second, this view confuses the situation of January, 1979, when the shah himself came to accept the hopelessness of his position, and that of the months before, when his government might still have saved itself. By the time of the Huyser mission, Washington was reconciled to the fact that even the most unified and concerted military action could not have crushed the opposition. Public opinion and political conditions in Iran were in early 1979 already at a point opposite those prevailing in August, 1953, when many were eager to see Mossadegh fall.

Finally, such an analysis misstates the motivation of the White House. By early 1979 American policy was based on a desperate attempt to adapt to clearly changing conditions. The decision to support a peaceful transition to opposition rule was dictated by a combination of wishful thinking and an absence of options. Though none in the United States government actually preferred that Khomeini take power, the frequently expressed hope was that political processes would allow the moderates to come out on top. In analyzing the actions of the Carter administration during the last days of the shah's regime, errors in judgment and limited choices, rather than a conspiratorial intent, must provide the essential explanation. Before discussing the causes of the Iranian revolution in detail it is useful to evaluate the part played by the American arms-transfer program in this event. After all, military sales were the most visible connection between the two countries. They affected Iranian attitudes toward the shah and towards the United States on two levels—those of legitimacy as well as those of economics.

The former issue has been summarized by Shahram Chubin: "Few [Iranians] understood why a $10 billion defense budget had become a necessity overnight or why a war on the Horn of Africa threatened them. Nor could the majority of Iranians comprehend why large loans were being made to other countries when Iran's own countryside was deteriorating." [5]

Many Iranians concluded that if the petroleum income was not serving their country's needs, as they understood them, then they must be designed to meet American interests. Petrodollars were being squandered, they believed, in exchange for "worthless" arms. Such attitudes could even be found among shah loyalists. A typical statement, from a Majlis member and union leader just before the shah's departure, complained, "the United States Government, by frightening the Iranian people with the spectres of their neighbors, by selling us used weapons at exorbitant prices, has poured billions of rials into the pockets of U.S. military cartels" and for United States military advisors. [6]

In Iranian eyes, it was the arms-sale program, more than any other aspect of the alliance between the United States and Iran, that compromised the shah's image with Iranians and led them to believe that the shah was America's "man." Bani-Sadr, after criticizing American military sales, aid, training, and advisors, concluded: "The economic health, social welfare and cultural integrity of the nation are all being sacrificed so that the Shah can continue to rule within the framework of American strategic objectives." [7]

Officially, Iran spent about 25 percent of its governmental budgets of the 1970s on the military, though hidden costs might have raised this figure another 5 percent. Although aggressive corporate salesmen oversold certain specific systems, the United States government hardly forced the material on the shah, who bought these weapons to meet what he saw as real threats. Though his purchases were quantitatively and qualitatively excessive, the Soviet invasion of Afghanistan and other regional events may yet demonstrate that his fears about aggressive neighbors were not completely foolish.

Nor should it be assumed that a transfer of money from military spending to economic development would necessarily have avoided the revolution. After all, such a shift might only have further accelerated Iran's "modernization," a central cause of the discontent. It is interesting to note that after the revolution Bani-Sadr advocated slowing down petroleum production, thereby generating less overall revenue and making possible a slower pace for Iran's civilian sector.

On the American side, there is no reason to doubt that the primary motive for the Nixon-Kissinger policy was a strategic one. The May, 1972 commitment to sell the shah unlimited amounts of equipment and the government's later handling of arms sales can certainly be called shortsighted and almost criminally careless, but this does not mean that there were additional hidden motives behind the administration's choices. The arms-sale program helped to discredit the shah at home, to stir Iranian antagonisms toward the United States, and to create problems for the Iranian economy. Nevertheless, the overall importance of this program should not be overestimated in assessing the contributing factors to the revolution, and it may well be that these purchases were more significant in undermining the shah's legitimacy than they were in terms of the economic damage they did to Iran.

An overall examination of the many factors leading to the

revolution would have to include a series of long-range factors that helped forge the unique Iranian political culture, medium-range factors that shaped the attitudes of various Iranian social and economic groups toward the shah's regime, and immediate issues that turned this strained relationship into a mass uprising. The Iranian revolution and its outcome can only be understood as a combination of these various factors:

• The traditional antagonism of peasants, tribes, and outlying ethnic groups toward the central government encourages these groups to thwart their rulers wherever possible. The shah's forces represented the unwelcome intrusion of military conscription, tax collection, and the concentration of power outside of the local identity groups. The 1978–79 revolution graphically demonstrated also the bandwagon effect of any seemingly successful uprising—everyone wanted to be on the winning side.

These strong antagonisms, however, have once more reasserted their influence now that the revolutionary forces have themselves become the central government in the Azerbaijani, Kurdish, and Arab revolts and in the proliferation of political power centers in competition with the central authorities. The tension between extremes of tyranny and anarchy, so often visible in Iranian history, has often produced an autocracy dependent on an individual—the shah and Khomeini are both examples. It is not yet clear whether the 1979 revolution has broken this cycle, but it can probably not tame the strong Iranian rebellious streak.

• Religion has always been a source of either reinforcement of or challenge to ruling authority. Zoroastrianism was the state religion of pre-Islamic Iran but heretical offshoots produced revolutionary movements. Islam also blurred the distinction between religion and "secular" politics, since social life and the conduct of public affairs were supposed to conform to the laws of God, as set down in the Koran and the subsequent theological commentaries. The Abbassid revolution of 750 used this ideology to bring down the caliphate. Iran's form of Shi'a Islam, which stressed descent from Muhammad's family as a precondition for serving as ruler, was also united with the Safavid dynasty, becoming the official religion in 1502. The Safavids even launched an international Shi'a propaganda campaign, as had the pro-Abbassid revolutionaries before them, to win converts, particularly in the domains of their enemies. While the mainstream Sunni Muslim sect tended to become tamed and bureaucratized by the ruling authority, the Shi'a clergy kept their parallel and semi-independent hierarchy, as well as their popular base among the masses.

In the Christian West various sects broke off from the Catholic church, the pope's power was defeated by secular monarchs during the early Middle Ages, and the separation of church and state was gradually recognized. Even Jesus made the distinction between that which was to be rendered to God and that which was to be rendered Caesar's. The Reformation and the Renaissance, as well as the widespread acceptance of Darwinism and the scientific method, further undermined religion's role as supplier of philosophy, ethics, and law. None of this happened in the Islamic world.

In Iran, for example, a relatively small number of those educated in Western liberal, technocratic, or Marxist world views dominated politics from the capital city. The overwhelming majority of Iranians remained in their traditional life-styles and maintained traditional values. In Turkey, Ataturk made some basic changes, through his imposition of modernism and Turkish nationalism on the people. In the Arab world, Arab nationalism gained ideological dominance during the decades before and after World War II.

There was no such mediation of the Islamic role in Iran and, consequently, the clergy there played a greater role in the nationalist and anti-imperialist movement than did the clergy in the Arab and Sunni worlds. In this context, the West was suspect not only because of its alien and non-Muslim nature but also because of the East's thwarted feelings of superiority. Why was the Muslim world, more ethical and spiritual than the West, subjected to Western power? The answer given was that the West had immorally suppressed Muslim rights. Modernism was seen as a further conspiracy to hold down the Muslims politically and economically; even worse, it threatened to strip them of their very culture and religion.

• Under the decaying Qajar dynasty, in the late nineteenth and early twentieth centuries, the shahs acquired bad reputations as antinationalists. Their dependence on the British and the Russians and their concessions to the powerful foreigners undermined their legitimacy. On more than one occasion, an alliance of merchants, intellectuals, and clergy—reminiscent of the 1978 coalition—saw the Qajars and foreign influence as a single enemy to be fought.

As an example, when in 1890 the ruling shah gave a tobacco monopoly to a British subject, those opposed to his regime cried out against corruption, against misgovernment, and against the dominance of foreign powers simultaneously. The merchants also charged that the shah had sacrificed their material well-being for that of a foreigner, the intellectuals rallied for Iran's incipient nationalism, and the clergy declared imperiled the laws of Islam. The mullahs issued a decree ordering Muslims to abstain from tobacco products. The shah was forced to abrogate his deal.

During the constitutionalist revolution the clergy was split into pro- and anti-shah factions. But the efforts of the latter were recognized in the 1906 constitution (which the demonstrators of 1978 sought to revive) that provided for a panel of five clerical representatives to ensure that no law violated Islamic precepts.

• Reza Shah ended the decadent Qajar era but he also destroyed the constitutionalist forces by revitalizing the monarchy. His attempts to rebuild the centralized state led him to attack the clergy, regional elites, the ethnic minorities and tribes, and the aristocracy. His pressure for modernism, including the campaign to unveil women, brought him into collision with the clergy. Few were sorry to see him go and their antagonism carried over to his son, Muhammad Reza Shah.

• The events of August, 1953 further put the shah in an antinational, unfavorable light and associated him with foreign and un-Islamic forces. The fact that Kashani and others also took an anti-Mossadegh stance was forgotten, as were the shortcomings of the National Front regime. Opposition elements believed the shah to be a traitor, dependent on American influence for his very throne.

The shah's policies after 1953 also provoked a number of medium-term conflicts.

• The shah's enervation of the Majlis and the premiership as power centers made possible a more decisive government but at a price—by reducing the right to participation of various groups, he lost the support of these forces. In addition, the buffers that protected his exalted status as head of state did not shield him from harsh criticism once he assumed the role of head of government, particularly once he decided to exercise one-man rule. The politicized class could hope only to be bureaucrats, executing his policy.

The White Revolution further alienated the landlord part of the elite and some religious leaders, though the shah continued to have many supporters among the clergy. The 1962–63 riots were, at one and the same time, protests against land reform and the changing status of women—symbols of modernization—and protests against the growing power of the shah.

• While the urban middle classes, the merchants, and professionals might have been thought beneficiaries of the system, they too shared the political complaints noted above. As well, they expressed a whole range of economic and personal objections to the shah's rule. Though corruption, for example, was by no means a phenomenon unknown in Iranian history (during the Mossadegh era, parents sometimes reportedly had to bribe teachers in order to have their children promoted to the next grade), the main impetus of the new corruption, from the 1960s on, was not its existence but its social impact. The spending on arms, imports, and construction seemed to disproportionately benefit a group of new-rich, who became wealthy through their particular connections with the shah, the court, and the Americans. These opportunities were generally closed to the 60,000 bazaar merchants in Tehran, as well as to their counterparts in provincial towns. Moreover, large-scale imports of mass-produced goods threatened to drive these artisans and merchants out of business. The cultural challenge of the West thus became intertwined with an economic one. Insult was often added to such injury, as in the persistent talk of a superhighway that might be run through the bazaar.

• SAVAK and government repression also hit hardest the modern sectors of the urban population, those who might have been expected to support the shah. One aspect of this was the ripple effect of arrests—each victim or prisoner had dozens of relatives who were turned against the regime.

That Iran was a country prepared for parliamentary democracy was by no means clear, nor are the shah's successors known for their adherence to human rights or to due process of law. Much of SAVAK has been simply taken over, though renamed, by the Khomeinists. Yet the anti-shah movement had an element of emotional appeal never to be matched by the shah—it was able to mobilize the masses, inspiring ideas of populism and group participation. In much of the Third World such mechanisms have seemingly produced viable governments. Repression by the post-shah regime cloaked itself in the psychologically satisfying rationalization that it was getting revenge for the majority over the minority, rather than vice versa.

• Association with foreigners made the shah appear fair game for xenophobic appeals. He was, his enemies said, the hireling of the Americans, more interested in helping them than in aiding his own people. The shah's toleration of both the Jews and the hated but inoffensive Bahai sect provoked similar reactions.

The exchange of petrodollars for arms, leaving Iran with "worthless" weaponry, was viewed by many Iranians as a giving away of their country's wealth for the Americans' double benefit—an advantage for both their economic and strategic interests. The handling of foreign labor also created problems. When Iran imported technology it also imported advisors and technicians. Saudi Arabia and Kuwait had similar problems, but top-level jobs in those countries were reserved for citizens. The large-scale use of Arab guest workers at all levels also lessened the cultural dissonance. Finally, of course, those countries had enough money to amply reward their nationals, whose small number made per capita oil income several times higher than that of the Iranians. To the inhabitants of the Arab petroleum producers, the foreigners seemed to be serving them; in Iran the foreigners were perceived as being on top.

From the Iranian point of view, diplomats, military advisors, and businessmen from abroad were housed by employers in expensive villas or apartments, had access to duty-free or subsidized food, drink, and household goods, employed servants, and gave lavish parties. It was not a question of these people doing anything wrong—they were simply living the way they had at home—but the cultural and material contrast between American and Iranian life-styles and living standards was simply too great at close quarters. "The public feeling is that members of these groups are particularly pampered" at Iranian expense, said one Tehran magazine during the revolution.[8]

Under the surface grew darker resentments, to be manifested after the revolution in the taking of United States hostages. This was the view that Iran was an American colony. "The embassy was the real center of power in Iran," claimed Bani-Sadr, and he added, "If you U.S. people, after 35 years of interference in and rule over your affairs by an embassy, were to carry out a revolution and achieve victory, would you consider the employees of that embassy as normal employees?" And, again: "All that happened in Iran: It was not the imperial court that made the decision, it was the United States Embassy."[9] Ayatollah Khomeini would be fond of saying that the United States was the cause of all Iran's troubles and this was a constant theme of the other radical leaders.

• Perhaps the most important factor behind Iran's internal strains was the rapid inflow of such vast amounts of oil revenue into the country, with the subsequent headlong rush into modernization and disproportionate military spending. The general American view of this process contained two misleading assumptions. First, it was assumed that life was being significantly improved for the average Iranian. Second, was the dichotomy perceived between a promodernization shah and a reactionary opposition.

In fact, some sectors of Iran, particularly in the rural areas, faced declining fortunes, and within the overall population disparities increased. The most prosperous Iranians, who made up 20 percent of the population, received 57.5 percent of the income in 1972 and 63.5 percent in 1975. The share of the middle 40 percent decreased from 31 percent to 25.5 percent over the same period, and that of the poorest 40 percent declined from 11.5 percent to 11 percent.[10]

For many individuals, "modernization" became associated with negative things—anomie, disorganization, waste, corruption, incompetent administration, dependence on foreigners, inflation, and uncomfortably dizzying change. Specific aspects of the poorly planned crash modernization damaged Iranians economically and culturally at the same time. Every village, for example, had its potter who made earthenware vessels for storage and cooking. Imported plastic goods destroyed the livelihood of these artisans. Imported plastic shoes made in Japan or Iran destroyed not only the traditional shoemaking industry but also cut the demand for leather, and hence damaged herders, middlemen, and retailers. Natural fibers could not compete with artificial fibers; the government thought it cheaper to import food than to invest in helping the Iranian peasantry. Importers and contractors with special connections benefitted while several strata of workers, artisans, and merchants were driven to the wall. Ironically, the plastic and fibers that had this effect were made from petrochemicals, in other words, from Iran's own oil. Efficiency, in its narrowest sense, dictated policies that were socially disastrous. Thus, Western goods seemed to combine with Western culture and Western power as threats to Iran.

• Iran's culture shock resulted from foreign goods and ideas coming into the country and from the internal mobility of Iranians themselves. As for the former aspect, Ayatollah Khomeini called television and advertising the two worst enemies of Islam, as perpetrators of alien concepts. Nor did the Western media always present the best of Western life or the most favorable views of those societies.

As early as 1932, Dr. R. E. Hoffman, an American missionary in Iran, wrote that "our films are suggesting to the Persians that American life consists chiefly of cow-punching, rescuing abducted girls, gangster warfare, and walking like Charlie Chaplin."[11] The next generation was able to watch the modern equivalents on their television sets: "Baretta," "Cannon," "Ironside," "The Six-Million Dollar Man," westerns, detective shows, and the worst "B" movies. American programs averaged 30.6 percent of broadcasting time. Although Iran produced many films itself, Western features dominated the theatres.[12] All this material was un-Islamic and Khomeini would convince many that it was in fact anti-Islamic. If Iranians still wanted these goods, Khomeini tried to redirect their desires by force or persuasion.

• The other aspect of culture shock struck the thousands of villages and the millions of peasants who had historically looked up to the shah as an almost superhuman figure, an allegiance later transferred to Ayatollah Khomeini. The ignoring of rural needs encouraged migration to the cities. There the peasants, lacking modern skills and experience with twentieth-century mores, turned to their trusted leaders—the mullahs. The White Revolution had given land titles to hundreds of thousands and then had quickly forgotten them.

From 1959 to 1972 the disparity between urban and rural incomes rose from 2:1 to 3:1. Tehran grew from 1.5 million in 1956 to 2.7 million in 1966, and to 4.5 million in 1976, tripling in twenty years. Other cities expanded at a similar pace. The urban population went from 31.2 percent in 1956 and to 41.9 percent in 1972. This completely changed the balance of Iranian politics. In the Mossadegh era, only the urban artisans, merchants, and workers had mattered; these sectors supported the "secular" elements of the National Front rather than Ayatollah Kashani. However, the newly arrived peasants were more likely to back clerical leaders than to support moderate politicians. This shift in constituency meant that the symbol and shaper of the new revolution would be not Bazargan or Sanjabi but Ayatollah Khomeini.

The villagers also turned away from the shah. They had to buy water from private landowners at a high price. No govern-

ment bank or institution would give them the money they
needed to buy a motor for their deep wells except at high interest rates. Their transistor radios, however, gave them access
to events in the outside world. During the revolution, they
decided they wanted an Islamic regime, which meant, peasants told a Le Monde correspondent, "a government with Khomeini as its leader. A government that respects us and respects our religion and customs." [13] They would believe
whatever Khomeini told them.

If the long-range factors were the quiescent dynamite and
the middle-range factors the fuse, several immediate issues
provided the explosive force of the revolution.

• The recession, resulting from falling oil sales, when combined with the shah's excessive spending, forced project cutbacks and increased unemployment at a time of serious inflation. Before 1976, Iran had so much money coming in that it
could afford the waste, corruption, and incompetence of the
government. By 1977 these shortcomings were imposing
serious costs. The construction industry, which employed
many of the unskilled village immigrants, was particularly
hard hit. Wages declined as much as 30 percent for such
workers. University graduates found it hard to get jobs, a
problem they tended to blame on the presence of foreign advisors.

One money-saving cutback was the government's reduction
of the religious establishment's subsidy from $80 million to
$30 million a year, a move that did not inspire increased loy-
alty from the mullahs. The bazaar merchants helped make up
the difference, cementing the alliance between the two
groups. The shah once asked an American long a resident in
Egypt why King Farouk had fallen in 1952. The reason, replied the American, was that Farouk had tried to govern without governing well. The opposition was not to a royal regime
per se but to an inept ruler, whatever his title.

• To the extent that the shah's programs had raised living
standards and created expectations, the situation had reached
a critical threshhold. The growing numbers of students and
the enlarged middle class were increasingly conscious of the

gap between promise and delivery. The shah had nurtured his own enemies, who now, feeling their strength, demanded a redistribution of power.

• The shah's illness and personal paralysis made it impossible for his regime to respond to the challenges of 1978. To some extent, this was due to his personality and in part to the effects of his cancer. Yet it was also the failure of a system that could not produce alternate initiative or leadership from its own military and civilian elite.

• These built-in weaknesses particularly plagued the armed forces. The generals could not and would not act without the shah's direction. Their jealousies and mutual mistrusts as well as the importance of conscripts and air force homafars further prevented decisive action.

• The shah, on the basis of his experience in the 1950s and 1960s, adopted an incorrect strategy of trying to wait out the disturbances and to divide radical from moderate factions within the opposition. Whether or not this strategy could have worked, its execution was badly flawed. The shah offered too little too late.

• The hesitation and slowness of an American response between January and December, 1978 was far more important in terms of the shah's downfall than were the actions actually carried out by Washington in January and February, 1979. "Seldom have the limits of American power or the lack of a strong policy been so obvious," criticized *Time Magazine*, but the media had also helped create the shah's misleading image and the underestimation of revolutionary forces in 1978 that lulled Washington to sleep.[14] Even if the shah, the Iranian army, and the United States had acted otherwise there were no guarantees that the shah could have stayed in power. Possible outcomes included a military government or a limited monarchy under the shah's son, but there was also a range of less pleasing results—full-scale civil war, a strengthening of Soviet influence, or direct American involvement in a major conflict.

• Even given all this, the revolution might not have succeeded, and would certainly have had a far more moderate result if not for the emergence of Ayatollah Khomeini. History has repeatedly shown that even the most "revolutionary" situation does not produce change without the presence of strong insurgent leadership. Not only did Khomeini impose his inflexible determination to bring down the shah, but he also provided a countercharismatic figure capable of appealing to the masses.

• Khomeini and his aides, along with a great number of allies, produced an opposition ideology that fit their country's historical/cultural predispositions and also supplied a complete set of explanations for Iran's problems. Embodied in this system were also a series of proposed solutions. To create a liberal or Marxist in the Islamic world takes much time and experience, but almost every citizen carries a Muslim orientation within himself. Even—one might say especially—the illiterate masses receive the bulk of their intellectual experience through the mosque, the mullahs, and the Koran.

• Failure to properly understand the importance of this ideological aspect has repeatedly led to faulty evaluations of the uprising and of post-shah Iran. The Islamic rhetoric was seen as a mask, as a convenient vehicle for expressing accumulated economic, political, and social grievances. Consequently, posited this analysis, the mullahs would soon return to their usual duties, leaving decision-making to political and technical specialists. Yet Islamic ideology was not only the rebellion's powerful motor—the masters of that weapon were also determined to remain in the driver's seat.

The ancestors of Ruhollah al-Musawi ibn Mustafa ibn Mustafa ibn Ahmad al-Musawi al-Khomeini came from Kashmir to the town of Khomein in Iran.[15] The future leader, born in 1900, was the youngest of seven children and was only nine-months old when his father died. His grandfather, father, and eldest brother were all ayatollahs. When he was sixteen he went to Arak to continue his religious studies and he later traveled to Qom, where a distinguished gathering of theologians made that city the Oxford and Harvard of Iranian Shi'ism.

His memories of Iran's humiliations at the hands of for-

eigners were similar to those of the shah. Khomeini later recalled: "During World War I, I also observed—I was small but
I was going to school—the Soviet troops in the center we had
in Khomein. We were subjected to an invasion in World War
I." In World War II: "We were subjected to an invasion by the
three powers—America, Britain, and the Soviet Union. Their
troops were nearly everywhere in our country." The lesson he
drew from this was that weak nations "are subjected to invasions and bullying in peacetime and in time of war." [16]

Because he had never been exposed to Western-style education or to travel outside of Iran, Khomeini's concepts of this
cultural and intellectual style came from second- and third-
hand sources. Yet his unapologetic isolationism, his memories
of Western mistreatment of Iran, and his identification of the
shah's regime with America, guided his footsteps:

> Let them erect a wall around Iran and confine us inside this
> wall. We prefer this to the doors being open and plunderers
> pouring into our country. Why should we want to achieve a
> civilization which is worse than savagery, a civilization
> which behaves worse than the way wild beasts behave to-
> ward one another? The gate to civilization that the deposed
> shah proposed to open to us—that is to subject us to outside
> powers and rob all our wealth and bring us in return a few
> dolls; . . . what do we want with this great civilization? Is
> this a civilization? [17]

Khomeini was never a great original thinker but he was a
skillful popularizer. Moral principles, unity, and faith in God
would make Iran a great and free nation, he preached, but
these values could gain ascendancy only in a society that returned to Islam's fundamental teachings, as he interpreted
them. Khomeini wanted to establish a stable, traditional, mor-
ally controlled society where everyone knew his or her place
and understood the rules of conduct. In contrast to the Western commitment to progress, the Islamic world looked back to
two earlier periods: the early years, when Islam was most
purely implemented and the middle years when it was most
politically powerful.

But, in order to reconstruct society along Islamic lines, Khomeini knew, one must sacrifice freedom for order. Within this disciplined framework, however, an effort would be made to maximize happiness and to provide benefits for all. Khomeini and his followers not only had a counterutopia to that state of Communist perfection proffered by the left, but his was more desirable and comprehensible to Iran's conservative poor and peasantry. Even in the West, until almost a century ago, this kind of static, structured, interdependent vision was the philosophical ideal.[18]

In achieving this stable society, consecrated by both Islamic theology and an idealized picture of the early Muslim states of the caliphs, the means were a matter of secondary importance. Dictatorship was perfectly acceptable as long as it was supported by the people; in fact such a system would certainly be preferable to a democracy that did not adhere to the laws of Islam. In Khomeini's words, "Nobody can exercise absolute power without the consent of the people."[19] This combination of populism, totalitarian control, and clearly defined ideology places Khomeinism in the mainstream of twentieth-century antiliberal political theory. To the Khomeinists, the shah was not bad because he was ruthless and repressive but because he performed these deeds for a bad cause, for unacceptable goals.

This ideology also had an explanation for opposition to Khomeinist policies. The achievement of an Islamic state ought to be a simple matter since all Muslims of goodwill would naturally agree on these principles. Islam is monotheistic, Bani-Sadr explained, and "monotheism means that we should guide the community toward one identity and give it one heart, one tongue, one instinct and one conscience."[20] Those who criticize or try to block this single voice, therefore, cannot be true Muslims: dissent equals treason. Moreover, given this view of dissent, it follows logically that since conflict imperils the Islamic revolution and aids its enemies— most obviously the United States—those who cause conflict are agents of the United States.

By this process, any foreign country, like Iraq, or any internal force, like the Kurds, the Azerbaijanis, or liberal dissidents, are called American puppets under this "unity of enemies" theory. Obviously, such a formula does not predispose the Tehran government toward compromise with its foes and it intensifies the use of America as scapegoat for all the revolution's problems.

Political philosophy followed similar channels. If the ruler were personally just and motivated by correct values, there was little need for institutionalized protections of citizens' rights or for checks and balances. "Was the commander of the faithful, Imam Ali, who was the vali of the people, a dictator? Was the prophet [Muhammad] himself a dictator?" asked Khomeini. Obviously not; it was because they spoke justly that the people followed them.*

This statement was made in the context of a debate over whether or not to establish under the new constitution the position of Velayat-e faqih, a special position of religious governor, which would be reserved during his lifetime for Khomeini. In a discussion between Professor of Religion Reza Esfahani and a cleric, Hojjat al-Islam Ali Hojjati Kermani, the former obviously representing a more Western style of political science, the difference between the two attitudes clearly emerged.

Esfahani asked how, since the Velayat-e faqih would have "absolute power in the Islamic society and . . . [hold] the reins of government, economy and administration of the country in his hands," he might be removed if he violated legality. How could society protect itself against a dictatorial, despotic ruler of this type? For Kermani this was no problem. The people would simply remove him. "In an Islamic society, the people will be clearly able to see the boundary between dictatorship and decisiveness and will fight for it."[21]

From the Khomeinist/Kermani position, ethical values are more than sufficient protection against evil rulers. Their own revolution seemed to offer an example of how ideas could overcome military strength. Thus, the post-shah regime stressed cultural change rather than the reconstruction of the

* Ali, Muhammad's close companion and son-in-law, is seen by Shi'a Muslims as his rightful political heir.

economy and the restoration of calm. Khomeini's most striking statement on the revolution's causes further demonstrates
this belief: "I cannot believe, I do not accept that any prudent
individual can believe that the purpose of all these sacrifices
was to have less expensive melons, that we sacrificed our
young men to have less expensive housing. . . . No one
would give his life for better agriculture."[22]

The ayatollah saw the Western concept of freedom as dissolving Iranian social institutions: "They want the gambling
casinos to remain freely open, the bars to be freely open . . .
the fleshpots . . . heroin addicts . . . opium addicts." He denounced such things as "mixed bathing, cinemas designed to
drag [the people] to corruption," arguing that "this would
emasculate our youth and make them indifferent to political
and spiritual affairs."[23]

Iranian culture, Khomeini demanded, must fight against
Westernization. He cited pharmacies, thoroughfares, textile
factories, and other places that, the ayatollah claimed, became
popular only when they took Western names. He even criticized any reference in scholarly works to Western writers. The
Iranians were forgetting their own heritage, culture, and even
language, he warned.[24] Given this orientation, the standard
methods of Western diplomacy and political analysis could
not deal successfully with post-shah Iran. "For them [the
West] politics is nothing but a mathematical process," said a
Radio Tehran commentary on the West. "Two plus two equals
four." But Iranians did not play by these rules: "Dignity is better than full bellies."[25]

Since the Khomeinists advocated struggle against the West,
they assumed that the West would respond with hatred and
subversion.[26] "Your government has not yet given up the idea
of ruling Iran," said Bani-Sadr to Americans in November,
1979. "Within the country and its marches your government's
hand is implicated in bloody incidents." All opposition was
attributed to American conspiracies. Even rumor-mongering
and food-hoarding, rational responses to the chaotic situation
in Iran, were said to be fomented by either servants of
America or by those deceived by the CIA.[27]

While such alleged foreign threats made Iranians feel insecure, the Khomeini revolution also offered an antidote. The Iranians had long viewed themselves as pawns of great powers and their conspiracies. By building up the nation's military and economic strength, the shah had hoped to overcome this inferiority complex by making Iran a great power in its own right. Khomeini's answer was to emphasize Iran's spiritual strength but—and this was potentially dangerous for the country—the weakness of the armed forces and the collapse of industrial production threw into question the efficacy of this strategy.

In contrast to the shah's formula for progress and independence—a foreign policy resting on an alliance with the United States, Khomeini hoped to keep all foreign powers at arms length and to liberate Iranian minds from those feelings of subservience and humiliation that had weighed them down for so long. In the hostage crisis, against a nonaggressive United States, this strategy worked. Khomeini claimed that Washington was afraid of a united Iran willing to face martyrdom and of a worldwide Muslim uprising in Tehran's support. But his regime was really preserved by American restraint; against less conscientious foes the thinness of such defenses might have been quickly revealed.

"All the problems of the East stem from those foreigners from the West, and from America at the moment," said Khomeini. "All our problems come from America." To him, America was the richest, most oppressive, most savage, and bloodthirsty country in the world, an international plunderer and Satan. "Iran was in turn enslaved by Britain and then America," he told Iranians. Now, "the downtrodden must triumph over the dominant elements," in a global revolution, "not only those exploited economically but those mistreated socially." If other peoples did not choose to follow Iran's example, it was only additional proof of the power wielded by America and its servants.[28]

The Khomeinist view of American domestic politics and society was equally unsophisticated. Khomeini's close advisor, Ayatollah Montazeri, argued that "the American nation itself is among the oppressed and is under the bondage of five or six million Jews and Zionists who have controlled the power in the United States."[29] Khomeini believed that American blacks might rise up in support of Iran. He could not conceive that the American people supported the American government and that the taking of diplomats as hostages would hopelessly end for all but a very few any sense of friendship with Iranian revolutionaries.

This insistence on endless attacks against past American perfidy and on present imagined hostility poisoned any possibility of amicable relations after the shah's departure. It also predetermined the reaction of Iranians to the shah's admission into the United States for medical treatment. "This is part and parcel of the clever and calculated plan worked out by the United States . . . in order to turn back the wheel of history and to retrieve its lost interests," said a Radio Tehran commentary.[30]

The fact that such insecurity played a central role in the radicalization of the revolution was most clearly articulated by President Bani-Sadr, who eventually recognized that things had gone too far. "In my view what has jeopardized Iran's security more than anything else," he said in a January, 1980 newspaper interview, "is the problem of an entire generation's fear that the revolution could fail and fear of what the future may hold."[31] Iranian leaders were paralyzed in their attempts to go forward in rebuilding their country by the haunting spectre of August, 1953. It was logical within this mindset that a good follower of Ayatollah Khomeini's line should be willing to take any action—including the kidnapping of American hostages—to forestall any possible treacherous reconciliation with Washington. Any moderate who objected to such actions would merely betray himself as an American lackey.

One additional psychological factor might be added to the list of those contributing to the Iranian obsession with proving America responsible for the sins of the shah's regime. Despite the blood sacrifice of the revolution, Iranians knew well that only a small minority had ever resisted the shah's regime. The young, who had the luxury of never having collaborated with the old order, were particularly harsh in their judgment of elders. Officers were considered guilty in the Islamic courts merely because they were officers. Why had they followed orders? Why had they not overthrown the shah themselves? Seeing the United States as the real power behind the throne lessened the burden of self-criticism over Iranian passivity toward a despotic government that fell within a year, once seriously challenged.

Iran's petroleum wealth, according to Khomeini's analysis, was another example of American-inspired betrayal and corruption. The resource had been wasted in exchange for military bases and weapons. Further, having been so often victimized by international power conflicts, Iranians, he felt, now yearned for isolationism. Relations with either the United States or the Soviets, said Khomeini, were inherently like those between a sheep and a wolf or those between a goat and a butcher. "They want to milk us, . . . they have no desire to give us anything. . . . If only we could totally divorce ourselves from them, we would be better off."[32]

"The oil revenues," Khomeini said on another occasion, "have at no time been spent to serve the people's interests." Instead, the production and export policy "serves the interests of the oil companies and the rich consumer countries . . . who plunder our resources, impose on us the purchase of weapons and then set up on our lands military bases to defend their interests and their policies." For their own purposes, he said, "they have turned us into the area's policeman. At the same time, they have sabotaged our agriculture so that they may become the source supplying us with wheat, rice and other food supplies."[33]

Now, with the revolution, Khomeini and his followers believed, Iran would finally have the upper hand. "You have the resources and mines," said Ayatollah Montazeri in a sermon broadcast to the Muslim world. "You do not need the United States. The United States needs you." Since Muslims should follow their own path, avoiding alignment with the Soviets as well as with the Americans, both the left and the liberals were seen as foreign agents. Further, because the United States was the main threat under the "unity of enemies" theory, even Marxists may be considered Washington's agents as much as those of Moscow. Khomeini aide Ibrahim Yazdi went so far as to argue that "Communism was created in Iran by the Americans and the British" to destroy the "nationalist liberation movements." More than once, Khomeini himself accused the main leftist group, the Fedayeen-i-Khalq, of receiving weapons and money from the United States.[34]

Nor was Khomeini any less virulent in his attack on Iran's intellectuals, who, said the ayatollah, carried within themselves the poisons of liberalism and that of Marxism and were largely responsible for Iran's degradation. Their "opposition to Islam, which is 100 percent revolutionary, opened the way for imperialism and the influence of voracious imperialists, the onslaught of consumption and the decline of thought and intelligence in Iranian society." Khomeini welcomed reports that many middle class people were leaving Iran. "Let these moribund brains drain away; these brains have worked for the aliens; these brains were part and parcel of [SAVAK]—let them flee the country."[35]

Taken together, these precepts led to the increasing radicalization of the revolution from February, 1979 on, intimidating the moderates—who might have preferred rapprochement with the United States—but maintaining the allegiance of the Iranian masses to the cause. Hatred of the United States was stoked daily by both the Khomeinists and by much smaller Marxist groups, which were at least in full agreement over the issue of anti-Americanism.

Indeed, one of the earliest acts after the revolution began was the first attack on the United States Embassy in Tehran.* By February 14, 1979, the capital was a nightmare of fire and smoke, with undisciplined armed bands roving the city. As

---

* On that same day, the American ambassador in Afghanistan, Adolph Dubs, was kidnapped by unknown terrorists in Kabul. A few minutes after the takeover in Tehran, Afghan police and their Soviet advisors decided to attack the hotel room where Dubs was being held. Dubs was shot to death during the battle.

many as 300,000 weapons of all types, including 75,000 sub-machine guns, had been passed out to various factions. That afternoon about 150 members of the Fedayeen-i-Khalq, a group, many of whose members had been trained by the ter-rorist Popular Front for the Liberation of Palestine, launched a military assault against the embassy compound.

Wearing recently captured Iranian army and air force uni-forms and carrying military-issue rifles, they opened fire on the Marine guards. While Ambassador Sullivan directed the defense, embassy officials destroyed classified files and valu-able communications equipment. Seeking to avoid bloodshed, Sullivan ordered the badly outnumbered guards to fire into the air and to use tear gas to try to drive off the attackers. After an hour it was clear that the defenders could not prevail. Sul-livan called for a surrender. The guerrillas rushed in, shooting down in cold blood an unarmed Iranian employee, wounding and kidnapping a Marine.

To some of those taken hostage it was only a continuation of the previous days' horror. Among the prisoners were American advisors, technicians, and businessmen who had taken refuge in the embassy until they might get out of Iran. The growing pattern of violence and the harassment of foreigners made flight seem wise, though no full-scale evacuation had yet been ordered.

Khomeini's supporters denounced the attack. They had not yet consolidated their power and the leftists were quickly turning from allies into competitors. Deputy Premier Ibrahim Yazdi, who had spent a number of years as an exile in the United States, and Foreign Minister Karim Sanjabi quickly ar-rived on the scene. Negotiating with the armed band they managed to effect the release of the hostages.

The disorganization of the country was graphically illus-trated by a February 14 communiqué from the Iranian air force: "All the struggling people of the Iranian revolution are hereby informed that since the Iranian Air Force helicopters have started flight activities between Mehrebad Airport and Doshah-Tapeh, the struggling people are hereby asked to avoid shooting at these helicopters."[36] A few hours later the offices of the National Iranian Radio and Television network came under attack. Khomeini's pleas for the return of firearms to designated mosques were ignored.

Moscow tried to further intensify anti-American sentiment in Iran. Commenting on the embassy attack, their National Voice of Iran station aired a commentary entitled, "The U.S. Embassy is the headquarters of antirevolutionary plots." All embassy officials, it claimed, "are plotting to create a pretext for American military intervention in Iran." The United States lodged a protest with the Soviets.[37]

But the American government never really appreciated how filled with hatred the new Iranian government was toward the United States and how the simplest bilateral contacts were fraught with danger. Once some time had passed, American policymakers thought, things would calm down. They still hoped that Prime Minister Bazargan would stabilize Iran and that Khomeini would retire to Qom.

To improve relations, Washington tried friendly gestures. Iran was sold spare parts and some oil products, as well as wheat and rice. Moderates continued to visit the embassy and express their hope that the serious misunderstanding between the United States and Iran would soon be successfully resolved. On February 12, the day after Bakhtiar's fall, President Carter told a press conference that he hoped to work with the new rulers and noted Bazargan's promise to ensure the safety of Americans in Iran. Newspaper editorials endorsed Carter's statement of "continued hope for very productive and peaceful cooperation."[38]

American activities in Iran were adjusted down to a relatively low profile. The United States would seek to continue oil purchases and to maintain diplomatic and business ties with Iran. But Bazargan's apparently lessening capability to honor his pledge of protecting the United States Embassy, though his ministers did succeed in freeing the hostages taken on February 14, led to a recommendation on February 15 by the State Department that all Americans leave the country.

Other signs seemed to indicate a still-possible normalization. The United States granted Bazargan formal recognition and, on February 21, Sullivan met with the prime minister. Iran's new Armed Forces Chief of Staff General Muhammad Vali Qarani announced that Iran would honor its agreements not to transfer American weapons elsewhere. American military personnel might still be allowed in the country to maintain equipment, although experts from other countries would be preferred.

But too much hope could not be invested in the Iranian military, which was already beginning to disintegrate under a fierce purge. Executions started on February 16, with the shooting of Generals Nasiri and Rahimi, and they continued through the following weeks. Qarani's chief aide, Colonel Nasrullah Tavakoli, was forced to resign when he was quoted as making pro-American remarks. Khomeini said that the revolution was only beginning and that all forms of American influence must still be eliminated. Bazargan's attempts to restore peace were frustrated by the interference of Khomeini's Revolutionary Council, which began at this time to act as a separate government.*

* The membership of the Revolutionary Council has never been officially announced. Even the number of participants has been kept secret, though most sources put the total at thirteen. The following were identifiable as members between February, 1979 and August, 1980; Ayatollah Moussavi Ardebeli, prosecutor general; Abol-Hassan Bani-Sadr, president of Iran; Mehdi Bazargan, former prime minister; Ayatollah Muhammad Beheshti, leader of the Islamic Republican Party and chief justice of Iran's supreme court, Hojjat al-Islam Muhammad Javad Bahonar, Khomeini's representative to the ministry of education and culture and a member of the special committee for reorganizing Iran's universities; Ayatollah Mehdi Ali Mahdavi Kani, supervisor of the interior ministry (which included jurisdiction over the Revolutionary Guard); Hojjat al-Islam Muhammad Ali Khamenehi, Khomeini's representative to the regular armed forces and leader of Tehran's Friday prayers; Ali Akhbar Mo'-infar, petroleum minister; Sadeh Ghotbzadeh, foreign minister; Hojjat al-Islam Ali Akhbar Hashemi Rafsanjani, former minister of the interior, having resigned to become speaker of the Majlis; and Ezzatollah Sahabi, deputy minister of budget and planning. Ayatollah Mahmud Teleghani, a political moderate and most influential of the Tehran clerics during the revolution, was a member until his death in 1979. Nasir Minachi, former minister of national guidance and of information, propaganda, and religious endowments, was a member until the embassy occupiers provoked his arrest in late 1979. Ayatol-

At first, the White House had implied that the shah would be welcome to come to America. The exiled monarch had hoped to stay at the estate of former Ambassador Walter Annenberg in California until he could find his own property there. Yet in February the American attitude changed, prompted in large part by the first embassy seizure. The shah's admission into the United States would hardly help Washington's efforts to rebuild ties with Iran. In Morocco, the shah was told that his personal security could not be guaranteed in the United States, nor could the government protect him against possible lawsuits by the new Iranian government and others.

Former Secretary of State Kissinger who, along with Chase-Manhattan Board Chairman David Rockefeller, was pressing for the shah's admission into the United States, argued that such treatment of a former ally was indecent, but President Carter announced in March, just before the shah left Morocco for the Bahamas, that such a move could endanger Americans living in Iran. Some of them might even be taken hostage by armed Iranians, the president warned. When Radio Tehran broadcast false rumors that the shah might be given American asylum, Yazdi stressed that any such action would be considered unfriendly and would adversely affect bilateral relations.[39]

While Ayatollah Khomeini did go to Qom on March 1, it was clear that he would continue to guide the revolution from there. The Iranian government announced plans to try the shah in absentia. Khomeini's committees, not Bazargan, were running the country, and the moderates, despite American hopes, showed little ability to wrest power from their hands.

lah Hussein Ali Montazeri was probably a member though this cannot be confirmed. Another possible member was Muhammad Hashem Sabaqian. Public spokesman for the Council was Hassan Habibi, the Islamic Republican Party's unsuccessful candidate for president in 1980. A number of these men were former Khomeini students and several had played key roles in organizing and propagandizing for the revolution in 1978. Teleghani went to school with Khomeini as a youth, Beheshti studied under Teleghani in Tehran, and Montazeri was a pupil of Khomeini. Both Montazeri and Teleghani were released from the shah's prisons in late 1978.

Not only did the radicals have the support of Khomeini, the revolution's unquestioned leader, but they also had the guns. The purge of the army destroyed the only force on which Bazargan might have relied.

The moderates suffered one humiliation after another. Bazargan originally promised autonomy for the ethnic minorities but was forced to renege by the hard-liners. He tried to stop the summary trials and executions but had little success. Even the civil service did not respond to his appeals. The Iranians were obviously not ready to settle down and rebuild.

It is important to note that the National Front leaders, Bazargan, Shariat-Madari, and most other moderates—virtually never attacked the United States. They wanted friendly relations. Asked if the United States was trying to ambush the new regime, Shariat-Madari replied that there was no evidence of such interference. Iran's main problems, he explained, were internal and not of external origin. Others like Mehdi Rowghani, a Khomeini confidant and businessman—he had the Ford automobile franchise in Iran—tried privately to patch together new bilateral ties. Before Khomeini's exile to Iraq, Rowghani's family had sheltered the ayatollah in their home. Now Rowghani sought to establish a liaison committee to improve relations between Bazargan and Khomeini; he also helped to free the United States Marine kidnapped and imprisoned after the February 14 embassy takeover.[40]

But the radicals kept up the pressure, particularly through the radio and television stations, now controlled by Ghotbzadeh. For example, Ali Safa, a frequent Radio Tehran commentator, said that the United States originally panicked after the shah's fall but was now showing its teeth and hatching plots. Carter wanted a counterrevolution and this was to be done, "by creating the movements of separatism, as well as by creating and spreading tension among the Iranian people." This was said to account for Kurdish autonomy demands and for women's demonstrations refusing to give up rights they had been granted by the shah.[41]

At the same time, on March 13, around 50,000 Iranians marched to the new PLO office—established in the former

Israeli mission building—and to the United States Embassy. Anti-American speeches were made and United States flags burned. The march was organized and carefully directed by the Khomeinists. PLO representative Hanni Hassan exhorted the crowd to protest Carter's Middle East policy and claimed that the aircraft carrier USS Constellation had been dispatched to the Persian Gulf "to destroy the Iranian revolution."[42]

In Washington, American policymakers were asking what Khomeini would do next and whether Bazargan could hold off the clerical challenge to his government. The prime minister was a good speaker, if not a good governor, and those unfamiliar with the ways of Middle East politics and of Iranian society simply found it difficult to understand the continued momentum of the radical forces and the seriousness with which Khomeini's ideology was taken. By the end of the summer the working-level specialists understood that Bazargan had become a frustrated figurehead; the intelligence experts, recovering from their mistakes of the previous year, also foresaw a victory for the Iranian hard-liners, but top-level decision-makers continued for much longer to believe that the secular technocrats would eventually win out.*

The main focus of administration concern was not on whether Bazargan or the fundamentalist clergy would win out but instead on the left. CIA Director Stansfield Turner, in a March, 1979 interview, said that Marxists would be the main beneficiary of any split between Khomeini and Bazargan.[43]

In addition to its overoptimistic evaluation of internal Iranian politics, Washington may have made an additional mistake in trying to be too friendly to the moderates. This was the paradox of United States-Iranian relations in the Khomeini era: Iranians wanted America to stay away. The friendlier the United States tried to be, the more suspicious were the hard-liners. Anyone perceived as being soft on America became a

---

* Ironically, Bazargan was a victim of his own ideology. In 1965 he gave a public lecture entitled "The Boundary Between Religion and Social Affairs," which subsequently was widely discussed. In the speech he saw a role for religious leaders in social and political affairs.

target for abuse and political excommunication. It was time for a low profile on the part of the United States.

April, 1979 was a difficult month for Iran. The upheavals in Azerbaijan and Kurdistan, the assassination of some Khomeinist leaders, and the clashes between Islamic and leftist forces all heightened fear of foreign involvement, of some new August, 1953-type counterrevolution. Increasing disorder fed anti-Americanism simultaneously with the strengthening of the radical Khomeinists. One symbol of this was Sanjabi's resignation as foreign minister on April 16 because of Yazdi's interference in international affairs. But even Yazdi was suspect because he had taken American citizenship during his long stay as a political exile in Texas. In retrospect, Yazdi would seem a relative moderate compared to what was to follow.

Khomeini set the new tone: "We are still at war with the superpowers," he told a meeting of 100,000 workers rallying at his home in Qom. "The purging of the country is still ahead of us. . . . Those creating trouble here and there are agents of the United States of America." Two weeks later, on April 18, he warned that "mysterious hands were creating disunity in the nation. Satanic plans are under way by America and its agents."[44]

The Khomeini and Bazargan views of how the revolution should proceed continued to diverge. While Khomeini complained that reconstruction in agriculture and industry was being blocked by traitors and by "lackeys of America" instigating opposition, Bazargan called for calm and for an emphasis on reconstruction. Drawing an analogy with the damage done to China by the Cultural Revolution there, Bazargan decried extreme antagonism toward all Western influence. Iran "should not exercise fanaticism with regard to world technology, social principles and the principles of natural law." Indeed, he charged, "the atmosphere of enmity, suspicion, and of purging and revenge" was proving the main barrier to progress. Witch-hunts were counterproductive. Bazargan's aides, like Deputy Prime Minister Abbas Amir Entezam, said that "we need foreign nationals for the development of the country." Yet such counsel could not prevail in the heated and emotional atmosphere created by Khomeini's uncompromising anti-Americanism.[45]

Ayatollah Khomeini himself became more and more angry as his utopian goals, whose achievement had seemed so immediate when he returned to Iran, were not fulfilled. Since all good Muslims must follow him, according to his view, the persistence of conflict meant outside, anti-Islamic forces were at work. That there might be sincere differences or factional disputes within the revolution was unintelligible to him. Thus, when General Qarani was assassinated, he reasoned, this could only be an American attempt to prevent Iran from escaping "the United States's clutches."[46]

The average Iranian, of course, had far more in common with Khomeini's patterns of thought than with Bazargan's cold rationalism. They tended to view the moderates as weak men, counterrevolutionaries, and even as agents of American imperialism. When Bazargan tried to take steps toward normalization—terminating the kangaroo courts and executions, for example—his actions were offered as proof of his unreliability. Why would anyone have sympathy with those butchers and criminals of the old regime? They were guilty and they should be executed. Calls for careful investigation of individual guilt or attention to due process rights were drowned out by a desire for vengeance.

Some of those shot had been soldiers or SAVAK agents accused of torture or of killings during the revolution, but many of them were civilian officials tried on vague charges. More than a few had been denounced by individuals seeking to settle personal scores and a small number were condemned primarily because they were Bahai or Jews. Their judges were generally members of the clergy and defendants were permitted no defense counsel during the one-day trials. Bazargan was forced to explain that Khomeini felt these measures were necessary because of "fantastic popular pressure. . . . If we do not execute the guilty people," rationalized the prime minister, "there is a strong danger that the people will start a massacre."[47]

When the United States criticized the summary trials and firing squads this was regarded as proof of American complicity in the crimes of the defendants. According to Radio Tehran, for instance, Washington appealed for the life of former Prime Minister Hoveyda, who, ironically, had been imprisioned by the shah, because he was "their lackey and slavish mercenary in Iran."[48] Ambassador Sullivan's many meetings with Iranian officials assuring them that no intervention in Iranian affairs would occur and the State Department's continual denial of Khomeini's charges had no effect.

On May 17, the United States Senate adopted a resolution condemning the killings. Iran responded by asking for an American delay in sending Sullivan's replacement, Ambassador Walter Cutler. The State Department tried everything possible to put the human rights criticism in a friendly context. It praised the revolution's objectives of freedom, justice, and democratic institutions, wished Iranian leaders well, and called for putting the past behind. At the same time it voiced concern over the executions, expressing the hope that basic standards of justice and human rights would be maintained.

During this period the Soviets did everything possible to curry favor with Iran and to stir up animosity toward the United States. Their ambassador went out of his way to call to Yazdi's attention the reinforcement of United States military units in the Indian Ocean. The Moscow-controlled National Voice of Iran radio said: "The government of the United States is the Number One enemy of the people and the revolutionary government of Iran" and was "conspiring and agitating against the revolutionary achievement of our nation." America was even planning to admit the shah as "a link in the chain of conspiracies."[49] But the Russians had to run hard to keep up with Radio Tehran's invective.

In particular, the United States Senate resolution of May 17 set off a storm. Radio Tehran sarcastically remarked that the Senate did not object to the "massacre of Iranian revolutionaries in the streets a few months earlier." Ayatollah Khomeini saw the criticisms as being due to the damage inflicted on American interests by the revolution: "No other country was receiving the same benefits from Iran as was the United States. They must condemn us."[50]

When some Iranians worried that the United States-Iranian relationship would be damaged beyond repair, Khomeini continued: "May God cause it to be endangered. Our relations with the United States are the relations of the oppressed with the oppressor, they are the relations of the plundered with the plunderer. . . . What need have we of the United States?" The implication was that the destruction of any possibility for reconciliation would be a praiseworthy act. In this speech the ayatollah made a reference to foreign embassies, saying that such diplomats were more concerned over protecting their furniture and "did not attach any importance to the fact that an ambassador or others might be killed."

Yazdi, in contrast, called for calm. Iran, he explained, was "desirous of friendly relations with all nations" and compared Iran's struggle to the American Revolution. He dismissed the executions as the "provocations and conspiracies of a minor group." He drew on his own experiences in the United States, in distinction to Ayatollah Montazeri's wild views of Jewish cabals and an imminent black revolution, to explain that all power was "not in the hands of the Zionists" and that legislative action did not necessarily reflect the views of the White House.

Like Bazargan and Ghotbzadeh, Yazdi (also the product of a mercantile family) had been a National Front supporter and later a follower of Bazargan. He had left Iran in 1960, studied in several American universities, and settled in Houston, Texas. There he worked as a pathologist, specializing in cancer research, and he organized students. He fought leftist influence in Iranian student groups and when the shah's regime revoked his passport he took up American citizenship. For several years, he also served as Khomeini's representative in the United States, though the position was more symbolic than real. While loyal to Khomeini, Yazdi also remained especially close to Bazargan.

There were "contradictions among the American people," Yazdi stressed, and many of them wanted friendly relations.

Nor was it likely that the United States would militarily threaten Iran. Ayatollah Shariat-Madari, whose Azerbaijani constituents were already demonstrating against Khomeini's policies and who vividly remembered the Soviet intervention of 1946, also called for calm. He advocated cooperation with Egypt—Khomeini had broken relations with Cairo over the Camp David peace agreement—and expressed concern about the infiltration of Soviet agents and about possible Soviet intervention in Afghanistan.[51]

Moderates also continued discussions with the United States Embassy. Chargé d'Affaires Bruce Laingen, who ran the mission in the absence of an ambassador, met, for example, on June 21 with Deputy Prime Minister Entezam, who was working to normalize relations. "We and you have to be patient," Entezam said. Nor was the government responsible for everything that was taking place. People outside the regime, with no knowledge of how to conduct a government, would not let them do their job. According to Laingen, Entezam sighed at this point and commented, "A consequence of this revolution is that everyone considers himself the voice of the people."

"Immediately after the revolution," Entezam explained, the new cabinet concluded "that everyone, including the Imam [Khomeini], the Komitehs [independent Islamic political/military committees], the Revolutionary Guards, and the Revolutionary Tribunals were working against" them. Hundreds of requests were made by Bazargan for Khomeini's aid against these forces without result. Bazargan understood, Entezam concluded, that reactionary religious rule could set the country back one thousand years. But the moderates would still try to bring a return to order at home and amity abroad.[52]

Even the documents released by the student/terrorist occupiers of the United States Embassy later on in November would show American reluctance to become involved with Iranian internal conflicts. When individuals approached the embassy seeking help for armed opposition activities they were turned down. After Vietnam and Watergate, explained an embassy political officer, the American people would not stand for any such foreign adventures. At most, American diplomats simply interviewed Iranian officials and dissidents and gathered material for reports on political conditions.[53]

The proclamation of an Islamic republic on April 1 and deliberations on a constitution designed to centralize power and to institutionalize Khomeini's leadership led to further conflicts in Iran. Anti-American rhetoric in Iranian politics was also escalated. Demonstrations against the Senate's criticism of the executions were held on May 25. Over 150,000 people marched to the American Embassy in separate Islamic and leftist parades, chanting "Death to the United States," and "Death to Carter." "We consider the entire ruling system of the United States the most criminal against humanity," said the rally's spokesmen. "We consider it as the Number 1 enemy of our Islamic revolution; we consider this system a plundering and criminal system."[54]

That evening, Ayatollah Ali Akhbar Hashemi Rafsanjani, a Revolutionary Council member, was wounded by unknown assailants. Radio Tehran, referring to the fact that Rafsanjani had given one of the main speeches at the demonstration, attributed the shooting to the United States. It repeated Khomeini's call for Iranians to unite and to mobilize themselves against America: "Today our chief enemy is the same eternal supporter of the Shah: The United States," it announced. A few days later, the Iranian government asked that Cutler's nomination as ambassador be withdrawn.[55]

By the end of May an Arab revolt in the strategic southwest province of Khuzistan led to a great deal of bloodshed and a state of emergency was declared there on May 31. Four days later, the board of the National Iranian Oil Company resigned to protest the pressures of the hard-line Islamic faction. June saw a series of border clashes between Iran and Iraq. The shah's fall had given Baghdad an opportunity to reopen all the old issues dividing the two neighbors. Fighting between leftists and Khomeinists led the ayatollah to warn that he might move to destroy the former. Responding to what it took as a signal, Islamic mobs sacked the Tudeh offices; the event led to Moscow's first criticism of Khomeini.

For the moment, amidst all this turmoil, the shah himself

seemed forgotten. On June 10 he arrived in Mexico, having traveled from the Bahamas. A number of members of Congress were already voicing support for providing him refuge in the United States. Senator Charles Percy of Illinois remarked, "I have talked to ambassadors from Arab countries who feel that it would destroy the credibility of this country if we do not do something. . . . If we were to turn our backs at this time on a long-time friend, despite his problems, we would somehow betray our principles." Senator Claiborne Pell of Rhode Island agreed: "Since we have done all we could to cozy up to the shah in the last 20 years, I think it does not reflect well upon our country were we to give him a cold shoulder in his time of need." Loyalty, Pell continued, was a two-way street. How could America hope to enjoy the trust of other friendly political leaders who knew that they might some day meet the same fate?[56]

Within Iran itself, increasing instability intensified the fear that the revolution might be overthrown. There was, Khomeini admitted, sabotage in the southwest, the forced cancellation of school exams, the conflict between a Communist government and Islamic rebels in Afghanistan, Iraqi hostility, trials and purges, derailed trains, bombed bridges, strikes, wild rumors, and fighting in Kurdistan, Azerbaijan, and Khuzistan. The only explanation that Khomeini could accept was that CIA agents and people trained by them were working to create chaos, prevent employees from working, ruin harvests, and sabotage factories. "We suspect that those who pose as leftists and who think they are supporting the people are agents of the United States," he charged. When his student supporters took over the American Embassy on November 4, the first thing they did was to look for proof of these accusations. What they found was generally unimpressive: documents showing that the embassy had, for example, written reports on the situation in Kurdistan, in the army, and in various government ministries. Despite the lack of evidence, however, most Iranians firmly believed all these accusations.[57]

Radicals found it far easier to stir the passions of mobs than it was for the moderates to calm them. Bazargan tried his best to restore order. "The masses, especially those who are in the forefront of the revolution . . . ask us: why don't you act in a revolutionary way, why don't you arrest, why don't you beat up, why don't you kill, why don't you nationalize, and why don't you take and confiscate? They ask for harsh extreme actions to satisfy the feeling of hatred and revenge." Yet, the prime minister complained, "they very seldom pay any attention to the operation of the country," only protesting when something goes wrong. Iran could only be rebuilt through positive cooperation, pleaded Bazargan.

The conspiracy mentality, however, was still in an ascendant phase. A vivid example of these perceptions was a program aired by Radio Tehran on July 11. Iran's problems, it said, "are parts of a larger plan which imperialism implements in countries such as ours." Such measures included sabotage, assassinations, and psychological warfare. "The West tries, on the one hand, by exerting economic pressure, such as refusing to export manufactured goods or by increasing the prices of exported goods, the West tries to force these countries to submit to their demands."

Various secret meetings were being held to implement these plans, the broadcast continued, and the Western press spread lies as part of the scheme. The next step was the formation of terrorist groups, acts of murder, and the creation of uprisings and false demonstrations. The final stage was direct military intervention. Even the energy crisis was involved because Western fuel shortages were blamed on "the oil-exporting countries, in particular Iran."[58]

Other detailed accounts in the Iranian press and on radio purported to reveal eight American contingency plans for overthrowing the revolutionary government. Washington was supposed to be implementing "anti-human plots and conspiracies," "weaving evil separatist conspiracies," and seeking to "create domestic discord and an atmosphere of fear and intimidation." Sometimes this propaganda campaign was almost humorous in its ironies. Thus, Radio Tehran complained that America "has always given asylum to criminals and antinational elements who flee their countries; it gives them protection in various ways." The shah's regime had taken a similar attitude toward the protection offered by the United States to such Iranian dissidents as Ghotbzadeh, who now directed Radio Tehran's operations, and Foreign Minister Yazdi.

More seriously, the United States Embassy in Tehran, which supposedly coordinated the anti-Iran effort, was often the target of abuse. Radio Tehran and the organ of the Khomeinist Islamic Republic Party even accused Laingen of being himself "a prominent CIA agent."[59] Such theories, of course, were not entirely based on fantasy; during the Nixon administration there had been a conspiratorial undercutting of the Chilean regime of President Salvador Allende. But the fact was that no economic pressures were being applied against Iran and no plots were being hatched in Washington.

For top American policymakers, who were more attentive to official Iranian government statements and might well have been unaware of the hard-line speeches and media distortions, there seemed some reason for continued optimism. Yazdi gave interviews calling for improved bilateral relations and expressing the belief that America had accepted the Islamic regime. The foreign minister also hoped that ambassadors would soon be exchanged; when he visited the United Nations in October his talks with American officials were fairly cordial.[60]

Although Americans in Iran had helped several officers and shah-era officials to escape, no visas had been officially issued between February and September, 1979. Now the Iranian government asked that this service be reopened and several consular officials were dispatched to Tehran for this purpose. The left-leaning American Embassy Committee, which provided "security" for the embassy after the events of February 14, was disbanded and replaced by Revolutionary Guards, supposedly more reliable. Laingen gave interviews to a number of Iranian newspapers stressing his attempts to promote friendly relations between the two countries and pointing to the successes achieved in that regard.[61]

Laingen returned to the United States in September and gave several talks in Washington before journalists and academics, criticizing those who saw the situation in Iran as one of extremism and chaos. Things were now settling down, he explained, and though ties with Bazargan had been established there could not be instant results. Brzezinski was also confident that these were people with whom the United States could deal.

Bazargan continued to hammer away at the domestic situation with articulate speeches but with little visible progress. The main cause of disruption, he noted, was the revolution itself. Its full benefits could be enjoyed only when the economy began to function again. He rejected the obsession with American conspiracies: "There may be . . . many problems in the world . . . for which, although not acceptable, no one has been responsible. They may be the necessary and logical result of a natural cause." Many people naively believed that after the shah left all would be well, he chided, citing an Iranian poem: "When the demon departs, the angel shall enter." Such views were doctrinaire, part of "the destructive and negative" side of the revolution. This kind of thinking led to irrational ends: "If you say 2 and 2 makes 4, he says you are satanical . . . hostile, and are not acting in a revolutionary way."[62]

The shah's worsening cancer and the White House decision to admit him for treatment in the United States brought about a dramatic change in the situation, although it did not really change the existing balance of power within Iran. Bazargan's regime had long been unable to act, given its lack of effective executive power and its reliance on Khomeini for popular support.

Throughout 1979, with American policymakers trying to rebuild friendly relations with Iran, the United States government opposed granting the shah asylum. Despite the appeals of David Rockefeller and Henry Kissinger, Vance in particular stuck to this position. When the shah's friends informed the White House of his serious condition, however, Washington asked the embassy for an assessment of the situation.

"We should not take any steps in the direction of admitting the shah until such time as we have been able to prepare an effective and essential force for the protection of the Embassy," Laingen reported. "We have the impression that the threat to US personnel is less now than it was in the spring. . . . Nevertheless, the danger of hostages being taken in Iran will persist."[63]

Nevertheless, Rockefeller's doctor reported from Mexico on October 20 that the shah needed a gallbladder operation and special cancer treatment not available in Mexico. An argument was later made that dependence on a single report from a physician employed by an individual who was strongly advocating the shah's admission was careless on the part of the administration though the State Department said three other doctors were consulted. Other critics noted that the necessary care was available in Mexico even if the shah were to prefer that American doctors travel there to treat him.*

Nevertheless, humanitarian considerations apparently prevailed on Carter and Vance. The shah entered the United States and checked into the New York Hospital-Cornell Medical Center on the night of October 22. Henry Precht flew to Tehran earlier to inform Bazargan and Yazdi of this possibility. They protested but they also promised to continue protection of the American Embassy. Bazargan's request that two Iranian doctors be permitted to examine the shah was refused by the shah.

The hard-liners were not bound by Bazargan's agreement. The shah's illness was only a pretext for a counterrevolutionary plot, they charged, and their government's response to this threat was too mild. A demonstration organized for November 1 drew 3 million participants according to Radio Tehran. Yazdi defended himself: "Whatever has been possible to do through diplomatic channels we have done. . . ."[64]

A second simultaneous event further enraged the militants. Bazargan and Yazdi had flown to Algeria for that country's in-

---

*The physician, Dr. Benjamin Kean, later said that he conferred with two of the shah's French doctors, who warned of several problems including the monarch's increasing resistance to chemotherapy and who said that his life was in danger. The State Department also checked with a Mexican doctor who said that the necessary facilities did not exist in Mexico.

dependence anniversary celebrations and there they met briefly on November 1 with Brzezinski, who was representing the United States at the celebration. Eager to undermine his old rival Yazdi, Ghotbzadeh ordered Iranian television to broadcast pictures of the encounter. The hard-liners claimed that Khomeini had not been informed that this meeting would take place.[65]

As a response to American asylum for the shah and to the alleged treason of their own government, a group of pro-Khomeini students seized the American Embassy on November 4, 1979; all the American employees there became hostages. A demonstration of some 30,000 people had been organized after several inflammatory speeches by Khomeini. As they marched by the embassy several hundred militants, who had planned their operation in secret, split off from the column and scaled the compound's walls.

The students appealed to Khomeini, basing their actions on a desire to block an alleged American-sponsored counter-revolution and to destroy the moderate regime. "How can we tolerate this, when the responsible officials sit around one table with American wolves, while you angrily shout that the United States is the major enemy of the Muslim and oppressed masses?" The revolution was not finished with the removal of the shah and his old system; the most important work of the revolution lay ahead—"the elimination of the economic, cultural and political sovereignty of the West" and the triumph of an Islamic society.[66]

As they had hoped, Khomeini supported their action. He had been told, the ayatollah said, that the embassy was a lair of espionage: "America expects to take the shah there, engage in plots, create a base in Iran for these plots, and our young people are expected simply to remain idle and witness all these things." But the blood of "100,000 martyrs" had not been shed in vain. The whole revolution was at stake, for these plots threatened to force Iran to "return to the past." Now Iran was about to initiate a new revolution; "a revolution greater than the first one."[67]

At first there were hopes of a quick solution, as there had

been the previous February. Yazdi communicated to Laingen on the first day of the takeover that he hoped to have all of them out by morning. The Americans also asked for Iranian troops to dislodge the occupiers but Tehran's promise to protect the embassy went unhonored. Indeed, the Iranian cabinet could not even keep itself in power.

The Bazargan government had reached an impasse. The Revolutionary Council, and behind it Khomeini himself, had long been making the real decisions. "What made my colleagues weary," Bazargan would later say, "was the friction, the resistance, the opposition, the interference. They did not know what to do." Unable to govern, unable to honor its pledges to protect the American Embassy, having lost all control of the situation, Bazargan and Yazdi resigned.[68]

Khomeini's long-voiced prophecy had finally fulfilled itself: at last Iran would have its confrontation with the United States.

10
Iran's Second Revolution 1979–80

United States-Iranian relations could not possibly have been worse in the months following November 4, 1979. From the American point of view, the central problem was obtaining the release of fifty-three American diplomats being held hostage at the American Embassy in Tehran. To the Iranians the capture of the American Embassy and its occupants marked a successful end to one revolution and the opening shots of a second. For Iran, like Russia in 1917, was to undergo both a February and a November revolution—the first a political struggle to unseat the old regime, the second a social, economic, and cultural revolution to build a new Islamic society.

In Iran's case, it was the fundamentalist mullahs and their Islamic Republican Party who were seeking to achieve what the Bolsheviks had done in Russia—monopolize power. Like Lenin, Khomeini would in time turn against moderate segments of the revolutionary coalition and purge their members from positions of authority; like the Bolsheviks, the fundamentalists, once in power, would refuse to compromise with those ethnic movements that had aided the revolution; and like the Leninists, Khomeini's supporters would try to create a totalistic structure, subsuming into their ideological framework all aspects of national life, from the courts to the schools, from the military to the conduct of commerce, and even the daily behavior of the citizenry.

Khomeini and his fundamentalist followers felt fully justified in centralizing power in their own hands. Unlike Lenin, who had played no direct role in the overthrow of the czar, Khomeini had been the revolution's most visible ideological guide, its most influential international spokesman, and its acknowledged strategic leader. Yet in the first days after the flight of the shah, American policymakers mistakenly assumed that Khomeini's role had been only a symbolic one and that the moderates had come to power. Many Iranian politicians made the same error.

Iran's first post-shah premier, Shahpour Bakhtiar, upon assuming office, covered up the shah's portrait with an Iranian flag and, as he thought proper, hung a portrait of Mossadegh, not one of Khomeini, in his office. Even after the fundamentalists had driven Bakhtiar into exile, they did not believe the revolution complete. Bakhtiar's successor, Mehdi Bazargan, despite his piety, represented a constituency made up of the same urban, liberal, middle class professionals and technocrats who had always supported the National Front. With their modernistic and relatively secular views of the governing process, this group was ideologically bent, certainly, more toward nationalism than toward Islamic piety.

Very soon after its assumption of the trappings of power the Bazargan government was forced to face the reality that, in fact, it occupied the governmental offices only at the pleasure of the top-level Khomeinists—Ayatollahs Beheshti and Montazeri, for example—who thought the moderate politicians potentially dangerous. Behind the hard-line leaders stood the student militants, the Revolutionary Guards, the "komitehs" that ran local government, the revolutionary courts, and the Islamic Republican Party. These ad hoc institutions—rather than the state apparatus—were the rulers of the country.

During the struggle over control of the direction the revolution would take, the clerics mobilized the masses and by consistently taking the most radical positions, were able to divide and defeat their opponents. Bazargan and the National Front helped them remove Bakhtiar; Yazdi conspired against Sanjabi; Ghothzadeh eliminated Yazdi; Bani-Sadr undermined Bazargan; and so on. As the treatment of Yazdi, Bazargan, and Bani-Sadr illustrated, the mullahs were not content to rule through even the most sympathetic "civilians"—they wanted full power in their own hands, the only hands they really trusted.

Dr. Mahmud Qashani, a member of the Islamic Republican Party's central committee, explained these views with remarkable candor in May, 1980:

> This revolution is a revolution by religious men under Imam Khomeini's leadership. It has been joined by . . . politicians who do not believe absolutely in the imam's line, that is, they are not radicals. Our experience with Dr. Mehdi Bazargan and the National Front is still on our mind, and we do not want a repetition of the mistake which the religious revolution made in Mossadegh's time. . . . Bani-Sadr today wants to pursue Mossadegh's policy. . . .

Bani-Sadr, Qashani claimed, worked with "all the factions opposing control by those who [had] staged the revolution, that is, the religious men." [1] This rewrite of recent history, giving credit largely to the clergy, ignored the role of the many others in the very broadly based coalition that had brought about the shah's downfall.* But the mullahs, who had been the nationalists' junior partners in 1906 and again under Mossadegh, were not about to accept that status a third time; in-

* Conversely, many high clerics had supported both Reza Shah and his son over the years, right down to the fall of the imperial regime. Another strong group preached neutrality on political issues. Not only did many mullahs welcome the shah's return to power in August, 1953, but a number of them helped to organize the August 19 demonstrations that ousted Mossadegh. During the 1950s the shah worked carefully and with a fair amount of success to ensure their support. Even in later years, most of the ayatollahs limited their criticisms to specific issues dear to the protection of the Shi'a moral/legal code. Up until the autumn of 1978, the Khomeinist view was in a clear minority among them, and those who acknowledged Khomeini as the primary leader came mostly from the ranks of his own former students.

deed, they argued that the revolution's very survival depended on their leadership. They were able to have their way on virtually every single issue.

The concept of ideology first (in Maoist terminology, "politics in command") pervaded their thoughts and actions. "The revolution does not succeed by providing electricity, work and housing for the citizen before the citizen understands and becomes aware of his revolution's principles," said Dr. Hadi Modaressi, a leading clergyman close to Khomeini. To accelerate this radicalization process, said Modaressi, "we wish and we welcome military aggression against us because it strengthens the revolution and rallies the masses around it." Even Iran's friends, he added, did not understand that their intent in taking the United States Embassy was to challenge the international order and to help build this "struggle against counterrevolutionary forces" at home.[2]

Within this context, it is easier to understand the reasoning behind the kidnapping of the fifty-three American diplomats. Ostensibly the embassy was taken over to force the return of the shah and his money, but there were other motives involved—motives that, when understood, help explain the intractability of the Khomeinists in the face of American attempts at reconciliation and reassurance.

First, the prisoners were seen as hostages in the classical meaning of that word: the threat to their lives would protect the Iranian revolution from American plans for intervention that the Khomeinists assumed were being hatched regularly in Washington. Despite the bravado in all their rhetoric, the revolutionaries were very insecure, not fully convinced of their ability to prevent a dramatic reversal of the revolution and the restoration of the shah to power—as, after all, had occurred in August, 1953. In Bani-Sadr's words, this represented "a whole generation's fear that the revolution could fail and fear of what the future may hold."[3] Khomeini and his supporters believed that the United States was behind all the regime's domestic problems and all the violence that continued to convulse the country. The shah's presence in America, they reasoned, might be a prelude to some imminent coup attempt.

Possession of the hostages would give Iran leverage against
any attempt to carry out such a plan.

According to Khomeini, all events were connected in this
grand American design to subvert the revolution. The United
States wanted "to make the world believe that . . . anarchy
rules here. . . . They want to say to the world that such a
country needs a guardian—and who is the guardian? Mr. Carter." The abortive American attempt to rescue the hostages in
April, 1980 was portrayed in this light. Bani-Sadr's message to
the United Nations protesting this raid made many references
to other coup attempts and announced "that the recent military aggression by the United States has been carried out with
the intention of toppling the revolutionary regime in Iran and
reestablishing U.S. domination over Iran." The hostage-rescue
operation was deemed to be only a convenient cover for the
Americans' real goal.[4]

Second, the embassy takeover was designed to make impossible any normalization of relations between Iran and the
United States. Khomeini's followers argued that Washington
was so powerful and devious that Iran would be safer in open
conflict with the United States than within a dangerous
"friendly" relationship. Since the United States was supposedly seeking to impose control on Iran and since there
were within Iran many "traitors"—both pro-shah elements
and moderates like Bazargan—who were prepared to renew
old ties, it was good preventive medicine, said the radical
mullahs, to wreck bilateral relations beyond hope of restoration. The Bazargan-Brzezinski meeting in Algiers was as influential in sparking the embassy takeover as was the shah's arrival in the United States.

Third, just as the hostage-taking was immediately seized
upon by the fundamentalists as a means of forcing the resignation of Bazargan's government, a hard line toward the release
of the hostages and in favor of continued anti-American confrontation was maintained as a reminder to Bani-Sadr and
other moderates of the futility of trying to dilute the radical
fervor of the revolution. "Without the embassy attack there
would never have been any radicalization [of the govern-
ment], still less a change in the government team," remarked

one leftist leader.[5] But this process was aimed as much against the Marxists as it was against the moderates. For the clerical Khomeinists it was not only a policy of ideology in command but also one of domestic politics in command.

Aimed first against the anti-shah coalition of the liberal, middle-class center and the Marxist left, this new revolutionary stage was next aimed at those nonclerical elements whose radical, fundamentalist credentials were genuine enough but who were seen as capable of providing an alternative leadership to clerical domination. Even such men as Bani-Sadr were now portrayed as having been tainted by Western influence. The Islamic constitution, drawn up by an almost exclusively clerical assembly and adopted in a December, 1979 referendum, helped complete the first stage in this process. Beheshti was the assembly's acting chairman.

Most of the openly expressed opposition to the new constitution was based on regionalist resistance to a continued strengthening of the centralized authority to which the Pahlevi dynasty had devoted such effort. When such opposition was expressed, however, by the Kurds, who demanded autonomy, as well as by many of the Arabs and Baluchs, they were confronted by the central government's army and the Khomeinist Revolutionary Guard.* The fighting was most in-

---

* Two other minorities faced discrimination even though they remained politically quiescent. Of the 80,000 Jews in Iran in 1979, some 25,000 to 30,000 left the country. Although Khomeini repeatedly promised them religious freedom, the violent attacks against Israel and Zionism frightened many into leaving. The passports of Jews who had visited Israel (where 120,000 former Iranian Jews live) were impounded and Jews were fired from civil service and university posts. Antisemitic pronouncements were common. Several dozen Jews were imprisoned and several more were executed, often on the flimsiest of charges. Even more precarious was the situation of tens of thousands of Bahai. Although their religion is an extremely peaceable and humanitarian one, Bahaism is a splinter sect, which left Islam. Consequently, it is not recognized by Muslims as a legitimate religion and those followers of the Bahai faith have long been persecuted in Iran, where the split originated. Under the shah, the Bahai were protected despite the mullahs' campaigns against them in the 1950s, and a number of Bahai were successful in business or government. A number of former officials were executed primarily because they were Bahai; others were falsely accused and punished for belonging to the sect.

tense in Azerbaijan, where Ayatollah Shariat-Madari condemned the constitution's undemocratic character, establishing as it did a special position through which
Khomeini could exercise almost unlimited powers. Those criticizing the constitution on more general libertarian
grounds—including Hassan Nazieh, chairman of NIOC, and
Hedayatollah Matin-Daftari, Mossadegh's grandson and leader
of the left-liberal National Democratic Front coalition—were
forced to go underground or into exile. The National Front itself disintegrated.

Finally, once undertaken, the holding of the hostages and
consequent defiance of the United States became a symbol of
Iran's independence. While even Khomeini's closest collabo-
rators had their own doubts about the course they were on, the
temptation to exploit any sign of support for compromise on
the part of one of their factional opponents was irresistible.
Beheshti went so far as to accuse Bani-Sadr, after the latter's
election to the presidency, of representing the "danger of liberalism."

To Beheshti, liberalism meant a capitalist economy, compromise with imperialism, and imitation of the West's disso-
lute way of life. Still, Beheshti added, "It has to be confessed
that there are several million Iranians who prefer a liberal government to a militant Islamic government." But Beheshti had
no intention of indulging them.[6] In collaboration with the radical mullahs, the students holding the embassy tried to use
some of the documents found there to discredit leading moderates, a tactic used in the early 1950s both against Mossadegh's opposition and by his political allies against their
rivals within the National Front.

The takeover was justified by the perceived American
threat; the failure of that alleged threat to be carried out after
the takeover was portrayed by the Khomeinists as an Iranian
victory. America, though still dangerous, had been defeated.
In short, Washington's failure to take bold steps to overthrow
Khomeini did not cause them to question the whole theory of
American conspiracy. Rather, Iranians attributed the American lack of success to the effectiveness of Khomeini in antici-

pating President Carter's conspiratorial designs and beating him back with threats of retaliation.

"Our youth should be confident that America cannot do a damn thing," Khomeini said repeatedly. The United States, he explained, was too impotent to interfere by direct military force and, if necessary, Iran could defeat such a move by mobilizing its own people, who were willing to become martyrs.[7] If traditional Iranian political culture had bred in the nation excessive deference toward foreign powers, Khomeini would restore their pride, drawing inspiration from the successful wars of early Islam.

As this new confidence expressed itself in repeated challenges to United States power, it confronted the USSR with only a slightly more cautious bravado, despite the overwhelming power of that great northern neighbor. There is an old anecdote that relates how a mullah once commented to a Turkish officer within hearing of the famous German General Von Moltke, "Why should even today ten thousand [Turks] not rise and with firm belief in Allah and sharp swords ride to Moscow?"

"Why not?" answered a Turkish officer. But in French, so the clergyman would not understand him, he added, "As long as the Russians stamp their passports."[8]

Even after the Soviet invasion of Afghanistan, the threat of Soviet intervention did not cause the fundamentalists to seek protection through a rapprochement with the United States. Khomeini's vision of foreign affairs led him to believe that his leadership had created an Iran impervious to attack by either of the superpowers.

Within Iran, this stance had great psychological impact. Hitherto, Iranians had seen themselves as pawns of foreigners and their conspiracies; at best, they could only occasionally, and with great cunning, manipulate these powers so as to serve Iran's purposes. Now Khomeini proclaimed liberation to be at hand. If the United States, with all its power and satanic determination, could not free its own diplomats, how could it bring down the Iranian revolution? Washington might continue to fuss and fume, but if Iranians were united behind

Khomeini's leadership the revolution would be invincible. If piety could bring about such a remarkable transformation, most Iranians believed, then their slogan, "God is great!" was indeed appropriate.

A few semi-realists among Khomeini's followers, however, were not about to rely solely on divine protection. Defense Minister Mustafa Ali Chamran suggested that if Moscow attacked Iran the United States would be forced to come to Tehran's aid no matter what the status of the hostages; the Soviets could be similarly used to intimidate America. Iran would thus be protected by a new Cold War equilibrium.[9] Yet this was a minority view, maintained quietly by relative moderates to remain calm in the dangerous situation Khomeini had created.

But others expressed the fear, as the hostage crisis dragged on into 1980, that it would prove too great a burden. Many became concerned that their plans to implement the Islamic revolution by restructuring Iranian society would be lost in the fervor directed daily against the United States. Such concerns did not illustrate the moderation of those expressing them, but rather a sincere eagerness to get on with the revolution's work and to fulfill its goals.* Hopes of freeing the hostages became bound up with these doubts about the price Iranians were paying for holding them. Washington tried to emphasize these

---

* Bani-Sadr and Ghotbzadeh, the two main advocates of a negotiated settlement in 1980, had been among Khomeini's most hard-line advisors in 1978–79. The son of a popular ayatollah, Bani-Sadr first met Khomeini in 1972, while the ayatollah was attending his father's funeral in Iraq. As an advisor, Bani-Sadr brought to his role a strong Islamic orientation but one tempered by Western academic training. As a student in Paris, in fact, Bani-Sadr had continually postponed defending his Ph.D. thesis to delay his return to Iran. While in Paris he was strongly influenced by the "small-is-beautiful" school and wanted a decentralized, self-reliant Iran. Ghotbzadeh, the son of a wealthy lumber merchant, left Iran in 1959 at the age of twenty-four and lived in Europe, the United States, and Canada. He organized anti-shah activities in the United States but flunked out of Georgetown University. Finally, his passport was revoked and he lived in the Middle East for several years. During the prerevolutionary period, he worked as an important go-between linking Khomeini and the Arabs, including the PLO, Libya, and Syria. Despite American hopes, neither man was moderate—except in a tactical sense—and both lacked a political base and political talent.

hidden costs in negotiating for the release of the American diplomats.

"The United States enslaved Iran for 25 years," said the influential Ayatollah Montazeri, "and the Iranians want to be finally released from this subjugation." Yet, he added, it was "impractical to sever relations between us and the United States."[10] Even Beheshti, in late December, 1979 and in early January, 1980, spoke out for freeing the hostages. The problem for the Khomeinists was to find a way to end the confrontation without losing face or without being outflanked in militancy by some other group. They considered and rejected tactic after tactic. In terms of domestic politics, of course, it was safer to do nothing; as long as the hostages were held there would be no challenge to their rule.

Bani-Sadr, who, like Bazargan before him, stressed the priority of social-economic reconstruction, saw the hostage crisis as endangering the normalization of domestic affairs. A few days after the embassy takeover, he praised the student militants for bringing down a government that "was following a conciliatory policy toward the United States." But he also spoke of negative results. That the occupiers ignored the formal governmental apparatus, conducted their own propaganda campaigns, invited their own foreign delegations, and professed faith only in Khomeini's direct link with them, "highlighted the multiplicity of decisionmaking centers." The regime's inability to control them diminished its prestige. "The absence of a strong central government and the spread of anarchy will eventually undermine Imam Khomeini's authority too," Bani-Sadr warned. "It is impossible to govern a country with permanent spontaneity."[11]

In time, Bani-Sadr's complaints about the seriousness of Iran's situation intensified. "Today our economy is paralyzed, our political atmosphere is plunged into discord, our culture is no longer operative and our social environment is disorganized," he told hundreds of thousands of Iranians at a rally marking the revolution's first anniversary.[12] In a desperate attempt to reach his countrymen Bani-Sadr even argued that the hostage-taking was an American plot to provide an excuse for

310   PAVED WITH GOOD INTENTIONS

their intervention. His pleas met with little response. As a political radical but a tactical moderate, Bani-Sadr was too alienated from either camp to build a strong base of support.

Shariat-Madari, whose views were more democratic and decentralist than those of Khomeini, also called for a period of construction. A few days before the embassy takeover he criticized the hard-line faction: "They imagine that if there is no severity, confusion and ruin will result, and progress will be impeded. Contrary to this, I believe that it is the very situation now being brought about which is impeding progress in the affairs of the country." He concluded: "Today, anyone who criticizes is called a counterrevolutionary and is said to be going against the revolution, whereas in my view it is the man who does not listen to criticism who is the counterrevolutionary." [13]

But in December, 1979, heavy fighting broke out in Tabriz, Azerbaijan's main city, in which Shariat-Madari's supporters took over the town, protesting the newly ratified constitution. During the following spring, a number of the leading supporters of Shariat-Madari were executed by the Khomeinists. Apparently not willing to throw his fellow Azerbaijanis into bloody, all-out confrontation with the central government, the more moderate ayatollah was forced to retreat and pledge his support to Khomeini.

When Bazargan resigned on November 6, 1979, the Khomeinists began consolidating their power, with nominal control of the government passing to the Revolutionary Council. Its membership was divided between clerics like Beheshti and pious laymen like Bazargan and Bani-Sadr. Khomeini, of course, had the final say. Council decisions growing out of the embassy seizure included directives to withdraw financial reserves from American banks (on the same day that President Carter froze them) and the repudiation of foreign debts.

Although Khomeini freed some of the black and female hostages, the conflict quickly settled down into a long seige. Fifty Americans were kept in the embassy grounds and three, including Chargé d'Affaires Bruce Laingen, were semiprisoners in the Foreign Ministry. The new factor in this affair was not the holding of hostages by terrorists—an increasingly common phenomenon in the world—but the support given this act of terrorism by the host country's government.

This support created special problems for the White House. While the president could not have been blamed had terrorists kidnapped American citizens it was quite another thing when the affront came from another government. Not eager for a direct confrontation President Carter embarked on a course that combined conciliatory gestures and a gradual escalation of pressure. He quickly ruled out an immediate rescue attempt; proposals to capture Iran's oil depots on Kharg Island were rejected because of possible Soviet reactions and potential reprisals against the hostages themselves.

Although Carter did authorize secret long-range planning for a rescue raid as a last resort, he committed the United States to a public policy of gradually escalating countermeasures, including appeals to the United Nations Security Council and to West European allies for economic sanctions against Iran. American Navy units were dispatched to the Arabian Sea. Washington ended imports of Iranian oil and froze billions of dollars of Tehran's assets within the country; the White House ordered a reduction in the number of Iranian diplomats in the United States and an immigration check on the tens of thousands of Iranian students in the country.

These actions did not bring quick results. The Europeans and Japanese were not eager to invoke sanctions that would damage their trade and petroleum purchases with Iran but, they argued, likely do little to help the hostages. As *The Economist* later summarized their case, they believed that "the denial of material things is unlikely to have much effect on minds suffused with immaterial things, and to the extent that sanctions do move Iran they will move it economically closer to Russia." [14]

Moreover, American courts temporarily blocked the special check of Iranian students' visas and Washington lost track of the number of Iranian diplomats. The stream of would-be negotiators going to Tehran—some of them self-appointed—and the promises of Iranian officials—which were generally reversed within twenty-four hours—delayed the application of stronger steps.

Khomeini refused to meet with Ramsey Clark, the former United States attorney-general, and William G. Miller, Senate Select Committee on Intelligence staff director, both of whom Carter had asked to go to Tehran. (Clark would later make a second trip to Iran not under government auspices to participate in a "crimes of America" conference.) Iran's ambassador in Washington, Ali Agah, furnished a more successful conduit for communications. State Department task force members also spoke via telephone and telex to Laingen, who was under "house arrest" at the Iranian Foreign Ministry, but they could not get Iranian officials to communicate with them directly. Among the various other intermediaries employed were the Swiss ambassador in Tehran, the Vatican, the Algerian government, the Irish international civil servant Sean MacBride, an Argentinian political operative, and some leftist French lawyers.

Only gradually did Washington understand that there were no governmental spokesmen or officials in Tehran capable of keeping pledges made to negotiators. In April, 1980 the White House finally gave up hopes for a diplomatic solution and launched an ill-fated rescue mission. When this attempt failed, President Carter gave the hostage question a lower priority.

Between November, 1979 and that point, however, President Carter had made the hostages' freedom the central issue in American foreign policy, a decision paralleled by extremely high levels of media coverage and the emotional involvement of the American people. Putting the hostages' safety first, Carter downplayed the possibility of a military response. But the White House's failure to use the abilities of Iran specialists made it difficult for the American government to understand Tehran's thinking and responses. Policymaking was increasingly in the hands of White House political operatives whose attentions were distracted by a challenge to the president's renomination from Senator Edward M. Kennedy.

In the fight for the Democratic presidential nomination, the

Iran issue seemed to help the incumbent. The feeling on the part of many voters that in a moment of national crisis they must unite around the current president helped defuse the challenge of Senator Kennedy, who criticized past United States-shah relations. For his part, conservative Republican Ronald Reagan advocated permanent American asylum be granted the shah, though all candidates agreed to refrain from debating the Iran question while the hostages were still being held.

The predominant public sentiment, particularly during the first six months of the crisis, was one of anger. At its most extreme—though expressed in a mere handful of instances—this ire led to some less-than-noble acts. The state legislatures of Louisiana and New Mexico ordered their state universities to stop enrolling Iranian students, while their Mississippi counterpart passed a bill doubling the tuition for the 430 Iranian students attending school in that state. As another example, an Iranian student who had earlier been chosen valedictorian of her New Jersey high school was pressured into withdrawing. Much more frequent signs of American anger found expression on local radio and television programs, particularly those soliciting call-ins, in boycotts against Iranian-owned businesses, and with the appearance of a slew of anti-Iranian bumper stickers. More serious, were a couple of bomb threats that brought out the local police. Yet such incidents, despite the ample publicity they received, were relatively uncommon.

More typical was the widespread refusal of most Americans to make any distinction between the pro- and anti-Khomeini Iranians living in the United States who numbered, in total, more than 150,000 at the time of the hostage seizure. Many of these Iranians were not sympathetic to the new rulers in Tehran; the same could be said of the 50,000-plus Iranian students in the United States, only a minority of whom participated in demonstrations backing the Islamic regime.

The slow pace of escalation was designed to lay the groundwork for a peaceful resolution of the crisis. In response to a proposal by Foreign Minister Ghotbzadeh, backed by Beheshti and by the Revolutionary Council, that the administration agree to a United Nations or congressional investigation into the activities of the shah and of the United States in Iran, the president let it be known that he would look favorably on such a step only after the hostages were released. When the student militants rejected this plan, the acting Iranian government was not strong enough to force it on them. The shah's departure for Panama on December 15, intended to cool the crisis, only further enraged the Iranians, who saw it as an American maneuver to avoid responsibility for returning him to trial in Tehran.

By the time the administration resolved to press ahead with the escalation of pressure a whole new set of problems had emerged. An attack on the great mosque in Mecca, the most important shrine in Islam, actually carried out by Islamic extremists, was blamed by many Muslims on the United States. Demonstrations against a number of United States embassies followed, most violently in Pakistan where the building was burned down with two American fatalities. Even more serious was Moscow's stage-managed coup in Afghanistan on December 27. There, a friendly government, unable to suppress nationalist and Islamic insurgents, seemed seriously threatened by the popular anti-Communist fervor. The Soviets eventually sent over 80,000 troops into that country with the strange mission of overthrowing their own semi-puppet government and installing a new, more subservient one, as well as to suppress the Islamic and nationalist resistance to Communist domination.

The brutal Soviet invasion provoked a major reconsideration of American foreign policy. "Let our position be absolutely clear," said President Carter in his State of the Union message. "An attempt by any outside force to gain control of the Persian Gulf region will be regarded as an assault on the vital interests of the United States of America, and such an assault will be repelled by any means necessary, including military force." [15]

This new stand foretold an increase in defense spending and a strengthening of the American military, a de-emphasis of attempts at detente with Moscow, and a recognition of the continuing reality of Cold War conflict. It also elevated the priority placed on building alliances with Islamic countries in the region. In essence, it was an abandonment of the Nixon Doctrine approach: direct American military presence was once more seen as the way to encourage regional peace and to protect American interests. The failure of the shah as a surrogate made such a revision necessary; the changed attitude of the American people made this new orientation possible.

Yet in this context, Iran was no longer the main American adversary or problem in the area—attention now had to be turned to the Soviet threat. Consequently, it was necessary to ease the friction between Washington and Tehran. The administration began to argue that it was in both countries' interests to work together against the Soviets. The best way to free the hostages, the White House argued, was to persuade the Iranians of this new reality.

The rhetoric in Washington eased off and plans for increasing the pressure against Iran were shelved. State Department briefings started to blame the embassy takeover on Marxists and terrorists, separating them from the Iranian government and suggesting that they might be a serious threat to that regime's survival.

"The Iranians know that the real threat to" Iran's national independence and territorial integrity "comes from the north and not from a distant country such as the United States," said National Security Advisor Brzezinski. "My belief," explained President Carter, "is that many of the responsible officials in Iran now see that this major threat to Iran's security . . . is becoming paramount, and that there will be an additional effort on their part to secure the release of the hostages and remove the isolation of Iran from the rest of the civilized world." Secretary of State Vance added, "as the Soviet threat has increased, the leaders of Iran have added reason to bring about the prompt and unconditional release of the hostages. . . ."[16]

Some of the Iranian leaders were indeed worried about Moscow's intentions and about the continued disorder at home.

The first break came on January 12, 1980, thirty minutes before the United Nations Security Council was scheduled to vote on anti-Iranian sanctions. A message from Ghotbzadeh, supposedly with Khomeini's authorization, suggested an investigation of the shah's alleged crimes in exchange for the release of the hostages. When Tehran failed to clarify the proposal, however, the vote went ahead. Although the council supported sanctions by a margin of ten to two (with two abstentions), Moscow's veto defeated the American request.

Up to that point, Vance had tried to go through more than ten secret channels to discuss a settlement of the crisis and he personally made three undisclosed trips to United Nations headquarters in New York to talk with Iranian officials. During the first months of the hostage conflict, this had been a frustrating task since Tehran kept changing both its negotiators and its positions. Finally, in mid-January there were some reasons for hope.

Ghotbzadeh offered further details of his plan on January 14. In addition to the investigation, Ghotbzadeh communicated, the United States must recognize Iran's right to extradite the monarch and to sue for the return of his wealth, not particularly onerous requirements. Further, the Revolutionary Council's refusal to turn over Laingen and the two other American diplomats residing in the Iranian Foreign Ministry to the student militants also seemed to indicate a change in course. On January 18, Revolutionary Council spokesman Hassan Habibi admitted that it had no control over the terrorists but stated that the new president would take control over Iran's foreign policy and over the hostage negotiations.

Bani-Sadr's election as president ten days later, with about 75 percent of the vote cast, gave additional credence to a diplomatic settlement. Born in 1933, Bani-Sadr attended Tehran University where he was active in the National Front under Mossadegh and later in its underground movement. He was arrested twice by SAVAK and was wounded in the 1963 riots, after which he spent four months in jail. Permitted to leave the country, he went to Paris to study and later to teach at the Sorbonne, developing his theories of Islamic economics.

As an outspoken critic of the embassy takeover, he was a likely candidate to solve the problem. Indeed, his victory was cautiously celebrated in Washington as a triumph for moderation. For him, the higher priority was settling Iran's economic problems, albeit within an Islamic fundamentalist framework. Bani-Sadr wasted no time in endorsing the Ghotbzadeh proposals, adding that Washington must acknowledge its errors in supporting the shah and must promise not to interfere in Iranian affairs in the future. He refused offers of American aid against the Soviets and explained that Khomeini would have to approve any arrangement leading to the release of the hostages.

The militants' opposition to Bani-Sadr's earlier plan to refer the hostage question to the United Nations had forced his resignation at the end of 1979 as supervisor of the Foreign Ministry. As the students continued to gain support from the state-controlled radio and television stations, whose directors were not sympathetic to Bani-Sadr, and used their special access to the news broadcasters to attack the regime's decisions, the new president accused them of trying to create a rival government. The hostages, he suggested, should be quickly tried or quickly released.

"We want American policy to change," said Bani-Sadr, suggesting that normalization was possible—an idea hitherto abhorrent to the hard-liners.[17] Once inaugurated on February 4, Bani-Sadr set about trying to forge unity. The students openly defied him, insisting that they would obey only a direct order from Khomeini; to the students and their clerical supporters, Bani-Sadr was simply another Bazargan. The terrorists in the embassy attacked moderate newspapers and politicians and provoked the arrests of National Guidance Minister Nasir Minachi and former Deputy Prime Minister Entezam—both of whom had friendly contacts with the United States Embassy during the Bazargan period—by claiming that captured embassy documents showed them to be CIA agents.

Bani-Sadr sought to isolate the terrorists. The day after he took office, the new president fired radio-television director Muhammad Kho'ini, the only outsider consulted by the students before their attack on the embassy and a member of their central council. The best way for those loyal to Imam Khomeini to act, Bani-Sadr lectured the embassy occupiers, would be to submit to revolutionary discipline. Only the diversity of decision-making centers allowed the revolution's enemies "to hatch a plot every day." "How," he asked, "can one govern a country when a number of individuals . . . act in a self-centered manner and create . . . a government within a government . . . ?" "These children" might have good intentions but they were damaging the revolution, and some of them might be deliberate subversives.[18]

Bani-Sadr, who after all had never been a political moderate, regarded men like Bazargan, Entezam, and Minachi "as reformists and pro-American," but conceded they were not spies and should not be slandered. Instead, "Certain uncontrollable Islamic committees which are rife in the country" must be disbanded.[19]

At the same time, Bani-Sadr and other Iranian leaders held out hopes of a quick settlement. The secret talks conducted through the United Nations produced a United Nations investigating commission that would come close to success. Later, Iranian officials would argue that there had never been any link between this committee and the freeing of the hostages but their contemporary statements belied these claims.

Waldheim had worked out a package deal. Once underway, the commission would visit Tehran and meet the hostages. The American diplomats would then be turned over to the Iranian government and subsequently to the Swiss or to International Red Cross representatives. The commission would return to New York to file its report and would then return to pick up the hostages. The United States would accept the United Nations report in some mutually satisfactory language, recognizing Iranian grievances. The State Department supported this proposal on January 30, promising cooperation with the commission—a change in the earlier policy of opposing any such investigation until the hostages were freed. Further sanctions would also be held in abeyance. Hodding Carter, the State Department spokesman, said that the United

States would not admit guilt in past relations with Iran, but implied that some formula could be worked out.

The Americans still did not understand that the embassy takeover was due to "our people's desire for independence," said Bani-Sadr, but if Washington examined its actions regarding past intervention in Iranian affairs and recognized Iran's right to obtain extradition of the shah and his fortune a solution was possible.[20]

Even the hard-liners seemed to indicate a change of heart. Iran must continue the anti-American struggle, Khomeini said on February 11, the anniversary of Bakhtiar's fall, though, "later, provided that our alert and noble nation grants permission, we will establish our very ordinary relations with Americans just as with other countries." Two days later Beheshti said that Iran wanted the hostage issue resolved quickly and that the American diplomats could be released even without the shah's extradition if Iranian public opinion agreed. Radio Tehran explained that Iran would seek the shah's extradition "until doomsday" but noted that this effort could continue even once the hostages had been released.[21]

On February 13, Bani-Sadr said that Khomeini had accepted the plan, though the embassy militants refused to believe this. Optimistic statements abounded. Beheshti said that the whole conflict would be settled by mid-March; Bani-Sadr spoke of a release within forty-eight hours; Ghotbzadeh estimated a month would be necessary; the White House said a solution might come in a few weeks.

"I am now in position to resolve the problem," President Bani-Sadr announced. The people wanted a strong central government and the students must leave the embassy and return to their schools. "Otherwise, in six months' time there will be nothing left of this country."[22] While Beheshti cautioned on February 14 that there was not yet complete agreement and that Bani-Sadr's statements only reflected his personal opinions, the hopeful projections continued. Two days later, in a trial balloon of self-criticism, President Carter expressed American regrets for any misunderstandings with Iran and looked forward to normal relations with Tehran in the future.

After hearing the names of the five-man United Nations commission on February 18—its members included jurists and diplomats from Algeria, France, Sri Lanka, Syria, and Venezuela—Bani-Sadr announced that both the Revolutionary Council and Ayatollah Khomeini had approved the commission. Waldheim predicted that the hostages would be released two weeks after the commission began its meetings in Tehran, but now Ghotbzadeh said the release of the hostages and the commission's work were unrelated. This was not the understanding of the group's members, who replied that their report would not be released until after the hostages had been let go.

These early misunderstandings boded ill for the commission's success. The Iranians interpreted the panel as a court investigating the crimes of the shah and America; Waldheim portrayed it as a fact-finding mission to hear Iranian grievances and to promote an early settlement of the hostage crisis. The White House claimed that it would explore American grievances against Iran. Now Revolutionary Council spokesman Habibi also said that the commission's work was not related to the release of the hostages, a view challenged by the group's cochairmen. The militant students also rejected any role for the commission.

In a stunning announcement Khomeini called for supporting the terrorists and endorsed their continued demand for the return of the shah and his wealth. Now backed by the only unchallengeable authority in Iran, the students hardened their line. The militants "have by their revolutionary deed dealt a crushing body blow against the world-devouring United States, and have thereby made the nation proud," said the aged ayatollah from his hospital bed. Iran's Majlis, when elected, would settle the hostages' fate, though the Revolutionary Council would continue to handle matters until that time.[23] The State Department argued that Khomeini's statement was meant only for internal Iranian consumption and would not affect the work of the commission. The problem was that this unyielding stand was a far more accurate picture of his views than the more flexible position presented in the diplomatic exchanges.

By the end of February, the situation in Tehran broke down into complete confusion. The international commission heard testimony on the shah's repression and corruption, but the key issue came to be the panel's visit with the hostages, the signal for the turnover of the prisoners. Contradictory reports were issued by Iranian officials every few hours. Beheshti began to shift over to support of the intransigent militants. In a test of wills between them and the Revolutionary Council, the students refused, then agreed, and then refused again to allow the commission to meet the American diplomats. Despite Bani-Sadr's and Ghotbzadeh's promises to the contrary, nothing was done about the students' independence.

On March 6, it was even announced that the Revolutionary Council would soon take custody of the hostages, and the frustrated United Nations investigators postponed their departure to New York. In a conciliatory move the White House indicated its willingness to express concern over past United States relations with the shah, though there would be no outright apology. As Khomeini was alternately portrayed as being for, against, or neutral on going ahead with the United Nations plan, the Revolutionary Council stayed in almost continual session. Large demonstrations and statements by the leadership of the Revolutionary Guards indicated support for continued confrontation. Finally, Khomeini said that the hostages would meet with the panel only after its report had been issued and only if that conclusion was satisfactory to Iran.

Celebrating the ayatollah's statement as a victory for their position, the student kidnappers refused to turn over the hostages. On March 11 the weary United Nations group left Tehran. The United States complained that the Iranian government had broken its promises; Bani-Sadr blamed the Revolutionary Council for being weak and indecisive. By mid-March, negotiations were back to where they had been in November. Beheshti explained that the Revolutionary Council's majority favored releasing the hostages only after the shah and his treasure had been returned to Tehran.

It is no easy task to untangle for examination this incredibly complex process, but some conclusions can be made over the

failure of the United Nations mission. The unyielding stand of
the student militants, the hysterical atmosphere in Tehran,
and the intransigent stand of Khomeini, all contributed to the
inability of Bani-Sadr and Ghotbzadeh to deliver on their
promises. Yet the issue was not a straight battle between students and government: without Khomeini's support the militants could not have prevailed and without the split in the
Council, Khomeini might have been swayed.

Two examples help illustrate the Iranian mood. The United
Nations commission's appointment, claimed Radio Tehran's
international service, justified the embassy takeover. Yet all
the American responses to the kidnappings—the appeals to
the United Nations and the International Court of Justice; the
real and potential sanctions—were simply new "fiendish
methods . . . to suppress the Islamic revolution."[24]

At a rally in front of the United States Embassy on February
25, Ayatollah Mahdavi Kani, a Revolutionary Council member
and supervisor of the Interior Ministry, quoted the Koran to an
approving crowd: "No individual, no official and no Muslim
has the right to show forbearance or compromise toward an
enemy who is not defeated and is not overthrown." Therefore,
he continued, all Iranians must support the militant students
and "imprison the agents and spies of the enemy according to
the command of the Koran until such day that the enemy con-
fesses its guilt and openly announces its defeat to the world."
Yet the proof of this submission would be "to return the criminal shah to us."[25] If this stand is any indication of the position of hard-liners within the Revolutionary Council, it clearly
shows why the United Nations commission failed to release
the hostages.

But none of this is surprising given the often-professed
ideology of the revolution. According to this creed, the shah
was a United States puppet and the American Embassy in
Tehran was the real center of government. After the revolution, Washington and the embassy allegedly did everything
possible to subvert the Islamic state. Since even an American
apology would hardly convince them otherwise, the new Iranian rulers had little reason to release the hostages.

Certainly, the embassy takeover had produced an explosion of Iranian national pride—they had slain the dragon their thoughts had conjured up. Given the fact that most Iranians were daily cheered by the continued holding of the hostages, the only appeal of the moderates could be to the best long-range interests of the revolution. Some could not so quickly forget Mossadegh's example. As Bani-Sadr pointed out, as a country ungoverned, with sporadic outbreaks of violence everywhere, a sick economy, and enemies all around its borders Iran was vulnerable and so was its revolution. Continued confrontation with the United States could easily endanger the regime's survival.

On the other hand, the embassy takeover helped keep at least the ethnic Persian parts of the nation united and provided a strong base for the fundamentalist leaders. To make some dramatic initiative on the hostage issue might undermine the credibility of some of the major individuals and factions; to hold onto the hostages seemed safer from this perspective.

Thus, the hard-line members of the Revolutionary Council were not blind to questions of realpolitik. Before one could exercise power, they reasoned, one had to maintain it at home. They did not care how much Iran was hated in Washington, D.C., or in Columbus, Ohio. The priority for them was the thinking of people in Tehran, Isfahan, and in the villages. The old rule that the successful Iranian political leader did not allow himself to be outflanked in militancy prevailed. Besides, while an inability to compromise had done more to bring down Mossadegh than all the efforts of the CIA in 1953, the very fact that the United States was not actively trying to bring down Iran's government in 1980—irony of ironies—made intransigence a less risky proposition.

Here lay the leverage of the militant student terrorists who held the embassy. They were able to invoke Khomeini's name without public contradiction from him because they did represent the logical extension of his thinking. They provided a high point of radicalism that Iranian politicians—particularly the hard-liners among them—were challenged to match. Their intransigence presented the clerical fundamentalists on the Revolutionary Council with both a danger and an opportunity, both to be exploited in the fundamentalist drive for power.

Among the kidnappers of the American diplomats, the conspiracy theory reached its most exhaustive proportions. It was claimed that the failures in Iranian agriculture were due not to the shah's errors but to deliberate United States efforts to keep Iran dependent. The arms sales were not a response to the shah's demands but an American plot to steal Iran's oil money and to protect Washington's interests. These young revolutionaries firmly believed that they were the vanguard of an international revolution. The success of the Canadian Embassy in safeguarding and smuggling out six American diplomats who had escaped the American Embassy on the day of the takeover, and the continuing existence of moderate factions within the revolution convinced them that they were surrounded by enemies.

There was much speculation on the identity of those who held the United States Embassy, particularly on the questions of Soviet KGB and Palestine Liberation Organization influence. There is no doubt that some of the occupiers were Marxists and that some were trained by the PLO, but neither the Soviets nor the PLO had any real control over their collective actions. Most of them were Islamic fundamentalists and followers of Ayatollah Khomeini's ideology—they had their own world view and had no need for the direction of outsiders.[26]

They were strongly aligned with the hard-line faction of the revolution. Much of their fire was directed against such moderates as Nazieh and Matin-Daftari, Entezam and Minachi, Admiral Madani and the newspaper *Bamdad*. Their access to the mass media, even after the removal by Bani-Sadr of their sympathizer and advisor Kho'ini from control over radio and television, was also a powerful weapon.

The average age of the approximately four hundred militants was only twenty-two years; one-quarter of them were women, some of whom wore a dark-blue head scarf while others wore the full *chador*. The men dressed in khaki United States army jackets. Islamic fundamentalists among them wore a light beard while leftists tended to cultivate thick moustaches. Most of them were indeed students—and mostly in the faculties of mathematics, chemistry, engineering, and medicine rather than in theology. Some of them were Arabic-speakers from Khuzistan, but most were ethnic Persians.

Gradually, they developed a tight, disciplined organization with six committees for information, documentation, operations, security, logistics, and guard duty. The public relations office dealt with Iranian and foreign journalists—banning reporters whose writing displeased them, favoring those who seemed to be more sympathetic. At the top stood an eight-member central council, meeting on alternate days. Aside from Khomeini himself, their most important theoretical guide was the late Ali Shari'ati, whose political philosophy combined a militant defense of traditional Islam with a radical emphasis on social justice.*

The seven identified members of that central council included: Muhammad Kho'ini, forty-one years old, who had been with Khomeini in Paris and was considered his representative to the students; Mohsen Mirtamadi, in his early twenties, who had been jailed for anti-shah activities in 1977; Naimi (a code name), twenty-two, the public relations officer; Hussein (a code name), twenty-three, an engineering student, and Hassan Habibi (a code name—not to be confused with the Revolutionary Council spokesman), early twenties, the only one of the group considered to have Marxist tendencies. Other probable members include Nilofar Ebtekar, twenty-one, a second-year chemistry student who, as "Mary," became well known in the United States through her television appearances. As a child, she had lived for several years in Upper

* Shari'ati combined a strong familiarity with Western thought and a very firm grounding in Islamic law and philosophy. He spoke against Western cultural influences but for a revolution in favor of Iran's poor. The term "Islamic-Marxist" often applied to his writing is somewhat misleading. Arrested several times under the shah's regime, he was allowed to leave Iran for England. He was mysteriously murdered there, probably by SAVAK. His work had a tremendous influence on many of those who participated in the revolution and in post-shah politics.

Darby, Pennsylvania. Finally, there was Shahpour, twenty-three, a third-year medical student.

None of them had much experience with international politics or with the workings of embassies. This, coupled with their ideology, made their analyses of the United States Embassy's operations inaccurate in the extreme. For them, a State Department report on the Kurdish insurrection or on the anti-Khomeini Islamic terrorist group Forqan was proof that the United States was in contact with these movements, if not directing them. Any meeting between an Iranian official and embassy employees was proof of the former's treason and the latter's espionage. What was the most remarkable was their failure, after months in the embassy files, to produce any hard evidence of their accusations; some of the material circulated as evidence within Iran consisted of the most transparent forgeries.

Nonetheless, their credibility within the country remained high. They knew that the eyes and ears of the world were focused on their every deed and pronouncement. It must have been a heady experience.

For President Carter, these events were far less pleasant. White House political operatives, who had more and more influence on the conduct of policy as 1980 wore on, tried to turn the humiliating hostage crisis, in which the president was daily being vilified by foreigners on America's own television news programs, into a campaign asset. One television political advertisement early in the primary season told voters: "Iowa will send a clear signal to the world . . . do we or do we not support the president as he makes the hard decisions in response to Iran and the Soviet aggression in Afghanistan. Let's join the fight for a stronger, more secure America. . . . President Carter—he's fighting for all of us." [27]

The president announced his abandonment of partisan campaigning to cope with the Iran issue, although he continued to call political allies to firm up support and to give interviews. During most of the primary season, he stayed close to Washington. At the same time, his Republican rivals, although kept cautious by the delicacy of the issue, tried to use the slowness of progress over the hostages against the president.

After the failure of the United Nations commission, American public opinion reflected both impatience and continuing, if slowly eroding, support for the president. A March, 1980 Harris poll found that voters who five weeks earlier had judged Carter's handling of the crisis a success—by a 51 percent to 32 percent margin—now considered it a failure by a 47 percent to 31 percent plurality. Whereas in mid-December, a 66 percent to 32 percent majority supported President Carter's strategy, by mid-March this had turned into a 55 percent to 43 percent negative assessment.[28]

By overwhelming majorities, Americans felt personally and emotionally involved with the hostages' fate, were willing to wait as long as necessary to get them back unharmed, favored tightening trade restrictions on Iran, and expressed frustration at America's seeming helplessness at resolving the issue. On a tactical level, 60 percent (against 31 percent) felt it had been a mistake not to give Iran an ultimatum to release the hostages during the first seventy-two hours after the takeover. By a closer margin, 53 percent (against 34 percent) rejected the idea of apologizing for past United States-shah relations, seeing such a step as "humiliating and wrong" even "if it was the only way to get the hostages back unharmed."

Before further escalating the pressure against Iran, which had already been delayed by the Soviet move into Afghanistan and by the United Nations plan, the White House was willing to try one more diplomatic effort. If this failed, Carter and aides agreed at a Camp David meeting on March 22, then more economic and political sanctions would be imposed. West European allies were alerted to the possibility of an embargo.

This timetable was somewhat disrupted by the shah's decision to leave Panama. He was nervous at the Iranian attempts to extradite him from that country, though such efforts seemed unlikely to succeed. Washington preferred that he stay in Panama so that as the extradition procedure slowly moved forward, the Iranians would have some incentive to make concessions on the hostage question. Despite a personal attempt by top White House aide Hamilton Jordan to dissuade him, the monarch insisted that he would go elsewhere.

On March 23 the shah departed for Egypt, leaving behind him charges and countercharges in which Panama, the United States, Iran, and the shah's own aides accused each other of bad faith and duplicitous actions. One issue of contention involved the December, 1979 agreement between the White House and the shah, reached just before the shah left for Panama, on a variety of questions. The United States, the shah's friends claimed, had originally promised the stricken monarch that he could return to America if he so desired. Now, they said, the promise was abandoned.

Meanwhile, the second American diplomatic initiative was put into operation. Known in Washington as "the French connection," because of its use of several French lawyers as intermediaries, the effort began with a message from President Carter to Tehran, the contents of which have been hotly debated. Apparently, belief in the potential success of this attempt had arisen out of earlier indirect exchanges between President Bani-Sadr and the United States government.

According to some sources, the letter carried a significant warning: it set down a short deadline for the hostages to be transferred to Iranian government custody before tough sanctions would be imposed. As released by the Iranians, however, the communication was quite conciliatory. It warned Iran of Soviet designs, said that the administration had inherited its earlier relationship with the shah, but now accepted the new situation and wanted to have good relations with Iran's revolutionary government. This seemed to meet some of the conditions publicly set down by Bani-Sadr. At the same time, Secretary of State Vance announced that he would not oppose a historical investigation of bilateral relations by the Senate Foreign Relations Committee.

The problem, though, was that the message was altered en route—either by the Iranians or by some of the intermediaries—to make it much more apologetic than it had been originally. The White House then denied all knowledge of or involvement with the message. Bani-Sadr persisted, making a relatively moderate statement proposing an arrangement in which the hostages, with or without the embassy grounds, would be turned over to the custody of the Revolutionary Council. Yet it is clear that this time Bani-Sadr did not have the council firmly behind him. Ayatollah Khomeini himself, enraged by the shah's flight to Egypt, was in no mood for a settlement. There was also some confusion over whether the United States had accepted a new condition—that the hostages' fate be determined by Iran's new parliament, which was to convene in June.

Once again, Iranian officials made contradictory statements every hour and the council convened in day-long sessions. When Ayatollah Khomeini made a hard-line speech on April 1, marking the Islamic republic's anniversary, everyone once again fell into line behind his position. The statement, read by the ayatollah's son Ahmed in its original form, despite Bani-Sadr's attempts to tone it down, blamed an American plot for the shah's movement to Egypt and reaffirmed that only in the upcoming Majlis session could the hostage issue be settled.[29]

With no further hope of a diplomatic solution, the White House now moved to the measures originally considered for the previous December. Relations with Iran were broken off, a full-scale attempt was made to encourage American allies to isolate Iran economically, and plans for the rescue mission were accelerated.

Khomeini welcomed this severance as a further proof of Iran's independence and the Revolutionary Council persisted in portraying the whole hostage issue as a secondary question. Their communiqué of April 8 stated:

> The American President tries to hide the imperialist ambitions of his government under the cover of the issue of the hostages . . . while we know and the events of the past year have clearly demonstrated that the essential question for the American Government is not the holding of the employees of the American Embassy . . . [but] the Islamic revolution and the severance of the aggressive hands of that government from Iran.[30]

Obviously, given this attitude on the part of the Iranians, any attempt to convince them of Washington's conciliatory intentions was doomed to fail.

In response to the impasse, President Carter initiated the long-deferred economic embargo, broke diplomatic relations with Iran, and began to inventory $8 billion in frozen Iranian assets against outstanding United States claims. He also pressed American allies, particularly Japan and Western Europe, to join in the economic and political isolation of Iran. "For long months, ours has been a restraint of strength despite outrageous provocation," he said in a speech. "But it has become necessary, because Iran would not act in accordance with international law and with their own interests, for us to act again."[31]

The frustrations within the administration had reached a boiling point. When Iranian Chargé d'Affaires Ali Agah and another official met with Henry Precht and Deputy Secretary of State Warren Christopher to discuss the closing of their embassy, the two visitors spent much of the time criticizing the United States. Some of the hostages preferred to stay in Iran, they said, and they were being protected by the Iranian government. "Bullshit!" Precht replied, and the two Iranians stormed out.

That usually calm State Department specialist was not alone in his anger. National impatience was reflected in all the American polls. A Harris survey in mid-April found that 68 percent thought the sanctions were too little, too late. A contemporary Newsweek inquiry found the public disapproved of past strategy by a margin of 49 percent to 40 percent, the former group demanding stronger action. Another study found two-to-one support for military action even if it imperiled the hostages' lives. Most of those questioned doubted whether the sanctions would bring a solution.[32]

American allies were reluctant to press sanctions, but were even more eager to prevent military action on Washington's part. They did not want to lose a source of oil and a trading partner and they also worried about pushing Iran into Moscow's arms. Perhaps most important was their desire to prevent any action potentially disruptive to the stability of the Persian Gulf area, which supplied 70 percent of Western European and 67 percent of Japanese petroleum imports.

But the White House had already decided on a daring rescue mission. On April 11 President Carter ordered the Joint Chiefs of Staff to go ahead with the plan. Vance set forth his objections: such an operation might endanger two hundred American nationals still in Iran and could threaten relations with Persian Gulf and European allies. The White House decided, however, that the importance of the issue and the need to take firm action took precedence.

Eight helicopters from the aircraft carrier USS Nimitz and six C–130 cargo planes, carrying a ninety-man assault team and another ninety support and flight personnel, set off on the night of April 25. They were to travel from the Gulf on a northwestern course, flying above uninhabited desert and mountain areas, and refueling in a desolate spot. From there, they would fly 208 miles more to a site 50 miles southeast of Tehran, arriving early in the morning.

At this point the commando team would be unloaded and the helicopters flown to a place where they could be hidden, camouflaged, and guarded by troops in Iranian uniforms. The rescue unit itself would spend the day hidden in a garage. At midnight, they would drive into Tehran in five trucks, heading for Amjadieh Stadium opposite the embassy. The assault team would attack the embassy—using folding ladders to scale the walls—and neutralize the terrorist guards. The hostages would then be taken to the stadium where they could be airlifted out. A smaller unit would rescue the three diplomats held in the Foreign Ministry. Four helicopters would carry the hostages, two more would provide air cover or be held in reserve. The whole group would rendezvous with the C–130s and would fly out of Iran, protected by American fighter planes.

Events did not turn out as planned. Three helicopters suffered incapacitating damage, forcing the mission's termination. To add to the debacle one of the helicopters collided with a C–130, causing an explosion in which eight servicemen died.

The failure provoked extensive criticism of the Carter administration at home and abroad. Some questioned the timing and propriety of the mission; others criticized the White House's decision-making and planning processes or the military's performance. Secretary of State Vance resigned, stating that he could not, in good conscience, support the resort to the use of military means. His departure was also a response to his loss in the administration power struggle—President Carter failed to inform him of the key meeting that gave the go-ahead signal.

The United States could not have waited any longer, Carter explained, because the shorter nights, unfavorable winds, and hot temperatures of Iran's summer would have made any future attempt increasingly difficult. He added that the United States had "exhausted every peaceful procedure" and defended the rescue effort as a humanitarian mission undertaken in self-defense and not a military attack upon Iran.[33]

The Soviet media, which for months had predicted a full-scale American attack against Iran, described the rescue attempt as a cover for a planned coup d'état. The Iranians celebrated the American failure, seeing it as proof of the correctness of Ayatollah Khomeini's leadership and perhaps even as proof of divine intercession for their cause. To discourage any follow-up effort, the student militants announced that they had scattered their prisoners to a half-dozen cities.

*   *   *

By May, 1980, then, with the hostage-rescue option abandoned, with other avenues of negotiation having been tried and found fruitless, the prospects for the release of the fifty-three American diplomats had, if anything, worsened. The American position was one of resignation. Though no one would say so publicly, the feeling in the Carter administration had become that the hostages would be released only when the Iranians decided to do so. Washington's leverage on the issue had shown itself to be minimal, whether because of objective conditions or government policy.

Yet from the Iranian perspective, the failed rescue-mission had major psychological importance beyond what it said or did not say about the will or the ability of the United States to act. By May, 1980, the fundamentalists had clearly gained the upper hand in the internal power struggle that had been joined in November, 1979 with the capture of the American Embassy. In mid-May, the results of the balloting for the Majlis made this official. While Bani-Sadr had won 75 percent of the vote in the earlier presidential election, the Islamic Republican Party took a clear majority of the seats in the parliamentary election. Having beaten back Bani-Sadr's leadership challenge, the militant leaders of Iran's 180,000 mullahs quickly escalated their demands, now seeking to purge the universities and the government bureaucracy of all but the most committed fundamentalists. Many of those fired had been long-time, anti-shah activists who found themselves, to their surprise, accused of collaborating with the imperial regime. Major efforts by the fundamentalists were also undertaken to pressure women out of public life and to restrict their activities. Prosecutor-General Ayatollah Ali Qoddusi admitted in May to holding 1,500–1,700 political prisoners, a number gradually approaching shah-era figures. Large numbers of executions continued through the summer as did barbarous stonings of Iranian sinners.

For Bani-Sadr, still nominally charged with running a government, the subsequent consolidation of power in fundamentalist hands made his job very nearly impossible. "We cannot fight imperialism simply by shouting hostile slogans," he declared, trying to orient the nation forward and direct its attention to the real problems that lay ahead. And clearly, those problems, left unresolved, had the potential to undermine the revolution even in the face of United States impotence or reluctance to act. Even Khomeini, absolutist that he was, began to express concern about the revolution's failure to produce a government capable of restoring order, about the constant rumors of military coups, about the intermittent violence that was erupting in different parts of the country. By March, 1980, inflation had risen in Iran to 25.6 percent over the previous year; the price of rice had climbed 30.6 percent.[34] The continued emigration of skilled Iranians, Bani-Sadr noted, would severely hurt the revolution, particularly while Iran remained very much dependent on the outside world. In words reminiscent of Bazargan's, he warned the people that they must settle down to work.[35]

Nor did the opening of the Majlis on May 28 seem to foretell a speedy resolution of matters, either within Iran or in regard to the United States. Members of the new parliament continued to talk of a trial for the hostages; many remained fixed on the goal of punishing the United States for its past and present relations with Iran. As one Majlis deputy put it: "Our purpose in holding the hostages is to put America on trial, so that we can prove to the world the oppression and tyranny suffered by this deprived nation at the hands of the American Government and the CIA organizations, and to expose their crimes." [36]

As Bani-Sadr's power continued to wane, the Islamic Republican Party tightened its hold on the country. The ailing Khomeini, though still the unchallenged leader, moved slightly toward the background. Semi-official assassination teams successfully murdered the shah's nephew in Paris and the outspoken Ali Akhbar Tabataba'i in Washington; an attempt against Shahpour Bakhtiar in Paris came close to success. These events in July were matched in Tehran by a new coup scare, involving several former or current military officers. The armed forces, already weakened, were once again purged and several dozen people were executed. Again, an attempt was made to link proregime moderates to these activities. Madani, for example, was forced out of the Majlis.

If any final event was necessary to demonstrate the new era in Iran it was furnished by the death of the shah in Cairo on July 27, 1980. The revolutionary leaders' fears that somehow their revolution might be undone and the shah restored to power once again were finally put to rest. So too was the misplaced belief among Americans that the passing of the shah could, in and of itself, lead to the release of the hostages. The shah's role in the hostage crisis had long ago become symbolic. The focus had shifted—from the holding of American diplomats as bargaining chips to force the return of the shah and his money to the holding of these people as spies and enemies.*

---

* On July 2, 1980 the militants released hostage Richard Queen, who was later diagnosed as suffering from multiple sclerosis. This reduced the number of hostages to fifty-two.

The shah's death once again highlighted the question of the historical relations between the two countries. Some Americans argued that their country had deserted a long-time ally in his hour of need; others said that America should never have so closely associated itself with the shah. It will take a more detached generation to examine the evidence and determine whether America's error lay in doing too little or too much for the shah.

Important as the hostage issue remained for Americans, there was more and more discussion of the problem of United States-Iranian relations outside the hostage crisis. Many government people began to express the feeling that even if the hostages were eventually freed, relations between the United States and Iran were unlikely to improve dramatically, other than through long years of reconstructive diplomacy. Neither Iranian domestic politics nor the will or whim of Ayatollah Khomeini would allow the country to be responsive to any American initiative any time in the near future. At the same time, more hawkish approaches might threaten broader United States interests. The United States had to consider the price of revenge against Iran in light of its broader interests in the Persian Gulf region, its relations with other Islamic countries and with its European allies, and the newly perceived need to strengthen the international anti-Soviet united front, particularly in light of new Soviet expansionism as manifested in Afghanistan.

Furthermore, history had taught the United States that Third World revolutions often brought in their wake extensive and long-term diplomatic ruptures in relations, especially where regimes relatively friendly to the United States were overthrown.* While a leftist victory in Iran seemed unlikely, the revolution's whole point had been to establish itself as an independent power force, based on an Islamic regime and ideology and distinguishable from both the Marxist-

* The 1955–57 break between America and Egypt took twenty years to resolve; the 1958 Iraqi revolution, despite several later changes of government, has produced continued hostility; United States reconciliation with China took twenty-five years. Many other examples could be cited. Often a whole political generation must pass before such wounds are healed.

Communist philosophy of the USSR and the Western-democratic traditions of the United States. Such an entity could be just as opposed to America and to American interests as any Communist regime, even while remaining equally hostile toward Moscow.

Thus, the United States and Iran, two countries whose friendship had begun with such high expectations and whose relations had included fine moments of selfless cooperation as well as many shameful episodes of corruption and insensitivity, were now the bitterest of enemies. A new historical era had opened—one of uncertainty for the two nations and for the whole world as well.

The Role of the Media

Much has been written recently about the role of the media vis-à-vis Iran. The Iranian crisis brought the American media its biggest and toughest news story since Watergate. A year-long revolution, the rise to international celebrity status of an unfamiliar Islamic clergyman and the holding hostage of fifty American diplomats provided the news media with a series of events as difficult to understand as they were sensational. For long periods at a time, developments in Iran ate up the lion's share of the American news media's resources, and overall, the combination of the new phenomenon of satellite broadcasts, the assumption by American correspondents of the role of de facto political intermediaries, and the almost unprecedented scope of international press coverage focused extended worldwide attention on Iran, with an intensity and immediacy rarely before equaled.

Yet for all their efforts, American newspaper and television journalists were subjected to an almost unprecedented level of criticism. Just as the shortcomings of the United States government were blamed on the failure of its intelligence community, the public's confusion over the meaning of the Iranian revolution were pinned on the shortcomings of the American press, despite the fact that among the many, often very different Iran stories published over the past decade, were some that were very well done, indeed. The variance in media performance provides one of the most illuminating examples of the diverse strengths and weaknesses of the American media's coverage of foreign affairs, particularly when their news is coming from a foreign country with which the American media has only modest familiarity.

Over the years, leading specialists on Iran have often been strong in their criticism of reportage in Iran. Writing in 1967, Professor Richard Cottam complained that "the American press seemed to treat the Iranian regime as sacrosanct," ignoring its pattern of repression and the dictatorial management of its political system. No American journalists were stationed in Tehran, he noted, and Iranian stringers could hardly be expected to write stories that might lead to their own arrests. Cottam even argued that this failure in proper coverage was a contributing factor in the middle-class opposition's growing disillusionment with the United States.[1]

More than a decade later, in the midst of the Iranian revolution, Professor James Bill found little improvement in the news media's handling of Iranian tensions: "The American mass media's coverage of Iran has over the years been consistently sparse, superficial and distorted. Major newspapers such as The New York Times, The Washington Post, and Wall Street Journal," Bill claimed, "have been especially weak in their reporting on Iran, misrepresenting the nature and depth of opposition to the Shah."[2]

Other journalists echoed these evaluations. Just after he and his colleagues had been expelled from Iran in January, 1980, Douglas Watson noted in the Baltimore Sun: "If Iran had been covered half as well by the American press during the decades of the shah's modernizing but arrogant, friendly but cruel and corrupt rule [as it was during the hostage crisis] Americans might have understood better how to avoid the disaster that has occurred there."[3]

Many similar comments came from Iranian revolutionaries

themselves, and from sympathizers in the United States. "By and large the American news media routinely have characterized the Iranian conflict as the work of turbaned religious zealots in league with opportunistic Marxists, rather than—as they might have—the reaction of people outraged by a repressive regime. By doing so the press has helped to misinform American public opinion and narrow the range of debate on this bellwether foreign policy crisis," wrote William Dorman, head of the journalism department of the California State University in Sacramento, and an anonymous Iranian co-author in the *Columbia Journalism Review.** Ayatollah Shariat-Madari, the popular, moderate religious figure who led the revolution from inside Iran, remarked, "The journalistic community of the world has continually made the libelous charge that we religious leaders are reactionary and against progress. But that is not true. We want science and technology, educated men and women, doctors and surgeons."[4]

Even the Russians got into the act, as Western press coverage became a major issue within Iran. Many broadcasts by the Soviet-backed National Voice of Iran and Radio of the Patriots condemned, "the liberal American press, which at first . . . spoke of human rights in Iran, [but] changed its tune when the people began lighting their sacred fires. All at once they joined in step with the most conservative papers in the world" to support the shah. "In discussing the demonstrations," continued this January, 1979 commentary, "the *New York Times* and the *Washington Post* never forgot to mention that those involved were a group of fanatics who are opposed to the so-called liberal programs of the shah. According to them several million demonstrators in the streets of cities all across Iran were opposed to freedom and they wanted to go back to the past. Consequently, their torture . . . was ignored when done by the liberal shah." Despite the source of these remarks, they seem to reflect popular Iranian sentiment as well.[5]

Indeed, Iranians in the postrevolutionary period seemed

* According to some sources, the co-author, who used the pseudonym Ehsan Omeed, was actually Mansour Farhang, the Iranian ambassador to the United Nations in 1979–80.

willing to believe even worse reports about the Western press. Siamak Zand, head of the protocol section of the shah's press office and responsible for liaison with important visiting journalists, defected to England in November, 1978. Zand charged that Western reporters, mostly Europeans, had accepted free plane flights, lavish hotel accommodations, and valuable gifts in exchange for favorable articles.[6]

While Zand admitted that most American journalists insisted on paying their own way in Iran, his charges were widely accepted within the country. Shortly after the revolution's victory, Abbas Amir Entezam, deputy prime minister and government spokesman, attributed *Time Magazine*'s critical coverage of the revolution to its alleged receipt of millions of dollars since 1953 from the shah and the National Iranian Oil Company. The Iranian government, he claimed, permanently financed hundreds of Western periodicals. One assumes that he was at least partly led to his beliefs by the many paid advertisements placed by the shah's regime in various publications, as part of its public relations efforts in the West.[7]

Lacking their own tradition of a media free from government control, the Iranians saw Western news organs as arms of the government. They were deemed to be full partners in a supposed American plan of psychological warfare, sabotage, and terror aimed at overthrowing Ayatollah Khomeini's government. This is why, Radio Tehran repeatedly told its listeners, "the Western press without exception shamelessly attacked the Iranian revolution and spread all sorts of lies. . . ."[8]

At times, though, Iranian officials bragged about their success in reaching Western public opinion through the news media. In April, 1979, for example, the Iranian Embassy in Washington publicized at home its successes in defending the positions of the Islamic movement "through dozens of television, radio and press interviews," including network appearances before 20 million American viewers. The revolution's first prime minister, the relatively moderate Mehdi Bazargan, actually thanked the Western press for its support. "It is thanks to the truth and legitimacy of our struggle and revolution," he told a February, 1979 press conference, "that the attention and cooperation of world public opinion and the press has been attracted." This was especially significant given the "riches and treasures" squandered by the shah in attempts "to buy" European and American public opinion.[9]*

Yet the dominant opinion remained that American newsmen were essentially acting as spies and saboteurs, linked to the American government in a sub rosa attempt to destroy Khomeini's new order. As such, they were no better than the "spy" diplomats held hostage in the American Embassy. Though this suspicion was most likely the main reason for the expulsion of American reporters in January, 1980, there were also two other factors contributing to the decision. First, the Iranian regime was fearful and resentful of the generally accurate American reporting about divisions and conflicts within Iran, particularly the uprisings among the Kurdish and Azerbaijani minorities. Second, many Iranian leaders seemed naively to have believed that if the American public could only be made to hear their side of the story large blocs of Americans would rally to support them. When this did not happen, the most palatable explanation was that the media had not made their case fairly or well enough.

Within the Iranian understanding of the role of the American news media, then, newspaper and television reporters were as much actors in the evolving political developments of the Iran crisis as they were journalists. Within America, the extensive and highly dramatized coverage led many to argue that it was the press that made Iran one of the main issues in the early part of the presidential primary campaigns, creating pressures on the Carter administration for action. The actual extent of media influence in either Iran or the United States will be hotly debated for years to come.

But what about the accusations cited above of superficial

---

*Even Ayatollah Khomeini commented: "Coming to France allowed me to inform international opinion of the shameful exploitation of the Iranian people by the Shah and his regime. . . . So, we were able by the information media to expose our problems to the peoples of the whole world and to their respective governments." Cited in Jennifer Parmelee, "Firemen to Diplomats: The Western Media and Iran Before and After the Revolution," senior thesis (Princeton, 1980) pp. 39–40.

coverage during the years before the revolution? Was coverage really sparse and misleading? Did the press misinform the American public? Should the journalism profession shoulder a large degree of responsibility for the unpleasant turns taken by this particular crisis?

The answer is not a simple one. While the shortcomings of the media in this area are far greater than many editors and journalists will admit, even to themselves, the problems are often in categories different from those identified by their challengers. If one goes back and reads news articles and editorials in the *Washington Post* and *The New York Times* day by day during the four years before the revolution, dozens of pieces citing Iran's economic problems and instability, the rampant torture and political repression can be found. There were more than a few editorials warning of the need to distance United States policy from the shah, challenging the massive arms-sales programs, and critically analyzing Iran's new international role.

This does not completely invalidate Bill's criticisms, for the media's greatest shortcoming was in the failure of its coverage to foster greater awareness among Americans of Iran's domestic politics and culture. Nor do Dorman and his colleague entirely miss the mark. There were many oversimplifications in the stories that appeared in such respected magazines as *Time* and *Newsweek,* as well as in many of the smaller daily newspapers. Nevertheless, the emerging myth that coverage of Iran was a media disaster is quite misleading.[10]

The real problem is that foreign news coverage is simply too often the major basis of public policymakers' perceptions of what life in other countries is really like. In general, many policymakers do not read the many dispatches and reports that come in through embassy and intelligence sources but do avidly and carefully read their daily newspapers and watch the evening television news. Congress, which lacks access to most of the sources available to the executive branch, is even more dependent on publicly disseminated information.

While international news coverage is not exactly an orphan in the makeup of newspapers and television reports, it leads a somewhat precarious life. Most editors assume that their readers have little interest in overseas affairs, unless the events have some direct impact on their own lives. Thus, those who define the news are constantly influenced by this perceived public disinterest. If such stories take up more of the editor's limited time and space than the public wants, it is argued, the effect will eventually be felt in declining circulation and ratings. On the other end of the journalism spectrum are those members of the press who see it as one of the duties of a free press to provide facts and analyses of those events that shape history, whether they occur domestically or in far-off lands.[11]

Of course, American periodicals range from the half-dozen or so prestige newspapers, which place a high emphasis on foreign news and employ their own foreign correspondents, to the hundreds of dailies that focus overwhelmingly on local developments and publish only abbreviated, event-oriented reports of foreign events culled from the dispatches of the wire services. The network news programs tend to fall between these two groups, thus playing an important supplementary information role in many parts of the country. Weekly news magazines fill a similarly complementing, rather than self-sufficient, journalistic part.

Each of these forms of reporting has its own special constraints. Television is restricted by self-defined needs for brevity, drama, and visual appeal. Since most stories run less than three minutes and since abstract ideas are notoriously hard to communicate through a camera lens, such coverage is usually insufficient. Further, if an editor of a major daily errs in his judgment on a story's importance it appears on page 8 rather than on page 1; if a television editor makes the same error the story appears not at all. Certain innovations, like Public Broadcasting's "MacNeil-Lehrer Report," which spends thirty minutes on a single important story, hold promise but have not yet caught on to any great extent. At any rate, until the revolution—and in a real sense until the hostage crisis—Iran remained largely a print-journalism story.

Throughout the 1940s, 1950s, and 1960s, the press—with

some notable exceptions—generally held a higher view of the shah's achievements and abilities than did the United States government. On the other hand, beginning around 1972, coverage of Iran's international and economic role began to generate more attention, and a gradually more critical evaluation. While many stories continued to ratify the conventional wisdom of the Nixon-Ford years, by 1974 others began to appear seriously questioning the basis of the alliance.

Before late 1977, outside of interviews with the shah on Sunday panel shows and on news-magazine programs, there was sparse television coverage of Iran. What little there was tended to emphasize the issue of arms sales even more heavily than did the print media. One notable television scoop, however, was the shah's admission, on CBS's "Sixty Minutes," of SAVAK activities in the United States. Television reporting on the revolution itself was even more upbeat than that of the press, with some stories holding out hopes for the shah's victory as late as December, 1978. Most of the evening news features ran only one or two minutes in length; the longer items tended to focus on the story's American angle: the statements of President Carter, threats to Iranian oil production, and the problems of Americans in Iran.

It would perhaps be most useful to analyze media coverage through three different periods: 1972 through 1977, the years we call in hindsight the prerevolution period; January, 1978 through February, 1979, the era of the revolution itself; and March, 1979, to the present, a time characterized by the confusing nature of the new Islamic regime and, after November, 1979, by media preoccupation with the American hostages.

1972–77

Iran's drive for modernization and for great power status was marked by a number of events in the early 1970s, including the shah's lavish celebration of the Persian empire's twenty-five-hundred-year anniversary; President Richard Nixon's May, 1972 promise to sell the shah all nonnuclear weapons he desired; Iran's nationalization of oil production; and the OPEC price increases in 1973. These events produced a number of stories, each covering some aspect of Iran's international policies and actions.

The American press did a good job in explaining Iran's role in the new Nixon Doctrine strategy, United States arms sales to Iran, and the Iranian role in the petroleum upheavals of 1973. Much attention was also devoted to United States-Iranian relations and to public and official moves of the Tehran government. During the first few years of this period, Cottam's earlier criticisms remained valid—coverage of the shah's government remained fairly uncritical. By mid-1974, however, a turning point had been reached; thereafter there was increasing discussion of the shortcomings of the Iranian regime and of its internal problems.

Even during this latter period, though, there was a tendency within the press, as well as within academic and congressional circles, to focus on the regional dangers facing Iran and America: Was the American military buildup of the shah producing a regional arms race? Might it lead to a war in which America would be involved? Would money being spent for armaments perhaps be better applied to Iranian social and economic development? If there was relatively little attention paid to those who stood in opposition to the shah, it was for the simple reason that by 1965 the shah had crushed any organized or vocal dissidence. Only urban terrorism remained as an active antigovernment force.

Typical of the lengthier early stories was Jonathan Randal's report, headlined, "The Shah's Iran: Arms Debts and Repression Are the Price of Progress," in the *Washington Post*. Despite some shoot-outs, he wrote, the guerrillas "remained an isolated island of extreme discontent in Iran's otherwise go-go success story." Under the shah, he continued, Iran was one of the few Third World states "whose problems are the consequences of its own success." The shah, "complicated, devoted, authoritarian and impatient," was responsible for many of these difficulties because of his determination to make Iran a major Middle East military power "no matter what the strains on his still vulnerable oil-based economy." [12]

Similar articles appeared in the *Washington Post* and *The*

New York Times over the following two years. The 1973 Arab-Israeli war, with its confirmation of the fragility of regional stability, called attention to the growing United States-to-Iran arms-sales program. Yet the real escalation in news coverage came with the sudden realization that OPEC had the power to raise oil prices almost at will. This trauma tended to end concern over the vulnerability of Iran's single-product economy, as long as the single product was oil.

During 1974, however, there was some divergence in approach between *Washington Post* and *The New York Times* correspondents. James Clarity, writing for the latter, produced relatively upbeat, lighter stories about Iran's rising living standards and about its rush to development, while Lewis Simons, the *Washington Post's* South Asia correspondent, produced some critical, more insightful pieces. According to Simons, Iran's new oil wealth made the Iranian government confident it could overcome whatever internal problems still existed in Iran, but United States specialists were predicting mounting discontent as promises were being made but not being kept. The shah ran "a police state" and his drive for development in record time "is broadening a gap between the shah and the people." Though American diplomats saw the regime as stable, the monarch's ability to control events was decreasing while those around the throne were cutting him off from accurate information on Iran's problems.[13]

By 1975 Iran was being better covered, receiving more attention than practically any other Third World country. If the story was seen more in terms of strategic issues, petroleum, and United States-Iranian relations these were, after all, the most active questions of the day. No one reading the *Washington Post* or *The New York Times* even by that early date could fail to sense the very real and serious problems already beclouding the Iranian economic "miracle." There were also reflections of congressional concern that American strategy toward Iran was being formulated without adequate consideration of the long-term consequences and that Congress should examine Washington's arms-sale policy.[14]

This does not mean that the administration's arguments

were summarily deprecated. A number of well-done thought pieces examined both sides of the debate about arms sales, the role of American technicians in Iran, and the shah's ambitions. In one such article, Marilyn Berger expressed the view that the shah "is a ruler who is trying to improve the lot of his people economically; yet he is dictatorial and repressive." The United States was placing its bets on this ambitious and unpredictable ruler because "for the time being there is a coincidence of interest. But nobody wants to look more than 10 years ahead." The point of the article was the seeming lack of American options: the shah was said to be "the only one around with any power in an area of weakness."[15]

Editorialists and correspondents became much more doubtful of this policy as time progressed. The United States was making a "profound mistake" selling so much weaponry in the Persian Gulf, concluded *The New York Times*, and the governments in that region were making an equally profound mistake by squandering their wealth on military display. *Washington Post* editorials criticized "a network of commitments that are becoming steadily more dangerous and onerous," that were likely to get both America and Iran into trouble. As long as the shah concentrated on military hardware to the exclusion of Iran's other needs, "the outlook for stable growth [was] obscure."[16]

Investigative journalists turned their attention to problems in the arms-sales programs. Leaked documents, congressional reports, and other materials were used to demonstrate the serious shortcomings, as well as the corruption, that were involved. Iranian complaints about malfeasance, about the rising costs of arms purchases, and about the problems created by private American commercial ventures were thoroughly aired.[17]

Greater concern was also directed toward repression in Iran. Simons repeated his "police state" analysis and called the shah's relatives the worst offenders in corruption; there were articles on press censorship and on SAVAK and torture. "Iran Secret Police Held 'Law Unto Self,'" proclaimed one *Washington Post* headline in presenting the reports of respected in-

ternational organizations on the subject. Another *Washington
Post* article, this one on SAVAK operations in the United
States first exposed by American television journalists,
pointed out that despite the repression it was now difficult to
find any Iranian students who supported the Tehran government.[18]

Finally, throughout 1976 and 1977, Iran's economic problems became the subject of a continuing string of stories. For
one thing, the country was not selling enough oil to pay its
bills. Bungling by Iranian officials was also being blamed for
the end of the boom.[19] A full year before the revolution began,
the best American newspapers were clearly telling a story of
a country with a harsh dictatorial government, severe economic difficulties, and an unhealthy emphasis on importing
weapons it was unprepared to use for years to come. Editorials
warned Washington that a re-examination of American policy
was necessary.

This does not mean that media coverage of Iran in these
years was an unbroken pattern of accuracy and profound insight. The Washington-datelined stories on strategic and oil
issues were just that, Washington stories. Although they represented some good reporting, it was clear that correspondents had failed to understand the effect of events on Iranian
society. Even where the stories were datelined Tehran, it was
obvious that correspondents found it difficult to get beyond
what officials in Tehran were prepared to let them see and
hear. Seldom did reporters succeed in breaking through or
communicating to readers the cultural and political context of
Iranian life. The major frictions were uncovered but because
there was a dearth of first-hand reports about these problems,
they were dealt with in a few general sentences. By the time
the few available facts reached the news magazines, the ratio
of hard news to the shah's public relations' press releases, was
even lower.

Interviews with reporters show that while there was no censorship of American reporters' dispatches, the Iranian government tried to intimidate or buy the loyalty of many journalists. They were given gifts and free junkets while red tape

was used to limit their investigations or to curb critical writers. The shah tended to grant interviews only to a select group of journalists and other high officials were often inaccessible. There was an approved list limiting those to whom the latter group could speak.

Correspondents had to submit a list of everything they wanted to cover to the Ministry of Information for approval; cameramen needed written permission to film any scene at all. When the American Cultural Center in Tehran was bombed, just before President Carter's visit in 1977, an NBC team attempting to film the site was briefly arrested.

Consequently, the three safest story types were those based on interviews with the shah or the prime minister, pieces on Americans in Iran, and travel/scenery stories. This, of course, was in addition to the internationally-oriented coverage. Sources were limited by the fact that many Iranians were afraid to meet with or talk to foreign reporters; many local Iranian stringers were also employed by the Ministry of Information and thus functioned as conduits for the official government line.

Much of the difficulty lay in the nature of the American press. The American media system, in contrast with European practice, encourages reporters to be generalists, moving from story to story and region to region; assignments rarely last beyond three-to-five years. Reporters, therefore, generally lack the ability to speak the native language, were never a continuing presence in Tehran, and did not have the reliable sources that can be cultivated only by long service in a country. As a consequence, few American journalists were familiar with Iran, and even fewer were knowledgeable about Islam or the values of Muslim societies.*

In addition, American journalism lacked a strong tradition of scholarship. Reporters have been good at investigatory work or at combing through documents, but rarely do they do the hard research so apparent in the work of their British and

_____

* After The New York Times closed its Tehran bureau in February, 1977 there were no full-time American newspaper correspondents in the country until November, 1978, though many reporters were sent in on a temporary basis.

French colleagues. To compare American stories on Iran to the detailed expositions of *Le Monde*'s Eric Rouleau is a sobering exercise, as are comparisons with a number of other European newspapers.

Writing in 1973, Rouleau described the poverty of the south Tehran slums, the "mixed blessing" of the shah's agricultural reforms, and the effects of inflation: "Some observers are amazed that the absence of safety valves, like independent trade unions, a representative parliament and genuine opposition parties, has not led to mass outbursts. One reason for this is that the country's economic progress has been really beneficial—even modestly—for some sections of the population, and this in turn has given rise to hopes in other strata."[20] Although many of Rouleau's conclusions were not altogether absent in the stories of his American counterparts, Rouleau's long experience and detailed knowledge lent his stories an aura of authority those of many Americans lacked.

Reporting the Revolution, 1978
Beginning in January, 1978, a massive, twelve-month-long revolution demonstrated the depth of opposition to the imperial regime. The American media, like the American government, found it difficult to gauge the movement's breadth and political direction. Reporters and editors were often confused over the grievances of anti-shah demonstrators, the motives of their leadership, and the likelihood of their success.

Critics see a great deal of ignorance and cultural bias in the coverage of this period. They point to the charged-language descriptions of "mobs" following leftists and backward-looking "black-robed mullahs" in acts of "riot," "anarchy," and "rampage." In comparison, the shah was favorably portrayed. While the opposition was pictured as fanatical and irrational, critics of the media coverage claim, the shah's motives and goals—if not always his methods—remained unchallenged. Consequently, the American public received a picture of a ruler who, with all his shortcomings, was far preferable to those who might take his place.[21]

There is much to be said in support of these criticisms. The lack of knowledge displayed by many journalists was nothing short of appalling. At the same time, it should come as no surprise that the media did far better on their home turf—the detailed coverage of daily events—than in their more vulnerable area—the analysis of political forces. Looking back from the perspective of events in Afghanistan and at the United States Embassy in Tehran, many of these early perceptions may have been more accurate than contemporary critics of the press would have thought possible.

Once the revolution triumphed in January, 1979, it was presumed that any good observer would have been able to predict the outcome in January, 1978. Such hindsight ignores the fact that history's dramas do not always follow set scripts. The final act could quite easily have turned out differently; some of the factors—particularly the shah's paralysis in the face of the crisis and Khomeini's takeover of the opposition—could hardly have been foreseen.

Nevertheless, it is interesting to compare the media's performance to that of the intelligence agencies. The contrasts are often in the press's favor. While the *Washington Post* and *The New York Times* reported in May and early June, 1978 on the alliance between Islamic political forces and other opponents of the shah, the CIA's daily reports to the president, which had earlier noted such a possibility, did not take note of the alliance until June 17, and then only with some uncertainty. On the other hand, while the press was relatively optimistic about the shah's future in August and September, the president's sources—those from the State Department somewhat more than those from the CIA—pointed out the difficulties blocking any easy resolution of the crisis.[22]

The media should beware of any excessive pride on this point. In discussing the "intelligence failure," the *Washington Post* complained that as early as February it had been clear that things were getting out of hand, although the United States Embassy in Tehran was still insisting at that time that there was no trouble.[23] By August, when even senior Iranian civil servants were saying that the shah would have to go the American diplomats stood by their earlier confident analyses.

Yet if all this was so obvious so early, one might well ask, why didn't the *Washington Post* tell its readers the score until October and November?

Yet the media's real failure lay not in its predictions (or lack thereof) but in its analysis. The American system of assigning overseas events did not require in-depth background knowledge of the actors and forces involved in the story being covered. The items reporters had followed the week before their Iran assignments and those they would turn to next, in most cases, were not linked together in any consistent manner conducive to building a commanding understanding of the material upon which the stories were based.

Anyone dealing with the press in those heady days has amusing stories to tell about attempts by the more conscientious to obtain instant education. Network news reporters asked Middle East specialists to describe the differences between Sunni and Shi'a Muslims, the relationship between religion and politics in Islamic countries, and the concept of *jihad*—all in one five-minute phone call. The reporter had to know all about these things by that evening when in his network news story he would authoritatively educate millions of viewers. There can be few experiences more disconcerting than watching highly paid reporters—who a few hours or days earlier had never heard the word "ayatollah" or "Shi'a"—discourse learnedly on these subjects to viewers coast to coast. Ordinarily, such trivialization of knowledge is annoying to the scholar, but of no great moment to the viewer. But when understanding the role of Islam in a Middle East country is tantamount to understanding why a crisis has occurred in that region and, more important, why one's country has chosen to respond to this crisis in a particular way, trivial and tragic no longer seem so far apart.

What the media repeatedly failed to communicate, both during and after the revolution, was the world view of the Iranian revolutionaries. I do not mean here that the media did not give fair time and space to Ayatollah Khomeini and his colleagues and aides. On the contrary, they were given more free television time and more interviews in print than any other foreign politicians within recent memory. But Khomeini could not adequately explain himself to an American audience—only an American reporter could do so. Yet the American reporters did not understand his message themselves. They did not read the Iranian press or listen to the Iranian radio—even in translation. Time and time again, they were scooped by the European press, whose journalists had area expertise and better developed and maintained sources.

Most surprisingly, American journalists often seemed to have forgotten their own pre-1978 stories. They had shown why Iranians were motivated to hate the shah's regime, they had documented the economic disaster facing Iran. Yet all this material was rarely tapped as explanation for the revolutionary response.

Further, despite the media's alleged overemphasis on "black-robed mullahs," American reporters in fact tended to underestimate their influence. Since Islamic fundamentalists, it was believed, could not possibly emerge as leaders of any lasting postrevolutionary state, it was only necessary to await the emergence to power of a new middle-class pragmatic elite, whose world view would be intelligible to an American television audience. Finally, there was no consistent American media "line" or level of quality. Stories differed drastically from day to day and from week to week. Top-notch analyses were often followed by simplistic clichés, sometimes in stories written by the same reporters.

The technical difficulties and the danger of appearing biased while covering the story were also factors that colored the reception of news from Iran. During the revolution the revolutionaries generally criticized the foreign media as being partial to the government: "Newspapers throughout the world should support us against the shah's regime," said Ayatollah Khomeini. From the other side, the shah's supporters often acted as if Khomeini had received his wish. The shah-controlled Radio Tehran attacked the foreign press for "sensationalism" and for "false and fabricated reports." This enemy "attacks people's minds and thoughts and, by creating a psychological war, would like to see an atmosphere of chaos and anarchy." Similar statements would be made a year later by the Islamic Republic's controlled media.[24]

Although Prime Minister Sharif-Emami urged the Iranian media to report accurately on revolutionary events—"If our radio doesn't broadcast it, the BBC will"—the shah's men did not make it easy for foreign reporters. About seventy-five reporters and a few resident bureau chiefs played a cat-and-mouse game to circumvent these obstacles. For days Iran was shut off from the outside world. Outgoing overseas calls and incoming messages were delayed or disconnected. The telex network collapsed, wire service teleprinters shut down, government agents monitored calls. SAVAK expelled UPI's chief and temporarily impounded office records. After September, 1978 the Ministry of Information stopped giving out information and top officials refused interviews.[25]

One American reporter was killed by a stray rifle shot. Three other Western correspondents, accused of attacking an army officer and joining an antiregime demonstration, were briefly arrested. Rumors flourished and even the most basic facts or casualty figures could not be accurately established. Tehran-based correspondents, for example, had to cover the August, 1978 Isfahan fighting via telephone.[26]

Early reports attempted both to understand the revolution's causes and to communicate the high degree of confidence freely expressed by the shah and his officials. "Rarely would contemporary history appear to provide such an example of a people's ingratitude towards a leader who had brought about an economic miracle of similar proportions," wrote Jonathan Randal. But, he quickly added, there was another side to it. The shah's haste in forcing modernization, the cost overruns, and poor management had brought on grave problems.[27]

Yet through early 1978 Randal and William Branigan judged the shah to be "firmly in control" and to have "more than enough resources to crush any serious challenge to his regime."[28] Randal had not pulled this judgment out of thin air: Mehdi Bazargan agreed with the assessment.

Newsweek saw the uprising only in terms of the Muslim mullahs' opposition to land reform, liquor stores, and movie theatres. Two months later they had grasped the alliance between "urban liberals" and the "conservative Moslem coalition," but they still saw it as having "little chance of sparking a full-scale revolution." [29]

Even as late as September, *Time Magazine* still defined the revolution's motive power as "Islamic puritanism" sparked by the shah's "rigorous modernization campaign." Discontent had also been encouraged by the Russians and by Palestinian groups. Branigin also continued to portray complaints as primarily religious in nature. Yet only five days later, William Claiborne wrote a splendid think piece on the causes of the revolt in the *Washington Post.* [30]

By the end of October, the picture of the shah's future began to look decidedly gloomier. The *Washington Post* reported that the country was out of control and that while moderate opposition leaders were seeking a peaceful transition, Khomeini's power was so great that none dared disagree with him in public. The *New York Times*, whose coverage had generally been superior, had reported in depth on the views of Khomeini and National Front leaders for some time. Now, the *Times* noted the revolution's unity behind Khomeini and the swing of all opposition forces in his direction. Jay Ross explained that the frustrated middle class had almost entirely deserted the shah and that the ruler's great dreams had ended in failure and corruption.[31]

Nevertheless, repenting of their earlier criticisms of the shah, both *The New York Times* and the *Washington Post* saw the opposition as a serious threat to American interests and to regional stability. *The New York Times* called on the White House to support the shah while keeping lines open to the opposition. The *Washington Post* concluded: "It is possible to see with new clarity why Americans have good reason to hope [the shah] rides out the storm," though his survival was uncertain. For him to be swept out would "be a misfortune for the United States." As for the two main elements of the shah's opposition—antimodern theologians and communist subversives—they were "in their separate backhanded ways, tributes to his vision for Iran" as a modern and non-Communist nation.[32]

The media's underestimate of the opposition's prospects, so

similar to that made by government sources, demonstrated
major misunderstandings of events in Iran even as they were
occurring. As for the opinions expressed in editorials, they
would not soon be forgotten by the victorious rebels.

The Hostage Crisis, 1979–80
With the kidnapping of fifty-three American diplomats as hostages in November, 1979, the Iran story attained the ultimate
American angle. The drama of this unprecedented act led to
saturation coverage. Television cameras, on an endless stake-
out around the American Embassy, showed thousands of
Iranian demonstrators shaking their fists and shouting anti-
American slogans. Every available detail on the hostages' well-
being, every statement by the militant students, and every hint
of any new development was carefully scrutinized. The media
played a central role in promoting concentration on the issue
across America. If reporters had not improved their understanding of Iranian politics and ideology, at least they now
had a story more responsive to standard treatment.

    Since there was no direct contact between the Iranian and
American governments, the press and television became diplomatic intermediaries. United States officials asked the American media to avoid antagonizing the Iranians; Iranian leaders
sought to use journalists to carry their message to Americans.
More than a few people understandably felt that the great
amount of attention focused by the press on Tehran only in-
flamed the conflict. Perhaps it would be better, they reasoned,
for the news people to go away and give quiet diplomacy a
chance to settle the issue.

    Iranians sincerely believed that if Americans could be made
to hear their story they would support Ayatollah Khomeini's
policies. Abol-Hassan Bani-Sadr, then Iran's foreign minister,
told reporters in late November, 1979 that the press alone
could solve the crisis. The hostages would be released only if
the shah were extradited to Iran. This would require a shift in
American public opinion capable of being brought about only
by the American press. He even offered to hold a one-day seminar with journalists to instruct them in how this might be
done, an offer that was declined.

What kind of articles and television stories did the Iranians want? Most likely, ones showing the extent of repression, torture, corruption, and oppression during the shah's regime— stories Americans were more familiar with than Iranians believed. Second, they wanted more coverage of the "constructive" accomplishments of the revolution, fewer reports on its chaos and its summary executions of "enemies" of Islam. Finally, they sought greater attention focused on American "responsibility" for the "crimes" of the old regime. While Iranian contentions that the shah was a mere American puppet were roundly rejected by informed reporters as absurd, there were other areas in which the problem was not one of different perceptions but of different levels of interest. In Iran, for example, CIA participation in the 1953 pro-shah coup or in the origins of SAVAK five years later were living issues of tremendous importance; to correspondents, these events were ancient history.

Western press comment on the summary trials and executions in revolutionary Iran provoked a wave of anger. "We Iranians cannot understand," said then-Prime Minister Bazargan in May, 1979, "the sentiments and support displayed by the Western press for the traitors and criminals . . . who ruled this country for more than 25 years in the most oppressive and barbarous manner." Correspondents did not understand that the struggle was continuing against the shah's regime, he continued. "A nation which has given up so many dead and wounded and has been plundered is not prepared to become calm the moment the shah leaves and his regime is overthrown."[33] Bazargan pleaded for understanding from journalists, speaking of "fantastic popular pressure" for the executions and warning that without such measures a much larger-scale massacre was possible.[34]

Ayatollah Khomeini and the Revolutionary Council leadership, however, saw Western media coverage as no less than part of a carefully planned plot to undo their revolution. In speech after speech, Khomeini pressed home this theme. "There is a great deal of propaganda against us," he said in a May 19 speech. "In their newspapers, in their magazines, they write that Khomeini has said that the breasts of all women should be cut off." When Western reporters wrote about the Arab uprising in Khuzistan province, Radio Tehran explained that "imperialism, American intelligence," and other hostile forces were orchestrating the media.[35]

The frustration of Iran's new leadership at their inability to wield the same absolute control over their country the shah had exercised was a prime factor behind the seizure of the hostages. Rather than coping with the real internal problems behind the chaos, as Bazargan attempted to do, Ayatollah Khomeini and the Iranian media saw the frequent strikes, demonstrations, and demands of the ethnic minorities as springing from United States plots. The first step in this campaign was psychological warfare and "in this connection," Radio Tehran explained, "the Western press without exception shamelessly attacked the Iranian revolution and spread all sorts of lies. . . ."[36]

The Iranian Islamic leaders have a conception of the role of the press similar to that held by many other Third World rulers today. The duty of the mass media, Ayatollah Khomeini told employees of the Tehran newspaper *Kayhan* in a speech, is to reflect the nation's aspirations: "The press must write what the nation wants, not that which runs counter to the nations' courses. . . . If the press still wants to write anything in support of criminals and traitors, this will not be our press— this will be treachery."[37]

Given this philosophy, which also characterized the shah's regime, it was very logical to the Khomeinists not only that those in control of the government also be in control of their own media but that friendly nations would naturally seek to regulate what was printed about Iran abroad. Further, they made the second assumption that foreign newspapers and television news were also controlled by the state—if not formally then behind the scenes. Hence, the American media was consistently seen, despite its denials, as an arm of United States foreign policy, rather than a variety of independent institutions. Just as the shah saw Western press coverage of his student opponents overseas as a hostile act, Khomeini interpreted the publication of interviews with the exiled former

Prime Minister Shahpour Bakhtiar as an attack on Iran. Each questioned not only the motives of those who would write such stories but the intentions of governments that would allow them to be published.

Khomeini's followers even began by mid-1979 hiring people just to read the foreign press reports, and these readers kept the government informed about critical reporting. Stories particularly singled out included those criticizing the political power of the clergy, suggesting the existence of corruption, or comparing the Islamic government with the shah's regime. David Lamb of the *Los Angeles Times* was expelled three days after breaking a story about the spread of opium production, addiction, and smuggling as a symptom in the breakdown of order.

One story had fatal repercussions. In May, 1980 two reporters from the French magazine *L'Express* interviewed Dr. Chahin Bavafa, director of the Choada hospital in Sanandaj, the major city of southern Kurdistan. She told them about atrocities committed by the Khomeinist Revolutionary Guards during fighting there. She insisted that her name be used to lend authenticity to her accounts. Shortly thereafter, she was captured by government forces and tried by an Islamic court. Charged with sabotage in her work and with publication in a foreign journal of a counterrevolutionary and insurrectional appeal, she was shot on June 17.*

Ironically, those who claimed that the American media was being manipulated by the Iranian militants were operating on the same premise as the propagandists in Tehran. Both accepted the idea that the more coverage Khomeini, Iranian leaders, and the kidnappers received, the more easily they might justify their actions with the American audience. In fact, the exact opposite happened: the more Americans heard themselves being attacked from Tehran, the more hostile they

---

*The incident is described in detail by Jean-Francois Revel in *L'Express*, July 12, 1980, p. 44. "Dictators of the Third World have for several years led a campaign to stifle information. The ayatollah has found the ideal method: to kill the oppositionists cited in the free press." This strategy was also used by the shah's regime.

became. Thus, NBC's controversial decision to agree to broadcast a speech from one of the student terrorists in exchange for an exclusive interview with one of the hostages may have set a dangerous precedent—as well as being in questionable taste—but turned out to be much less of a public relations victory than the militants had thought it would be.

Viewing correspondents as spies who were magnifying and fomenting internal disorders, the Iranian authorities began to crack down on the foreign press even before the embassy takeover. As early as June, 1979, Minister of Information Nasir Minachi called for the expulsion of all foreign journalists, on the grounds that the Western mass media was directed by international Zionism and imperialism. Its object, he said, was to mobilize public opinion against the revolution so that people abroad would prefer the shah's return.[38]

Petty harassment accompanied new, restrictive regulations. On a number of occasions, satellite communication of television stories was blocked by technical means. The ground station, which had been built by the shah, allowed a faster sending of stories; this technical innovation, like so many of the shah's other infrastructure improvements, was turned to another use by his enemies. The networks began to fly film out to London. In August, four American reporters and a CBS film crew were expelled for filing reports before obtaining prior clearance by local revolutionary committees.

Washington Post journalists were told that they could not report from outside Tehran without notifying the Ministry of National Guidance. They had to be accompanied to all interviews by a representative of that institution.

There were some differences among the Islamic revolutionaries over how to proceed. Dr. Mehdi Momken, the deputy minister of national guidance, said that while the majority of foreign reporters were serious persons, some, especially the Americans, were spies who deliberately spread incorrect news. Bani-Sadr, just after his election as president, took a softer line. "Of course many of them have written abominable or ridiculous things about us," he told *Le Monde*, "but others have done their job honestly." On the whole the presence of

Western journalists was "positive for us and for world opinion which understands better what is happening in Iran."[39]

Nevertheless, a number of American reporters were forced out of Iran in the closing months of 1979 and all were entirely barred for about ten weeks beginning in mid-January, 1980. At the time of the general expulsion, each of the television networks had about thirty-five people in Tehran.[40]

Immediately prior to the expulsion decision a CBS report from Washington by Marvin Kalb claimed that Foreign Minister Ghotbzadeh had told foreign visitors that Ayatollah Khomeini was out of touch with political reality. As soon as Ghotbzadeh saw wire-service reports of the story, CBS was deprived of satellite facilities. Next, impartial coverage of Ayatollah Shariat-Madari's followers, including their anti-Khomeini demonstrations, became the last straw and all American reporters were ordered to leave.

By the end of July, after a major coup scare, American reporters were again forced out of the country. Several European correspondents were also arrested and charged with furnishing dispatches to American networks and publications. Given the growing power of the independent revolutionary committees, even the Foreign Ministry could not guarantee these journalists protection. Several Iranian nationals working for the television bureaus were taken into custody and simply disappeared. Tehran newspapers ran front-page pictures calling the Intercontinental Hotel, where most journalists stayed, "a nest of spies," the term earlier applied to the American Embassy.

At the same time, the media was also under a certain amount of pressure from the White House. Telephone calls were made to the three networks to postpone certain segments because, according to United States government officials, they might interfere with delicate negotiations to free the hostages. Most of the targets of these efforts were retrospectives on United States-Iranian relations during the shah's regime.

In April, when sanctions were invoked against Iran, Carter made an unprecedented and largely ignored appeal to news organizations to minimize their presence and activities in

Iran. These requests seem to have had relatively little effect on the overall coverage of the crisis. The networks continued to buy pictures of the hostages from Iranian sources; ABC even obtained copies of the plans to rescue the hostages, documents that had been captured after that mission's failure.

The entanglement of media coverage with diplomatic efforts made the analysis of the former a more difficult task. For example, on May 6, 1980, *The New York Times* carried a front-page article by Washington correspondent Bernard Gwertzman claiming that President Carter had assured outgoing Secretary of State Cyrus Vance that he was ruling out the use of military force to settle the crisis in the forseeable future. He would now emphasize political and economic strategies to free the fifty-three Americans.

The "ABC Nightly News" opened the next evening with a dramatic report by correspondent Sam Donaldson. President Carter had ordered the Pentagon, he revealed, to begin preparations for a second rescue attempt. But knowledge of this plan might, he added, encourage the Iranians to free their victims and avoid such a confrontation.

Was Donaldson's "scoop" an irresponsible leak that jeopardized American plans? Or was it merely a statement of the obvious dressed up in impressive language? Of course, the Defense Department always has unlimited numbers of contingency plans drawn and filed away, including, until recently, one proposing reactions to a Canadian invasion of the United States.

On the other hand, the ABC story might have been an administration signal to Iran, another particle of pressure to gain the hostages' release. Equally possible was the idea that Gwertzman's story might have been planted to misdirect the Iranians into complacency, or a leak from Vance's entourage aimed at holding Carter to his private promises. In short, as the air filled with leaks designed to support or justify the strategies of various factions, departments, and individuals in Washington, the contents of articles and television stories on Iran took on a dual meaning. This media-political relationship was by no means new in Washington, but never before had it become so central to the policymaking process. Given the absence of direct communication between Washington and Tehran the media filled the task usually performed by embassies and back-channel exchanges.

As usual, the American media did a good job in covering the events of the Iran crisis. Demonstrations, riots, press conferences, political announcements, interviews, and briefings were generally factually reported to the American people. Policy decisions in Washington, with some notable exceptions, were also reported with reasonable speed and comprehension, though undoubtedly the close attention paid the hostage crisis tended to create overreactions to the ups and downs of United States-Iranian negotiations, producing unnecessary pressures.

The Iran crisis became an overwhelming national fixation in 1980, in part due to this mutual reinforcement between White House and media. An image-conscious administration, particularly so in the midst of a presidential-primary campaign, carefully gauged the tone of everything written. As middle-level officials noted their superiors' responses to each day's headlines they were given an incentive to leak their own positions and thereby bump them onto the agenda, much as many journalists traditionally passed their stories on to counterparts at The New York Times in order to catch their own editor's attention and command space in their own papers.

The heavy front-page, opening-minute coverage of the hostage crisis may have backfired on the White House and damaged American policy by seeming to demand quick results and the fostering of optimism. The former factor encouraged an acceleration of diplomatic initiatives that might have been more effective through calmer, quieter, and slower procedures. The latter tended to give United States-Iranian relations a roller-coaster effect. Such issues can only be evaluated after the passage of more time.

There are no easy solutions to the problems revealed in the history of Iran coverage. Certainly, the media should encourage more specialization by reporters, along with basic reading and research regarding the countries and regions they are likely to cover. More time and space should also be devoted to explaining how local peoples and regimes see current issues and problems. Foreign leaders cannot do this directly— without adequate and accurate context, the shah's statements proved misleading and Khomeini's were often incomprehensible—these ideas must be packaged by American reporters for American audiences.

Nowhere is this more true than in the Middle East, where complex historical and ideological factors have created a world view often at variance with Western conceptions, but it also applies to the rest of the Third World and beyond. The dual extremes of "global village" (the perception of an increasingly homogenous world) and of exoticism (seeing these peoples as inscrutable or irrational) must be replaced by more sophisticated levels of understanding.

United States-Iranian Relations Chronology of Events 1978–80

PREPARED BY BONNIE KOENIG*

January 1, 1978:   The shah of Iran entertains President Carter and Jordan's King Hussein in Tehran.

January 9, 1978:   Police fire on a crowd of religious demonstrators, killing between six and one hundred people, depending on which side's estimates are to be believed.

February 21, 1978:   Police patrol the streets of Tabriz after a weekend of rioting in which nine persons are killed and hundreds injured. The demonstrations spread to other cities.

March 7, 1978:   The government announces that several SAVAK agents and police officials will be disciplined for allowing the February disturbances to get out of hand.

March 29, 1978:   Hundreds are arrested in Tabriz for demonstrating against the shah.

---

* Some of the material used in this chronology was drawn from Congressional Research Service chronologies prepared by Clyde R. Mark and by members of the "Iran Task Force."

May 11, 1978:   The shah personally leads Iranian troops against demonstrators in Tehran.

May 15, 1978:   A general strike called by religious leaders closes shops and keeps motorists off the streets of Tehran. Troops patrolling the streets stop demonstrations.

June 6, 1978:   General Nematullah Nasiri is removed as head of SAVAK, the Iranian secret police.

August 27, 1978:   Jamshid Amouzegar resigns as prime minister. The shah appoints Jaafar Sharif-Emami to form a new government.

October 26, 1978:   The shah grants amnesty to fourteen hundred political prisoners.

October 31, 1978:   The government releases the names of thirty-four SAVAK officials recently relieved from duty.

Iran's oil workers go on strike, reducing oil production in one week from 5.8 million barrels per day to 1.1.

November 1, 1978:   Troops are deployed in the oil fields to prevent sabotage by striking oil workers and to protect those workers not on strike.

November 2, 1978:   National Front leader Dariush Foruhar calls for a referendum on a new government. (Over the next few days, violent demonstrations and strikes sweep through the major cities of Iran.)

November 6, 1978:   The shah appoints General Gholam Reza Azhari as prime minister of a predominantly military government. The day before, during the worst wave of violence in the continuing crisis, Sharif-Emami had resigned. The State Department announces United States support for the new military government.

November 7, 1978:   In Paris Ayatollah Khomeini says that an Islamic Republic will be formed by force if necessary.

November 9, 1978:   The shah orders an investigation of the imperial family's wealth and the activities of the Pahlevi Foundation. Twenty-four hours earlier, the government stops all foreign currency exchanges to halt the flow of money out of Iran into foreign bank accounts.

The United States ships riot control gear to Iran.

Ayatollah Khomeini says in Paris that all contracts with foreigners will be renegotiated under an Islamic Republic.

November 11, 1978: Dariush Foruhar and Karim Sanjabi of the National Front are arrested for holding an illegal press conference, at which they charge that the shah's government is illegal.

November 26, 1978: According to press reports in Washington, President Carter criticizes the United States intelligence agencies for their failure to see the crisis in Iran coming.

November 27, 1978: The *Washington Post* reports that the United States government has initiated secret contacts with the Iranian opposition forces.

Following a meeting with the shah, Senate Majority Leader Robert Byrd says that the United States will not interfere in Iranian affairs and will view "with utmost gravity and concern" any other nation's interference. The senator's visit to Iran is seen as a reaffirmation of United States support for the shah.

November 30, 1978: President Carter reaffirms his full confidence in the shah and says that the United States will not intervene in Iranian affairs. The president denies reports that he has ordered a review of the intelligence community's evaluations of Iran.

December 2, 1978: Ayatollah Khomeini says that when his forces take over Iran, oil shipments to Israel will be stopped and military ties to the United States will be re-examined.

December 29, 1978: Oil production falls below 300,000 barrels per day. (Iran's domestic consumption is 900,000 barrels per day.)

December 30, 1978: The National Front expells Shahpour Bakhtiar for agreeing to establish a cabinet under the shah.

December 31, 1978: General Azhari resigns as prime minister as demonstrations against the shah continue in most Iranian cities.

January 1, 1979: Bakhtiar tells an interviewer that he will form a cabinet if four conditions are met: that the shah leave Iran; that

SAVAK is disbanded; that police and military personnel responsible for shooting demonstrators are tried; and that civilians are put in charge of Iran's foreign affairs.

January 3, 1979:   The Majlis (parliament) approves the appointment of Shahpour Bakhtiar as prime minister. Bakhtiar begins forming a cabinet and a government program to present to the Majlis for a vote of confidence.

January 4, 1979:   State Department spokesman Hodding Carter says that the Carter administration has offered to cooperate with the new government of Iranian Prime Minister Bakhtiar and that the administration has no intention of influencing the shah either to stay or to leave Iran.

January 16, 1979:   Shah Muhammad Pahlevi leaves Iran for an extended "vacation" abroad. Most observers agree that his departure marks the end of his thirty-seven-year-old reign. In his departing message, the shah appeals to his people to support the government of Prime Minister Bakhtiar.

January 18, 1979:   In Paris, Ayatollah Khomeini rejects President Carter's appeal to give Iranian Prime Minister Bakhtiar's government a chance to succeed and declares that the big powers should stay out of Iranian affairs.

January 22, 1979:   In Paris, Khomeini receives former United States Attorney General Ramsey Clark.

January 25, 1979:   An estimated one hundred thousand people march through the streets of Tehran in support of Bakhtiar.

January 27, 1979:   All airports in Iran are closed.

January 28, 1979:   Thirty people are killed in Tehran as supporters of Bakhtiar, the shah, and Khomeini continue to clash.

January 30, 1979:   Iran's airports reopen after being closed for three days.

January 31, 1979:   Ayatollah Khomeini returns to Iran and is greeted by crowds of supporters estimated to be in the hundreds of thousands.

February 5, 1979:   Khomeini announces that Mehdi Bazargan is his choice for prime minister of a provisional Islamic government.

February 11, 1979:   Prime Minister Shahpour Bakhtiar and the members of the Majlis resign. General Glarabaghi, armed forces chief of staff, declares the military to be neutral in the near civil war.

February 14, 1979:   The American Embassy in Tehran is attacked by Marxist guerrillas, who kill an Iranian employee, wound a United States Marine guard, and hold an estimated one hundred hostages, including Ambassador William Sullivan, for nearly two hours, before forces supporting Ayatollah Khomeini arrive to disperse the attackers.

February 25, 1979:   The American Embassy in Tehran announces that it can no longer protect American lives in Iran and "strongly recommends" that all Americans (in nondiplomatic roles) leave the country.

February 16, 1979:   The United States announces that it will maintain diplomatic relations with the new Iranian government, signaling formal recognition.

February 18, 1979:   Iran breaks diplomatic relations with Israel.

February 19, 1979:   PLO leader Yasir Arafat assumes control of the former Israeli Embassy in Tehran as PLO headquarters.

February 21, 1979:   Iran announces that the United States will not be permitted to continue operating its monitoring installations in northern Iran.

February 28, 1979:   Iranian Prime Minister Bazargan warns that he will resign if Khomeini's Revolutionary Council continues to interfere with his government.

March 1, 1979:   Khomeini leaves Tehran to guide the revolution from his new headquarters in the holy city of Qom.

March 5, 1979:   Seven more former government officials (under the shah) are executed, bringing the number of twenty-four such executions to date after trials by Khomeini's committee courts.

March 6, 1979:   The revolutionary government announces plans to try the shah in absentia.

March 30, 1979:   The shah of Iran, accompanied by his family, ends his temporary exile in Morocco and flies to the Bahamas.

April 30, 1979:   Ayatollah Khomeini orders diplomatic relations with Egypt to be terminated as a result of the signing of
the Egyptian-Israeli peace treaty.

May 17, 1979:   The United States Senate adopts a resolution
condemning the summary executions in Iran.

May 20, 1979:   Iran asks the United States to delay sending
its new ambassador, Walter Cutler, to Tehran in response to
the United States Senate resolution of May 17.

June 4, 1979:   State Department spokesman Hodding Carter
announces that the Iranian government has requested the
United States to withdraw the nomination of Walter Cutler as
ambassador-designate to Iran and comments that "the action of
the Iranian government is not helpful in helping to restore a
constructive relationship."

June 19, 1979:   The Khomeini "committees" execute three
more former members of the shah's regime, bringing the estimated total of such executions to three hundred.

July 10, 1979:   The former shah is granted a six-month tourist
visa and takes up residence in Mexico, after his sixty-day visa
in the Bahamas expires.

July 19, 1979:   Prime Minister Bazargan announces that he has
reached agreement with Ayatollah Khomeini on the sharing of
power between his government and Khomeini's Revolutionary
Council.

August 1, 1979:   Iran announces the cancellation of $9 billion in
United States arms agreements made during the shah's regime.

August 17, 1979:   The United States consulate in Tabriz is
slightly damaged by a rifle grenade attack. No injuries are reported.

September 15, 1979: Radio Tehran reports the repeal of the 1947 law
authorizing the presence in Iran of a United States military
mission.

October 5, 1979:   The Department of Defense announces that the
United States has resumed delivery of spare parts for Iran's
United States-built military aircraft. (The Iranian government
sends its own aircraft to pick up the parts.)

October 22, 1979:   The exiled shah arrives unannounced in New York to undergo medical examinations at the New York Hospital-Cornell Medical Center.

October 23, 1979:   State Department spokesman Hodding Carter says that the United States notified the Iranian government that the shah would be admitted to the United States strictly for medical reasons and that he would return to Mexico after American and European doctors had completed their treatments.

November 1, 1979:   Khomeini's office in Qom issues a statement encouraging Iranian students to "expand their attacks" against the United States to force the United States to return the deposed shah.

November 3, 1979:   The Iranian Foreign Ministry formally protests the United States decision to admit the shah to the United States and the American refusal to allow Iranian doctors to examine him.

November 4, 1979:   Iranian students stage a sit-in at the American Embassy in Tehran that ends in violence and the taking of approximately one hundred hostages as the students storm the embassy and call on the United States to extradite the deposed shah.

November 5, 1979:   Ayatollah Khomeini condones the takeover of the American Embassy saying that, "if they do not give up the criminal . . . then we shall do whatever is necessary. . . ."

November 6, 1979:   Prime Minister Bazargan and his government resign. Khomeini gives their power to the Revolutionary Council, and directs the council to manage the transition and prepare for new elections.

November 7, 1979:   Ayatollah Khomeini refuses to meet with a special United States delegation that includes Ramsey Clark.

The United States reaffirms that the shah will remain in the United States until his medical treatments are completed.

November 8, 1979:   The United States halts the shipment of spare military parts to Iran.

November 9, 1979:   The United Nations Security Council appeals to the Iranian government for the immediate release of the hostages being held at the American Embassy in Tehran.

November 10, 1979: President Carter asks the United States attorney general to inform the 50,000 Iranian students in the United States to report to the nearest immigration office. Any student found to be in violation of the terms of his or her visa is to be deported.

November 12, 1979: President Carter announces that the United States will stop importing oil from Iran.

Iranian officials announce that Iran has suspended all oil sales to United States companies.

November 14, 1979: President Carter freezes Iranian assets in United States banks and their foreign branches.

November 17, 1979: Khomeini orders the release and immediate deportation of blacks and females among the hostages being held at the American Embassy.

November 20, 1979: In a statement issued by the White House, the United States mentions the possibility of taking military action should Iran decide to put the remaining hostages on trial.

November 23, 1979: Finance Minister Abol-Hassan Bani-Sadr announces that Iran is repudiating all foreign debts.

November 27, 1979: U.S. Attorney General Benjamin Civiletti urges Americans not to discriminate against Iranians in the United States "despite our justifiable anger."

President Carter says that the release of the hostages will not "wipe the slate clean" at the end of the current crisis situation in Tehran.

November 29, 1979: The United States petitions the International Court of Justice at the Hague for a speedy legal judgment against Iran demanding the immediate release of the hostages.

December 2, 1979: Shah Pahlevi leaves the New York hospital where he has been undergoing treatment for six weeks and is flown to an Air Force hospital near San Antonio, Texas.

Iranian voters approve a draft Islamic constitution prepared by Khomeini's Revolutionary Council, though voter turnout is light and a number of groups boycott the election.

December 8, 1979:   Iranian Finance Minister Bani-Sadr calls for the release of the hostages and says that he is working to convince his colleagues on the Revolutionary Council to adopt this course.

Foreign Minister Ghotbzadeh calls for the creation of an international tribunal to investigate "wrong-doing" in Iran under the shah's regime. Ghotbzadeh holds out the possibility that such an inquiry can be part of an overall plan leading to the release of the hostages.

December 10, 1979:   In response to Iranian Foreign Minister Ghotbzadeh's call for an international tribunal to investigate the crimes of the United States in Iran, the State Department reiterates that only after the hostages are freed will the United States be ready to discuss with Iran the "differences which remain between us."

December 13, 1979:   The Foreign and Defense Ministers of the fifteen NATO countries issue a statement in Brussels condemning the seizure of the American hostages and demanding their release.

December 15, 1979:   The White House announces that the shah has left Texas for Panama, where he will establish residence.

The International Court of Justice unanimously rules in favor of the United States and orders Iran to release the hostages and restore United States property.

December 19, 1979:   United Nations Secretary-General Kurt Waldheim asks the United States to delay its appeal to the United Nations Security Council for economic sanctions against Iran because he is in the midst of intensive discussions with the Iranians. President Carter agrees to a temporary delay.

December 27, 1979:   A coup by the most pro-Soviet faction in the Afghan Communist government takes place. Even before this regime is formally in power, about 30,000 Soviet troops start to pour across their common border. In the following months the number builds to over 80,000.

December 31, 1979:   Waldheim is given permission by the Security Council to travel to Tehran to mediate for the release of the hostages, with the stipulation that further discussion on the

imposition of economic sanctions against Iran would be postponed only until Waldheim reports back to the council on
January 7.

January 1, 1980:   Secretary-General Waldheim arrives in Tehran.

January 3, 1980:   Waldheim meets with the Iranian Revolutionary Council but is denied a meeting with Ayatollah Khomeini.

January 4, 1980:   Returning to New York from Tehran, Waldheim
says that he is "glad to be back, especially alive." Waldheim
predicts "no quick solution" to the Iranian crisis in the absence of a single authoritative decision making center in Iran.

January 6, 1980:   President Carter meets with Waldheim to
discuss his trip to Iran. Carter rejects a proposal that a United
Nations commission to investigate the regime of the deposed
shah be part of a "package deal" to obtain the release of the
hostages.

January 11, 1980:   Secretary of State Cyrus Vance says that the
United States can "not rule out" the possibility that it will use
a naval blockade in the Persian Gulf to prevent goods from
reaching Iranian ports.

January 12, 1980:   Panama receives a warrant for the arrest of
"Muhammad Reza Pahlevi" from the Iranian government.

January 13, 1980:   The Security Council votes on a United States-
proposed economic sanctions measure. The vote is ten to two,
with a Soviet veto canceling the measure.

January 14, 1980:   Iranian Foreign Minister Ghotbzadeh criticizes
the United States for applying too much pressure on Iran and
says that Iran can hold the hostages "more or less forever."

The Revolutionary Council votes to expel American journalists from Iran for alleged "biased reporting and insulting the
revolution."

January 17, 1980:   The United States aircraft carrier Nimitz enters
the Indian Ocean. Two aircraft carriers, Kitty Hawk and Mid-
way, are already on station in the Arabian Sea.

January 18, 1980:   State Department spokesman Hodding Carter
suggests coordinating a "Washington-Tehran" reply to the So-

viet intervention in Afghanistan. He then says that the United States is ready to cooperate with Iranian authorities regarding their security requirements if they will release the American hostages.

January 20, 1980:   In one of his few public statements on the crisis since November 4, President Carter says that we must "protect first of all, the short-term and long-range interests of our country and then secondly protect the safety and lives of the hostages themselves."

January 22, 1980:   President Carter tells Congress that the United States has "no basic quarrel with Iran" once the hostages are released, paving the way for possible cooperation with Iran on countering the Soviet presence in Afghanistan.

January 27, 1980:   Finance Minister Bani-Sadr appears to be an easy victor in the election for Iran's presidency, claiming between 75 percent and 80 percent of the vote.

January 29, 1980:   A Canadian newspaper reports that Canadian embassy officials in Tehran have smuggled six American diplomats out of Tehran on forged Canadian diplomatic passports. United States and Canadian officials confirm the story. The six had been hiding at the Canadian Embassy and in embassy housing in Tehran since Nov. 4, 1979.

The conference of Islamic foreign ministers meeting in Islamabad denounces Soviet activity in Afghanistan, condemns "pressure" on Moslem countries by "Western powers," and calls on both Iran and the United States to resolve their differences by using "peaceful means."

February 2, 1980:   Iranian President-Elect Bani-Sadr calls upon the United States to "block the wealth" of the shah as a "gesture of goodwill" to help end the deadlock over the hostages.

February 4, 1980:   Bani-Sadr meets with Ayatollah Khomeini in Khomeini's hospital room to be sworn in as the first president of the Islamic Republic of Iran.

February 6, 1980:   President Bani-Sadr begins trying to assert his authority over the militants holding the American Embassy saying that the "government within a government" that they are attempting to create is "intolerable."

February 7, 1980:   The State Department announces a delay in the implementation of unilateral economic sanctions against Iran. State Department spokesman Hodding Carter says that the "administration is holding the sanction regulations in abeyance while diplomatic activities continue."

February 13, 1980:   President Carter says at a press conference that the United States will accept the creation of an international commission with a "carefully defined purpose" to investigate the shah's regime. Carter says that recent "positive signs" in negotiations with Iranian officials through the United Nations could lead to a resolution of the hostage crisis but warns against "excessive optimism."

February 16, 1980:   Bani-Sadr tells an interviewer that the hostages will be released after the United Nations commission reports its findings and after the United States meets Iran's conditions: an admission of guilt, recognition of Iran's right to return of the shah and his wealth to Iran, and a promise not to interfere in Iran's affairs in the future.

February 18, 1980:   United Nations Secretary-General Waldheim announces the names of the five-person commission that is to hear the charges against the deposed shah of Iran: Algeria's United Nations delegate, Muhammad Bedjaoui; Venezuela's former ambassador to the United States, Andres Aguilar; a French jurist, Louis Pettiti; Adib Dawudi of Syria; and Jayewardene of Sri Lanka.

February 21, 1980:   The White House issues a statement welcoming the appointment of the United Nations commission, emphasizing that the commission will explore United States grievances against Iran. Iranian President Bani-Sadr's cable of acceptance, received in New York, refers to the "court of inquiry" and United Nations Secretary-General Waldheim speaks of the commission's "fact-finding" purpose. To compound the uncertainty, Khomeini and Bani-Sadr both refuse to link the work of the commission to the release of the hostages, while Commission Cochairmen Aguilar and Bedjaoui make reference to a "gentlemen's agreement" concerning the release of the hostages.

February 23, 1980:   Ayatollah Khomeini issues a statement leaving a decision on the fate of the American hostages to the Islamic Assembly, not scheduled to be elected until May.

February 26, 1980:   The Revolutionary Council announces that American journalists, barred from Iran since mid-January for alleged biased reporting, can be readmitted if the Iran Embassy in the United States "vouches for their impartiality."

March 2, 1980:   Ayatollah Khomeini leaves the hospital where he has been a heart patient for several weeks. He does not return to his Qom headquarters but remains in Tehran.

March 10, 1980:   After days of conflicting signals, it becomes apparent that the United Nations commission will not be permitted to see the hostages.

March 11, 1980:   The United Nations commission leaves Tehran admitting defeat in helping to resolve the crisis.

March 12, 1980:   Bani-Sadr expresses frustration in dealing with a divided Revolutionary Council and criticizes the militants holding the hostages for not cooperating with the government.

March 16, 1980:   In early returns from Iran's parliamentary elections, the right-wing clerical Islamic Republic Party appears to be heading towards a strong showing. The Islamic Party has often sided with the militants in the hostage crisis, and against President Bani-Sadr.

March 23, 1980:   The deposed shah leaves Panama for Egypt, accepting a long-standing offer from President Anwar Sadat. The shah leaves Panama the day before Iran is to present Panama with formal extradition papers.

March 27, 1980:   During a hearing before the Senate Foreign Relations Committee, Secretary of State Vance says that the administration is reviewing the options available for dealing with Iran, and that a military option has not been ruled out.

April 7, 1980:   President Carter announces the severing of diplomatic relations with Iran, the implementation of an economic embargo against Iran, an inventory of Iranian assets in the United States, an inventory of United States financial claims against Iran to be paid from the Iranian assets, and the cancellation of all entry visas for Iranians. The president orders the Iranian Embassy in Washington and Iran's five consulates closed and Iran's 35 diplomats and 209 military students in the United States out of the country by midnight, April 8.

April 8, 1980:   Ayatollah Khomeini reacts to the United States diplomatic break as a "good omen" that proves that the United States can no longer dominate Iran.

April 9, 1980:   Secretary of State Vance calls twenty-five ambassadors of allied nations to a meeting in order to urge these countries to take actions against Iran.

April 10, 1980:   At a meeting in Lisbon, the foreign ministers of the Common Market and the Council of Europe demand the release of the American hostages, but delays any decision to impose sanctions on Iran.

April 22, 1980:   In Luxembourg, the Foreign Ministers of the nine European Community countries agree to reduce their diplomatic representation in Iran, suspend arms sales to Iran, require visas for Iranians traveling in Common Market countries, and discourage purchases of Iranian oil at prices above the OPEC standard.

April 25, 1980:   The White House announces that a military operation to rescue the hostages has been attempted and has been cancelled because of equipment failure. After the cancellation, a collision between two aircraft results in eight deaths. President Carter takes full responsibility for the operation.

April 27, 1980:   Secretary of State Vance resigns his post. (Vance had actually presented his resignation on April 21, after having failed to persuade President Carter not to attempt the rescue mission, but asked Carter to delay its announcement until after the operation.)

April 28, 1980:   Iran's Revolutionary Council agrees to turn over the bodies of the eight dead United States servicemen to representatives of the Vatican and the Red Cross, who then arrange for their return to the United States.

April 30, 1980:   In London, three Iranian Arab gunmen seize the Iranian Embassy and take twenty people inside the embassy hostage. The terrorists threaten to kill the hostages and blow up the embassy unless the Iranian government releases ninety-one Arab political prisoners.

May 2, 1980:   The militants holding the American hostages announce that they have scattered their captives to eight cities around Iran to deter any future attempt to rescue them.

May 5, 1980:   The hostage seizure in London ends when British commandos storm the embassy building, killing three of the Arab terrorists and rescuing nineteen of the hostages.

May 10, 1980:   Radio Tehran reports that the Islamic Republican Party will hold a majority in the new parliament.

May 11, 1980:   United Nations Secretary-General Kurt Waldheim announces that Syrian diplomat Adib Dawud (formerly a member of the "commission of inquiry" sent to Iran on Feb. 20) will go back to Tehran as Waldheim's representative.

May 18, 1980:   In Italy, foreign ministers of the European Community approve limited economic sanctions against Iran effective May 22, but exclude from the planned trade embargo all contracts signed before the Nov. 4 takeover of the American Embassy.

May 22, 1980:   In Islamabad, Pakistan, the 11th Islamic Conference ends with resolutions condemning the United States for the attempted hostage-rescue mission, requesting that the United States and Iran resolve their differences through negotiations, and asking the Egyptian nation to "pursue all possibilities for handing over the deposed Shah" to Iran.

May 28, 1980:   Iran's new parliament convenes. President Bani-Sadr tells the Majlis that it "must act swiftly" to ease the frustrations of the Iranian people, adding that Iran should remain neutral and not ally itself with either the Eastern or Western blocks. Yadollah Sahabi, the acting speaker of the Majlis, says that a decision on the fate of the hostages must await decisions on pressing domestic issues.

June 2–5, 1980:   Despite an executive order banning American citizens from traveling to Iran, a ten-person delegation (including former Attorney General Ramsey Clark) attends a conference in Tehran on "U.S. crimes." The mission appears to do little to help the current state of affairs between the two countries.

July 11, 1980:   Ayatollah Khomeini orders the release of one of the fifty-three hostages, Richard Queen, who was found to be suffering from multiple sclerosis.

July 22, 1980:   Ali Akhbar Tabatabai, an anti-Khomeini activist, is shot at his home in suburban Washington, D.C., by an assassin linked with the Iranian government.

July 27, 1980:   The former shah of Iran, in exile in Egypt, dies at the age of sixty of terminal cancer.

Notes

Chapter 1

1. Mihyar al-Daylami cited in Bernard Lewis, ed. and trans., *Islam* (New York, 1974) vol. 2, p. 207.
2. Ibid., p. 52.
3. Ibid., p. 54.
4 American Consulate in Tabriz to United States Minister John Jackson, RG 59, 5931/377 April 3, 1909; 891.00/510 May 3, 1910 and May 20, 1910; RG 59, 391.1163B/29 September 19, 1927, National Archives.
5. W. Morgan Shuster, *The Strangling of Persia* (New York, 1912) p. 333.
6. Cited in Robert McDaniel, *The Shuster Mission and the Persian Constitutional Revolution* (Minneapolis, 1974) p. 198.
7. RG 59, 123 Imbrie, Robert, particularly /201 and /245 August, 1924, National Archives.
8. For a detailed discussion of U.S.-Iranian relations during the war years, see Barry Rubin, *The Great Powers in the Middle East: The Road to Cold War* (London, 1980) ch. 5.
9. Text in J. C. Hurewitz, *Diplomacy in the Near and Middle East* (Princeton, 1956) vol. 2, p. 232.
10. RG 226, Office of Strategic Services Report 25065 October 25, 1942, National Archives.
11. For example, Memorandum of Conversation with Muhammad Schayesteh, Iranian minister to Washington, RG 59, 741.9111/66 March 20, 1942 and memorandum of April 11, 1942, National Archives.

12. RG 59, OSS Research and Analysis Report 517 February 20, 1943; Dreyfus to Hull, RG 59, 741.9111/69 May 13, 1942, National Archives.
13. RG 59, Memorandum of John Jernegan, 711.91/98 January 23, 1943, National Archives.
14. Hull to Roosevelt, RG 59, 891.00/2042a August 16, 1943, National Archives.
15. Ibid., enclosure, "American Policy in Iran."
16. Cordell Hull, Memoirs (New York, 1948) vol. 2, p. 1507; Roosevelt to Churchill, February 29, 1944, in Francis Loewenheim et al., Roosevelt & Churchill (New York, 1975) p. 499n.
17. Jonathan Daniels, White House Witness (New York, 1975) pp. 221–22; Roosevelt to Hurley, RG 59, 123 Hurley, Patrick, J. /128½ March 25, 1944, National Archives; for the State Department report, see the Hurley file above, January 12, 1944.
18. Text in Department of State Bulletin, December 11, 1943, p. 409–10; William Leahy, I Was There (New York, 1950).
19. RG 226, OSS L47580 October 16, 1944, and OSS L48058 October 17, 1944, National Archives.
20. George F. Kennan, Memoirs 1925–1950 (Boston, 1967) pp. 209, 222–23.
21. Cited in W. Averell Harriman, Special Envoy to Churchill and Stalin (New York, 1975) pp. 345–47.
22. Cited in Beatrice Berle, Navigating the Rapids (New York, 1973) pp. 462–68.
23. Harriman to Stettinius, RG 226, 861.9111/1–1045 January 10, 1945, National Archives.
24. On Soviet intelligence operations and activities in Azerbaijan, see RG 84, 400.1 Espionage 1950 file, Box 2250, Washington National Record Center, particularly the interrogation of Lev Vasilev, a defector from the Soviet Embassy, in 320 Iran-USSR file. On the Kurdish question, see William Eagleton, Jr., The Kurdish Republic of 1946 (New York, 1963) particularly pp. 44–46.

Chapter 2

1. Barry Rubin, The Great Powers in the Middle East: The Road to Cold War (London, 1980) ch. 9; Murray to Byrnes, RG 59, 891.00/9–2545 September 25, 1945, National Archives.
2. RG 218, JIS 80/9 October 26, 1945 in CCS 092 USSR (3/27/45) Section 2, Appendix B, National Archives.
3. Washington Post, January 1, 1946.
4. "Attitude of the Soviet Press and Radio Toward Iran," text in RG 226, Office of Strategic Services Research & Analysis Report 3526.6 nd, probably January, 1946, National Archives.
5. For Byrnes's statement see Edwin Wright's account, U.S. State Department, Foreign Relations of the United States, 1946 (Washington, D.C., 1967) vol. 7, p. 347.

6. George F. Kennan, *Memoirs 1925–1950* (Boston, 1967) p. 556.

7. *The New York Times*, March 1 and March 14, 1946.

8. Joseph Goodwin, letter to *Washington Post*, October 8, 1979; Robert Rossow to Byrnes, RG 59, 761.91/3–546 March 5, 1946, National Archives; see also RG 59, 861.24591/3–646 and /3–746, National Archives.

9. Geo ge V. Allen to John Jernegan, January 21, 1948, George V. Allen papers, Duke University Library. During this time, Allen recounts, he became personally friendly with the shah. One night the shah said laughingly: "My sister Ashraf asked me yesterday whether I was a man or a mouse." Turning more serious, the shah then asked Allen: "Do you mean that I should stay in my palace at Saadabad, selfishly enjoy my pleasant gardens, dogs and horses, and do nothing about the tragic situation in my country with Pishevari (the Azerbaijan Communist leader) about to steal the most important province of Iran?"

    "Well, yes," Allen answered with some astonishment. Allen was not sure whether the king should be meddling in politics anyway and was not certain where the shah might stop once he became so involved.

10. "Evidence of Soviet Interference in Iran," RG 59, Office of European Affairs Box 16 May 27, 1946, National Archives.

11. RG 59, 740.00119 Council/10–146 October 1, 1946; Hilldring to Reid, RG 59, 711.91/9–2646 September 26, 1946; RG 353, SWN–4776 SWNCC 091, Box 76, SM–6874 October 11, 1946, and RG 353 SWN 4818 October 12, 1946; RG 59, 711.91/10–1246 October 12, 1946, National Archives.

12. Allen to Byrnes, RG 59, 891.00/12–1746 December 17, 1946, National Aechives.

13. Lovett to United States Embassy in Iran, December 9, 1947, in *Foreign Relations of the United States, 1948*, vol. 5, pp. 88–90.

14. Memorandum of Conversation, RG 59, 891.00/3–1948 March 19, 1948, National Archives.

15. Wiley to Acheson, RG 59, 891.001 Pahlevi, Reza Shah /6–1449 June 14, 1949, National Archives.

16. *The New York Times*, May 17, 1949.

17. Ibid., November 17, 1949.

18. Ibid., February 11, 1950.

19. Princeton Seminars May 15–16, 1954, Dean Acheson papers, Harry S. Truman papers, Harry S. Truman Library.

20. *Foreign Relations of the United States, 1949*, vol. 6, pp. 574–79.

21. Joseph J. Wagner, "The Peculiar Position of the British in Iran," enclosed in Richards to Acheson #83, July 29, 1950, RG 84, 400.1 Espionage 1950 file, Box 2250, 320 Iran-Great Britain file, Washington National Records Center.

22. *Foreign Relations of the United States, 1950*, vol. 5, pp. 13–15.

23. Wiley to Acheson, January 30, 1950 in ibid., p. 463.

24. Ibid., p. 510. *See also* pp. 510–26.

25. Interview with Arthur L. Richards, June 3, 1980.

26. "Iran: A Year of Danger," March 17, 1952, RG 84, Box 2248, 300 Iran, Washington National Records Center.
27. Wiley to George McGhee, January 10, 1950, ibid.
28. Arthur Richards, memorandum of conversation, August 3, 1950, ibid.; Wagner report, note 21 above.
29. Richards, November general report, December 15, 1950, note 26 above; Stutesman to Richards, "Decline of United States Influence and Prestige," November 20, 1950, RG 84, 400.1 Espionage 1950 file, Box 2250, 320 Iran-United States file, Washington National Records Center.
30. Henry Grady to Harry Eaton, February 1, 1951, Henry Grady papers, Harry S. Truman Library.
31. Roy Melbourne, "America and Iran in Perspective: 1953 and 1980," *Foreign Service Journal*, April, 1980, p. 16.
32. Acheson's account is in *Present at the Creation* (New York, 1969). Grady blamed Acheson for the policy's failure. "Had Britain and the United States backed Razmara, the former Iranian prime minister who was a friend of the West and who was fighting that nationalization movement, this present situation would not have developed. Nor would Razmara have been assassinated." He continued, "During my tenure as Ambassador to Iran I made at least half a dozen requests, all of which were ignored or flatly turned down by our Government under British influence and assistance." *The New York Times*, October 18, 1952.
33. Shah Muhammad Pahlevi, *Mission for My Country* (New York, 1961).
34. *The New York Times*, March 8, 1951.
35. Report of January 12, 1951 #539, cited in note 26 above.

Chapter 3

1. *Time Magazine*, January 7, 1952.
2. Princeton Seminars, May 15–16, 1954, Dean Acheson papers, Harry S. Truman Library, p. 1607.
3. U.S. Congress, Senate, *Executive Sessions of the Foreign Relations Committee*, 82nd Cong., 2nd sess., testimony of January 14, 1952, pp. 18–27.
4. Ibid., 83rd Cong., 1st sess., testimony of April 29, 1953, p. 387.
5. Princeton Seminars, note 2 above, p. 1662.
6. Acheson to Grady, June 7, 1951, RG 84, Box 2250, 300 Iran file, Washington National Records Center; see also Grady to Acheson, April 27, 1951, 320 Iran-Great Britain file.
7. *The New York Times*, May 3, 1951.
8. United States Congress, Senate, Committee on Foreign Relations, Subcommittee on Multinational Corporations, *Multinational Oil Corporations and U.S. Foreign Policy*, 93rd Cong., 2nd sess., January 2, 1975, p. 58.
9. The following account draws on Vernon Walters, *Silent Missions* (New York, 1978) pp. 241–63; Dean Acheson, *Present at the Creation* (New York, 1969), and the Princeton Seminars, note 2 above.

10. *The New York Times*, September 23, 1951.
11. Ibid., and January 8, 1952.
12. Ibid., November 25 and December 7, 1951.
13. Richards to Grady, October 20, 1951 and Stutesman to Richards, October 19, 1951, note 6 above, 320 Iran-U.S. file.
14. "Iran: A Year of Danger," March 17, 1952, note 6 above.
15. Henderson to Acheson, February, 16, 1952, note 6 above.
16. *The New York Times*, July 15, 1952.
17. Ibid., July 20, 1952.
18. Ibid., August 11, 1952.
19. Henderson to Acheson, July 28, 1952, note 6 above, 320 Iran file.
20. Note 8 above.
21. Mossadegh to Eisenhower, January 9, 1953, and Eisenhower to Mossadegh, January 10, 1953, Dwight Eisenhower Library.
22. Interview with Kermit Roosevelt, March 20, 1980. See *also* Kermit Roosevelt, *Countercoup* (New York, 1979).
23. Henderson to Dulles, March 19, 1953, RG 84, Box 2667, 350 Iran file, Washington National Records Center.
24. *The New York Times*, April 5, 1953.
25. Smith to Eisenhower, "Memorandum for the President," May 23, 1953, Eisenhower Library.
26. Kermit Roosevelt, *Countercoup* (New York, 1979) pp. 1–19. The overthrow of Mossadegh was actually an Anglo-American operation, a fact still not generally understood today. When Roosevelt's book was submitted to the CIA for screening, the agency pressured him to attribute certain British actions to the AIOC to avoid embarrassing the British government. When AIOC's successor, British Petroleum, implied it might take legal action, the book was withdrawn from circulation soon after its release.
27. Roy Melbourne, "America and Iran in Perspective: 1953 and 1980," *Foreign Service Journal*, April, 1980, p. 15.
28. Kennett Love, "The American Role in the Pahlevi Restoration," unpublished manuscript (1960).
29. *The New York Times*, August 4, 1953.
30. Note 26 above; Loy Henderson oral history, Harry S. Truman Library, pp. 210–17; Roosevelt and other interviews.
31. Zahedi to Eisenhower, August 26, 1953, Eisenhower Library.
32. *The New York Times*, August 21, 1953. In an August 6, 1954 editorial, the *Times* concluded in reference to these events: "Underdeveloped countries with rich resources now have an object lesson in the heavy cost that must be paid by one of their number which goes beserk with fanatical nationalism." On the other hand, the West must study and take into account "before and not after great losses have been incurred—of the great forces which now move the people everywhere in Asia, Africa and South America."
33. Allen Dulles, *The Craft of Intelligence* (New York, 1963) p. 224; Dwight Eisenhower, *Mandate for Change 1953–1956* (New York, 1963) pp. 3, 83,

NOTES

166, 435, and 574; Robert Branyan and Lawrence Larsen, *The Eisenhower Administration 1953–1961: A Documentary History* (New York, 1971)
vol. 2, p. 216.
34. Richard Cottam, *Nationalism in Iran* (Pittsburgh, 1964) p. 229.

Chapter 4

1. *The New York Times*, January 5, 1954.
2. Ibid., April 12, 1956, January 4 and January 25, 1957.
3. Ibid., August 6, 1954.
4. Dulles to Eisenhower, "Visit of the Shah of Iran," December 13, 1954,
   Eisenhower Library. Iran's inability to absorb sophisticated equipment
   was but one important reason for limiting military aid. A United States
   military study mission reported, for example, that Iranian maintenance
   crews filled the crankcases of new Sherman tanks with olive-drab paint,
   thinking it was lubricating oil.
5. Interview with Raymond Hare, former acting assistant secretary for Near
   East Affairs, February 9, 1979; *see also* Norman Hannah, letter, *Foreign
   Affairs*, vol. 52, no. 3 (April, 1974) pp. 649–50.
6. Shah to President Eisenhower, November 20, 1956, Eisenhower Library.
7. Dulles to Eisenhower, memorandum and background information, June
   28, 1958, Eisenhower Library.
8. *The New York Times*, July 13 and December 2, 1956, February 14, 1959.
9. Ibid., April 2, 1957.
10. Ibid., August 21, 1955.
11. Ibid., January 2, 1958.
12. Wailes to Herter, September 15, 1959, Eisenhower Library.
13. Hall to Eisenhower, July 15, 1958 and Eisenhower to shah, July 19, 1958,
    Eisenhower Library; *The New York Times*, July 22, 1958.
14. Herter to Eisenhower, December 31, 1959, Eisenhower Library; *The New
    York Times*, December 15, 1958.
15. Herter to Eisenhower, April 21, 1960 and September 19, 1960; Wailes to
    Herter, March 14, 1960, and Dillon to Eisenhower, May 18, 1960,
    Eisenhower Library.
16. On these issues *see* Marvin Zonis, *The Political Elite of Iran* (Princeton,
    1971), particularly pp. 305–6, and Richard Cottam, *Nationalism in Iran*
    (Pittsburgh, 1964), particularly pp. 230–35.
17. *The New York Times*, January 29, 1960.
18. Ibid., January 2, 1958.
19. Ibid., January 26, 1960.
20. Ibid., January 29, 1960.
21. *The New York Times*, May 30 and June 2, 1960; *see also* Manfred Hal-
    pern, "Perspectives on U.S. Policy—Iran," *SAIS Review*, vol. 6, no. 3
    (Spring 1962) pp. 27–31; *The New York Times*, June 2 and August 9,
    1961; E. A. Bayne, *Persian Kingship in Transition* (New York, 1968) p.
    191.

22. *The New York Times*, December 4, 1961.
23. National Security Council Action proposal 2447 and Rusk to Kennedy, "Proposed Approach to the Shah of Iran," March 8, 1962, and Rockwell to Rusk, May 14, 1962, John F. Kennedy Library, NSF: NSC Box 340.
24. Interview with Kermit Roosevelt, March 20, 1980.
25. *The New York Times*, January 23, January 28, and June 10, 1963.
26. Ibid., September 17 and September 20, 1963.
27. Ibid., September 26, 1963.
28. *Tehran Journal*, January 16, 1979; Nawal Azhari, "Secrets in Khomeini's Life . . . ," *Al Watan al-'Arabi* (London), March 2–8, 1979; *Kayhan* (Tehran) May 14, 1979, all texts in *Joint Publications Research Service* (hereafter *JPRS*) June 6, 1979, pp. 74–79.
29. Director of Central Intelligence, "Special National Intelligence Estimate 34–63: The Iranian Situation," April 10, 1963, John F. Kennedy Library.
30. Bureau of the Budget memorandum for Robert Komer, May 7, 1963, John F. Kennedy Library.
31. Rusk to Kennedy, April 20, 1963, "Report on U.S. Strategy for Iran," and Holmes to Rusk, May 15, 1963, John F. Kennedy Library.
32. William Gaud, Oral History, John F. Kennedy Library, p. 41; United States Information Agency reports R–15–64 (1/3/64), R–212–64 (7/64), R–220–64 (12/64) and R–203–65 (12/65).
33. E. A. Bayne, *Persian Kingship in Transition* (New York, 1968) pp. 220–22.
34. Ibid., and *The New York Times*, September 9, 1965.
35. See his account in Martin F. Herz, ed., *Contacts with the Opposition*, Institute for the Study of Diplomacy, Georgetown University (Washington, D.C., 1980) pp. 26–27.
36. U.S. Congress, Senate, Committee on Foreign Relations, Subcommittee on Multinational Corporations, *Multinational Oil Corporations and U.S. Foreign Policy*, 93rd Cong., 2nd sess., report of January 2, 1975, pp. 115–31, and parts 7 and 8 of hearing records.
37. *The New York Times*, November 24, 1967.
38. Rostow to Johnson, November 4, 1966, and Rostow to Fulbright, November 11, 1966, Lyndon B. Johnson Library.
39. U.S. Congress, Senate, Committee on Foreign Relations, *Arms Sales to Near East and South Asian Countries*, 90th Cong., 1st sess., hearings March–June, 1967, p. 17; *Department of State Bulletin*, July 1, 1968; *The New York Times*, June 13, 1968.
40. Martin F. Herz, "A View from Tehran—A Diplomatist Looks at the Shah's Regime in June 1964," Institute for the Study of Diplomacy, Georgetown University (Washington, D.C., 1979).
41. U.S. Congress, House, Committee on Foreign Affairs, *Foreign Assistance Act of 1968*, 90th Cong., 2nd sess., June–July, 1968, p. 258.
42. Robert Paarlberg, "The Advantageous Alliance: U.S. Relations with Iran 1920–1975," in Paarlberg et al., *Diplomatic Disputes* (Cambridge, Mass., 1978) p. 43.

Chapter 5

1. U.S. Congress, Senate, Committee on Foreign Relations, Subcommittee on Multinational Corporations, *Multinational Oil Corporations and U.S. Foreign Policy,* 93rd Cong., 2nd sess., report of January 2, 1975, pp. 107ff.
2. *Times* (London), June 10, 1969.
3. "Meet the Press," October 26, 1969, cited in Shahram Chubin and Sepehr Zabih, *The Foreign Relations of Iran* (Berkeley, 1974) p. 242.
4. Ibid., p. 239.
5. Anne Hessing Cahn, "United States Arms to the Middle East 1967–1976: A Critical Examination," in Milton Leitenberg and Gabriel Sheffer, *Great Power Intervention in the Middle East* (New York, 1979) pp. 102–4.
6. Henry Kissinger, *White House Years* (Boston, 1979), p. 1264.
7. Ruhollah Ramazani, *Iran's Foreign Policy 1941–1973* (Charlottesville, 1975) p. 381.
8. *The New York Times,* July 17 and November 26, 1970.
9. Cited in Richard Preece, "U.S. Policy Toward Iran, 1942–1979," *Congressional Research Service,* May 23, 1979, p. 84; U.S. Congress, House, Committee on Foreign Affairs, *New Perspectives on the Persian Gulf,* 93rd Cong., 1st sess., 1973, p. 69.
10. *Washington Post,* October 10, 1971. According to the CIA's deputy chief of station in Tehran in the 1960s, Princess Ashraf's patronage was necessary to obtain many contracts. He told an executive of the Vinnell Corporation that it failed to land contracts to construct several airports because Ashraf had already gone into partnership with another firm. This construction was being financed by American aid money. Wilbur Crane Eveland, *Ropes of Sand* (New York, 1980) p. 318.
11. Note 1 above, part 17, 191ff.
12. Smith to Eisenhower, May 23, 1953, Eisenhower Library.
13. U.S. Congress, House, Committee on Foreign Affairs, Subcommittee on International Organizations, *Human Rights in Iran,* 95th Cong., 1st sess., hearings of October, 1977, p. 56.
14. U.S. Congress, House, Committee on Foreign Affairs, Subcommittee on Near East and South Asian Affairs, *U.S. Interests in and Policy Toward the Persian Gulf,* 92nd Cong., 2nd sess., hearings of February–August, 1972, pp. 6–7; *Washington Post,* May 14, 1973.
15. See, *Washington Post,* January 16 and February 27, 1974; *The New York Times,* March 7, September 27, October 4, and November 3, 1974.
16. *The New York Times,* February 24, 1974.
17. U.S. Congress, House, Committee on Foreign Affairs, *New Perspectives on the Persian Gulf,* 93rd Cong., 1st sess., 1973, pp. 2–4.
18. Ibid., p. v.
19. Sisco to Hamilton, August 17, 1973, in ibid., pp. 194–95. A similar exchange between Sisco's successor, Alfred Atherton, and Hamilton took place at the August, 1974 hearings. See U.S. Congress, House, Committee on Foreign Affairs, Subcommittee on Near East and South Asian Affairs,

The *Persian Gulf 1974: Money, Politics, Arms, and Power,* 93rd Cong., 2nd sess., March 6, 1975, particularly pp. 73–85.
20. This and the following is from note 9 above, 67ff.
21. Note 9 above, p. 70.
22. *Manchester Guardian,* International Edition, October 27, 1973.
23. *Washington Post,* May 26 and 27, 1974.
24. *The New York Times,* June 3 and October 14, 1974; *Business Week,* June 22, 1974; *Newsweek,* March 24, 1975. The quotation from *Newsweek* well illustrates the difficulty for Western journalists in understanding the revolution four years later. Its implication was that the faster the pace of development the greater the country's political stability; in Iran, of course, the speed of change led to heightened instability.
25. *Wall Street Journal,* August 29, 1974; *Washington Post,* August 16, 1974.
26. Cited in Hamid Mowlana, "U.S.-Iranian Relations, 1954–1978: A Case of Cultural Domination," paper presented at the Middle East Studies Association conference, November 8, 1979. Ironically, Ambassador Zahedi provided one of the best analyses of the revolutionary sentiments held by many Iranian students abroad: "Think of all those boys and girls going to school in America, fresh from Iran. Here they see a haven of democracy. Unique in industrialization. Unique in power. And they see the gap between America and home. Being young, leaving your native Iran, having ambition, and seeing America, it makes you unhappy, disappointed, frustrated." *Washington Post,* November 10, 1978.
27. Interview in *Yediot Aharnot* (Tel Aviv), text in *Foreign Broadcast Information Service (FBIS)* April 4, 1980; cited in Barry Rubin, *How Others Report Us* (Los Angeles, 1979) p. 55.
28. U.S. Congress, House, Committee on Standards and Official Conduct, *Report of the Staff Study of Alleged Misconduct by Members of the House of Representatives Involving the Former Government of Iran,* 96th Cong., 1st sess., October 24, 1979, plus extensive interviews.
29. *Department of State Bulletin,* March 10, 1975, p. 293 and December 15, 1975, p. 864.
30. Max McCarthy, unpublished report to Zbigniew Brzezinski, December 3, 1976, part I, p. 1.
31. See, for example, *The New York Times,* February 5, and March 2, 4, and 15, 1976; *Washington Post,* January 28 and February 9, 1976.
32. *Washington Post,* February 13, 1976.

Chapter 6

1. Shahram Chubin, "Implications of the Military Buildup in Non-Industrial States: The Case of Iran," in Uri Ra'anan et al., *Arms Transfers to the Third World* (Boulder, Colorado, 1978) pp. 262–63.
2. Ibid., p. 262.
3. *Business Week,* November 17, 1975; *Le Monde* (Paris), March 1, 1976.

4. Note 1 above, p. 267.
5. John Hoagland, "The U.S. and European Aerospace Industries," in note 1 above, p. 216.
6. Anne Hessing Cahn, "United States Arms to the Middle East 1967–1976: A Critical Examination," in Milton Leitenberg and Gabriel Sheffer, *Great Power Intervention in the Middle East* (New York, 1979) p. 117.
7. U.S. Congress, Senate, Foreign Relations Committee, Subcommittee on Multinational Corporations, *Multinational Oil Corporations and U.S. Foreign Policy*, report of January 2, 1975, part 17, p. 121.
8. U.S. Congress, House, Committee on International Relations, *The Persian Gulf 1975: The Continuing Debate on Arms Sales*, 94th Cong., 1st sess., June–July, 1975, pp. 133–36.
9. U.S. Government Accounting Office, *Inspection Report: Contract, Administration Services Security Assistance Program, Iran*, June 25, 1976; *Inspection Report: Automatic Data Processing Program Security Assistance Program, Iran* June 30, 1976.
10. *Washington Post*, December 9, 1976.
11. *The New York Times*, February 4, 1976; *Washington Post*, September 11, 1976.
12. *Washington Post*, February 22, 1976.
13. *The New York Times*, March 4, 1976.
14. *The New York Times*, February 13, 1976.
15. See, *The New York Times*, February 5 and March 2, 4, and 15, 1976; *Washington Post*, January 28 and February 9, 1976.
16. *Middle East* (London), March, 1976.
17. *Washington Post*, August 7, 1976.
18. *Washington Post*, October 11, 1976.
19. *Christian Science Monitor*, November 11, 1976.
20. *Amnesty International Report 1975–76* (London, 1976) pp. 182–83; *Washington Post*, December 16, 1979. None of this is said to excuse the behavior of the shah's regime, but comparison with neighbors and with other countries does raise two important questions. First, the level of repression cannot be used as a single-factor explanation for the revolution. If so, then why does the regime in, say, Iraq still prosper? One must look at the style and targets of repression and at the popular perception of whether such actions are justified, as well as at a large variety of other issues. Second, if most or all of the states with a similar political culture employ the same methods the task of changing that situation becomes more complicated: a mere change of government will not necessarily produce a democratic society: more deep-seated changes in society or ideology are needed to produce a respect for human rights. See Walter Laqueur and Barry Rubin, *The Human Rights Reader* (New York, 1980) and Barry Rubin and Elizabeth Spiro, *Human Rights and U.S. Foreign Policy* (Boulder, Colorado, 1979) for a broader consideration of these questions.

21. Max McCarthy, unpublished report to Zbigniew Brzezinski, December 3, 1976, section 2, p. 2.
22. Ibid., pp. 2–11.
23. U.S. State Department, text in *Bureau of Public Affairs* release, September 8, 1976.
24. Thomas Powers, *The Man Who Kept the Secrets* (New York, 1979) p. 243.
25. *Washington Post*, August 4, 1976.
26. *The New York Times*, October 7, 1976.

Chapter 7

1. Theodore H. Moran, "Iranian Defense Expenditures and the Social Crisis," *International Security*, vol. 3, no. 3 (Winter 1978–79) p. 179.
2. U.S. State Department, *Country Reports on Human Rights Practices,* (Washington, 1978).
3. U.S. State Department, *Report on Human Rights Practices in Countries Receiving U.S. Aid* (Washington, 1979).
4. Congressional Research Service, *Human Rights Conditions in Selected Countries and the U.S. Response* (Washington, 1978) pp. 124–28.
5. Interview in *Al Nahar Al-'Arabi wa al-Duwali* (Paris), December 24–30, 1979, text in *Joint Publications Research Service* (hereafter *JPRS*) January 29, 1980.
6. Hubert Humphrey to President Carter, July 27, 1977; Clifford Case and Hubert Humphrey "dear colleague" letter, September 19, 1977.
7. *Washington Post*, July 28 and September 13, 1977.
8. Ibid., December 1, 1977.
9. Ibid., November 18, 1977.
10. Ibid., December 31, 1977.
11. *The New York Times*, January 2, 1978.
12. U.S. Congress, House, Committee on Foreign Affairs, Subcommittee on Evaluation, Permanent Select Committee on Intelligence, *Iran: Evaluation of U.S. Intelligence Performance Prior to November 1978,* 89th Cong., 1st sess., 1979.
13. Jesse Leaf, "Iran: A Blind Spot in U.S. Intelligence," *Washington Post,* January 18, 1979.
14. See, for example, Paul Blackstock, *The Secret Road to World War Two* (Chicago, 1969) pp. 260–61.
15. Thomas Powers, *The Man Who Kept the Secrets* (New York, 1979), p. 36.
16. *Washington Post*, February 5, 1979.
17. Ibid., November 18, 1979.
18. The causes of the revolution are discussed at greater length in Chapter 9.
19. *Washington Post*, March 6, 1978; *U.S. News & World Report*, June 26, 1978.
20. *Washington Post*, April 2 and May 29, 1978.
21. Herman Nickel, "The U.S. Failure in Iran," *Fortune*, March 12, 1979, p.

97; Bill's paper is cited in Nicholas Wade, "Iran and America: The Failure of Understanding," *Science*, vol. 206 (December 14, 1979) p. 1281.

22. U.S. Congress, House, Committee on International Relations, Subcommittee on Europe and the Middle East, *Review of Developments in the Middle East*, 95th Cong., 2nd sess., 1978.

23. Speech to National Iranian Radio & Television Organization, October 4, 1978, text in *Foreign Broadcast Information Service (FBIS)* October 5, 1978.

24. *Kayhan* (Tehran), August 10, 1978, text in *JPRS* September 14, 1978.

25. *Kayhan* (Tehran), August 28, 1978, text in *JPRS* October 25, 1978.

26. *Stern* (Hamburg), August 31, 1978, interview by Franz Tartarotti and Rolf Winter.

27. Reza Shah Pahlevi in *Now* (London), December 7, 1979.

28. Interview with Agence France-Presse (hereafter AFP), September 5, 1978, text in *FBIS* September 6, 1978.

29. Interview with *Le Figaro* (Paris), September 12, 1978.

Chapter 8

1. *Le Matin* (Paris), September 14, 1980.

2. U.S. Congress, House, Committee on International Relations, *Arms Sale Policy and Recent Sales to Europe and the Middle East*, 89th Cong., 1st sess., 1979.

3. Speech of October 6, text in *Foreign Broadcast Information Service (FBIS)* October 11, 1978.

4. *Kayhan* (Tehran), October 18, 1978, text in *Joint Publications Research Service (JPRS)* November 29, 1978; *FBIS* October 31, 1978. There is a complex and intriguing story behind Khomeini's relations with the French government during this period. Some sources claim that French intelligence wanted Khomeini admitted to the country because he was seen as Iran's future leader; others credit the French Foreign Ministry with this foresight. While Paris periodically told the ayatollah to moderate his fiery anti-shah rhetoric, his hosts went out of their way to let him stay. For their part, Khomeini's advisors warned that they would never leave without publicly blaming France for expelling them—they would take their revenge at some future time. Meanwhile, the French saw some advantages in their position—for example, all foreign airline offices in Tehran were wrecked except for those of Air France—and hoped to keep their bets on both Khomeini and the shah. Khomeini's visa was renewed in January, 1979. There is some evidence, however, that the French had high hopes for Bakhtiar, to whom France was virtually a second homeland. Consequently, Khomeini returned to Tehran just in time; his welcome was definitely wearing out.

5. Cited by Joseph Kraft, *Washington Post*, October 29, 1978; *FBIS* November 1, 1978; Agence France-Presse (AFP), October 28, 1978, text in *FBIS* October 30, 1978.

6. Interview with Oriana Fallaci, *Corriere Della Sera* (Milan), September 30, 1979.
7. Letter to the editor, *Washington Post*, October 2, 1978.
8. *The New York Times*, November 1, 1978.
9. Ibid., November 6, 1978.
10. Interviews in *The New York Times*, November 7, 1978; *Time Magazine*, November 6, 1978; *Stern* (Hamburg), November 6, 1978.
11. *The New York Times*, November 7, 1978.
12. *Washington Post*, November 7, 1978.
13. Texts in *FBIS* November 6 and 7, 1978.
14. *Times* (London), November 21, 1978.
15. See Radio Tehran broadcast, November 27, 1978, text in *FBIS* November 28, 1978, and Austrian radio interview, text in *FBIS* November 30, 1978.
16. *Washington Post*, December 15, 1978.
17. Text in *The New York Times*, December 8, 1978; *Washington Post*, December 8, 1978.
18. *The New York Times*, December 14 and 13, 1978.
19. Interview with *Manchester Guardian*, December 13, 1978.
20. *Dagens Nyheter* (Stockholm), interview with Sanjabi, December 22, 1978; text in *FBIS* December 22, 1978.
21. The shah's accounts imply that he asked Sadighi before Sanjabi to form a government. Probably, negotiations were going on between the king and the opposition on a number of levels and these talks were far more extensive and detailed than opposition leaders, for obvious reasons, were later willing to admit.
22. Khomeini's interviews in *Le Monde* (Paris), December 13, 1978; and AFP, December 17, 1978, text in *FBIS* December 18, 1978.
23. Abol-Hassan Bani-Sadr, "Instead of the Shah, an Islamic Republic," *The New York Times*, December 11, 1978.
24. *The New York Times*, December 28, 1978.
25. Ibid., December 30, 1978.
26. Reported on by Sadegh Ghotbzadeh, *Washington Post*, January 19, 1979; and by Ibrahim Yazdi over Radio Tehran, August 7, 1979, text in *FBIS* August 7, 1979.
27. Martin F. Herz, ed., *Contacts With the Opposition*, Institute for the Study of Diplomacy, Georgetown University (Washington, D.C., 1980).
28. *Washington Post*, January 2, 1979; *Le Monde*, January 10, 1979.
29. *Monday Morning* (Beirut), January 8–14, 1979, text in *FBIS* January 16, 1979; *L'Express* (Paris), January 20, 1979; *Le Monde*, January 10, 1979.
30. Khomeini interview, *Le Monde*, January 10, 1979; Bazargan in *Le Figaro* (Paris), January 2, 1979.
31. Press conference of January 3, 1979, text in *FBIS* January 5, 1979.
32. Speech to Senate, January 13, 1979, text in *FBIS* January 15, 1979.
33. AFP report, January 16, 1979, text in *FBIS* January 17, 1979.
34. *Washington Post*, January 22, 1979.
35. Radio Tehran, January 31, 1979, text in *FBIS* February 1, 1979.

36. *Le Monde,* January 31, 1979.
37. *Washington Post,* February 2, 1979; National Voice of Iran radio, January 29, 1979, text in *FBIS* February 2, 1979.
38. Interview on Paris radio, February 2, text in *FBIS* February 2, 1979; speech on Radio Tehran, February 4, text in *FBIS* February 5, 1979.
39. *Elevtherotipia* (Athens), February 7, text in *FBIS* February 8, 1979; *Ayandegan* (Tehran), February 8, text in *FBIS* February 9, 1979.
40. *Washington Post,* February 8, 1979.
41. Interview with *Manchester Guardian,* September 18, 1979.

Chapter 9

1. Interview in *The Economist* (London), February 10, 1979.
2. *Washington Post,* January 26, 1979.
3. Interview in *Al-Nahar Al-'Arabi wa al-Duwali* (Paris), September 17–23, 1979, text in *Foreign Broadcast Information Service* (hereafter FBIS) September 19, 1979, pp. R6–R7.
4. *Khandaniha* (Tehran), December 16, 1978, text in *Joint Publications Research Service* (hereafter JPRS) January 26, 1979.
5. Shahram Chubin, "Local Soil, Foreign Plants," *Foreign Policy,* no. 34 (Spring 1979) p. 22.
6. Majlis deputy Qorbani-Nasab, Majlis debate, January 14, 1979, text in *FBIS* January 15, 1979.
7. Abol-Hassan Bani-Sadr, "Instead of the Shah, An Islamic Republic," *The New York Times,* December 11, 1978.
8. *F.Y.I. Iranian Political Digest,* November 6, 1978, in *JPRS* December 4, 1978.
9. Speeches over Radio Tehran, November 10 and 11, 1979, texts in *FBIS* November 14 and 13, 1979.
10. U.S. State Department, *Report on Human Rights Practices in Countries Receiving U.S. Aid* (Washington, D.C., 1979).
11. Cited in John De Novo, *American Interests and Policies in the Middle East* (Minneapolis, 1963) p. 296.
12. K. Motamet-Nejad, "Image of America in Iranian Mass Media," unpublished paper, author's possession.
13. *Le Monde* (Paris), January 2, 1979.
14. *Time Magazine,* January 15, 1979.
15. The fact that Khomeini's ancestors came from Kashmir several centuries ago led some of his enemies to charge that he is not a real Persian; similar accusations have been made about Reza Shah, albeit with less genealogical basis. So vital is ethnicity in Iran that there are constant rumors that such and such a political figure is "really" a Kurd or an Azerbaijani, as if such a designation would in itself prove discrediting. At the same time, one of the reasons for Bani-Sadr's easy triumph in the 1980 presidential elections was that the Islamic Republican Party's candidate turned out to

have too much Afghan blood and was disqualified. One is reminded of the great nineteenth-century Islamic reformer (and sometime anti-shah activist) Jamal al-Din al-Afghani. His critics charged that he took the name al-Afghani ("the Afghan") but that he was really an Iranian, a charge that may have been true. As such, he would have been a Shi'a and, consequently, his teachings would have had less impact on the majority Sunni Muslim world.

16. Khomeini speech at "Crimes of America" conference, June 4, 1980, text in FBIS June 5, 1980.

17. Ibid.

18. And indeed, it bears a striking resemblance to Marxist utopias, and even to those of the 1960s countercultures, though Khomeini's strictness and—in Western religious terms—"Puritanism" would not be welcome to the latter.

19. Cited in Le Monde, November 15, 1978.

20. Interview in Ettela'at (Tehran), February 2, 1980, text in FBIS February 7, 1980.

21. Radio Tehran, October 3, 1979, text in FBIS October 9, 1979.

22. Speech to radio workers, Radio Tehran, September 8, 1979, text in FBIS September 10, 1979.

23. Speech to Feyziyeh Theological School in Qom, August 24, 1979, text in FBIS August 27, 1979.

24. Speech to Feyziyeh School, September 8, 1979, text in JPRS September 19, 1979.

25. Radio Tehran, November 12, 1979, text in FBIS November 13, 1979.

26. Again, it should be noted that many of these patterns of analysis were similar to those made by the pro-shah forces in the previous regime. After an extended trip to the West, Hussein Ramtin, an Ettela'at commentator, wrote that the United States was trying to undermine Europe by manipulating oil and the dollar and he suggested that the Soviet invasion of Angola and the Marxist coup in Afghanistan were results of a secret superpower agreement. While praising "the special American spirit of the love of freedom" and marveling at American social mobility, Ramtin saw Americans in government as completely abandoning their own morality. Iranians and others, he concluded, "have been and are the prisoners of the wrongful decisions" of America. Ettela'at, October 17–18, 1978, text in JPRS December 6, 1978.

27. Radio Tehran, November 10, 1979, text in FBIS November 14, 1979.

28. See Khomeini's speeches to Islamic students in Qom, October 28, 1979, text in FBIS October 29, 1979, and his speech of November 5, 1979, text in FBIS November 6, 1979. On Khomeini's views of the international revolution see Rouhollah Ramazani, "Iran's Foreign Policy: Perspectives and Projections," in U.S. Congress, Joint Economic Committee, Economic Consequences of the Revolution in Iran, 96th Cong., 1st sess., 1979, pp. 79–80.

29. Radio Tehran, October 12, 1979, text in FBIS October 15, 1979.

30. Radio Tehran, October 27, 1979, text in *FBIS* October 29, 1979.
31. *Bamdad* (Tehran), January 27, 1980, text in *FBIS* January 31, 1980.
32. Speech of October 26, 1979, text in *FBIS* October 30, 1979.
33. Interview in *Al Safir* (Beirut), January 18–19, 1979, text in *JPRS* February 13, 1979.
34. Montazeri speech on Radio Tehran international service, November 9, 1979, text in *FBIS* November 13, 1979; ibid.; and Khomeini's speech of October 26, 1979, text in *FBIS* October 30, 1979.
35. Speech of October 30, 1979, text in *FBIS* November 1, 1979.
36. Radio Tehran, February 14, 1979, text in *FBIS* February 14, 1979.
37. *Washington Post*, February 16, 1979; National Voice of Iran broadcast, February 14, 1979, text in *FBIS* February 15, 1979.
38. *Washington Post*, February 13, 1979.
39. *Washington Post*, April 21, 1979; Radio Tehran, April 22, 1979, text in *FBIS* April 23, 1979.
40. Shariat-Madari interview in *Al-Watan al-'Arabi* (London), March 9, 1979, text in *JPRS* March 27, 1979. Rowghani's role is discussed in documents taken from the U.S. Embassy. *See, Kayhan* (Tehran), December 3, 1979, text in *JPRS* January 15, 1980.
41. Radio Tehran, March 14, 1979, text in *FBIS* March 15, 1979.
42. *Washington Post*, March 14, 1980.
43. *Washington Post*, March 17, 1979. The terms "left" and "right" on the political spectrum are often misleading when applied to Middle East politics. Many Americans were confused because of the Marxist sound of Khomeinist rhetoric, but the two philosophies have vastly different roots and implications. One might say that the insistence on forcing ideology and individual governments and parties in the region into left/right and East/West spectrums is one of the main reasons for erroneous analyses. *See* Walter Laqueur, "Is Khomeini a Neoconservative?" *The New Republic,* December 8, 1979.
44. Speech of April 6, text in *FBIS* April 9, 1979; speech of April 18, 1979, text in *FBIS* April 18, 1979.
45. Radio Tehran, April 28, 1979, text in *FBIS* April 30, 1979; Radio Tehran, April 24, 1979, text in *FBIS* April 26, 1979; Radio Tehran, April 9, 1979, text in *FBIS* April 11, 1979.
46. *Le Monde*, May 10, 1979. Qarani, of course, had been relatively friendly toward the United States.
47. *Le Monde*, May 15, 1979.
48. Radio Tehran, April 8, 1979, text in *FBIS* April 9, 1979.
49. National Voice of Iran, April 25, 1979, text in *FBIS* May 7, 1979.
50. Radio Tehran, May 19, 1979, text in *FBIS* May 21, 1979, for Khomeini's statement; Radio Tehran, May 18, 1979, text in *FBIS* May 18, 1979, for the Radio Tehran commentary.
51. Yazdi interview, Radio Tehran, May 21, 1979, text in *FBIS* May 22, 1979; Shariat-Madari interview in *Al Ahram* (Cairo), cited in *Kayhan* (Tehran), June 20, 1979, text in *FBIS* June 21, 1979.

52. This is from a dispatch by Laingen released by the occupiers of the American Embassy and published in *Kayhan*, January 20, 1980, text in *JPRS* March 11, 1980.
53. Embassy document published in *Kayhan*, February 21, 1980, text in *JPRS* April 11, 1980.
54. Radio Tehran, May 25, 1979 text in *FBIS* May 29, 1979.
55. Radio Tehran, May 28, 1979, text in *FBIS* May 31, 1979.
56. U.S. Congress, Senate, Committee on Foreign Relations, *Nominations*, 96th Cong., 1st sess., May 15, 1979, pp. 8, 14.
57. Khomeini's speeches of July 5 and July 24, texts in *FBIS* July 9 and 25, 1979. For an example of the militants' attempts to use the embassy's normal operations as proof of sabotage, see "Revelations Announcement No. 1," November 8, 1979, text in *FBIS* November 9, 1979.
58. Radio Tehran, July 11, 1979, text in *FBIS* July 11, 1979. The commentary drew in part on a rather wild article published in *Newsweek*, October 7, 1974.
59. See Radio Tehran, August 9, 20, and 17, 1979, texts in *FBIS* August 10, 24, and 21, 1979; *Bamdad*, July 18, 1979, text in *FBIS* August 10, 1979. For the attacks on Laingen, see Radio Tehran, October 12, 1979, text in *FBIS* October 15, 1979, and *Jomhuri ye-Eslami* (Tehran), October 1, 1979, text in *FBIS* October 2, 1979.
60. See Yazdi's interviews with *An Nahar* (Beirut), October 1, 1979, text in *FBIS* October 4, 1979, and with Radio Tehran, October 1, 1979, text in *FBIS* October 2, 1979, as well as Deputy Prime Minister Sadeq Tabataba'i in *Al Nahar Al-'Arabi wa al-Duwali* (Paris), October 15–21, 1979, text in *FBIS* October 16, 1979.
61. For example, see, *Ettela'at*, August 21, 1979, text in *JPRS* September 26, 1979.
62. Speech of September 23, 1979, text in *FBIS* September 24, 1979.
63. *Los Angeles Times*, November 9, 1979; *Washington Post*, November 11, 1979.
64. See Yazdi's interviews on Radio Tehran, October 31 and November 5, 1979, texts in *FBIS* November 1 and 6, 1979; Tabataba'i on Radio Tehran, November 5, 1979, text in *FBIS* November 6, 1979.
65. At the same time, Precht had spent ten days in Tehran trying to improve bilateral relations and offering to give further aid to the Iranian government. These initiatives might have contributed to the students' conclusion that the Bazargan government was about to take major steps toward normalizing relations with the United States. The embassy, whose staff had declined from a high of one thousand before the revolution (including a variety of related offices) to a low of forty, had climbed back up to seventy.
66. Radio Tehran, November 5, 1979, text in *FBIS* November 6, 1979.
67. Khomeini speech to employees of the Iran Central Insurance Company, Radio Tehran, November 5, 1979, text in *FBIS* November 6, 1979.
68. Speech of November 8, 1979, text in *FBIS* November 9, 1979.

398 NOTES

Chapter 10

1. Interview with *Ash-Sharq al-Awsat* (London), May 12, 1980, text in *Foreign Broadcast Information Service* (hereafter *FBIS*) May 14, 1980.
2. Ibid.
3. *Bamdad* (Tehran), January 27, 1980, text in *FBIS* January 31, 1980.
4. Khomeini speech of November 7, 1979, text in *FBIS* November 8, 1979; Bani-Sadr to Waldheim, Radio Tehran, April 29, 1980, text in *FBIS* April 30, 1980.
5. Pietro Petrucci, "Cultural Revolution, Iranian-Style," *Afrique-Asie* (Paris), December 10–23, 1979.
6. *Le Monde* (Paris), February 2, 1980.
7. See for example, his speech of November 7, 1979, text in *FBIS* November 8, 1979.
8. Roderic Davison, *Turkey* (Englewood Cliffs, New Jersey, 1968), p. 68.
9. *Washington Post*, March 21, 1980.
10. Interview in *Al Nahar Al-'Arabi wa al-Duwali* (Paris), December 24–30, 1979, text in *Joint Publications Research Service* (hereafter *JPRS*) January 29, 1980.
11. *Le Monde*, November 7, 1979.
12. Radio Tehran, February 3, 1980, text in *FBIS* February 4, 1980.
13. *Kayhan* (Tehran), October 28, 1979, text in *FBIS* November 6, 1979.
14. *The Economist* (London), May 21, 1980. The magazine also repeatedly suggested after the Soviet invasion of Afghanistan that Washington would be better advised to give priority to Moscow's new aggression rather than continue to focus on the Iran crisis.
15. President Jimmy Carter, State of the Union Address, text in U.S. State Department, Bureau of Public Affairs, Current Policy paper No. 132, January 23, 1980.
16. Interview in *The Wall Street Journal*, January 15, 1980; President Jimmy Carter, Interview on "Meet the Press," text in U.S. State Department, Bureau of Public Affairs, Current Policy paper No. 130, January 20, 1980; Secretary of State Cyrus Vance, Statement before Senate Appropriations Committee, text in Current Policy paper No. 135, February 1, 1980.
17. Interview in *Ettela'at* (Tehran), February 2, 1980, text in *FBIS* February 7, 1980.
18. Radio Tehran, February 10, 1980 and *Kayhan*, February 6, 1980, texts in *FBIS* February 11, 1980.
19. *Le Monde*, February 12, 1980.
20. Ibid.
21. Speech over Radio Tehran, February 11, 1980, text in *FBIS* February 12, 1980; Agence France-Presse, February 13, 1980, and Radio Tehran, February 12, 1980, texts in *FBIS* February 13, 1980.
22. Interview in *L'Expresso* (Rome), February 15, 1980.
23. Speech of February 23, 1980, text in *FBIS* February 25, 1980.
24. Tehran International Service, February 24, 1980, text in *FBIS* February 25, 1980.

25. Radio Tehran, February 26, 1980, text in FBIS February 27, 1980.
26. Especially useful in the following discussion has been the eyewitness account of Christos Ioannides, "The Hostages of Iran," unpublished manuscript, Athens: March, 1980.
27. Cited in The New York Times, January 27, 1980.
28. Washington Post, March 17, 1980.
29. Text of the speech is in FBIS April 1, 1980.
30. Text in FBIS April 8, 1980.
31. Speech to the American Society of Newspaper Editors, April 10, 1979, text in U.S. State Department, Bureau of Public Affairs, Current Policy paper No. 159.
32. Washington Post, April 13, 14, and 20, 1980.
33. President Jimmy Carter, Press Conference, text in U.S. State Department, Bureau of Public Affairs, Current Policy paper No. 170.
34. Times (Tehran), May 15 and 19, 1980, text in FBIS June 11, 1980.
35. Agence France-Presse, June 8, 1980, text in FBIS June 9, 1980.
36. Deputy Teyyebi of Esfara'in, Kayhan, May 28, 1980, text in FBIS June 4, 1980.

Appendix A

1. Richard Cottam, Competitive Interference and Twentieth-Century Diplomacy (Pittsburgh, 1967) p. 192.
2. James Bill, "Iran and the Crisis of '78," Foreign Affairs (Winter 1978–1979) pp. 323–24.
3. Baltimore Sun, January 16, 1980.
4. William Dorman and Ehsan Omeed, "Reporting Iran the Shah's Way," Columbia Journalism Review, January–Feburary, 1979. Shariat-Madari, cited in Washington Post, October 29, 1978. See also M. Reza Behnam, "Misreading Iran Through U.S. News Media," Christian Science Monitor, March 12, 1979; Edward Said, "Iran," Columbia Journalism Review, March–April, 1980 and J. C. Hurewitz reply, May–June, 1980.
5. National Voice of Iran, January 10, 1979, text in Foreign Broadcast Information Service (hereafter FBIS) January 11, 1979.
6. See, The New York Times, November 9, 14, 17, and 23, 1978. Antagonism toward the Western press might also have been created by the selective use of its coverage in the shah's press. "Only those cultural endeavors which help to uphold imperalist and capitalist ideology are permitted to enter," wrote dissident Ahmad Faroughy in an article reprinted in The New York Times. Western values were presented as superior while Iranian values were portrayed as retrograde, he added. The Iranian press "has become a great translating machine" carrying articles from the "conformist" American newspapers. Naturally, Iranians would never have seen, there or in imported periodicals, the articles critical of the shah and of his government.
7. Kayhan (Tehran), March 13, 1979, text in Joint Publications Research Service (hereafter JPRS) April 11, 1979.

8. Radio Tehran, July 11, 1979, text in *FBIS* July 12, 1979.
9. Radio Tehran, April 25, 1979, text in *FBIS* April 26, 1979; Radio Tehran, February 9, 1979, text in *FBIS* February 12, 1979.
10. Much of this, of course, comes out of a larger, still-ongoing political debate between those who see the men who made the revolution as fanatic reactionaries and those who do not. While the media often failed to see the broad popularity of the anti-shah movement, many critics went further in their criticism and castigated the press for being unsympathetic toward that struggle and for exaggerating the extremism of the revolution's leaders. Whether such characterizations were unjust may be better judged, perhaps, by a study of Ayatollah Khomeini and his advisors now that they have attained power.
11. For a general view of how the American media covers foreign news, *see* Barry Rubin, *International News and the American Media* (Beverly Hills, 1977). *See also* Barry Rubin, "The Press in Its Own Image," *The Washington Quarterly*, vol. 2, no. 2 (Spring 1979).
12. *Washington Post*, October 10, 1971.
13. For example, *see*, *The New York Times*, June 3, 1974, August 12, 1974; *Washington Post*, May 26 and 27, 1974.
14. *See*, *The New York Times*, October 7, 1974; *Wall Street Journal*, August 29, 1974; *Washington Post*, December 30, 1974.
15. *Washington Post*, January 13, 1975.
16. *The New York Times*, February 13, 1976; *Washington Post*, February 13, 1976. *See also*, *Washington Post*, August 4, 1976.
17. For example, *see*, *Washington Post*, August 16, 1974, Feburary 22 and September 11, 1976, January 2 and March 26, 1977; *The New York Times*, June 1, 1975.
18. *Washington Post*, February 23, 1976, November 11, 1975, May 29 and November 28, 1976; *The New York Times*, September 29, 1976; *Washington Post*, December 17, 1976.
19. *Washington Post*, Feburary 21 and 28, 1976.
20. Eric Rouleau in *Manchester Guardian*, October 20 and 27, 1973.
21. Note 4 above, p. 31.
22. U.S. Congress, House, Subcommittee on Evaluation, Permanent Select Committee on Intelligence of the House of Representatives, *Evaluation of U.S. Intelligence Performance Prior to November 1978*, 89th Cong., 1st sess., 1979.
23. *Washington Post*, November 25, 1978.
24. *Le Monde* (Paris), January 10, 1979; Radio Tehran, December 3, 1978, text in *FBIS* December 6, 1978; *see also* Radio Tehran, November 30, 1978, text in *FBIS* December 1, 1978.
25. *See* speech to National Iranian Oil Company, October 4, 1978, text in *FBIS* October 5, 1978; *Washington Post*, November 15 and 25, 1978.
26. *The New York Times*, December 3, 1978; PARS news agency, December 4, 1978, text in *FBIS* December 5, 1978.
27. *Washington Post*, April 2, 1978.

28. *Washington Post*, May 29 and April 2, 1978.
29. *Newsweek*, May 22 and July 24, 1978.
30. *Time Magazine*, September 11, 1978; *Washington Post*, September 10, 1978; *Washington Post*, September 15, 1978.
31. *Washington Post*, October 29, 1978; *The New York Times*, October 31, 1978; *Washington Post*, November 6 and 12, 1978.
32. *The New York Times*, December 14, 1978; *Washington Post*, November 12, 1978.
33. Radio Tehran, May 1, 1979, text in *FBIS* May 2, 1979.
34. Ibid.; *Le Monde*, May 15, 1979.
35. Radio Tehran, May 19, 1979, text in *FBIS* May 21, 1979.
36. Radio Tehran, July 11, 1979, text in *FBIS* July 12, 1979.
37. Radio Tehran, May 16, 1979, text in *FBIS* May 17, 1979.
38. *Kayhan*, June 26, 1979, text in *JPRS* August 20, 1979.
39. Radio Tehran, August 7, 1979, text in *FBIS* August 8, 1979; *Le Monde*, January 29, 1980.
40. Bert Quint, "Dateline Tehran: There Was a Touch of Fear," *TV Guide*, April 5, 1980. The CBS contingent included a bureau chief, three producers, four correspondents, five camera crews, a radio editor, two tape editors, a troubleshooting expediter, four translators, six automobile and two motorcycle drivers.

Bibliography

Primary Sources

PRESIDENTIAL LIBRARIES

Dwight D. Eisenhower Presidential Library: Abilene, Kansas.
Dwight D. Eisenhower papers; Loy Henderson, Oral History.

Lyndon B. Johnson Presidential Library: Austin, Texas.
McGeorge Bundy papers.

John F. Kennedy Presidential Library: Waltham, Massachusetts.
William Gaud, Oral History; National Security Files-National Security Council Files; Shah Muhammad Pahlevi, Oral History.

Franklin D. Roosevelt Presidential Library: Hyde Park, New York.
Franklin Roosevelt papers.

Harry S. Truman Presidential Library: Independence, Missouri.
Dean Acheson papers; Henry Grady papers.

OTHER PRIMARY SOURCES

British Public Record Office: Kew Garden, England.
Records of the Foreign Office.

Columbia University: New York City (Oral History Collections).
John Badeau; Loy Henderson.

Duke University: Durham, North Carolina.
George V. Allen papers.

Library of Congress: Washington, D.C.

William Culbertson papers; Herbert Feis papers; Cordell Hull papers; Harold Ickes papers; William Leahy papers; Henry Stimson papers.

National Archives: Washington, D.C.

Charles Bohlen papers, Record Group 59, Diplomatic Branch; James Forrestal papers, Record Group 38, Navy and Old Army Branch; Joint Chiefs of Staff, Record Group 218; Office of Naval Intelligence, Record Group 38, Navy and Old Army Branch; Office of Strategic Services, Record Group 226, Division of Modern Military Records; State-War-Navy Coordinating Committee, Record Group 59, Diplomatic Branch; U.S. State Department, Record Group 59, Diplomatic Branch, particularly Office of European Affairs; U.S. State Department, Record Group 84, United States Embassy in Tehran.

Princeton University Library: Princeton, New Jersey.

Allen Dulles papers; John Foster Dulles papers; Loy Henderson, Oral History.

Seeley Mudd Manuscript Library: Princeton, New Jersey.

James Forrestal papers; George Kennan papers.

U.S. Navy Operational Archives: Washington, D.C.

James Forrestal Diary; William Leahy papers.

University of Virginia: Charlottesville, Virginia.

J. Rives Childs papers; Edward Stettinius, Jr., papers.

Yale University Library, New Haven, Connecticut.

Henry Stimson Diary.

Books

Acheson, Dean. *Present at the Creation: My Years in the State Department*. New York: 1969.

Akhavi, Shahrough. *Religion and Politics in Contemporary Iran: Clergy-State Relations in the Pahlavi Era*. Albany: 1980.

Amirsadeghi, Hossein. *Twentieth Century Iran*. London: 1977.

Amnesty International. *Law and Human Rights in the Islamic Republic of Iran*. London: 1980.

———. *Report 1975–1976*. London: 1976.

Anderson, Matthew. *The Eastern Question: 1774–1923*. New York: 1966.

Arfa, General Hassan. *Under Five Shahs*. London: 1964.

Bayne, E. A. *Persian Kingship in Transition*. New York: 1968.

Berle, Beatrice. *Navigating the Rapids: 1918–1971*. New York: 1973.

Binder, Leonard. *Iran: Political Development in a Changing Society*. Berkeley and Los Angeles: 1962.

Blackstock, Paul. *The Secret Road to World War II: Soviet Versus Western Intelligence, 1921–1939*. Chicago: 1969.

Branyan, Robert and Lawrence Larsen. *The Eisenhower Administration, 1953–1961: A Documentary History*. 2 vols. New York: 1971.

Bullard, Reader. *The Camels Must Go: An Autobiography*. London: 1961.

Byrnes, James. *All in One Lifetime*. New York: 1958.

―――――. *Speaking Frankly*. New York: 1947.

Campbell, John. *The United States in World Affairs: 1945–47*. New York: 1947.

Chubin, Shahram and Sepehr Zabih. *The Foreign Relations of Iran: A Developing State in a Zone of Great-Power Conflict*. Berkeley and Los Angeles: 1974.

Churchill, Winston S. *The Second World War*. 6 vols. Boston: 1948–1953.

―――――. *Sinews of Peace: Post War Speeches*. Boston: 1949.

―――――. *War Speeches*. Vol. 2. London: 1952.

Cottam, Richard. *Nationalism in Iran*. Pittsburgh: 1964.

Daniels, Jonathan. *White House Witness*. New York: 1975.

De Novo, John. *American Interests and Policies in the Middle East: 1900–1939*. Minneapolis: 1963.

Dulles, Allen. *The Craft of Intelligence*. New York: 1963.

Eagleton, William, Jr. *The Kurdish Republic of 1946*. New York: 1963.

Eden, Anthony. *The Reckoning*. Boston: 1965.

Eisenhower, Dwight D. *Mandate for Change, 1953–1956: The White House Years*. Garden City, New York: 1963.

Elwell-Sutton, Laurence P. *Persian Oil: A Study in Power Politics*. Westport, Connecticut: 1976.

Eveland, Wilbur Crane. *Ropes of Sand*. New York: 1980.

Faischer, Michael M. J. *Iran: From Religious Dispute to Revolution*. Cambridge, Massachusetts: 1980.

Feis, Herbert. *Seen From E. A: Three International Episodes.* New York: 1947.

Frye, Richard and Lewis Thomas. *United States and Turkey and Iran.* Cambridge, Massachusetts: 1952.

Frye, Richard. *Iran.* London: 1960.

Gibb, H. A. R. *Mohammedanism: A Historical Survey.* New York: 1973.

Goodrich, Leland and Marie Carroll, eds. *Documents on American Foreign Relations.* Vol. 6. Boston: 1945.

————. *Documents on American Foreign Relations.* Vol. 7. Princeton: 1947.

Graham, Robert. *Iran: The Illusion of Power.* New York: 1979.

Halliday, Fred. *Iran: Dictatorship and Development.* New York: 1979.

Harriman, W. Averell and Ellie Abel. *Special Envoy to Churchill and Stalin, 1941–1946.* New York: 1975.

Heravi, Mehdi. *Iranian-American Diplomacy.* Brooklyn, New York: 1969.

Herz, Martin F., ed. *Contacts With the Opposition.* Washington, D.C.: 1980.

Holt, P. M., et al. *The Cambridge History of Islam.* Vol. 1. New York: 1970.

Hughes, Emmet J. *The Ordeal of Power: A Political Memoir of the Eisenhower Years.* New York: 1963.

Hull, Cordell. *The Memoirs of Cordell Hull.* Vol. 2. New York: 1948.

Hurewitz, J. C. *Diplomacy in the Near and Middle East: A Documentary Record.* Vol. 2. Princeton: 1956.

————. *Middle East Politics: The Military Dimension.* New York: 1969.

Issawi, Charles. *The Economic History of Iran 1800–1914.* Chicago: 1971.

Kennan, George. *Memoirs 1925–1950.* Boston: 1967.

————. *Memoirs 1950–1963.* Boston: 1972.

Kissinger, Henry. *White House Years.* Boston: 1979.

Kramer, Martin. *Political Islam.* Los Angeles: 1980.

Kuniholm, Bruce. *The Origins of the Cold War in the Middle East: Great Power Conflict and Diplomacy in Iran, Turkey, and Greece.* Princeton: 1979.

Lambton, Ann Katherine Swynford. *Landlord and Peasant in Persia: A Study of Land Tenure and Land Revenue Administration.* London: 1953.

Leahy, William. *I Was There.* New York: 1950.

Legum, Colin. *Middle East Contemporary Survey.* Vol. 2. 1977–78. New York: 1979.

Lenczowski, George. *Iran Under the Pahlavis.* Stanford, California: 1978.

————. *The Middle East in World Affairs.* New York: 1952.

Lewis, Bernard, ed. & trans. *Islam.* Vol. 2. New York: 1974.

Loewenheim, Francis, et al. *Roosevelt and Churchill.* New York: 1975.

Marshall, G. S. Hodgson. *The Venture of Islam.* 3 vols. Chicago: 1974.

McDaniel, Robert. *The Shuster Mission and The Persian Constitutional Revolution.* Minneapolis: 1974.

Millis, Walter, ed. *The Forrestal Diaries.* New York: 1951.

Millspaugh, Arthur. *Americans in Persia.* Washington, D.C.: 1946.

Odell, Peter. *Oil and World Power: An Economic Geography of Oil.* London: 1963.

Paarlberg, Robert. "The Advantageous Alliance: U.S. Relations With Iran 1920–1975," in Paarlberg et al. *Diplomatic Disputes: U.S. Relations With Iran, Japan, and Mexico.* Cambridge, Massachusetts: 1978.

Pahlevi, Shah Muhammad. *Mission for My Country.* New York: 1961.

Peterson, Sir Maurice. *Both Sides of the Curtain.* London: 1950.

Powers, Thomas. *The Man Who Kept the Secrets: Richard Helms and the CIA.* New York: 1979.

Ra'anan, Uri, et al., eds. *Arms Transfers to the Third World.* Boulder, Colorado: 1978.

Rabinovich, Itamar and Haim Sheked, eds. *From June to October.* New Brunswick, New Jersey: 1977.

Ramazani, Rouhollah. *The Foreign Policy of Iran: A Developing Nation in World Affairs, 1500–1941.* Charlottesville, Virginia: 1966.

————. *Iran's Foreign Policy 1941–1973: A Study of Foreign Policy in Modernizing Nations.* Charlottesville, Virginia: 1975.

————. *The Persian Gulf: Iran's Role.* Charlottesville, Virginia: 1973.

Rand, Christopher. *Making Democracy Safe for Oil*. Boston: 1975.

Reitzel, William. *The Mediterranean: Its Role in America's Foreign Policy*. New York: 1948.

Roosevelt, Kermit. *Countercoup: The Struggle for the Control of Iran*. New York: 1979.

Rubin, Barry. *The Great Powers in the Middle East 1941–1947: The Road to Cold War*. London: 1980.

————. *How Others Report Us: America in the Foreign Press*. Los Angeles: 1979.

————. *International News and the American Media*. Los Angeles: 1977.

Saikal, Amin. *The Rise and Fall of the Shah*. Princeton: 1980.

Saleh, Ali Pasha. *Cultural Ties Between Iran and the United States*. Tehran: 1976.

Semkus, Charles Ismail. *The Fall of Iran 1978–1979: A Historical Anthology*. New York: 1979.

Sheehan, Michael. *Iran: The Impact of United States Interests and Policies 1941–1954*. Brooklyn, New York: 1968.

Shuster, W. Morgan. *The Strangling of Persia*. New York: 1912.

Shwadran, Benjamin. *The Middle East, Oil and the Great Powers, 1959*. New York: 1959.

Speiser, E. A. *The United States and the Near East*. Cambridge, Massachusetts: 1947.

Stettinius, Edward R. *The Diaries of Edward R. Stettinius, Jr., 1943–1946*. Edited by Thomas Campbell and George Herring. New York: 1975.

————. *Roosevelt and the Russians: The Yalta Conference*. Edited by Walter Johnson. New York: 1949.

Truman, Harry S. *Memoirs*. Vol. 1. *Year of Decisions*. New York: 1955.

————. *Memoirs*. Vol. 2. *Years of Trial and Hope 1946–1952*. New York: 1956.

Upton, Joseph. *The History of Modern Iran: An Interpretation*. Cambridge, Massachusetts: 1961.

Walters, Vernon. *Silent Missions*. New York: 1978.

Watt, W. Montgomery. *Islam and the Integration of Society*. London: 1970.

Warne, William. *Mission for Peace: Point Four in Iran.* Indianapolis: 1956.

Woodward, Llewellyn. *British Foreign Policy in the Second World War.* London: 1962.

————. *British Foreign Policy in the Second World War.* Vol. 4. London: 1975.

Yergin, Daniel. *Shattered Peace: The Origins of the Cold War and the National Security State.* Boston: 1977.

Yeselson, Abraham. *United States-Persian Diplomatic Relations: 1883–1921.* New Brunswick, New Jersey: 1956.

Zabih, Sepehr. *The Communist Movement in Iran.* Berkeley: 1966.

Zonis, Marvin. *The Political Elite of Iran.* Princeton: 1971.

Articles

"An American in Persia: Intimidated." *School of Advanced International Studies Review,* February, 1979.

"Another Persia: A Survey of Iran." *The Economist,* October 31, 1970.

Azhari, Nawal. "Secrets in Khomeini's Life . . ." *Al-Watan al-'Arabi,* March 2–8, 1979.

Bani-Sadr, Abol-Hassan. "Instead of the Shah, An Islamic Republic." *The New York Times,* December 11, 1978.

Bayne, Edward. "Crisis of Confidence in Iran." *Foreign Affairs,* July, 1951, pp. 578–90.

Bill, James A. "The American Analysis of Iranian Politics." *Iranian Studies,* October, 1977.

————. "Iran and the Crisis of 1978." *Foreign Affairs* 57 (Winter 1978–79).

————. "The Plasticity of Informal Politics: The Case of Iran." *The Middle East Journal* 27 (Spring 1973): 131–51.

Burrell, Richard. "Iranian Foreign Policy During the Last Decade." *Asian Affairs* 61 (February, 1974): 7–15.

Cahn, Anne Hessing. "U.S. Arms to the Middle East 1967–1976: A Critical Examination." In Milton Leitenberg and Gabriel Sheffer, eds. *Great Power Intervention in the Middle East.* New York: 1979, pp. 102–17.

Chubin, Shahram. "Iran's Foreign Policy 1960–1976: An Overview."

In Hossein Amirsadeghi, ed. *Twentieth Century Iran*. London: 1977.

————. "Implications of the Military Buildup in Non-Industrial States: The Case of Iran." In Uri Ra'anan et al., eds. *Arms Transfers to the Third World*. Boulder: 1978.

————. "Local Soil, Foreign Plants." *Foreign Policy*, no. 34 (Spring 1979): 22.

Cooper, R. "The Crisis in Iran." *The World Today* 35 (February, 1979): 39–42.

Cottam, Richard. "Goodbye to America's Shah." *Foreign Policy* 34 (Spring 1979).

————. "The United States, Iran, and the Cold War." *Iranian Studies* 3–4 (Winter 1970).

Cottrell, Alvin. "Iran, the Arabs, and the Persian Gulf." *Orbis* 17 (Fall 1973): 978–88.

Doenecke, Justus D. "Iran's Role in Cold War Revisionism." *Iranian Studies*, Spring-Summer 1972, p. 96.

————. "Revisionists, Oil and Cold War Diplomacy." *Iranian Studies*, Winter 1970, p. 23.

Dorman, William A. and Ehsan Omeed. "Reporting Iran the Shah's Way." *Columbia Journalism Review*, January-February, 1979.

Fathi, Asghar. "Role of the Traditional Leader in Modernization of Iran 1890–1910." *International Journal of Middle East Studies*, February, 1980.

Grady, Henry. "Real Story of Iran." *U.S. News and World Report*, October 19, 1951.

————. "What Went Wrong in Iran?" *Saturday Evening Post*, June 5, 1952.

Hadary, Gideon. "The Agrarian Reform Problem in Iran." *The Middle East Journal*, May, 1951, pp. 181–96.

Halpern, Manfred. "Perspectives on U.S. Policy—Iran." *School of Advanced International Studies Review* 6 (Spring 1962): 27–31.

Hammeed, K. and M. Bennett. "Iran's Future Economy." *The Middle East Journal* 29 (Autumn 1975): 418–32.

Hannah, Norman. Letter. *Foreign Affairs* 52 (April, 1974): 649–50.

Harkness, Richard and Gladys. "The Mysterious Doings of the CIA." *The Saturday Evening Post* 227 (November 6, 1954): 34–35.

Heravi, A. "The Achievements and Aspirations of Modern Iran." *International Affairs* 22 (October, 1971): 22–24.

Herz, Martin F. "A View from Tehran—A Diplomatist Looks at the Shah's Regime in June, 1964." Institute for the Study of Diplomacy. Georgetown University, Washington, D.C.: 1979.

Hoagland, John. "The United States and European Aerospace Industries." In Uri Ra'anan et al., eds. *Arms Transfers to the Third World*. Boulder: 1978.

Howard, Harry N. "The United States in the Mid East Today." *Current History* 557 (July, 1969): 36–44.

Hunter, Robert. "American Policies in the Mid East." *Royal Central Asian Journal (RCAJ)* 55 (October, 1968): 265–75.

"Iran Applies Brakes to Boom: Shah Visits United States." *International Commerce* 75 (October, 1969): 2–8.

Irani, R. "The United States Involvements in Iran, 1942–1944." *Iranian Review International Relations*, no. 7 (1976), pp. 136–61.

Khaleeli, A. "Some Aspects of Iran's Foreign Relations." *Pakistan Horizon* 21 (1968): 14–20.

Laipson, Ellen B. "Congress and the Middle East." In U.S. House of Representatives. *Congress and Foreign Policy*, pp. 72–84. Washington, D.C.: 1980.

Lambton, Anne Katherine Swynford. "Impact of the West on Iran." *International Affairs* 33 (January, 1957): 12–25.

Laqueur, Walter. "Is Khomeini a Neoconservative." *The New Republic*. December 8, 1979.

———. "Trouble for the Shah." *The New Republic*, September 23, 1978.

Leaf, Jesse. "Iran: A Blind Spot in United States Intelligence." *Washington Post*, January 18, 1979.

Ledeen, Michael and William Lewis. "Carter and the Fall of the Shah." *The Washington Quarterly* 3 (Spring, 1980): 3–40.

Lenczowski, George. "United States Support for Iran's Independence and Integrity 1945–1959." *The Annals of the American Academy of Political and Social Science*, no. 401 (May, 1972), pp. 45–55.

Levy, Walter. "Economic Problems Forcing a Settlement of the Iranian Oil Controversy." *The Middle East Journal*, Winter 1954, pp. 91–95.

McLachlan, Keith. "Strength Through Growth: Iran on the March." *New Middle East*, June, 1973.

Meisler, Jurgen. "Iran's Naval Buildup." *Swiss Review of World Affairs*, July, 1973.

Melbourne, Roy. "America and Iran in Perspective: 1953 and 1980." *Foreign Service Journal,* April, 1980.

Motahedah, Roy. "Iran's Foreign Devils." *Foreign Policy* 38 (Spring 1980): 19–34.

Moran, Theodore H. "Iranian Defense Expenditures and the Social Crisis." *International Security* 3 (Winter 1978–79): 179.

Mossadegh, Muhammad. "Man of the Year." *Time Magazine,* January 7, 1952.

Neuman, Stephanie. "Security, Military Expenses and Socioeconomic Development: Iran." *Orbis,* March 22, 1978.

Nickel, Herman. "The United States Failure in Iran." *Fortune,* March 12, 1979.

Pahlevi, Shah Reza. In *Now,* December 7, 1979.

Pfau, Richard. "The Legal Status of American Forces in Iran." *The Middle East Journal* 28 (Spring 1974): 141–53.

Pietro, Petrucci. "Cultural Revolution, Iranian Style." *Afrique-Asie,* December, 1979, pp. 10–23.

Pranger, Robert J. and Dale R. Tahtinen. "American Policy Options in Iran and the Persian Gulf." *American Enterprise Institute Foreign Policy and Defense Review,* 1979.

Preece, Richard. "U.S. Policy Toward Iran, 1942–1979." *Congressional Research Service,* May 23, 1979.

Ramazani, Rouhollah. "Iran and the United States: An Experiment in Enduring Friendship." *The Middle East Journal* 30 (Summer 1976): 322–34.

————. "Iran and the United States: The Dilemma of Political Independence and Political Participation." *Journal of South Asian and Middle Eastern Studies* 2 (1978): 3–11.

————. "Iran's Changing Foreign Policy: A Preliminary Discussion." *The Middle East Journal* 24 (Autumn 1970): 421–37.

————. "Security in the Persian Gulf." *Foreign Affairs* 57 (Spring 1979).

Roosevelt, Kermit. "How the CIA Brought the Shah to Power." *Washington Post,* May 6, 1979.

Sadeghi, K. "American-Iranian Relations." *Iranian Review of International Relations,* no. 9 (1977), pp. 45–67.

Shapiro, W. "Arming the Shah: Alms for the Rich." *Washington Monthly* 6 (February, 1975): 28–32.

Shaplen, Robert. "The Eye of the Storm: David Newsom." *The New Yorker*, June 2, 9, 16, 1980.

Shari'ati, Ali. "Seven Letters from Valiant Struggler Dr. Ali Shari'ati." (1977) Translated by *Joint Publications Research Service* 73670, no. 1901, June 13, 1978.

Singh, K. "Iran—The Quest for Security: An Overview." *India Quarterly* 30 (April-June, 1974): 125–32.

"Struggles of Khomeini Revealed by His Brother." *Tehran Journal*, January, 1979, p. 4.

Szulc, Tad. "Oil and Arms." *The New Republic*, June 23, 1973.

"United States-Iran Joint Commission Joint Communique." *The Middle East Journal* 29 (Summer 1975): 345.

Wade, Nicholas. "Iran and America: The Failure of Understanding." *Science* 206 (December 14, 1979).

Watson, Douglas. "Ouster of Journalists Indicates Tehran Realizes Its Show Isn't an American Hit." *Baltimore Sun*, January 16, 1980.

Young, Cuyler. "The Race Between Russia and Reform in Iran." *Foreign Affairs* 28 (January, 1950): 278–89.

———. "The Social Support of Current Iranian Policy." *The Middle East Journal* 6 (June, 1952): 125–43.

Zabih, Sepehr. "Iran's International Posture: De Facto Non-Alignment Within a Pro-Western Alliance." *The Middle East Journal* 24 (Summer 1970): 302–18.

Unpublished Sources

Bakhtiar, Shahpour. "The Basis of Shahpour Bakhtiar's Political Concepts and Executive Programmes." Mimeographed. Paris: 1980.

Love, Kennett. "The American Role in the Pahlevi Restoration." Unpublished manuscript. 1960.

McCarthy, Max. Report to Zbigniew Brzezinski. December 3, 1976. Unpublished report.

Motamet-Nejad, K. "Image of America in Iranian Mass Media." Unpublished paper.

Mowlana, Hamid. "U.S.-Iranian Relations, 1954–1978: A Case of Cultural Domination." Paper Presented at the Middle East Association Annual Conference, November 8, 1979.

Parmelee, Jennifer. "Firemen to Diplomats: The Western Media and

Iran Before and After the Revolution." Senior thesis. Princeton: 1980.

United States Government Documents

U.S. Congress. House. Committee on Foreign Affairs. *Foreign Assistance Act of 1968.* 1968.

————. *New Perspectives on the Persian Gulf.* 1973.

————. Subcommittee on Evaluation. Permanent Select Committee on Intelligence. *Iran: Evaluation of U.S. Intelligence Performance Prior to November 1978.* 1979.

————. Subcommittee on International Organizations. *Human Rights in Iran.* 1977.

————. Subcommittee on Near East and South Asian Affairs. *The Persian Gulf 1974: Money, Politics, Arms and Power.* 1975.

————. Subcommittee on Near East and South Asian Affairs. *United States Interests in and Policy Towards the Persian Gulf.* 1972.

U.S. Congress. House. Committee on International Relations. *Arms Sale Policy and Recent Sales to Europe and the Middle East.* 1979.

————. *The Persian Gulf 1975: The Continuing Debate on Arms Sales.* 1975.

————. Subcommittee on Europe and the Middle East. *Review of Developments in the Middle East.* 1978.

U.S. Congress. House. Committee on Standards and Official Conduct. *Report of the Staff Study of Alleged Misconduct by Members of the House of Representatives Involving the Former Government of Iran.* 1979.

U.S. Congress. Joint Economic Committee. *The Political Economy of the Middle East 1973–1978.* 1980.

U.S. Congress. Senate. Committee on Foreign Relations. *Arms Sales to Near East and South Asian Countries.* 1967.

————. *Country Representatives on Human Rights Practices,* Report. 1978.

————. *Foreign Assistance and Arms Sales Issues.* 1975.

————. *The International Petroleum Cartel, the Iranian Consortium, and U.S. National Security.* 1974.

————. *Nominations.* 1979.

————. Subcommittee on Multinational Corporations. *Multinational Oil Corporations and U.S. Foreign Policy.* 1975.

————. *United States Military Sales to Iran.* 1976.

U.S. Congressional Research Service. *Human Rights Conditions in Selected Countries and the United States Response.* July 25, 1978.

U.S. General Accounting Office. Iran Inspection Report. *Contract Administration Services Assistance Program.* June 25, 1976.

U.S. Information Agency. *Attitudes and Values of Iranian University Students.* December, 1964.

————. *Attitudes Towards Nonalignment in India, Iran, and Pakistan.* December, 1964.

————. *Opinion of Teheran Literates on International Issues.* January, 1964.

————. *The Standing of the Major Powers in Teheran.* December, 1965.

————. *Survey Shows United States and Turkey lead in Teheran Esteem.* July, 1964.

————. *U.S. Enjoys High Standing in Teheran.* November, 1965.

————. *U.S. Maintains High Standing in Teheran.* November, 1965.

U.S. State Department. Attorney General Benjamin Civiletti. *Oral Argument on Iran Presented to International Court Justice.* Current Policy. No. 110. December 10, 1979.

————. Zbigniew Brzezinski. Current Policy. No. 173. April 27, 1980.

————. Warren Christopher. *Iran and America.* Current Policy. No. 173. April 13, 1980.

————. *Country Reports on Human Rights Practices.* 1978.

————. Don McHenry. *Statement to the UN Security Council.* Current Policy. No. 126. January 13, 1980.

————. *President Carter News Conference on Iran.* Current Policy. No. 115. November 28, 1979.

————. *Report on Human Rights Practices in Countries Receiving U.S. Aid.* 1979.

————. Harold Saunders. Current Policy. No. 152. March 24, 1980.

————. *World Court Decision on Hostage Case.* Selected Documents. No. 15. December, 1979.

Newspapers and Periodicals

UNITED STATES

Boston	*Christian Science Monitor*
Cambridge, Massachusetts	*International Security*
Chestnut Hill, Massachusetts	*Iranian Studies*
Indianapolis	*Saturday Evening Post*
Los Angeles	*Los Angeles Times*
New York	*Business Week*
	Columbia Journalism Review
	Foreign Affairs
	Fortune
	The New York Times
	Newsweek
	Time Magazine
	The Wall Street Journal
Philadelphia	*Orbis*
	Current History

Springfield,
Virginia   U.S. Department of Commerce, National Technical
               Information Service. *Federal Broadcasting In-
               formation Service*. Mideast and North Africa.
               U.S. Department of Commerce, National Technical
               Information Service. *Federal Broadcasting In-
               formation Service*. South Asia.
               U.S. Department of Commerce, National Technical
               Information Service. *Joint Publications Research
               Service*. Mideast and North Africa.

Villanova,
Pennsylvania   *Journal of South Asian and Middle Eastern
               Studies*

Washington,
D.C.   *American Enterprise Institute Foreign
               Policy and Defense Review*
               Congressional Research Service
               Foreign Policy
               Foreign Service Journal

International Commerce
The Middle East Journal
New Republic
School of Advanced International Studies (SAIS)
    Review
Science
U.S. Department of State Bulletin
U.S. News and World Report
Washington Monthly
Washington Post
The Washington Quarterly

FOREIGN

Cambridge,
  England   International Journal of Middle East Studies

London,
  England   Asian Affairs
                   Contemporary Review
                   The Economist
                   International Affairs
                   International Monthly
                   New Middle East
                   Now
                   Times (London)

Manchester,
  England   Manchester Guardian International Edition

New Delhi   India Quarterly

Paris   Afrique-Asie
                   Le Figaro
                   Le Matin
                   Le Monde

Zurich   Swiss Review of World Affairs

Index

Aaron, David, 223
Abadan, 207, 210
Abbasids, 5, 262–263
ABC (American Broadcasting Company), 362
Acheson, Dean, 62, 88; in Anglo-Iranian oil dispute, 43, 47, 63, 64, 65, 68, 72, 75, 77, 384[n]; on economic reform in Iran, 34–35, 42, 45, 51–52, 57; on Mossadegh, 58, 59, 61; on the shah, 38, 41–42
Afghanistan, 8, 9, 102, 108, 127, 160, 177, 280[n]; Soviet intervention in, 191, 200, 256, 258, 261, 291, 293, 307, 314, 326, 327, 335
Afshar, Nasser, 181
Agah, Ali, 312, 330
Ahvaz, 206
Alahi, Habib, 227–228, 247
Ala, Hussein, 13, 33, 67, 71, 106
Alai'i, Massoud, 179–180
Alam, Assadollah, 203
Algeria, 132[n], 138, 297, 312, 320
Allen, George V., 33, 34, 36, 37, 383[n]
Allies, World War II, 18, 19, 20–21, 23, 27, 29, 30, 55, 58, 273
American Cultural Center in Tehran, 349
Amini, Ali, 48, 105, 106, 109; in 1978–79 Revolution, 217–218, 222, 228–229, 233, 234
Amnesty International, 176–177, 192. See also Iran, political repression in
Amouzegar, Jamshid, 210
Anglo-Iranian Oil Company (AIOC), 11–12, 13, 24–25, 42–44, 46–47, 51–52, 58, 60,

61, 63–65, 68–69, 71, 72, 74–75, 77, 385[n]; nationalized by Majlis, 51; Supplemental Agreement (1949), 47, 51; takeover of refinery by Iran, 68. See also Acheson; Mossadegh; National Iranian Oil Company
Anglo-Russian rivalry in Iran, 4, 7, 8, 9, 10–11, 18–23, 29, 54, 134, 264
Annenberg, Walter, 243, 284
Ansari, Masud, 101
Arab Gulf. See Persian Gulf
Arabistan. See Khuzistan
Arab nations, 98, 103, 108, 116–117, 118, 119, 120–121, 125, 208, 263, 266–267, 293, 308[n], 335; conflict with Israel, 132[n], 139, 140, 141, 159, 184, 346; relations with Iran, 126, 127, 133. See also Middle East
Ardebeli, Ayatollah Moussavi, 283[n]
Aspin, Les, 170
Ataturk, Kemal, 14, 15, 263. See also Turkey
Atherton, Alfred, 154, 185–186, 197
Atlantic Charter, 21
Attaei, Ramzi, 172
Ayatollah Khomeini. See Khomeini, Ruhollah, Ayatollah
Azerbaijan, 47, 239, 262, 274; 1978–79 revolutionary turmoil in, 287, 291, 293, 306, 310, 341; Soviet-backed regime in, 19, 27–28, 31, 32, 33, 34, 35, 38, 40; Soviet Socialist Republic Council of Ministers in, 27, 28; Turkish-speaking people in, 19. See also Shariat-Madari
Azhari, Gholamreza, 224, 225, 227, 228, 239

417

424